Text Linguistics

Equinox Textbooks and Surveys in Linguistics
Series Editor: Robin Fawcett, Cardiff University

Published titles in the series:

Analysing Casual Conversation
Suzanne Eggins and Diana Slade

Multimodal Transcription and Text Analysis: A Multimodal Toolkit and Coursebook with Associated On-line Course
Anthony Baldry and Paul J. Thibault

Meaning-Centered Grammar: An Introductory Text
Craig Hancock

Language in Psychiatry: A Handbook of Clinical Practice
Jonathan Fine

The Power of Language: How Discourse Influences Society
Lynne Young and Brigid Fitzgerald

Genre Relations: Mapping Culture
J.R. Martin and David Rose

Writing Readable Research: A Guide for Students of Social Science
Beverly A. Lewin

Intonation in the Grammar of English
M.A.K. Halliday and William S. Greaves

Invitation to Systemic Functional Linguistics through the Cardiff Grammar: An Extension and Simplification of Halliday's Systemic Functional Grammar. Third edition
Robin Fawcett

The Western Classical Tradition in Linguistics. Second edition
Keith Allan

An Introduction to Irish English
Carolina P. Amador Moreno

An Introduction to Linguistics and Language Studies
Anne McCabe

An Introduction to English Sentence Structure: Clauses, Markers, Missing Elements
Jon Jonz

Learning to Write/Reading to Learn: Scaffolding Democracy in Literacy Classrooms
J. R. Martin and David Rose

Text Linguistics

The How and Why of Meaning

M. A. K. Halliday and Jonathan J. Webster

SHEFFIELD UK   BRISTOL CT

Published by Equinox Publishing Ltd.

UK: Office 415, The Workstation, 15 Paternoster Row, Sheffield, South Yorkshire S1 2BX
USA: ISD, 70 Enterprise Drive, Bristol, CT 06010

www.equinoxpub.com

First published 2014

British Library Cataloguing-in-Publication Data
A catalogue record for this book is available from the British Library.

ISBN 978 1 904768 47 0 (hardback)
978 1 904768 48 7 (paperback)

Library of Congress Cataloging-in-Publication Data

Text linguistics : the how and why of meaning / M.A.K. Halliday and Jonathan J. Webster.
pages cm.—(Equinox Textbooks and Surveys in Linguistics)
Includes bibliographical references and index.
ISBN 978-1-904768-47-0 (hb)—ISBN 978-1-904768-48-7 (pb)
1. English language–Semantics. 2. English language–Syntax. 3. English language–Tense. 4. Functionalism (Linguistics) I. Halliday, M. A. K. (Michael Alexander Kirkwood), 1925- II. Webster, Jonathan, 1955-
P325.T478 2014
420.1'43--dc23

2014010900

Typeset by S.J.I. Services, New Delhi
Printed and bound by Lightning Source Inc. (La Vergne, TN), Lightning Source UK Ltd. (Milton Keynes), Lightning Source AU Pty. (Scoresby, Victoria).

Contents

Acknowledgments vii

Preface viii

Part One: A functional approach 1

1. Functions and components of language 3
2. Experiential systems 24
3. Material, mental and verbal processes 52
4. Relational processes 78
5. Participants and circumstances 110
6. Things and 'meta-things' 139
7. Modality in English: 'Modals and pseudo-modals' 170

Part Two: Text and texture 181

8. Textual meaning 183
9. Rhetorical structure of texts 198

Part Three: Case studies in text linguistics 217

10. Stepping into meaning: A case study of Billy Graham's address at the National Prayer and Memorial Service at the Episcopal National Cathedral on 14 September 2001 219
11. Visualizing the architeXture of the text: Analyzing Obama's first inaugural address and Nixon's second inaugural address 272
12. Arriving at a theory of the text: A case study of the commencement addresses delivered by Steve Jobs and Susan Rice 367

Index 426

Acknowledgments

'National Day of Prayer and Remembrance on 14 September 2001', by Rev. Billy Graham at the Washington National Cathedral Appearances, Washington, DC. Reprinted with the permission of Billy Graham Evangelistic Association.

Preface

Working with Professor M. A. K. Halliday on his collected works, I have been privileged to come across a considerable body of unpublished work which he has produced over the years, including lecture notes covering such fundamental concepts in Systemic-functional theory as functions and components of language; experiential systems; material, mental and verbal processes; relational processes; participants and circumstances; things and 'meta-things'; modality in English: modals and 'pseudo-modals' and textual meaning.

In this book, Halliday's clear and concise explanation of the fundamentals of systemic-functional theory are complemented by examples of detailed analyses, accompanied by discussion, of Billy Graham's address at the National Prayer and Memorial Service at the Episcopal National Cathedral on 14 September 2001; Richard Nixon's second inaugural and Barack Obama's first inaugural speeches; and the commencement addresses delivered by Steve Jobs and Susan Rice at Stanford University.

The analyses cover transitivity structure – process, participant, circumstance; logical analysis – parataxis, hypotaxis; and theme analysis. The analyses for each text, however, should be thought of as contributing to a theory of each text, hopefully prompting discussion and even challenge. While alternative and more delicate analyses certainly are possible, nevertheless, what is provided here should serve as the basis for subsequent observations about patterning in choice which contributes to how a text is understood and valued.

Part One

A Functional Approach

1 Functions and components of language

1.1 The functions of language

One cannot answer the question 'what is language for?' in one simple sentence. Even an answer such as 'the function of language is communication', which at first glance seems broad enough, even though admittedly it does not say very much, is not really all-embracing; if 'communication' here is more than just a tautology, i.e. another name for 'using language', then it cannot be assumed that whenever we use language we are communicating. We may be expressing a purely private, and incommunicable, state of our own being – as we usually are when producing expletives or personal jingles of various kinds, or when singing. It would be a waste of a useful word to refer to these as 'communication'.

Even if we leave aside these non-communicative aspects of language, the communicative function itself connotes a variety of different purposes, one or other of which may seem more prominent at any given moment. These different purposes are often reflected in the definitions and characterizations of language given by different writers. For example, one well-known formulation comes from David Abercrombie: 'Language is a means of social control'. This emphasizes communication as a means of influencing people and getting things done; it calls to mind instances of the use of language such as the issuing of an order, or the filling up a form requesting some article or some service.

But Abercrombie is really making a much more general point. He is suggesting that the element of 'social control' is present in all interpersonal communication, even if it is not manifested directly in some tangible result. In the last analysis, we can probably always relate anything that is said or written to some more general, socially definable activity within which the speech or writing is playing a part; it is this principle, in fact, that is embodied in the notion 'field of discourse'. In some cultures, for example, a simple exchange of observations about the weather may serve the underlying purpose of establishing appropriate temporary social relations, which, in turn, facilitate transactions of various kinds, or may even serve as a bridge to more lasting interaction.

While there is no difficulty in agreeing with Abercrombie's formulation, the question that arises is its relation to other, apparently contradictory, statements about language, such as that language is 'the communication of ideas' or 'the expression of inner mental states'. These approach language from quite a different point of view, although they also represent some aspect of the truth.

We might seek to reconcile these different formulations by suggesting that different speech acts have different functions. One utterance may be expressive of the speaker's feelings, while another may be designed to persuade someone to do something; a third might be conveying technical information. This is the way in which it seems that those accounts which have been given of the different functions of language are intended to be interpreted. Perhaps the best known of such accounts is the tripartite scheme put forward by Karl Bühler in the 1930s. Bühler propounded the theory that language has three functions: ***conative***, ***expressive***, and ***representational***. These can be thought of as, respectively, language as social control, language as expression of speakers' feelings, and language as communication of ideas.

Such a framework does not, however, exclude another, rather different interpretation: namely that every speech act contains some element of each of the three functions. Every utterance might be, at the same time, conative and expressive and representational in function, rather than being limited to one only. Once it is recognized that language as a whole has more than just one function, then in order to understand the nature of language we shall need to show how the various functions are reconciled and combined.

We can approach this question through an investigation of language itself. A study of the internal workings of language indicates that different parts of the language system serve different functions. When we investigate the grammars of language, we find that they are made up of a small number of components; and each of these components corresponds to one of the functions that language is required to fulfil.

The way in which these components are combined in speech acts lies somewhere in between the two interpretations offered above. It is not the case that each speech act serves only one function. Nor is it the case that every speech act serves all functions in equal proportion, or in some other constant measure. Rather, most speech acts combine different functions; but the relative prominence of these may vary.

So, if we keep for the moment to the three functions suggested by Bühler, we may say that most utterances will contain conative, expressive and representational components simultaneously. But one or another may be more prominent; some utterances will lack one or other component entirely; and in certain cases an utterance may be restricted to a single component (e.g. 'Damn!').

However, other sets of functions have been suggested, being more or less closely related to the three above. In part, the functions that are recognized will depend on the point of view. Bühler was a psychologist, and was primarily interested in the role of language in the individual, although he took full account of the fact that the individual was also a social being. Bronislaw Malinowski started from a very different field of enquiry, in which his main concern was with the role of language in the community. His point of view is sociological and ethnographic, and the major distinction he draws is between a 'pragmatic' and a 'magical' function. Both of these comprise conative, expressive and representational elements; but the more 'social' function, the conative, is stressed in each case. Malinowski's distinction largely rests on the means whereby social control is achieved: whether directly, as in the language associated with social activities such as agriculture and fishing, or indirectly through the psychological effect on the people involved as in the language of ritual.

These two views, Malinowski's and Bühler's, do not contradict each other; they simply highlight different aspects of the multiple functions of language. They represent, roughly, a sociological and a psychological emphasis respectively, though neither excludes considerations of the other kind. In one respect, they are alike. Both of these scholars were adopting an instrumental approach to language: they were using language as a means of pursuing investigations whose goals lay outside language, in the study of society, or of the mind.

It is possible, however, to take the language system itself as a starting point, and to ask a specifically linguistic question: how is language organized in such a way that it is enabled to fulfill a range of different needs? We may express these needs in social or in psychological terms, but the question itself is directed towards a deeper understanding of language. If we adopt this as our starting point we will get a slightly different picture again; one that still does not contradict the other two but is, as it were, neutral between them, since it derives primarily from an investigation into the resources of language, and from a study of the composition of speech acts.

Even from this starting point we could derive more than one framework, since there are many ways of interpreting the facts of language. The one that is being put forward here is one that is consistent with the findings of linguists who have worked in this area (principally those of the 'Prague school', as it came to be called).

What we recognize as the different functions of language are, in effect, the demands that we make on language as speakers and listeners and writers and readers. These demands are, obviously, very many and varied: there is practically no limit to what we expect language to do for us. But they do group themselves into a small number of basic functions, representing the broad general requirements that all languages have to meet.

The functions of language are illustrated in the following extract from that point in *Alice Through the Looking-glass* where Alice is talking to the White Knight:

> 'What a curious helmet you've got!' she said cheerfully. 'Is that your invention too?'
>
> The Knight looked down proudly at his helmet, which hung from the saddle. 'Yes', he said, 'but I've invented a better one than that – like a sugar loaf. When I used to wear it, if I fell off the horse, it always touched the ground directly. So I had a very little way to fall, you see – But there **was** the danger of falling **into** it, to be sure. That happened to me once – and the worst of it was, before I could get out again, the other White Knight came and put it on. He thought it was his own helmet.'
>
> The Knight looked so solemn about it that Alice did not dare to laugh. 'I'm afraid you must have hurt him', she said in a trembling voice, 'being on the top of his head'.
>
> 'I had to kick him, of course', the Knight said, very seriously.

Many of the words, and the structures, used in this passage express what we might think of as 'content'. They have a representational function, in the sense that they are 'about' something. This is clearly the case with words like 'saddle' and 'sugar-loaf', or 'laugh' and 'kick'; these refer to classes of objects, or of events, which we can recognize and delimit.

As further examples, consider the following sequences:

> 'his helmet ... hung from the saddle'
> '... I fell off the horse'
> 'it always touched the ground directly'
> the ... White Knight came and put it on

These express processes of various kinds, e.g. spatial ('hang') or dispositional ('put on'), together with the various participants in these processes (e.g. 'I', 'his helmet') and the circumstances associated with them (e.g. 'off the horse', 'directly').

We may think of these expressions as the linguistic representation of processes that take place in the external world, in 'reality'; but if we do, two points need to be stressed. One is that such processes include those taking place in the internal world of our own consciousness, for example processes of perception ('looked down') or of cognition ('thought'). The other, perhaps less immediately obvious, is that the 'reality' that is represented in language is reality as interpreted through the speaker's experience – and this experience, being codified and transmitted in language, embodies interpretations of reality made by the members of the speech community over the whole of its history.

To say this is not to exclude the possibility of individual interpretations of experience, such as often underlie language that we recognize as 'poetry'. Indeed many of the White Knight's representations of experience are at variance with our cultural norms – for example, shortly after the above passage comes the sentence 'it was careless of him to put another man's helmet on – with the man in it, too'. Putting on a hat which has a man in it is hardly an everyday experience. Nevertheless we make fewer assumptions if we think of 'content' in terms of speakers' and hearers' experiences. To cite the White Knight again: when he says at another point 'then I stand on my head', we accept this without question as a phenomenon of our experience, although in fact it involves the interpretation of a particular posture as being a kind of 'standing', and thus as being related to the more usual human posture in which the foundation is provided by the feet. This interpretation is, as it happens, made generally by the English-speaking community and embodied in the English language. But in many languages this upside-down posture would not be referred to as 'standing', and an expression which was word-for-word equivalent to 'standing on one's head' would be either unintelligible or highly original and 'poetic'.

Thus there is some value in thinking of the representational element in language as the linguistic encoding of experience; and we use the term ***experiential*** to refer to that function of language which consists in expressing content – the function of being 'about' something. The use of this term may help to emphasize the fact that the reality which underlies this content includes mental as well as physical processes, abstract as well as concrete entities; and to suggest that it is the structure of collective and individual experience that provides the basis for the linguistic representation.

But the text is by no means entirely made up of words and structures expressing some recognizable content. We also find there are numerous expressions of what, in the broadest terms, we might think of as the speaker's own involvement with, or intrusion into, the situation – his comments, evaluations, attitudes and so forth. The passage quoted is largely a dialogue within a narrative; so the instances of this are mainly in the dialogue, with 'the speaker' being Alice or the White Knight (though the narrator does come into the picture at times). For example, there are words and phrases expressing the speaker's attitude of surprise or regret at what he himself is saying, such as 'curious', 'the worst of it was', 'I'm afraid'; there are his deductions, assessments of probability, and the like, e.g. 'of course' ('I take this for granted'), 'must' in 'you must have hurt him' ('I'm certain'), 'to be sure' ('I concede the fact').

More general than these, but still representing the speaker's personal participation, are the selections of mood: for example the use of questions, and exclamations. When Alice says 'Is that your invention too?' she is setting up a particular linguistic relationship between herself as speaker and the Knight as hearer: she herself is taking on the 'communication role' of questioner, and she is requiring of the Knight that he should provide an appropriate response. This choice of mood is an aspect of the speaker's involvement which runs throughout all use of language; the speaker must adopt some communication role or other, and at the same time he cannot avoid imposing one on the hearer, even if only that of listening.

Features of this type correspond to both the 'conative' and the 'expressive', functions as described by Bühler. It is difficult, in fact, to separate the conative and the expressive in language: both represent the speaker's intrusion into the communication process, and there is no clear linguistic distinction between them. The use of an interrogative, for example, might be explained either as expressing the speaker's uncertainty (expressive function) or as conveying his request for an answer (conative function). Even expressions of attitude, and other forms of comment, invite a reaction from the hearer, whether of confirmation, of sympathy or in some other mode. Rather than insisting on what is, in linguistic terms, a somewhat unreal distinction, it is more helpful to take the conative and the expressive together as a single function. We shall refer to this as the ***interpersonal*** function, since it is concerned primarily with the interrelations between speaker and hearer insofar as these are embodied in the speech act.

In defining the interpersonal function in this way, we are not intending to exclude it from the written language. The writer-reader relationship is in many ways more complex and more variable than that between speaker and listener; at the same time, as the example from *Alice* shows, many interpersonal features are found in writing – not merely in the dialogue, which in this respect would be likely to simulate speech, but in the expression of the narrator's own role. The selection of the narrative mode, with its accompanying pattern of statement in past time, is itself an aspect of the interpersonal function, since it defines the relation of writer and reader. But there are additional signs of the narrator's intervention, such as the component of kindly mockery in the words 'proudly', 'solemn' and 'seriously' which the narrator uses to describe the White Knight's appearance and manner of speaking.

But there is one important aspect of the content that we have been ignoring up to this point. Consider the expression 'if I fell off the horse, it always touched the ground directly'. Here we have two units of experience: a process of falling and a process of touching, each accompanied by a participant and a circumstance. But the two processes are linked, by a relationship of 'if ... then ...', or ***condition***. This is still an aspect of human experience; but it is represented indirectly, not as one composite unit but as two units with a logical relationship between them. We will refer to this distinctively as the ***logical*** function. But to fit this in to our total picture we will need to introduce the more general term ***ideational***, with the experiential and the logical recognized as its two subcomponents. Another example of the logical function would be the construction of 'so ... that ...' in 'the knight looked so solemn about it that Alice did not dare to laugh'.

We have so far identified two major components in the language of the specimen text, which we have accounted for in terms of two basic functions of language, the ***ideational*** function and the ***interpersonal*** function. On the one hand, the speaker is representing in language his experience of the persons, objects, abstractions, processes, states, qualities and relations of the real world, including the internal world of his own consciousness; and the ways in which one quantum of experience is related to another. Here language fulfils the function of expressing content, of communicating about something. On the other hand, the speaker is using language for his own direct participation in the speech situation: for the definition of his own and the hearer's communication roles, and the expression of attitudes and assessments. Here in the broadest sense language fulfils the function of establishing and maintaining social relations, of expressing individuality and of achieving 'social control'.

Neither of these two functions could be carried out effectively except through their combination with a third, which we will call the *textual* function, since it simply expresses the fact that language is used for creating texts. A *text* is defined as any coherent passage of language in use, whether spoken or written. We speak, and write, not in words or in sentences but in texts.

Many of the features of the *Alice* passage have to do with its structure as a text – as a connected and contextualized piece of discourse, as opposed to a random collection of unrelated sentences, The most obvious examples of this, perhaps, are the ***anaphoric*** words, words which refer back to something that has previously been mentioned, and thus provide ***texture*** (if we may use this term to designate the property of being a text). Examples are 'that' referring to 'helmet', 'he' referring to 'the Knight'. In the same general category is 'a better one', where 'one' is anaphoric by substitution (it substitutes for 'helmet') and 'better' is anaphoric by comparison – there must be something previously mentioned for it to be better than.

These anaphoric items have the effect of relating one sentence to another one that has preceded it, thus helping to build up an integrated piece of discourse. Other features that contribute to texture in this way, by relating sentences together, include sentence conjunctions such as 'too', 'so' and 'but'; and elliptical forms of response such as 'yes'. In all such cases, the hearer, or reader, has to make the appropriate link with some preceding sentence in order to interpret the sentence in question.

Sentence linking is an important aspect of textual structure. But there are, in addition, a large number of patterns internal to the sentence, particular ways of structuring a clause, which are textual features, in the sense that the speaker, in selecting among them, is selecting that form which expresses the appropriate meaning in the given context. These include patterns of emphasis, e.g. 'but there **was** the danger of falling **into** it', which reflects – and would enable us to deduce, if we did not already know – the fact that some other potential danger was avoided. Another type of pattern that figures prominently in the structuring of clauses in their appropriate textual function is the type involving 'it was … who …', 'that was what …', etc. These are well exemplified in a slightly later passage concerned with the discussion of the White Knight's song, which includes sentences such as 'that's what the name is called' and culminates with 'of all the strange things that Alice saw … this was the one that she always remembered most clearly'. The last is an example of a rather complex structure, here taking form 'of all the … things that … this was the one that …', which is entirely textual in its function.

The textual function is one that is purely linguistic, in the sense that it is the internal aspect of the operation of language; for this reason, perhaps, it is not taken into account in either Bühler's or Malinowski's analysis, since their work is oriented towards the investigation of questions outside language. It is a 'function' in a rather different sense, but we keep the term 'function' for it because, as with the other two, there is a corresponding component in the grammar. The textual function is an essential property of language, and is instrumental to both the others. By creating texts, the language makes the necessary links within itself and with the situation; this enables the speaker to communicate effectively, and indeed underlies the whole concept of 'rhetoric and composition'. Anyone who knows a language well can distinguish, in that language, between a passage of language in use and a random sequence of sentences; it is the textual function that makes the difference between them.

We have seen from the sample passage how these three functions of language, the experiential, the interpersonal and the textual, are all embodied in one text. Any sentence, in fact, is likely to provide illustrations of all three, since most sentences have some content, and involve some speaker-hearer (or reader-writer) relationship, and are part of a longer text.

What is less obvious is that the same is true of most of the elements within a sentence. To take one example, consider the word 'that' in 'Is that your invention too?' It refers back to 'the helmet' and thus, as pointed out already, has a textual role. At the same time it is the subject of the clause, and as such it combines with the finite element of the verb, namely 'is', to realize interrogative mood; mood, as we have seen, is an interpersonal option defining a particular type of relation between speaker and hearer. Third, it enters into a structure which expresses a kind of process, that of 'invention', and so contributes also to the experiential function of the sentence.

There are instances where we can pick out a particular word or phrase as fulfilling just one function. Perhaps 'how do you do?' has only an interpersonal function – it really has no content, and does not necessarily demand an answer or presuppose any preceding communication. Another example from the *Alice* text might be '*to be sure*', which has no other role here than that of expressing the speaker's comment. In general, however, most of the constituents of a sentence, like most sentences, embody all the functions of language. This is because it is not just the choice of words or phrases in the text, but their operation in particular structures, that is their contribution to the total meaning. As a word, 'that' has a textual meaning: it requires the hearer to identify some element in the text or in the situation. But at the same time it always has some structural role, and the structure or structures into which it enters will express other kinds of meaning.

The structural contribution made by a particular word may be an indirect one, through the mediation of some larger unit. For example, 'helmet' belongs to the 'content' side of the vocabulary and has a clearly experiential meaning. But it functions as the 'head' of a nominal group 'what a curious helmet', which is exclamatory and thus plays an interpersonal role. This nominal group also enters into a possessive relation ('... you've got'), which is an experiential one; and contains, in turn, the word 'curious' which is ambiguous, but in this instance is interpersonal insofar as it expresses Alice's attitude of surprise.

1.2 The components of a grammar

The significance of these three functions of language, ideational, interpersonal and textual, is not simply that they represent the varied nature of the demands that we make on language, but also that they are incorporated into its internal structure.

If we are right in putting forward this 'multiple function' view of language, there would be some reflection of the multiplicity of functions in the way language is organized. We have already seen that this is not to be sought in constituency, the division of a sentence into its parts: it is not the case that we can assign each constituent of a sentence uniquely to one function or another. The functional value of a particular segment, such as a word or a phrase, derives from the structural relations into which it enters, and the various structural roles that it occupies as a result.

By way of example, in the nominal group 'the other White Knight' the word 'other' has a textual function, in that it relates what is being spoken about to something already known to us (in this case the first White Knight, who happens to be speaking); at the same time it stands in a particular structural relationship to 'White Knight', that of a 'modifier' to its 'head', and in so doing it fulfils a type of ideational function. The word 'white' denotes a particular quality, but one that is being used not to describe but to classify; it thus has a complex ideational function, and in addition the whole phrase 'White Knight' has been used earlier, so that its occurrence has the textual function of giving cohesion to the parts of the discourse.

It is not, however, the structural relations themselves that constitute the core of the grammar of a language. Structure may be thought of as a means of putting into effect the options that the language makes available. The core of the grammar is the set of choices that the language has to offer. Structural relations are the channel for putting these choices into words.

As an example, we could refer to what is known as 'number', in the sense of 'singular number or plural number'. This is the name of an option, or choice, as shown by the 'or'. The significance of this option is that, under certain specifiable conditions (roughly, whenever one uses a noun), the speaker has to make a selection between two possibilities which are different in meaning. He expresses this selection through the medium of structure – in this case perhaps just by adding, or not adding, a plural marker on to the noun: a very simple device, but nevertheless a structural one.

The grammar of a language may be thought of as comprising a very large number of interrelated options together with the means whereby these options are 'realized' in the form of structures. The options are meaningful;

they are the choices open to the speaker or writer for expressing what he wants to say. Whenever he makes a selection within any one option, he is choosing to express one meaning rather than another.

In the last resort, every option in a language is related to every other option; there are no completely independent choices. The total 'network' of options is thus an extremely complicated one. But if one examines the actual way in which the various options are related to each other, the picture becomes simpler: the total network can be seen to be composed of a number of small networks, each of which is complex in itself but is connected to the others by links that are relatively simple.

By way of an analogy, we might think of a network of options as a piece of circuitry. The grammar as a whole would then correspond to some complex mechanism made up of a number of interconnected 'blocks' of wiring. Within each block the connections are extremely dense, whereas the interconnections between blocks are relatively straightforward.

The options that make up the grammar of a language are actually divided into blocks along two different axes; one (to continue the analogy) defines a relationship 'in series', the other a relationship 'in parallel'. The first is according to the structural unit with which the options are associated: there are clause options, phrase or group options, and word options, and each set is dependent on the preceding – though this is a logical dependence, not a temporal one: they are all expressed simultaneously. Blocks of options defined in this way are related 'in series', and we shall refer to the relationship among them as one of rank.

But it is the second axis that concerns us here. Here the options are grouped 'in parallel' according to the area of meaning to which they relate; and it is this that enables us to define the notion of 'the functions of language' from within language, because this grouping corresponds to the three functions described previously. Thus the fact that language fulfils different functions is reflected in the organization of the grammar: each function is expressed by one block of options. We shall call these blocks the components of the grammar.

We understand by a 'component' a relatively independent set of grammatical options defined by reference to one of the functions of language; together with the structural relations which realize these options. The components are not, of course, entirely un-interconnected; but in general the three sets of choices which the speaker or writer makes do not determine one another.

To summarize: we are describing the grammatical system of a language as a network of options that are open to the speaker as strategies for the

Table 1.1: Principal blocks of options in the grammar of English

Function / Rank	IDEATIONAL EXPERIENTIAL		LOGICAL		INTERPERSONAL	TEXTUAL	
CLAUSE	TRANSITIVITY types of process, participants and circumstances (identity as clause) (things, facts and reports)	HYPOTACTIC COMPLEXES OF CLAUSE, GROUP & WORD	condition addition elaboration report	PARATACTIC COMPLEXES (all ranks) co-ordination apposition	MOOD types of speech function modality (the WH-function)	THEME types of message (identity as text relation) (identification, predication, reference, substitution)	COHESION ('above the sentence': non-structural relations) reference; substitution and ellipsis; conjunction; lexical cohesion
Verbal GROUP	TENSE (verb classes)		POLARITY catenation secondary tense		PERSON ('marked' options)	VOICE ('contrastive' options)	
Nominal GROUP	MODIFICATION epithet function enumeration (noun classes) (adjective classes)		classification sub-modification		ATTITUDE attitudinal modifiers intensifiers	DEIXIS elements (qualifiers) (definite article)	
Adverbial GROUP, Prepositional PHRASE	'MINOR PROCESSES' prepositional relations (classes of circumstantial adjunct)		narrowing sub-modification		COMMENT (classes of comment adjunct)	CONJUNCTION (classes of discourse adjunct)	
WORD (incl. lexical item)	LEXICAL 'CONTENT' (taxonomic organization of vocabulary)		compounding derivation		LEXICAL 'REGISTER' (expressive words) (stylistic organization of vocabulary)	COLLOCATION (collocational organization of vocabulary)	
INFORMATION UNIT					TONE intonation system	INFORMATION distribution and focus	

speech act. The options are all interconnected, but they group themselves into sub-systems corresponding to the different functions of language. The sub-system, which is what we are calling a 'component', is a relatively independent clustering of options – that is, a set of options such that a high degree of interdependence within the set contrasts with a low degree of interdependence between sets. The selection by the speaker of one option in, say, the interpersonal component will tend to have a considerable effect in determining which other options he may select from within the same component (for example, his choice of mood will determine what are the available options in tone) but will be largely without effect on, and unaffected by, the selections he makes in other components.

Table 1.1 shows the principal blocks of options in the grammar of English, arranged on the two axes of rank and function. This gives a very broad and rough picture of the kinds of choice the speaker or writer of English makes when he expresses himself in words.

It is worth insisting on the point that all these choices are choices in meaning. Meaning is not limited to the experiential component. It is sometimes assumed that 'the meaning' of a passage corresponds solely to its factual and notional content. But this rests on a definition of meaning which is too narrow for an adequate understanding of language, and we shall maintain throughout that all components are concerned with meaning – that the interpersonal and textual functions of language are no less meaningful than the ideational.

To put this another way: we can construct pairs of sentences that differ only in respect of one component. There will be a different kind of difference between the members of each pair; we express this by referring to 'experiential meaning', 'interpersonal meaning' and 'textual meaning'. But in each case the difference is a difference in meaning. Given, for example, 'Mary's decided to marry Stephen. It must be Stephen she loves, after all' we could replace the second sentence by any of the following, of which (a) differs from it only ideationally, (b) only interpersonally, and (c) only textually:

It must be Stephen she wants, after all.

Could it be Stephen she loves, after all?

It must be Mary who loves him, after all.

It would seem somewhat arbitrary to suggest that only (a) involved a difference in meaning, especially as this would presumably be taken to imply that (b) and (c) were freely interchangeable with the original. (Note that only a change in textual structure is needed to alter 'they shook hands' into 'what they shook was hands', which is not really acceptable as a paraphrase!)

We are not, of course, rejecting the notion that two sentences, or words, or clauses, may be identical ideationally and differ in respect of one or both of the other components of meaning. This distinction is well established; in the description of lexical meanings, for example, we recognize words which are alike in denotation (ideationally) but differ in their connotations, for example one being favourable and the other unfavourable, like 'firm' and 'stubborn'. This distinction between 'purr words' and 'snarl words' is an interpersonal one. Similarly the clauses 'it's Mary who loves Stephen' and 'it's Stephen who Mary loves', while very different in textual meaning, could be said to be ideationally equivalent (although actually there is a subtle ideational distinction between them as well).

What is unsatisfactory is the restriction of the term 'meaning' to the sense of ideational meaning, with the suggestion that all other distinctions are 'meaningless'. This view ignores all the functions of language except that of communicating 'about' something. Related to this restricted view of meaning is a distinction that is sometimes drawn between language and its use, or, in another formulation, between 'the code' and 'the use of the code'. Here only the ideational component is considered to be part of language as a system; the textual and interpersonal functions are thought of as pertaining merely to 'the use of language'.

We shall not accept this distinction; instead we shall consider that all the functions here recognized have a place in the language system – are 'part of the language', like everything else. It does not seem necessary, in attempting to understand the resources and the special character of modern English, to postulate some ideal entity called 'the English language' to which those who speak and write it achieve only a rather inadequate approximation. This is not to deny that people make mistakes, or that one person's use of language may be more effective than another's. It is simply to assert that by 'a language' we mean all that the speaker of that language may 'do' linguistically: the total set of options that are available to its users and that define the range of their speaking, listening, writing and reading.

One function we need to say more about is the logical. It needs to be considered how far the linguistic expression of what might be thought of as certain fundamental logical relations, such as co-ordination and negation, constitutes a separate component in the grammar.

The philosophical and logical approach to the study of language has always, naturally, emphasized the logical component in the linguistic system, and the syntax of 'natural language' (real languages as opposed to formal systems of various kinds) has been investigated from the point of view of its deviation from logical syntax. Some linguists would take the view that the entire ideational component of language can be brought within a logical framework, by a further extension of the notion of the 'logic of natural language'. That is to say, if the analysis of negation and co-ordination and other such quasi-logical relations in language already involves a departure from strict formal logic, then the same approach can be extended so as to encompass, for example, the linguistic expression of all types of process, the various categories of the verb and the noun, and so forth. Or, starting from an opposite point of view, it may be held that, since there are no 'purely' logical relations in language, an adequate account of the ideational structure will necessarily take in all the so-called logical relations within its own compass.

In other words, either all ideational meaning is logical or none of it is; and both these views are alike in treating the linguistic expression of experiential and logical meaning under one heading (sometimes referred to as 'semantic structure' or 'the semantic function', but this has the drawback referred to above, of appearing to claim for this function a monopoly of meaning). We are not disputing this view. There is no clear line to be drawn between the logical and the experiential; and if language does express certain relations that we would wish to call 'logical' it must be assumed to do so because these are in some way embodied in our own structuring of experience. They are not purely conceptual relations divorced from our interpretation of ourselves and our environment.

However, there is a certain operational value in recognizing a partial and subsidiary distinction here, between what we might call the 'logical' area and the rest of the ideational component. This derives from a consideration of how the two are represented in the grammar; and in particular, of a type of structure that typically realizes what we would regard as logical relations. Logical relations tend to be expressed through the medium of 'univariate' (lineally recursive) structures whereas the structures expressing options of all other kinds are normally 'multivariate'. A clear example of the logical type of structure is co-ordination; this is a univariate structure of a 'paratactic' kind, one which can be extended fairly indefinitely both in length and in depth.

The fact that logical relations are often associated with a particular type of structure need not by itself suggest the existence of a distinct 'logical component' in the grammar. A component implies a fairly clearly definable function with, corresponding to it, a relatively discrete set of grammatical options. But since options are realized in the form of structures, a distinctive type of structure is likely to suggest underlying options that are also of a special kind; and in fact the options realized as logical structures are themselves, in part, recursive: having as it were entered the system by making one selection, the speaker can go round again and re-enter the same option.

There is therefore a recognizably distinct 'logical' type of option in the grammar. At the same time such options do not form an independent block; they are closely tied to other ideational choices in meaning. For example, the modification of nouns, which is structurally rather varied, would not fall clearly within or outside the logical component. This is why we have distinguished between 'ideational' and 'experiential', using 'ideational' as the wider form. We continue to recognize a single ideational component, but divided into two sub-components, the experiential and the logical.

Certain areas of ideational meaning are thus being thought of in terms of abstract relations not directly derived from experience. These areas, however, are those which are closely related to textual meaning, so that in a sense the 'logical' forms a bridge between the experiential and the textual. For example, the logical relation of 'apposition' is connected, in one direction, to the experiential relation of 'identity', and in the other direction to the textual relation of 'commentary':

> To-morrow is New Year's Day. (identity)
>
> To-morrow, New Year's Day, will be the great day in his life. (apposition)
>
> To-morrow is their great day. That is to say, New Year's Day is the day when ... (commentary)

This intermediate position between the experiential and the textual is typical of a number of logical structures, and gives a clue to the meaning of 'logical' when used in this connection: the logical options are those whereby the speaker expresses in 'pure' (abstract) form relations which appear experientially as processes.

These various factors – the distinct structural type, the recursive nature of the options, and the abstract, 'medium-neutral' character of the relations involved – suggest that there are some generalizations to be made under the heading of a 'logical' sub-component. At the same time one would not go so far as to recognize a distinct 'logical function' in language; if anything, it would rather be the case that the logical options in language are neutral, or universal, as regards the particular function they serve.

The kind of indeterminacy into which we have been led in the discussion of the logical element in language is not in any way exceptional; rather it is typical of the indeterminacy that has to be built into any account of language – since it is present in language itself. The framework of components that we are adopting here is far from being 'hard and fast'. In describing a language, we are operating within a highly abstract universe of discourse in which there are many different ways of accounting for the facts; or, simply, many different facts, since a 'fact' already presupposes some definite way of looking at the phenomena in question.

There are also, in language, many uncertain and borderline instances. The notion of a borderline itself denotes two different types of indeterminacy. One is the indeterminacy of the system. One part may shade into another, so that there are areas of overlap or fuzziness between the categories we have set up, precisely such as that between the ideational and the textual components which we are explaining in terms of the notion of 'logical'. Similarly the interpersonal and the textual merge in the area of 'commentary': items like 'as a matter of fact' express the speaker's view of the reality of the situation, but at the same time can be shown to link what follows in a specific way with the preceding text. Naturally the aim is to categorize in such a way as to minimize this kind of uncertainty; but it cannot be eliminated altogether without misrepresentation.

The other type of indeterminacy is that of instances. Particular classes of words or phrases may express a combination of two different functions, or may be ambiguous between them. For example there is a small set of words 'but', 'yet', 'so' and 'then' which combine the logical function of co-ordination with the textual one of conjunction. And the entire class of modal auxiliaries 'can', 'may', 'might', 'should', etc. is ambiguous as between the interpersonal function of modality, as in 'Henry can't be driving' ('I don't believe it'), and an experiential function as in 'Henry can't drive' ('he isn't able to').

Lexical items also often combine two functions. We tend to think of lexical items as expressing 'content', and – at least with 'open class' items – it is usually reasonable to regard their experiential (denotative) meaning as primary. But the vocabulary of English includes a large number of what have been called 'expressive words', words exhibiting at the same time a connotational component of interpersonal meaning, like 'trounce' ('defeat' + 'I approve'), 'whine' ('moan' + 'I disapprove'), including those where the interpersonal element consists in some shared context or social relationship, e.g. 'pussycat' ('cat' in baby talk), 'fiddle' ('violin' in context 'folk'). Sometimes, as in slang, the interpersonal element may be merely 'you and I belong to the same in-group'.

At the same time the repetition of a lexical item, or the use of one that is synonymous with (or in some other way related to) a preceding one, has a textual function, being an important form of cohesion between sentences: cf. the repetition of 'helmet', and of 'fall', in the specimen passage from *Alice Through the Looking Glass*; and the occurrence of 'serious' following 'solemn'. Lexical repetition even at a considerable distance constitutes a cohesive factor and thus affects the interpretation of a text, so that there is a strong textual element in the speaker's selection of lexical item. Thus there is usually more than one answer to 'why did he choose this word rather than that?'.

Finally, the above discussion concerns indeterminate 'types'; but there are also indeterminate 'tokens' to be reckoned with – particular occurrences which we are uncertain whether to account for in one way or in another. These are important in any study which involves text analysis, either as sample data for some linguistic research or where the text is of interest in its own right, as in the study of a poem. Poetic language has the special property that, unlike most other uses of language, it exploits this indeterminacy of tokens; a token which may be of more than one type has very often to be assigned to both.

The components of grammar, therefore, serve the functions of language; and thus reflect these functions in the way they are organized. We use the same names for both, subdividing the 'ideational' component into the two sub-components which we label 'experiential' and 'logical'.

1.3 Summary

The ideational component provides the resources for the expression of content, including on the one hand the persons, objects, abstractions, processes, qualities, states and relations that constitute the phenomena of experience, and, on the other hand, the abstract logical patterns relatable to experience only indirectly. This component is the one that is usually emphasized, often to the exclusion of the others, in the philosophical and psychological traditions in the study of language, the former tending to stress the logical and the latter the experiential element.

Falling within the ideational component is the system of transitivity which specifies the different types of process that are recognized in language, and the structures by which they are expressed. A process consists of three components: the process itself, participant(s), and circumstance(s).

Transitivity structure facilitates comparison between languages on a generally shared level of meaning. Other considerations, such as whether a participant is the grammatical subject, whether or not a participant is explicitly mentioned, or where the elements appear in the clause, are dealt with by other components, the interpersonal and the textual.

The interpersonal component involves the hearer as an essential participant in the speech act. Whereas in the more philosophical approaches to language the hearer has tended to be excluded, and the notion of a text (as opposed to words and sentences) left out of account, the more sociologically oriented approaches to language have naturally paid attention to the speech situation, and have examined those aspects of the language system which are concerned with the expression of interpersonal relations.

Falling within the interpersonal component are options related to mood-residue structure. In English, mood and residue are two constituents of the clause as exchange. The mood element consists of Subject plus Finite, the residue consists of Predicator, Complement and Adjunct. The mood element in a proposition serves to indicate whether the clause is a statement or a question, whether the speaker is giving or asking for information. The order of Subject before Finite realizes declarative; the order Finite before Subject realizes yes/no interrogative. In WH- questions, the Subject, if it is a WH-element, precedes the Finite; otherwise the Finite precedes the Subject.

The textual component has often been thought of – when thought of at all – as concerned solely with anaphoric and other relations between sentences; it is sometimes referred to, in fact, as 'the structure of discourse', or 'grammar above the sentence'. This is, as we noted, an important aspect of it; and there have been valuable studies of the structure of narrative, particularly oral narrative in unwritten languages, which in turn link up with the linguistic study of written prose and verse literature. But the intra-sentence aspects of textual structure – the distribution of information in the clause, various forms of emphasis, etc. – are no less fundamental to the creation of text. This component is also relevant to the speaker – hearer relation, since it is control over this part of the language system that enables one to interact appropriately with one's interlocutor, and to structure what one is saying, through the various thematic and other options, in such a way as to construct dialogue.

Falling within the textual component are those structures that contribute texture to a piece of discourse. Two such structures are thematic structure and information structure. When analysing for thematic structure, one must identify the theme of each clause, i.e. the point of departure for the message. Given a text, 'the thematic organization of the clauses (and clause complexes where relevant) expresses, and so reveals, the method of development of the text ... by analysing the thematic structure of a text clause by clause, we can gain insight into its texture and understand how the writer made clear to us the nature of his underlying concerns' (Halliday, 1985: 67).

Information structure consists of an optional element functioning as Given accompanied by an element functioning as New. The distinction between Given and New has to do with whether the information presented by the speaker is recoverable (Given) or not recoverable (New). The New information has a phonological realization in that it typically culminates in an element with tonic prominence called the Focus. Owing to this connection between tone group and information unit, analysis for information structure has been largely confined to investigations of spoken discourse, not written texts. One can identify the boundary between Given and New in written texts in much the same way one does in spoken discourse – the Given refers to something locatable, or already present in the verbal or non-verbal context. Whereas thematic structure (Theme-Rheme) is clause-based, information structure (Given-New) may extend beyond a single clause to over one clause and half of the next, or even to two or more clauses; or occur two or more times within one clause.

Each component consists of a very large set of options, which are realized through the formation of structures defining the functional roles taken on by the constituent words, phrases and so forth. It is thus through the medium of structures that the component makes its contribution to the final shape of any sentence that is spoken or written. To illustrate this in its simplest form, let us consider the structure of the clause 'you must have hurt him':

'You must have hurt him'

(Actor) (Process ......) (Goal) = ideational

(... (Modal) Propositional ....) = interpersonal

(Theme) (Rheme...................) = textual

Ideationally, the clause expresses a process in which there are two participants, one functioning as actor and one as goal. Interpersonally, it is a statement, expressed as a declarative clause, the subject ('you') and the finite verbal element ('must') together having the function of realizing the selection of mood. Textually it consists of a theme and a rheme; the theme is, as often (though by no means always), also both the actor and the subject. This illustration shows in a simplified form how the components of the grammar are embodied in the structure of the clause. The clause is the domain of many of the principal options in the grammar; primarily (grouped according to function) those of transitivity, mood and theme, which relate to the components as follows:

Table 1.2: Clause structure in terms of functions and components

Component:	Clause system:	Expressing:
ideational	transitivity	types of process (action, etc.)
interpersonal	mood	types of speech function (statement, etc.)
textual	theme	types of message structure

Table 1.3: Terms in functions and components of language

Component	a division of the grammar corresponding to a linguistic function and characterized by a relatively independent set of grammatical options
Constituency	the part–whole relation, whereby a linguistic unit consists of sequences of smaller units of the same kind
Experiential sub-component:	sub-component of the ideational component, comprising options concerned with the phenomena of experience
Ideational function	the function whereby language serves to express our experience of the phenomena of the 'real world', including the inner world of our own consciousness
Interpersonal function	the function whereby language serves to express the roles, attitudes, demands, etc., of the speaker, together with other factors of a social and personal nature
Logical sub-component:	sub-component of the ideational component, comprising options concerned with abstract and functionally neutral relations
Option	a choice, in language, among a small fixed set of possibilities
Text	the operational unit of language – an integrated passage of language in use
Textual function	the function whereby language serves to create texts; a prerequisite of the other two functions

2 Experiential systems

2.1 Introduction

2.1.1 Experiential structure of the clause

The ideational, or 'content', function of language can be subdivided into two, the experiential and the logical. There are two aspects to the use of language to express content. One is the ability to talk about our experience, to encode it linguistically in terms of some model of reality which is reasonably consistent and stable; this we refer to as the 'experiential' function of language. The other is the ability to make explicit certain fundamental logical relations, kinds of 'and' and 'or' and 'if' and 'not' which, although inherent in and apprehended through our experience, are manifested rather distinctly in the language system. In origin these things are part of our experience of the external world, but once incorporated into language they combine as well with interpersonal as with experiential elements: for example, we can negate an attitude as much as we can negate a process. Hence the 'logical' function emerges as partially independent from the experiential, and special grammatical mechanisms have evolved to express logical relations. So when we come to recognize the components in the grammar of a language which embody the means of expression of the different functions, we find it helpful to distinguish between an 'experiential component' and a 'logical component'.

The 'experiential' component in English grammar, i.e. the grammar of experience, is the potential that we have for putting our experience into words, which means being able to talk about processes and things – with, as always, the proviso that 'being able to talk about' is an informal way of saying 'having at our command a "meaning potential" whereby we can represent them in terms of systematic contrasts and combinations'. The experiential component is that part of the grammar by which we handle processes and the things that enter into them. And this enables us to put in perspective certain major divisions within the grammar of every language. Some interesting partial exceptions notwithstanding, every language contains the following elements in its grammar:

Table 2.1: Elements in grammar

Clause	expressing a process as an integrated phenomenon, i.e. the process plus the things involved in it ('participants') plus circumstances attendant on it ('circumstances')
Verbal group	expressing the process itself and its properties
Nominal group	expressing the participant itself and its properties
Adverbial group	expressing the circumstances and their properties

The part of the grammar that is concerned with the expression of processes as integrated phenomena is known as ***Transitivity***. Transitivity, in other words, is the experiential component in the grammar of the clause – or, in our functional perspective, it is the part played by the clause in the experiential functional component. This is an extension of a narrower meaning whereby the form refers simply to the types of process, as in 'transitive and intransitive verbs'; here we shall use it in the wider sense, to refer to all those features of the clause which contribute to the linguistic representation of the speaker's experience. In other words, ***Transitivity*** is the representation in language of ***processes***, ***participants***, and ***circumstances***.

Our experience of the world around us is, in fact, an experience of processes constantly taking place. These include natural processes like water flowing or clouds forming; movements of all kinds, of animate or inanimate objects, such as running, bouncing, wriggling, swaying; specifically human activities of throwing, striking, building and the like; and innumerable complex events that cannot be described in single words but are always part of the environment. But we are also aware of processes in ourselves, postures and physical states on the one hand and states of our own consciousness on the other: of the mental processes of perception, reaction and cognition – seeing, thinking, feeling, responding to – and also of the linguistic processes of talking and listening. All these events, actions and states, of the external world and of the internal world of our own consciousness, are part of our experience of processes, an experience which has to be expressible in language.

Processes, however, involve things; someone, or something, is taking part, so that our experience of processes is not one of processes in isolation but one of processes together with their participants. Moreover they do not take place in a vacuum; we are also aware of circumstantial features that may be associated with them, features of time and place, ways and means and so on. Hence the systems of transitivity in language are the means whereby we can represent in integrated form the ***processes*** of our experience, together with the ***participants*** in these processes, and the ***circumstances*** which surround them.

When we talk of representing processes in language, it is perhaps most natural to interpret this in the sense of having words for them. Obviously there must be words, and we have already seen that there are: the fact that we can use words like 'running' to cite examples of processes means that the word 'run' is the name of a process in English. But words are not the whole story. It is only through their potentiality of being combined in grammatical structures that words are of any use in expressing our experience. The grammatical structures are made up of sets of grammatical functions; and when words are used in structures they take on grammatical functions that relate to the kind of meaning we are expressing.

2.1.2 Kinds of process

So, for example, in a clause such as 'the little boy's throwing stones', which expresses a process in which there are two participants 'the little boy' and 'stones', one element, namely 'is throwing', has the structural function of ***Process***, and the others, 'the little boy' and 'stones', have the functions of ***Actor*** and ***Goal***, respectively. Actor and Goal are two of the types of participant function that the English language recognizes in the representation of processes of a certain type. But it is the structure as a whole, the total configuration of functions that make it up, that represents the process grammatically and interprets it as a process of a certain type. The words that express these functions, such as 'throwing', and also 'boy' and 'stones', are simply (the expression of) finer shades of meaning within the meanings 'process', 'actor', and 'goal', etc. (Of course they express other meanings as well in relation to other grammatical functions that they are occupying at the same time.)

The grammatical structures in which we encode our experience relate fairly directly to recognizable categories of that experience, to phenomena of the world that is around us and inside us. We construct sentences – or, more strictly, clauses – about processes by using structures in which the elements are generalized representations of the various functions that are associated with such processes: the process itself and various categories of participant and of circumstance.

Different languages have different 'ideas' about what kinds of process, and what kinds of participant and circumstance there are. For example, 'there's a bird flying' seems to us to be a simple case of a clearly perceptible process with just one participant involved. But it is not absolutely necessary to separate the process from the participant. It is perhaps useful to be able to talk about birds even when they are not flying and about flying being done by other things than birds, though even this does not require that we isolate two components elements in 'there's a bird flying' – it is not necessary to have a discrete word 'bird' which is used for both birds when they are flying and birds when they are not. In the clause 'it's raining' we do not recognize, in English, any participant at all – the 'it' is not serving a participant function in the structure – whereas some languages recognize one or even two ('the sky is dropping water').

Nevertheless all languages provide for talking about processes, and they do so in such a way which makes it possible for the child who is learning the language as his mother tongue to relate the linguistic structures to his own experience. The grammatical structure is meaningful as an interpretation of experience, and it allows significant generalizations to be made which link one area of experience with another, as we shall show: we can group together different kinds of process that are in some ways alike.

One can in fact follow up the developmental connection between the elementary structures whereby the child builds up his language system in functional contexts, and the structures of the adult language such as that composed of process plus ***Actor*** plus ***Goal***. When the young child says 'teddy', in a plaintive voice meaning 'I want my teddy', we can reasonably analyse this as a structure consisting of one element whose function is something like 'object of desire'. This simple structure is very clearly derivable from the particular purpose for which the child is here using language, which is for the satisfaction of his material and emotional needs; the grammatical function 'object of desire' reflects the social function which he is making language serve for him. But this is exactly the same as the way in which the grammatical functions of the adult language, those such as Process and Actor and Goal, reflect adult functions of language, in this case the function of representing our experience of the world around us. No doubt the transition from one to the other in the history of the individual gives us some indication of the stages that have been traversed in the history of language.

So although the patterns of the adult language, the grammatical structures that we use for talking about experience, are of a highly abstract character – otherwise we could not reduce the infinite variety and complexity of our experiences into a codable form, they relate fairly directly to our perception of the world around us and inside us; and this no doubt is what makes it possible for children to learn language so successfully and so quickly as they do. The patterns of the adult language, reflecting the potential of the mature speaker, are not static – both the individual and the community are constantly modifying their language system – but they are stable: they will not be replaced by any other forms of the same language. They provide the model to which the child is approximating, and a conceptual framework within which to interpret and make sense of what goes on around him.

We may summarize the principal systems within the experiential component in the grammar of English as follows:

Table 2.2: Principal systems within the experiential component in the grammar of English

EXPERIENTIAL SYSTEMS		
RANK	SYSTEMS	SCOPE OF SYSTEMS
clause	transitivity	types of process types of participant and circumstance things, facts and reports identity and ascription
verbal group	tense verb classes	temporal categories
nominal group	modification systems, noun and adjective classes	types of epithet and classifier numeration
adverbial (incl. prepositional) group	categories of time, place, manner, etc. adverb classes	types of 'minor process' (prepositional relations)
word (lexical item):	lexical meanings	taxonomic organization of vocabulary

2.1.3 Process, participant, circumstance

A process, in the sense of what is recognized as a process by the English language, may be an event, including an action by a human or other animate being; a mental process; a state; or an abstract relation. All the following are the expression of processes;

the little boy's throwing stones into the water	it's raining
can you see a light?	don't sulk
the blade's gone rusty	I don't believe you
justice had been done	Jupiter is the largest of the planets

Associated with the process there are, or may be, participants and circumstances; and, as noted earlier, we use the term 'process' also in the narrower sense to refer just to the action, event, etc. in contradistinction to the participants and circumstances. Thus 'the little boy is throwing stones into the water', taken as a whole, expresses a process (in the wider sense); and it consists of a process (in the narrower sense) expressed by 'throw', two participants 'little boy' and 'stones', and a circumstance 'into the water'. The grammatical function of ***Process***, in the structure of the clause, corresponds to process in this narrower sense.

There is a typical pattern in the expression of processes, participants and circumstances in the English clause:

processes	are expressed by	verbal groups
participants		nominal groups
circumstance		adverbial groups prepositional phrases

So for example the following is a typical instance:

in the evening	*they*	*ate*	*roast beef*	*and then*	*swam*
circumstance	participant	process	participant	relator	process
prepositional phrase	nominal group	verbal group	nominal group	conjunction	verbal group

However, it is possible to have quite a different form of expression, as in the following, where the processes, etc. remain the same:

their dinner of	*roast beef*	*was followed*	*by a swim*
participant + process + circumstance	participant	relator	process
nominal group		verbal group	prepositional phrases

Note that we are not saying that the two versions have the same meaning, which they undoubtedly do not; but they have the same meaning in respect of transitivity – the same experiential meaning. The second is an untypical, or 'marked', version, motivated by considerations related to its thematic nature.

It is obvious then that 'processes' may be of very different types, and may involve different numbers and different kinds of participants. For example, in 'it's raining' there is no participant at all, whereas in 'you are required by the regulations to pay the full fee to the examining board' there are four: 'you', 'the regulations', 'the full fee' and 'the examining board'. Moreover these four include participants of various kinds: persons, institutions and abstractions. The term 'participant' is in fact rather awkward here, since it suggests a human being, whereas a participant in the grammatical sense is not necessarily human or even concrete. The term ***participating entity*** would be clearer, but we shall stick to 'participant' as being less clumsy. Like the grammatical concept of a 'process', that of a 'participant' covers a number of more specific phenomena:

Process	includes	action, event, mental process, state, relation
Participant		person, other living being, object, institution, abstraction

2.2 A simple system of process types

2.2.1 Processes

Approaching this discussion of types of process in English from another angle, we will consider two possible systems, both of them imaginary but each representing a very simple model of transitivity in a pure and extreme form. English belongs to neither of these hypothetical, 'pure' types, and probably no other language does either, although some languages come fairly close to one or the other.

The simplest system, then, would be one which distinguished just two different kinds of process according to the number of participants involved. Any process involves either one or two participants:

> One-participant processes, e.g. 'the water was flowing', 'Mary smiled'
>
> Two-participant processes, e.g. 'they were pouring the water', 'John kissed Mary'

Probably no language has quite such a simple system as this, with only two possibilities; but the distinction that is being made is one that is important in many languages – it is the basis for the traditional distinction into intransitive and transitive verbs. In the imaginary language in which this is the only significant distinction, then, we have a simple system of process types as follows:

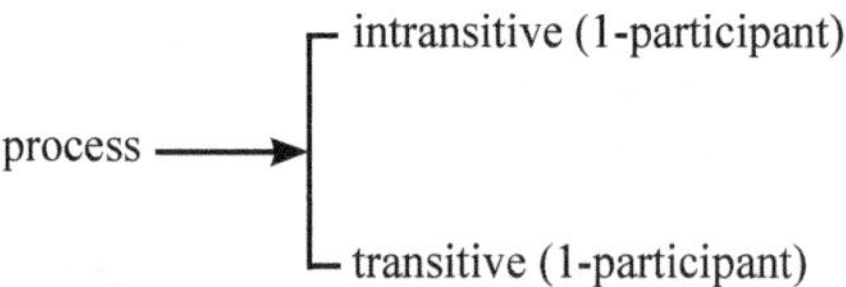

There are two possible versions of this system. In Version A, every verb in the language belongs to one of two classes; let us call these 'class I' and 'class II'. Class I verbs occur in intransitive (1-participant) clauses, and class II verbs occur in transitive (2-participant) clauses; and each verb belongs to one class only. The two process types thus have structures as follows:

> intransitive: participant + process (class I verb)
>
> transitive: participant_1 + participant_2 + process (class II verb)
>
> Note that as it stands the information about the process type has been given twice over: once by the number of participants and once by the class of the verb. There is a fairly high level of redundancy in the expression of the system.

In Version B there are no verb classes (i.e. all the verbs belong to one class, which is the same thing), and every verb can occur in a clause of either type. Here we have:

intransitive:participant + process (verb)

transitive: participant_1 + participant_2 + process (verb)

And the only indication of the type of process is provided by the number of participants – there is no redundancy in the expression at all, which is also rather unusual.

	Version A		Version B	
	intransitive	transitive	intransitive	transitive
participants	1	2	1	2
verb	class I	class II	any verb	any verb

Before turning to English we will take one further stop in considering our hypothetical transitivity systems. In Version B there is only one variable, the number of participants; if we take a clause that is transitive and leave out one of the participants it thereby becomes intransitive. In Version A, however, we have two variables; in principle, therefore, we can vary them independently of each other. Suppose we do this, and ask what is the nature of a clause that has a class II verb in it but only one participant. It may simply be ungrammatical – a mistake, in fact. But, on the other hand, it may be the case that another of the participants, though unexpressed, is nevertheless assumed to be present. Thus we are making a distinction between 'actual' and 'inherent' participants.

Any participant that is required by the nature of the process – whether it is present in the clause or not – is an 'inherent' participant; thus in Version A, class II verbs have two inherent participants and class I verbs have one. Any participant that is actually present in the clause structure we shall call an 'actual' participant.

To return to more familiar terminology. This is what happens when we have a 'transitive verb used intransitively (with the object understood)' (i.e. two inherent participants, one actual), or an 'intransitive verb used causatively' (one inherent participant, two actual). An example from English of the former is 'they're going to build here'; of the latter, 'they ran him out of town'. Notice that these examples assume the existence of verb classes, at least as far as these two verbs are concerned: 'build' must be class II and 'run' class I. This suggests that English has at least some of the character of Version A of our imaginary dual system, which indeed it has. The evidence for this is that there are many verbs in the language for which we can fairly readily assign a definite number of inherent participants. To go back to the earlier example, 'flow' and 'smile' both seem to have just one inherent participant, and so are labelled 'v. intr.' in the dictionary, while 'pour' and 'kiss' have two and are labelled 'v. trans.'. And if we meet an example like 'they're planning to flow the river into the sea', with two actual participants, we feel that it is very much a marked form and probably call it 'causative' rather than 'transitive'.

On the other hand, the picture is far from being as clear as this over the language as a whole. Suppose we invent a verb 'to snarp' and another verb 'to wendle'; here are two possible snatches of dialogue in which these verbs occur:

> It snarped. – Well who snarped it?
>
> I'm wendling the tegs. – My tegs never wendle properly.

Both the replies seem quite natural, although each one changes the number of participants – from one to two in the case of 'snarp', and from two to one with 'wendle'. This is in no way surprising if we consider the analogy with verbs such as 'break' and 'polish': given 'it broke' we can (and often do) answer 'well who broke it?' And a reply to 'I'm polishing the taps' might well be 'my taps never polish properly'.

The verbs 'snarp' and 'wendle', if they existed, would belong to that very large group of verbs in English labelled 'v. trans. & intrans.'. These make up about half the verbs listed in an average dictionary, though they are considerably more than half if only the more frequent verbs are taken into account. It is not the case that all the more frequent verbs belong to this type; but the more frequent a verb is, the greater the probability that it will be equally at home either with one or with two participants. In this respect, then, Modern English resembles our Version B; and this is the result of a considerable change that has taken place in the last five hundred years; it was not true of Middle English to nearly the same extent.

Summing up so far: in Modern English, we have one type of process characterized by one inherent participant, the 'intransitive', and another type characterized by two, the 'transitive'. But at the same time we have a third type which neutralizes this distinction, having either one or two participants **equally inherently** – that is, without either being the typical, or unmarked, form. In other words, we treat some of the processes which we experience as inherently involving just one participating entity, and others as inherently involving two; but many, including the majority of those we talk about most frequently, are treated as lying outside this type of restriction.

2.2.2 Participants

So far we have considered only processes having just one or two participants. But in fact English does not restrict itself to these two possibilities. On the one hand, there are processes that are treated as having no participants at all, as we saw with 'it's raining'. The 'it' is not a participant, as is shown by the fact that we cannot put anything else in its place, and we cannot ask 'what is?' It is there to function as a subject, because a subject is required in finite clauses as a marker of mood, but it has no function in transitivity. The verb 'to rain' has no inherent participants.

On the other hand, there may be more than two, as exemplified by the verbs 'give' and 'pelt': 'he gave his dog a bone', 'they were pelting the pigeons with pebbles'. The verbs 'give' and 'pelt' express processes which typically have three participants associated with them; with 'give', for example, a donor, a recipient and a gift, and with 'pelt', a pelter, a pelted and something to pelt with.

So we may have none, one, two or three inherent participants. An inherent participant, since it is one that is typically associated with a given process, can be asked for if it is not expressed. So for example the occurrence of each of these verbs implies that the accompanying question can reasonably be asked (or, of course, any part of it):

0 - *raining*	(none)
1 - *flowing*	what is?
2 - *pouring*	who is ... what?
3 - *giving*	who is ... what ... to whom?

However, as we saw earlier, the tendency in English is away from a pattern whereby each process is tied to a fixed number of participants – the 'Version A' model of experience – in the direction of one where the choice of type of process does not determine what participants are involved. We may represent the range of possibilities as follows:

Version A ('pure')	Version A ('impure')	Version B
fixed no. of participants determined by process type ('actual' always equals 'inherent')	fixed no. of 'inherent' participants specified by process type but 'actual' number may differ	no fixed no. of participants specified by the process (i.e. no 'inherent' participants)

English is now very mixed, having processes located at all points along this scale. But relatively few are of the 'pure' type of Version A, so even with those processes where we can show a fixed number of inherent participants it is usually possible to bring in others; and conversely one or other of the inherent ones may not be actually present. For example:

process	inherent participants	example	actual participants
rain	0	it's raining cats and dogs	1
flow	1	they're going to flow the Thames into the Wash	2
pour	2	the water poured through the gap	1
pour	2	have you poured the cat some milk?	3
give	3	please give generously	0

Note that we have not changed the sense of the verb here; the process is the same as that where just the inherent participants are actually present. We do of course find the same verbs in different senses, as in 'it's pouring', 'the roof gave', 'he's giving the inaugural address'; but here the processes are different so that the specification of inherent participants given above does not apply.

2.2.3 Participant roles

What we are calling the 'participant' is really a 'participant role'. Our analysis of structure is in terms of functions, and functions in structure can be thought of as roles rather than as entities.

In order to consider the nature of the process, and the functions of the participants within it, let us return for a moment to the simple model of an intransitive/transitive system, with just one or two participants respectively.

If we follow the accepted interpretation, then in an intransitive process, where there is just one participant, that participant has the function of Actor. He is the 'one who does', e.g. 'the little boy "in" the little boy ran away'. The term 'Actor' suggests a human or at least animate participant; this is not intended, and the participant in an intransitive process may just as well be inanimate or even abstract; e.g. 'the water flowed', 'their friendship grew'. But we shall see that this apparently purely terminological difficulty does conceal a real problem in the interpretation.

If there are two participants – that is, the process is transitive, as in 'shall I pour the water?' – then one of these two is analysed as Actor and the other as Goal (Patient, in earlier terminology). In other words, one of the two participants in a transitive clause process is assumed to be identical in function to the single participant in an intransitive clause process. The analysis goes:

intransitive		transitive		
the little boy	*ran away*	*the little boy*	*was throwing*	*stones*
Actor	Process	Actor	Process	Goal

the water	*flowed*	*the little boy*	*poured*	*the water*
Actor	Process	Actor	Process	Goal

One reason for identifying the participant in an intransitive clause with one – and with this particular one – of the participants in a transitive clause is the factor of case. In many languages, such as Latin, there is a 'nominative case' which is used for both. This also applies to English insofar as there are any cases left; that is, with the personal pronouns 'I', 'he', 'she', 'we', 'they' and, marginally, 'who'. So 'the little boy' would be 'he' in all the above examples; whereas in 'the dog chased the little boy', 'the little boy' is Goal and the pronominal form would be 'him'. The reasoning is that case corresponds to function; where the case is nominative, we have one function, labelled Actor, and where it is accusative we have a different function, that of Goal.

This is perfectly sound reasoning as far as it goes, but it is not conclusive: there are numerous instances in language where form and function do not match. This is indeed inevitable, since every element in a structure is likely to have a number of functions at the same time, and no one formal feature can be in regular correspondence with all of them. In any case this particular argument holds true only so long as the clause is active; if we make it passive, then the cases change and what we have called the Goal is now in the nominative:

The little boy (he)	*was chased*	*by*	*the dog*
Goal	Process		Actor

If we do not take into account the passive, and also build into the picture the possibility of a difference between inherent and actual participants, we find that whereas there is only one way of talking about a process that is intransitive there are four ways of talking about one that is transitive:

intransitive (one participant)

the water	*flowed*
Actor	Process

transitive (two inherent participants, one or two actual)

Henry	*poured*	*the water*			*Henry*	*poured*
Actor	Process	Goal			Actor	Process
the water	*was poured*		*by*	*Henry*	*the water*	*was poured*
Goal	Process			Actor	Goal	Process

> Note that we are not calling the intransitive form 'active', since it is not in contrast with a passive; the verb form is active, but the clause itself is outside this system. We shall refer to it as 'middle', using a traditional term that is in fact entirely appropriate; these clauses are middle in the underlying sense of this term. A 'middle' clause expresses a process that has just one inherent participant.

2.3 Alternative analyses

2.3.1 Process + Medium

The next question to arise is whether this form of analysis will still hold when we take account of the fact that English does not operate with this simple opposition of intransitive and transitive processes. What about processes such as 'snarping' and 'wendling', or 'breaking' and 'polishing', which we described as being 'equally at home' with one or with two participants? Let us take the example of 'open':

Intransitive (one participant)

the door	*opened*
Actor	Process

Transitive (two inherent participants, one or two actual)

Henry	*opened*	*the door*			*Henry*	*opened*
Actor	Process	Goal			Actor	Process
the door	*was opened*		*by*	*Henry*	*the door*	*was opened*
Goal	Process			Actor	Goal	Process

The analysis in terms of Actor and Goal now looks rather odd. The same participant 'the door' is shown as being Actor in 'the door opened' but Goal everywhere else; whereas as far as the process of opening is concerned, the relation of 'the door' to this process is constant throughout. The door is the entity that actualizes the process of opening; i.e. there is no process of opening that takes place in isolation from the door. This is true whatever the agency by which the opening comes about – whether Henry, the wind or some supernatural force – and whether that agency is specified explicitly or not. It is immaterial, in fact, whether or not an external agency is required in the real world; from the point of view of the English language 'the door opened' does not necessarily imply that 'someone or something opened it', even though we may claim that it implies this state of affairs.

In fact, the pattern represented by 'open' and 'door' (or '*open-door*') is no isolated phenomenon restricted to just a few verbs; rather it is the typical pattern of Modern English. Here is a set of examples:

the glass broke	*Fred broke the glass*
the curtain moved	*Jane moved the curtain*
the car turned	*Sam turned the car*
the wording changed	*the committee changed the wording*
the rumour spread	*Tom spread the rumour*
the house shook	*the explosion shook the house*
the ball bounced	*Jill bounced the ball*
the wire bent	*the pliers bent the wire*
the rice cooked	*Susan cooked the rice*
the toast burnt	*Harold burnt the toast*
the clothes dried	*Jenny dried the clothes*
the baby sat up	*Lynne sat the baby up*
the radio plugs in here	*you plug the radio in here*
her heart softened	*his pleas softened her heart*
a new process has evolved	*they've evolved a new process*
the platoon were drilling	*the sergeant was drilling the platoon*
the boys lined up	*the headmaster lined the boys up*
the donkey is feeding	*Robert is feeding the donkey*
rabbits breed	*he breeds rabbits*
the boat sailed out to sea	*we sailed the boat out to sea*
the two classes combined	*the instructor combined the two classes*

Notice however that it is often necessary to specify something of the nature or type of the central participant, that which is fundamental to and affected by the process. For example, with 'open' this pattern holds good with doors, windows, etc.; with eyes; with meetings; and with institutions (e.g. 'the new school opened'); but we cannot say 'the can of beans opened' or 'an account opened at the bank'. In this view of processes the essential element is really a complex of 'process plus participant'. It is this that provides the key to the situation – provided that we can identify the right participant. But this is not difficult, since in the intransitive form of the process there is only one. In 'the door opened', it must be 'the door'. At this point, however, the analysis in terms of Actor and Goal breaks down, because 'the door' turns up as Actor in the intransitive, but as Goal in the transitive. We need to replace this by an analysis in which 'the door' is shown as having the same function throughout. We therefore recognize a function 'Medium' which we assign to 'the door' in all instances. The function of 'Henry' – the other participant when the clause is transitive – we shall label 'Agent'. We can now rewrite the description as follows:

Intransitive (one participant)

the door	*opened*
Medium	Process

Transitive (two inherent participants, one or two actual)

Henry	*opened*	*the door*		
Agent	Process	Medium		
The door	*was opened*	*by*	*Henry*	
Medium	Process		Agent	

Henry	*opened*
Agent	Process
the door	*was opened*
Medium	Process

We have now made a different identification of the participants as between the intransitive and the transitive types. Where previously it was the 'nominative case' element in the active transitive clause that was regarded as having the same function as the participant in the intransitive clause – the function of ***Actor*** – now it is the 'accusative case' element with which the intransitive participant is identified, through the function ***Medium***. This replaces a 'transitive' form of analysis, which is one in terms of Actor and Goal, by what is known as an 'ergative' analysis, in terms of the functions of Medium and Agent.

2.3.2 Transitive and ergative interpretations

Essentially, the ergative and the transitive represent two different ways of interpreting our experience of the processes around us. In the transitive interpretation, the variable is the extension of the process. The theory is that the Actor 'does' something, which either extends beyond the Actor to the Goal, or does not. In the ergative interpretation the variable is the cause of the process: the Medium participant 'is involved in' or actualizes some process, whose cause either lies outside the Medium or does not. Whereas the notion of transitive involves 'do (X) to N', the ergative view is 'make N do (X)'.

In view of the predominance of patterns of the '*open-door*' type in Modern English it seems likely that our model of processes is as much an ergative one as a transitive one, and perhaps is more fundamentally ergative. In other words, the language treats processes in terms of cause and effect rather than in terms of action and extension.

A process that is intransitive has a Medium element but no Agent. This does not mean that it is seen as having no cause; it means that the cause, or agency, is treated as being within the Medium itself. Hence 'the door opened' is like 'John sat down' or 'Mary washed' (in the sense of 'she washed herself'). All intransitives are in that way reflexive, and this is why it is very often possible to add the reflexive pronoun without altering the pattern of the process; not only 'Mary washed herself' but also 'John sat himself down' and even 'the door opened itself'.

Now patterns of the type '*open-door*' occur equally readily in both intransitive and transitive forms. That is to say, the active/passive (or 'non-middle') form, in which a separate, external Agent is specified ('Henry opened the door', etc.), and the 'middle' form, in which there is no separate Agent ('the door opened'), not only are both acceptable but both represent equally well the fundamental nature of the process as it is conceived in English. The fact that this is the predominant type of pattern in Modern English makes it likely that our model of processes, at least the kinds we have been considering so far, is as much an 'ergative' as a 'transitive' one. Not that an analysis in terms of Actor and Goal is wrong; rather it fails to account for a lot of the facts, which the analysis in ergative terms can explain. Both contain elements of the truth, the ergative being probably the deeper and more fundamental. What this means is that English tends to interpret process as cause and effect rather than as action and extension.

In this view all processes are alike, in the sense that each one has one central participant associated with it, the 'Medium' as we are calling it. (When this analysis was first introduced, the term used was 'Affected'. But 'Medium' is a more functionally appropriate term.) The Medium is the participant role that is required for the process to be actualized; the process is not seen as an independent phenomenon but as something that is tied to a particular type of entity, through which it is realized. Hence the Medium is obligatory in all structures except those process types which have no participant roles at all.

From this in turn it follows that the essential component in a transitivity structure is the complex formed by 'Process-Medium', e.g. '*open-door*', and this has important consequences for the way the clause is built up in Modern English. It makes the clause atomic rather than molecular; with the complex of 'Process-Medium' constituting a clearly defined nucleus. The other functions in the clause then cluster around this nucleus. This is an abstract and metaphorical way of explaining the difference between a transitive and an ergative interpretation of processes; but we shall see later that it has some very concrete results as far as the remaining elements in the clause are concerned – particularly in respect of their potential for varying their status in the communication process.

Up to this point we have considered only processes of the 'action' type; a very broad category, but not exhaustive because it leaves out of account mental processes, linguistic processes (saying, etc.), and relational processes such as attribution. It is particularly for these non-action clauses that we have to have an analysis of the ergative type; they make little sense viewed in terms of Actor and Goal.

There is nothing surprising in the finding that, as far as action clauses are concerned, ergative and transitive components co-exist. This may be so in all languages – though, if so, it is also true that English is more 'mixed' than many. It may be, though this is speculation, that a mixture of this nature is unstable as a system; certainly in English it is the result of extensive changes over the last millennium, the change being away from a transitive towards an ergative pattern. What is interesting is that the move is away from the transitive type towards the ergative, whereas it appears that at a very early stage our 'ancestral' language (Indo-European) moved the other way, since there are traces of ergative-type constructions – expressed by totally different structural mechanisms – in the oldest forms that are accessible to us. Among the modern Indo-European languages, the other ones to show a significant ergative element are Hindi and certain other Indian languages, at the extreme eastern end of the geographical spectrum, and there is little or no trace of it in between, with the exception of Modern Greek where it is also fairly evident. There seems to be little evidence of it in most of the other languages of the family.

By way of reminder here, note that not all verbs in Modern English behave in this typically ergative, 'vb. trans. & intrans.' fashion. There are many that still reflect the interpretation of an action as being inherently of a two-participant type, like 'throw', or as being inherently of a one-participant type, like 'swim'; as well as those in between, which are inherently of one type but may be 'used as' the other (i.e. the actual participants may differ from the inherent) like 'polish' or 'shine'. 'Shine' is intransitive, but we talk of 'shining the silver'; 'polish' is transitive but we can say 'the silver polishes beautifully'; but we can see that these are more restricted uses – if 'polish' is used without a Goal, the Goal meaning is still transitive ('I'm polishing' means 'I'm polishing something'), whereas if 'shine' is used without a Goal it can never be interpreted in this sense ('I'm shining' couldn't mean 'I'm shining something'), showing that the Goal is inherent with 'polish' but not with 'shine'.

It may be useful to summarize the kinds of 'action' processes that are recognized in English in the form of a scale going from 'most transitive' to 'most intransitive':

	voice	example	participants
most 'transitive'	always 'non-middle' (active/passive)	*throw*	two participants obligatory ('actual' no. cannot vary)
↑	predominantly 'non-middle'	*polish*	two inherent participants (may be just one actual)
	unrestricted: the central type	*open*	either two or one participant(s) (no concept of 'inherent' as distinct from 'actual')
↓	predominantly 'middle'	shine	one inherent participant (may be two actual)
most 'intransitive'	always 'middle'	swim	one participant (only) ('actual' no. cannot vary)

The tendency is, then, for all verbs to move towards the centre of the scale, being neither transitive nor intransitive but facing either way. This tendency manifests itself even where it is not at first apparent, as a final illustration will show. A verb at the 'most transitive' end of the scale may pair with one at the 'most intransitive' end to make up what is, effectively, a single verb of the 'unrestricted' type. In other words, we find pairs of verbs which are related to each other as 'open'$_1$ (in 'the door opened') is to 'open'$_2$ (in 'he opened the door'). In older English, 'sit' / 'set' and 'lie' / 'lay' were related to each other in this way. With these particular words the relationship has been lost (though we have 'stand'$_1$ in 'the chair stood by the wall' and 'stand'$_2$ in 'he stood the chair by the wall'); but it turns up in other pairs, such as 'go' / 'send', 'die' / 'kill', 'learn' / 'teach', 'recover' / 'cure'. The second of these pairs is usually called 'causative'.

Some verbs belong to the class of verb for which there is apparently free variation between active and passive. The fact that we can say (or write) either 'derives from' or 'is derived from' with hardly any difference in meaning is no more than a natural consequence of the move towards an ergative perspective; such pairs are actually the same as '(the door) opens' / 'is opened'. But because these are abstract processes we do not notice the difference between the forms with and without Agent, as we do in the case of something as concrete as the opening of a door. The examples given are rather empty as they stand – such words usually occur embedded in more connected passages of speech or writing; but it is not difficult to supply a context:

this combines with / is combined with a passion for truth

this relates to / is related to what was said earlier

this derives from / is derived from the same source

Neither transitive nor ergative interpretation captures the whole truth about the representation of material processes in the grammar of English. Both analyses can be applied, and each explains some of the facts. For example, the 'transitive' analysis accounts for the following:

i. some verbs are intransitive (only), or transitive (only)
ii. intransitive verbs are active in voice
iii. the Subject of an active verb has the role of Actor in all instances
iv. active is more frequent than passive
v. transitive and causative are not the same thing
vi. there is a distinction between Actor and Goal, on the one hand, which are nominal elements, and all other elements in the clause, which are adverbial

On the other hand the 'ergative' analysis explains other aspects of the picture, which can be contrasted with those above:

i. many verbs are 'vb. trans. & intrans.'
ii. transitivity is a feature of the clause, and voice in the verb is not the expression of the transitivity of the process
iii. the choice of Subject is determined by theme; it is a matter of 'theme' not of transitivity
iv. passive is very frequent (i.e. by comparison with earlier English, or with other Indo-European languages having active and passive)
v. transitive and causative are very similar notions
vi. the distinction between nominals and adverbials does not reflect function in transitivity but status in the information (textual) organization of the clause

The ergative interpretation seems to reflect the direction in which the language is changing; and it also seems to see more deeply into the heart of the language. When we come to take account of factors that lie outside the central core of the transitivity system – that is, of considerations other than the process itself and its immediate participants – we find that the ergative viewpoint gives relatively greater insight. It helps to explain the pattern of organization of the other participants and circumstances in the clause, which has changed radically in Modern English in a way that is otherwise difficult to comprehend.

Second, the ergative view enables us to understand the relation between transitivity and the other functional system-complexes of the clause. The clause expresses not only transitivity but also mood and theme, and all three systems interact in various ways. One clear example is the category of Subject. The category of Subject is defined by the mood system; but the selection of which element in any given clause is to function as the Subject is made outside this system. In earlier English it was generally selected on the basis of transitivity: the normal choice for the Subject role was the Actor. But in Modern English it is selected thematically: it is the Theme, not the Actor, which combines with the role of Subject. Summarily:

i. the category of Subject (what Subject **means**) is determined by mood
ii. the potential for Subject (what **can** function as Subject in a given instance) is determined by transitivity
iii. the actual Subject (what **does** function as Subject in a given instance) is determined by theme

And this in turn is connected with the fact that the Actor is no longer the key role in transitivity – not even in material processes, still less in processes of other kinds.

This leads to the third point: the ergative analysis allows us to relate material processes to processes of other kinds, mental, verbal and relational. The Actor/Goal view will serve up to a point as a model of doing; but for thinking, saying and being it is unrevealing.

There is an apparent paradox here. The ergative interpretation seems to be at one and the same time both more general and more in line with recent changes in the language. One would expect that the more general, and therefore presumably more abstract and deeper, pattern of meaning would also be the one which was more persistent; the assumption being that a language changes on the surface but not, or only much more slowly, underneath. But we should be prepared to find that this assumption does not always hold. It may happen that a language, like a society, preserves superficial features whose persistence conceals quite significant underlying changes. We have already seen some evidence of this in our discussion of transitivity: Modern English preserves the category of Subject, and of active and passive in the verb, from earlier stages of the language; but both have changed considerably in their meanings. The choice of Subject has acquired a communicative, or textual, significance (it is 'that which I want to start from') rather than its earlier experiential one ('that which has the role of doer'); and the selection of active and passive in the verb is becoming more a matter of orientation towards the process (active) or towards the agent (passive) as in 'the ball rolled' versus 'the ball was rolled'.

2.3.4 Historical changes

We should not of course tie the discussion to the idea of a simple opposition between what is there on the surface and what lies underneath. We shall expect to find, in language, as we do in culture, various layers of patterning; some of these may be very deep-seated, and may come to light on the surface at different times and in different ways. It is possible to speculate about the ergative in these terms, although it must be stressed very clearly that such would be speculation. We made the point earlier that there is an ergative element in the grammatical representation of processes in some other Indo-European languages, notably those of modern India, which are geographically remote and remote also in time, in the sense that in order to postulate a 'common ancestor' of English and Hindi one has to go back six to eight millennia, perhaps more. It would be reasonable to postulate that Indo-European had a significant ergative component – it may be in fact that all languages base their transitivity structure on some admixture of the transitive and the ergative – and this component is overlaid, to a greater or lesser extent in different languages and in the same language at different times, by a transitive type of pattern. The situation in English would be that in the marked and very far-reaching changes that have been taking place in its semantic organization over the last millennium, the ergative element in its make-up has come into prominence, possibly thus reverting to an earlier balance of forces, although if so then in a very different form.

It is important to recognize that these changes that have taken place in English are in fact very far-reaching. The superficial changes over this period – the almost complete elimination of the inherited morphological structure – are so striking that, once they had been understood, it became customary to emphasize rather the underlying persistence and continuity from Old English to Modern English. Moreover such continuity is very real; English is still English, not some totally new creation. But this should not lead us to believe that everything in its deeper essential nature has remained unchanged. The morphological changes (though they are not completely unrelated) do not give us any direct clue to the semantic ones, and sometimes even obscure them; but it is the semantic changes we are primarily concerned with, the changes in the 'meaning potential' of the language. These have been extensive and, in places, fundamental.

Moreover any implication that a move in the ergative direction is a 'return' to an earlier state of affairs is an oversimplification and needs qualifying very carefully. There are good reasons for calling the Modern English transitivity pattern 'ergative', taking the term from the description of the case systems in those languages in which the Subject of an intransitive verb is expressed by the same case, not as the Subject but as the Object of a transitive verb. The pattern that we have seen in English is the same in principle: the Subject in an 'intransitive' (one-participant) clause patterns in many respects like the 'object' in a 'transitive' (two-participant) clause – but not, of course, in respect of case, because in general there are no cases in Modern English, and where there are they work transitively and not ergatively (they are a relic semantically as well as morphologically, at least as far as material processes are concerned). Hence while the ergative element in English is recognizable as the same semantic pattern as that expressed by the case system – the form in which it is found in non-Indo-European languages, and which it may be presumed to have taken in early Indo-European also – it is also likely to be substantially different in its meaning and scope. If there has been a return to an earlier type of focus, then the process must be seen as a dialectic one rather than as a simple oscillation.

The Russian linguist Marr considered that ergative represented a rather unsophisticated view of human actions, according to which the 'Actor' could not really be held responsible but was merely the means whereby some external and presumably supernatural agency put its designs into effect. The transitive view of material processes, on the other hand, is the technological one: it is concerned with the process as mechanics. It is 'Newtonian', to apply Whorf's characterization. 'Somebody does something', which is strictly classified in terms of its force, the extent of its effect on the surrounding matter. This model of experience draws a sharp boundary between entities that are capable of 'doing', basically human ones, and those that are not – basically inanimate, with the animal kingdom poised uncertainly on one side or the other. The ergative interpretation, by contrast, would be the magical one; it is concerned with causes, with explanations. A process is not 'done', by an Actor; but is rather brought into being, or actualized, through the intermediary of an 'Affected' entity (and compare here Whorf's account of Hopi metaphysics); and this can take place either spontaneously or through an external agency or cause. There is no sharp boundary here between different types of material process, nor is there any real difference in the potentialities, with respect of these processes, of human and inanimate entities. (Non-material processes, however, are marked off as distinct, and there is a difference; but the specifically human attribute in this schema of reality is consciousness, not mechanical genius.) But this view of experience would not only be the magical one; it would also be the scientific one, scientific theory being another expression of the magical concern with causes.

Thus Marr's argument can be turned on its head, making the ergative seem the more sophisticated model; and this is a characteristic finding if one tries to interpret linguistic phenomena in terms of some conception of 'progress' – the same phenomenon can be made to look progressive or retrogressive according to the way in which it is presented. The lesson usually drawn from this is that there are no irreversible trends in the history of language but only cyclical or pendular movements of a kind familiar in theories of history. Certainly it is foolish to attempt to relate features like transitive and ergative to aspects of social and economic development; and Whorf, the brilliant American linguist whose name is associated with the theory of 'linguistic relativity', saw and stated this very explicitly. But he also saw that it would be equally foolish to deny any possibility of a relationship between semantic organization in languages and systems of thought and of knowledge. And there is nothing inherently improbable in the suggestion – though in the present state of knowledge there is no way of verifying it – that these two meaning perspectives, the transitive and the ergative, represent what we might call the technological (mechanical) and magical-scientific (explanatory) elements in our interpretation of reality and of the processes going on around us. Both of these are essential elements in our mode of thinking, and both are present in language, probably in all languages at all times. But there are differences in orientation and emphasis, in the means of their expression, and in their interrelation with other elements in the semantic system.

This is quite compatible with our notion of the 'characterology' of a language. Although every language is unique, in that it represents a unique configuration of patterns of meaning, there is no implication with regard to any one phenomenon, or set of phenomena, that we describe, that it is to be found only in that particular language. This would in general be rather unlikely. Nor do we go to the other extreme and claim that all semantic patterns are the same in all languages, which is true only if tautological – that is, if we describe every language according to a theory which holds it to be true. Languages differ, as societies do, though we could always construct a social theory which proved them all to be variants of the same basic society; this would embody one aspect of the truth, but a rather obvious one, and it would be most unhelpful if it led us to conclude that all differences between societies were merely superficial. The 'Englishness' of English resides in the total balance, of its systems of meaning potential, their interrelations with each other and their internal contrasts and sub-systems; and likewise for every other language.

It follows that it is the various interrelations and correlations within the grammar of English that make up our picture of the 'character' of the language. The relative weakening of the Actor-Goal image of material processes in the modern language, as compared with Old and Middle English, might be connected with the fact that the Actor-Goal structure as encoded in the language English is appropriate only to material processes, and within these to those of a concrete more than to those of an abstract kind; since if it is true that clause types expressing mental processes and others falling outside the 'material' category have become relatively more prominent, the structure of these non-material processes, as the language interprets them, might tend to become the model for material processes just as much as the other way round. This would link developments in the meaning potential not to extra-linguistic factors but to a functional view of language itself. Our perspective here is, as we have stressed throughout, a functional one.

2.4 Processes and grammatical patterns

That there are semantic differences among the processes themselves, and also among the roles that are associated with them, is not by itself a sufficient reason for treating them as separate categories in the language. Doing, knowing, saying and being are, clearly, different kinds of process: and something 'done to' is different from something known or something 'been'. But purely on semantic grounds we would find many other different kinds; there would be no particular reason for stopping here, or even for starting here rather than with a distinction along some other lines.

When we are describing the meanings of a language we are concerned not only with the semantic system itself but also with what is above it and below it. What is above it is outside language: so here we are taking account of whatever higher level semiotic is most relevant to the functional component we are describing. Our present concern is with transitivity, which is an aspect of the experiential component: so in looking 'above' the level of meaning we are asking whether the system we have set up makes sense in terms of our experience. Concepts like 'doing', 'seeing, feeling and knowing', 'saying' and 'being' are not difficult to interpret as categories of everyday experience.

What is below the semantic system is the **lexicogrammatical** one; so we set up only such categories as are recognizably distinct in the grammar. The criteria we use must involve grammatical as well as semantic categories.

We stress all along that there is never a perfect match between any pair of adjacent levels in the linguistic system. (If there was, there would be no need to recognize them as distinct levels.) The multiple coding process that we call language is the means of establishing systematic relationships between what are qualitatively and quantitatively different orders of phenomena, namely meanings on the one hand and sounds on the other. The relationship between them is a symbolic one, or rather it is a **series** of symbolic relationships each of which involves approximations of various kinds. Hence in describing any part of the system we shall not find perfect categories, but transitional patternings which are fluid in extent and whose boundaries will appear different according to where we choose to home in on them.

Other than any variation in the number of participants, as noted above, there are other differences in the way that processes pattern in the grammar, such as, for example:

i. differential restrictions on the kinds of participant involved;
ii. variations in the potential with respect to other systems, such as voice or theme;
iii. differences in the syntagmatic environment – in the kinds of question to which each can stand in answer, and so on.

In English, there is one type of process which accepts the pro-verb 'do', where the doer need not be human, and which cannot take a 'that'-clause; and another type which does not accept the pro-verb 'do', requires a human participant, and can take a 'that'-clause. The former are the processes of 'doing'; the latter are the processes of consciousness – knowing, seeing, fearing and the like. No general labels will be very adequate; but let us call those of the first type 'material processes' and those of the second type 'mental processes'.

The statement, 'the thorrow flinced', can be queried by 'what did the thorrow do?' Notice that there are a number of possible interpretations of this clause, to which the question 'what did X do?' does not fit.

i. We can say, 'What did the glass do? – **The glass cracked**.' But hardly, 'What did the princess do? – **The princess feared**.' Similarly we can say 'what the glass did was (to) crack'; but not 'what the princess did was (to) fear'. 'Fear' is not a 'doing' kind of verb.
ii. To take another example: we can say 'the princess knew'. But we cannot expand this as 'what the princess did was (to) know'; and we cannot probe it with 'What did the princess do? – **The princess knew**.' The same applies to the verb 'see'. Like 'fear', 'know' and 'see' are also not 'doing' verbs.

iii. This restriction appears even more sharply if we add a second participant, using 'do to' as the corresponding probe. We can say 'what the boy did to the glass was crack it', but not 'what the princess did to the dragon was fear it'.

In the case of 'The thorrow flinced that all was lost', we cannot construct a probe with 'do to'. The form 'what did the thorrow do to that all was lost?' is impossible. The verbs that occur before a 'that'-clause are ones that can not be probed by 'do to'; verbs such as 'know' and 'see' and 'fear' (and also 'say').

i. These verbs cannot take 'do' as a pro-verb. The pro-verb occurs in probes and thematic expansions such as those we have been illustrating: in 'what was Mary doing? – Reading', and 'what Mary was doing was reading', 'do' functions as pro-verb for 'read'. ['do' as a substitute occurs anaphorically: in 'Is Mary reading? – She was doing', here 'do' functions not as pro-verb but as substitute for 'read'.]
ii. There is another feature that distinguishes 'know' and 'see' and 'fear' from the doing verbs. If I say 'the thorrow knew', or put 'the thorrow' in a context where the process must be of one of these kinds (i.e. followed by a verb plus 'that'-clause), you know immediately that 'the thorrow' must be human (or at least human-like) – that is to say, that it must be endowed with human-like consciousness.
iii. If I say 'it knows', or 'it fears', there is an element of incongruity which forces a re-interpretation of the 'it' as something that is in some sense anomalous, partly human and partly not human. This explains the effect of utterances such as 'It doesn't like me', said about a machine which refuses to work.

Now suppose that 'flince' is a word meaning 'boast' or 'claim'. This can take a 'that'-clause: 'the thorrow boasted that all was well' is quite acceptable. But note that it can also take pro-verb 'do' (though not 'do to'): 'What did the thorrow do? – The thorrow flinced that all was well' can readily be interpreted. It makes sense provided that 'flince' is a verb of a type different from either of those we have looked at so far – namely, a 'saying' verb.

i. A 'saying' process is like doing, in that it can take the pro-verb 'do', but it can take a 'that'-clause. In fact, it must take a 'that'-clause, or if not then some noun that is merely a general label for 'that'-clauses or for the act of saying.

ii. The sayer, although not necessarily human, must be emitter of signals, or at least an information source. A clause such as 'the proclamation claimed that all was well' does not imply that 'the proclamation' is endowed with consciousness. It merely implies that it is a source, a symbol-generator. It contains information, and information is not a specifically human attribute. [Note in this connection the very clear distinction between 'my watch says it's half-past eight' and 'my watch knows (or thinks) it's half-past eight'.]

In the example 'the thorrow flinced happy', 'flince' is probably unstressed. Here 'flinced' could be 'was', or a number of other verbs of similar meanings. It is not a matter of 'doing', or 'knowing' or 'saying', but rather of 'being'. The process is a kind of relation between the two parts. We shall refer to these as 'relational' processes.

i. In English, 'relational' processes **are indeed** processes, and are clearly treated as such in the grammar. Notice that they have to have to have a tense. In this respect they are subject to the same requirement as processes of all other kinds: they must be located in past, present or future.

Relational processes are of two kinds, known as 'ascriptive' and 'identifying'. In this one, the ascriptive, some Attribute is being ascribed to an entity, which can be of any kind, from the most concrete, like 'the bus was crowded', to the most abstract such as 'her resentment was understandable'. The commonest verb here is *be*, but there are many others like *seem, become, look, sound, feel, turn, go*. The entity carrying the Attribute is known as the Carrier.

In an identifying process, one entity is being equated with another; typically with some differentiation between them, such as that of performer to role, as in 'Sue is the class teacher'. Since the relation is one of identity, the direction can be reversed; we can equally well say 'the class teacher is Sue'. These two variants ensure different questions; in the first case, 'which is Sue?', the new information is 'the class teacher', while in the second case, answering 'which is the class teacher?', the new information is 'Sue'.

These different process types will be discussed in more detail in the next two chapters, 4 and 5. Meanwhile Table 2.3 summarizes the main grammatical distinctions by which they can be told apart.

Table 2.3: Main grammatical distinctions

	PROCESS		PARTICIPANT 1		PARTICIPANT 2		PROCESS TYPE	
	What… do?	What… do to…?	Non-human	Human	'that' clause	other		
1	√	√	√	√	×	√	material	doing, happening
2	×	×	×	√	√	√	mental	seeing, feeling thinking
3	√	×	√	√	√	×	verbal	saying
4	×	×	√	(√)	(√)	√	relational	being, becoming

Note: In Type 4, the first participant can be human, and the second participant can be a 'that' clause, but the two are mutually exclusive: no clause can contain both a human participant and a 'that' clause.

3 Material, mental and verbal processes

3.1 Material processes

3.1.1

Material processes have been glossed as those of 'doing', but this is really too active a term, as is the alternative name 'action clause' that has sometimes been used for this type. They include events as well as actions: not only doings, but also happenings.

The latter are processes involving non-human and inanimate participants, such as 'the tide came in', 'the snow damaged the roof'; and involuntary processes involving human participants, such as 'the king expired' (and including most passives).

This category also includes purely abstract processes of creation, destruction and change, such as 'a quarrel developed', 'the opportunity did not recur'. Such abstract processes do not form a separate class in the grammar of English; they simply fall in with concrete actions and events. The term 'material process' rather obscures this, but there seems no other obvious name for them. For the gloss, we ought rather to say **'doing or happening'**; these are the two pro-verbs that cover processes of this type.

Action clauses come in three forms known as ***voices***, which we will identify as ***operative***, ***middle*** and ***receptive***. (Operative and receptive could be known instead by their more familiar names 'active' and 'passive'. However, the division does not correspond to that between active and passive in the verb: receptive clauses may have active verbs, and in addition there is a 'middle' type of clause which has no corresponding special form of the verb.)

<table>
<tr><td>operative</td><td>'he is tying the string'</td><td>actor (= Subject) 'he'</td><td rowspan="3">active verb</td></tr>
<tr><td>middle</td><td>'he is waiting'</td><td>actor (= Subject) 'he'</td></tr>
<tr><td rowspan="3">receptive</td><td>'this string won't tie'</td><td>no actor</td></tr>
<tr><td>'this string has been tied very tight'</td><td>no actor</td><td rowspan="2">passive verb</td></tr>
<tr><td>'this string must have been tied by an expert'</td><td>actor (= Adjunct) 'an expert'</td></tr>
</table>

Processes of the 'action' type usually involve an ***actor***. The actor may be (i) grammatical Subject, (ii) an adjunct with 'by', or (iii) not expressed at all. If the clause is operative or middle, the verb will be active and there will be an actor as Subject.

If the clause is receptive, then either the verb will be active and there will be no actor or the verb will be passive, in which case either there will be an actor introduced by 'by', or there will be no actor. An actor expressed in the form of an adjunct with 'by' (or other preposition) in a receptive clause is usually known as an ***agent***.

A middle clause is one in which the action involves only one participating entity, which is thus always an actor:

John is waiting.

The sun is shining.

His popularity declined.

(You will) Behave yourself!

In non-middle clauses, on the other hand, the action involves two participating entities, even though one or other of these may not be present in the structure: it involves an ***actor*** and a ***goal***, respectively 'John' and 'the string' in 'John is tying the string'. Within the non-middle, the distinction between operative and receptive relates to the function of Subject: in the operative, the Subject is the actor while in the receptive the Subject is the goal. The other participant, the one which is not the Subject, may be absent in each case: 'you wrap and I'll tie' shows a 'goal-less' form of the operative, while 'this string won't tie' and 'this string has been tied very tight' show an 'actor-less' (agentless) form of the receptive.

The choice between operative and receptive – i.e. the factors affecting the speaker's decision whether to say 'Wren built this gazebo' or 'this gazebo was built by Wren' – concerns what should be the starting point of the message, i.e. Theme. The difference in meaning between the two is a textual one, and not related to transitivity.

Consider the following examples:

a. 'The lion ran.'
b. 'The lion chased the tourist.'
c. 'The tourist was chased by the lion.'
d. 'The tourist ran.'
   i. The difference between (a) and (b) is one of transitivity, (a) is intransitive, (b) is transitive. In (b) the action of running is extended to the tourist, who is being chased by the lion.
   ii. The difference between (b) and (c) is a choice between operative and receptive, or active vs. passive – a difference in textual meaning, i.e. whether the actor/agent or the goal is Theme, and thus identified first.

iii. The difference between (b) and (d) is a matter of ***ergativity***, in which the sentence pair expresses a cause and effect relationship. We understand that the tourist is running because the lion is chasing him, i.e. the lion is the **agent** causing the tourist to run. The tourist in (d) is the **medium**, the entity through the medium of which the process comes into existence, i.e. is actualized.

3.1.2

The distinction between ***transitive*** and ***ergative*** is not a distinction between different kinds of processes, but rather different ways of looking at the same process. A process is a semantic construct: and what we are suggesting is that in any one language the representation of processes in the semantics will be a mixture of these two modes. This means that certain regularities in the grammar will be brought out by an analysis in transitive terms and others by an analysis in ergative terms.

Below are additional examples illustrating the distinctions noted above:

- 'The tourist woke.' [middle] ['the tourist' = Medium/Actor] [non-ergatve; intransitive]
- 'The lion woke the tourist.' [non-middle, operative] ['the lion' = Agent/Actor; the tourist = Medium/Goal] [ergative; transitive]
- 'The tourist was woken (by the lion).' [non-middle, receptive] ['the tourist' = Medium/Goal; 'the lion' = Agent/Actor] [ergative; transitive]
- 'The glass broke.' [middle] ['the glass' = Medium/Actor] [ergative; intransitive]
- 'The heat broke the glass.' [non-middle, operative] ['the heat' = Agent/Actor; 'the glass' = Medium/Goal] [ergative; transitive]
- 'The glass was broken (by the heat).' [non-middle, receptive] ['the glass' = Medium/Goal; 'the heat' = Agent/Actor] [ergative; transitive]

One might suggest that a middle clause is simply one with an intransitive verb, such as 'wait' or 'shine', and a non-middle clause is one with a transitive verb, but it is no longer very useful to classify verbs simply into transitive and intransitive, because a large number of them, including probably a majority of the more common verbs, can be either.

The distinction between middle and non-middle voice in the clause provides an alternative basis for verb classification.

With verbs of action, a three-way classification suggests itself:

- A large proportion of the more frequent verbs in the language are equally at home with either one or two participants. These we will refer to as ***neutral verbs;*** examples of such are 'move', 'turn', 'open', 'change', 'spread', 'shake', 'pour', 'roll', 'bend', 'break', 'smash', 'mend', 'cook', 'boil', 'stew', 'burn', 'melt', 'dry', 'loosen', 'soften', 'quicken', 'plug in', 'fit in', 'mix', 'combine', 'evolve', 'drive', 'row', 'sail', 'drill', 'slide'. With such verbs it is not really possible to decide which is the more 'basic' form, whether with one participant, like 'the water poured out', or with two, like 'he poured the water out'. Such verbs, then, fit equally naturally into both middle and non-middle clauses, being associated indifferently either with actor alone or with actor and goal.

- Contrasting with verbs of the neutral type are those that reflect a more clear-cut treatment of an action as inherently, or preponderantly, of a two-participant type ('transitive', e.g. 'throw') or of a one-participant type ('intransitive', e.g. 'swim').
- There is a small class of action clauses with no participants at all: meteorological clauses such as 'it's raining'. In a transitive / intransitive classification, they are intransitive since they have no goal, and when a nominal is associated with them, as in 'it's snowing feathers', it does have a participant function (distinguish 'they rained down arrows' / 'arrows rained down', where 'rain down' is a neutral verb and 'arrows' is goal or actor).

Table 3.1 summarizes the points made above with respect to material processes.

Table 3.1: Material processes

<table>
<tr><td rowspan="12">Material processes</td><td rowspan="3">Process Type (transitive)</td><td>action (animate actor)</td><td>intention ('do')</td><td rowspan="5"></td></tr>
<tr><td>event (inanimate actor)</td><td rowspan="2">supervention ('happen')</td></tr>
<tr><td>natural phenomenon (no actor)</td></tr>
<tr><td rowspan="2">Voice</td><td>middle</td><td>active</td></tr>
<tr><td>non-middle</td><td>passive</td></tr>
<tr><td rowspan="7">Process Type (ergative)</td><td rowspan="5">concrete</td><td rowspan="3">spatial</td><td>existence</td></tr>
<tr><td>form & location</td></tr>
<tr><td>movement</td></tr>
<tr><td>material</td><td>operation</td></tr>
<tr><td></td><td>alteration</td></tr>
<tr><td rowspan="2">abstract</td><td>creative</td><td>cause, fusion, change</td></tr>
<tr><td>effective</td><td>disposition, control</td></tr>
</table>

3.2 Mental processes

3.2.1

The 'mental processes' are processes of consciousness. They fall into three sub-groups, (i) perception (e.g. seeing and hearing), 'seeing'; (ii) reaction (e.g. liking and fearing), 'feeling'; (iii) cognition (e.g. knowing and thinking), 'knowing'. This is the one type of process in English that is treated as distinctively human, so that any entity that is cast in the role of this activated entity in a mental process clause thereby becomes endowed with quasi-human consciousness. The participant that is 'seeing', 'feeling' or 'knowing' in a mental process clause is referred to as the **Senser.** Such a participant is obviously playing a very different part in the process from one who is doing something like 'running', 'breaking' or 'throwing'. There is a distinct role of 'one involved in a process of consciousness', treated in the language as different from 'one engaged in doing something'. The Senser is **narrower** than either Actor or Goal: not only must it be a 'thing' – it must be human, or endowed with human-like consciousness. The Phenomenon is **broader** than either Actor or Goal: not only need it not be human – it need not even be a 'thing', but can be a fact or a report.

Mental processes incorporate an option not found in action-type processes, an option that is an extension of an opposition related to voice (in the sense of active/passive): they can be viewed from either of two opposing standpoints. For example, we can say 'Nigel liked the play', but we can also say 'the play pleased Nigel', 'please' and 'like' represent the same process seen from different ends. But we cannot simply say that one of these is the passive of the other, because each has its own passive: 'the play was liked by Nigel' and 'Nigel was pleased by the play'. Similarly we have 'Tony believed the story', 'the story convinced Tony'; and their corresponding passives 'the story was believed by Tony', 'Tony was convinced by the story'. Notice that, of the two passive forms in each pair, those with 'please' and 'convince' are much more usual than those with 'like' and 'believe'.

It is not to be supposed that every word has an exact equivalent in the other set. Some pairs do match fairly closely, like 'please' and 'like', 'frighten' and 'be afraid of', 'amuse' or 'delight' and 'enjoy', perhaps 'strike' and 'notice'. But most of them do not, and even these are not totally equivalent. The point is that, once we are talking about a mental process, we have the choice of looking at it from either viewpoint; according to the choice we make, so we have one or another set of words to choose from, sets which correspond roughly as a whole but not one to one.

This is in fact a good illustration of the relation between vocabulary and grammar. Vocabulary is not something separate from grammar, as some metaphors suggest – one of the most misleading views of language is the 'bricks and mortar' theory, according to which the words provide the meanings (the bricks) and these are held together by structures (the mortar). Both grammar and vocabulary express meaning; the vocabulary is simply the most 'delicate' part of the grammar, the choice of words being the limiting stage when it comes to deciding on one's choice of meanings to be expressed. So in talking about a mental process we have various options to choose from – what kind of mental process we are talking about, for example – and these include the choice just mentioned, that of the vantage point. The choices made in all these options determine the set of lexical items available in the final selection. When we say 'determine' and 'final selection', we are not assuming any direct relation between this model of the decision-making processes of speech and whatever takes place in real time, in the brain. We have given a very simple model of what is an extremely complex process. But it is possible to conceive of there being some relation between the two, whereas the 'bricks and mortar' view of language does not seem to correspond to anything that we can imagine actually happening. The speaker does not first decide which words to use and then consider how to stick them together.

3.2.2

The selection of meanings in this area is in any case very complex. There are restrictions on the type of phenomenon – that which is being reacted to, perceived, etc. – that can occur under different conditions of choice. For example, we can say 'I liked his house' and 'I liked his wife'; we can also say 'his house pleased me', but not, or not in the same sense, 'his wife pleased me'. In some instances there is a third possibility: 'I liked his attitude', 'his attitude pleased me', and also 'he pleased me by his attitude'. But we cannot say 'he pleased me by his house', still less 'he pleased me by his wife'. A number of factors enter in to the specification of the total meaning potential.

In the second place – a rather minor point, but quite interesting – with action clauses we can almost always use an expanded form with the verb 'do' or 'happen': 'do' if the process is active, 'happen' if it is passive or 'superventive' (i.e. active in form but inherently 'passive' in sense):

Lionel jumped off the roof – what Lionel did was jump off the roof.

Lionel was pushed off the roof – what happened to Lionel was that he was pushed off the roof.

Lionel fell off the roof – what happened to Lionel was that he fell off the roof.

With mental processes none of these is really appropriate. We cannot say 'what Nigel did was like the play'; we might perhaps accept 'what the play did was please Nigel' and 'what happened to Nigel was that he liked the play', which is less inconsistent with our intuitions about what kind of a process 'liking' is. But none of these is very natural. Mental processes are not readily expressed in this highly generalized form, which is very common with action clauses (where it carries an important and specific meaning). Note that we are not talking here about the verb substitute *do,* which occurs for example in 'Nigel liked the play better than I had done'; in which verb substitute *do* has a different meaning, and has nothing to do with the type of process being talked about.

The main factor that distinguishes mental processes is the nature of the participants involved. It is not really surprising that the participants – or, better, the participant roles – in a mental process clause should be different from those in an action clause. The two are different types of process. The distinction is in fact rather clear cut; unusually so for grammar, where most distinctions are muddy and blurred.

Essentially, there are two participant roles in the expression of a mental process (sometimes there may be only one; we refer to these below); and both are different from any of the participant roles in action clauses. They differ not only in that they are different functions, but also as regards what kinds of participant can appear in them. One is more restricted, and the other less restricted, than the participant roles of action clauses.

One of the participants in a mental process is always 'human'. This includes the category of 'quasi-human': anything that is regarded as being like a human being, in the sense of being endowed with consciousness, and thus having ascribed to it the capacity for thoughts, feelings and perceptions can take on this particular function. The extent of this category varies considerably, not only from one speaker to another but also with the same speaker in different situations; but it generally includes some animals – pets or farm animals, those most closely associated with human beings – and may be extended ad hoc to others, often humorously. The category in question includes 'things that are referred to pronominally as "he" or "she" and not "it"'; this is why mental process clauses with 'it' in this function always sound slightly off. This is one source of the humorous effect, such as for example when the speaker who is tickling an octopus in a tank turns to his companion and says 'look, it likes it'. Expressions such as 'I couldn't convince it', 'Do you think it heard me?' 'It doesn't seem amused' are all perfectly possible but they suggest a self-consciousness on the part of the speaker which itself is a very good index of their slightly deviant quality.

Computers now tend to be credited with thoughts, feelings and perceptions and thus figure in expressions of mental processes, even though they are still usually referred to as 'it'. (On the other hand, the use of personal reference, 'she', for ships and cars, which is rather quaint or artificial for most speakers, does not extend to their participation in mental processes.)

This human or quasi-human participant is obligatory in all mental process clauses and plays the part of the one who experiences the process in question – who likes, sees, thinks or whatever it is. What is its function in the clause structure? Here any attempt to analyse in terms of Actor and Goal, an analysis which worked – even if only partially and imperfectly – with action-type processes, breaks down altogether. There is no way of saying which is Actor and which is Goal in a clause such as 'Jane liked the gift'. Jane is certainly not doing anything to the gift; and although we might perhaps argue that the gift is doing something to Jane (we even have an expression 'it does something to me' as evidence), we would hardly accept the transitive interpretation 'the gift is doing something, and the action extends to Jane'.

Of course, it is easy to make any such interpretation look absurd by paraphrasing it; the really significant point is the one already noted, namely that these are two forms of expression for mental processes, 'Jane liked the gift' and 'the gift pleased Jane'. In an Actor and Goal analysis we should have to say that 'Jane' was the Actor in the first instance and 'the gift' was the Actor in the second, which makes it impossible to make sense of the concept. The problem is rather like that of 'open–door': we did not want to conclude that 'the door' had a different function in the two clauses 'the door opened' and 'Henry opened the door' (see discussion in the chapter on *Experiential meaning*, #43–46). Here however the problem is more acute, for two reasons. The first that the difficulty of identifying the Actor would apply to **all** mental process clauses, whereas it arose only with **some** action clauses. The other is that, although we might be prepared to assign two different functions to 'the door' in these instances, we cannot get away with this in a mental process clause: the 'human' participant must be recognized as having the same function throughout, since that is the only way we can explain why it is always has to be human – namely because it is fulfilling this particular function in the structure.

So we shall not attempt to identify any of the roles in a mental process clause as an Actor. Instead, we shall recognize as a distinct function the role of the 'human' being that reacts, perceives or thinks. There is no very satisfactory term for this, but since the meaning of this role is that of apprehending or processing in the consciousness we shall refer to it as the ***Senser***.

3.2.3

Every mental process clause must contain a senser. This function may be combined with the function of Subject, as in 'Jane liked the gift', or that of Complement, as in 'the gift pleased Jane', as well as occurring with 'by' as in 'the gift was liked by Jane'. As far as transitivity is concerned, it is the same function in each case. When we investigate further, we find that the Senser is no so much human as 'human-like'; that is, treated as being endowed with consciousness – and so pronominalized as *he* or *she* rather than *it*.

By the same token, the other essential element in the mental process, the phenomenon that is 'sensed', likewise has the same function throughout the whole range of variations in the form of the clause. Let us call this simply the ***Phenomenon***. We now analyse as follows:

Jane	*liked*	*the gift*	*the gift*	*was liked*	*by*	*Jane*
Senser	Process	Phenomenon	Phenomenon	Process		Senser
the gift	*pleased*	*Jane*	*Jane*	*was pleased*	*by*	*the gift*
Phenomenon	Process	Senser	Senser	Process		Phenomenon

The Phenomenon can be anything that can enter into a process of the 'action' type, and certain other things besides, It is not limited to persons, objects and other phenomena on the plane of experience. The most distinctive feature of mental process clauses is that what is perceived or reacted to or thought of may also be what we might call a 'metaphenomenon'. To put this another way, in a mental process meanings as well as things may play a part in the process.

The components of a process – the process itself, and the participants and circumstances – are phenomena of our experience. We can list the types of such phenomena, using headings that reflect their categorization in the language: in English we recognize persons, other living beings, objects, institutions, abstractions, actions, events, qualities, states and relations. (It is a mistake to expect the categorization of phenomena to be expressed directly in the organization of 'parts of speech'; rather, they are reflected indirectly, through semantic patterns, throughout the lexicogrammatical system.) These together make up the ideational content of language, though the headings differ from one language to another; as, of course, do the means of their expression. In English any of these can be expressed in nominal form, and any of them can function as the Phenomenon in a mental process (e.g. 'approved', 'noticed', 'thought about'):

the president (person)	*his departure* (action)
the cat (living being)	*the ceremony* (event)

the table (object)	*her looks* (quality)
the government (institution)	*their loneliness* (state)
their intention (abstraction)	*the cost* (relation)

We shall refer to these collectively as 'things'. Some kinds of thing can also be expressed as clauses (nominalizations), for example 'I liked *what she was wearing*' (object), 'I heard *the rain falling on the leaves*' (event).

The phenomenon that is the object of reaction, perception or cognition may be a phenomenon of experience (a 'thing') – something that can figure also in a non-mental process. But it may, on the other hand – unlike the elements in an action clause – be a 'fact' or a 'report'. Facts and reports are not 'things' in our sense; they are 'mere words' – phenomena that have been as it were processed by language. Thus in addition to

I saw Helen

I saw the gazebo

I saw a discrepancy in the argument

I saw the game

I saw Leeds play(ing) Chelsea

we can say

I saw that he was exhausted

I saw that interest rates were going up

Of the last two, the first is a 'fact', the second a 'report'. In many instances we can actually insert the words 'fact' and 'report' to introduce these elements; 'I noticed the fact that he was exhausted', 'I read the report that the interest rates were going up'.

Facts and reports correspond to what is sometimes known as 'indirect speech'. But this term is sometimes used rather inconsistently; it includes reports, but it is not always clear whether it also includes facts or not. This is not entirely surprising; a fact is less closely related to speech than a report is, and the concept of indirect speech is derived from that of 'direct', or quoted, speech. Facts and reports are both, in one sense, simply language. They are not themselves phenomena of our experience; they are the representation of these phenomena in language, hence second order phenomena, or 'metaphenomena' as we termed them above. And the difference between a fact and a report is that the latter is a representation in linguistic form; it is a 'wording', of a phenomenon – technically, a representation of it at the lexicogrammatical level. A fact, on the other hand, is a 'meaning': a representation of a phenomenon at the semantic level. It is one stage more 'indirect' than indirect (reported) speech:

Senser	Mental Process	Phenomenon
I	*saw*	*Leeds win* [thing]
I	*saw*	*that Leeds were winning* [fact]
I	*saw*	*(the report) that Leeds had won* [report]

Thus, whereas in action processes only things can enter in, in mental processes language itself, in the form of meanings and wordings, can play a part. A mental process can involve either things, directly, or facts and reports about things.

This is the general pattern. Naturally, not every verb of mental process can accept phenomena of all kinds; and even where it can the meaning may be somewhat different in the different instances. For example a verb of perception such as 'see' feels to us rather like a different verb when we talk of 'seeing' a fact or report, as distinct from 'seeing' a thing; these are obviously different processes. But the difference in meaning can be explained precisely because in one case the phenomenon is a thing and in the other it is not; there is no need to say that there is more than one verb 'to see'. The senses – 'I perceived visually', 'I deduced from what I saw the fact that ...', 'I read the report that ...' – derive naturally from the type of phenomenon with which the process, 'to see', is combined. Even its use as a verb of cognition, as when we say 'I see' in the sense of 'I understand', follows in the same way: 'I perceive in my mind's eye', as it were. **The essential point is that mental processes as a whole are distinct from actions in that words as well as things can play a part.** The choice of the particular type of phenomenon will determine what verbs can be used and what their particular interpretation in the context is likely to be.

Nouns of the 'general' or 'cover' class corresponding to facts and reports can occur wherever facts and reports themselves can occur; this includes the words 'fact' and 'report', and others besides, for example 'I appreciate the fact', 'he didn't believe the rumour', 'I don't like the idea'. These 'cover nouns' can also occur as introducers of facts and reports; the nominalization expressing the fact or report then functions as a qualifier in the nominal group having the cover noun as head:

He didn't believe the rumour that they were going bankrupt.

I don't like the idea of your going there alone.

The occurrence of a nominalization as the phenomenon of a mental process clause can lead, under certain conditions, to ambiguity as between a thing and a fact. For example:

what she kept in the cupboard terrified him

This could mean either 'the thing that she kept in the cupboard ...' or 'the fact of what she kept in the cupboard ...'; the ambiguity arises because 'what' can mean both 'that which' (relative) and 'what?' (interrogative). Compare 'did you see what she was wearing?', which could mean either 'did you notice the object?', in which case an appropriate answer might be 'yes, wasn't it terrible', or 'do you know the answer to the question?', for which the appropriate answer might be 'yes, a short knitted dress'.

The difference is brought out by considering pairs such as the following:

the chair collapsed	*what he was sitting on collapsed*
it collapsed, the chair	*it collapsed, what he was sitting on*

The second of each pair, with 'it' at the beginning, is a 'substitution' form. Any Subject can be substituted in this way, giving the clause a particular textual meaning. Provided the Subject is a 'thing', as in these examples, then the substitute form is clearly the marked option; the typical form is that with the Subject at the beginning, whether it contains a nominalization or not. But where the Subject is a fact or a report, the typical pattern is the substitute one, and here it is the non-substitute form that appears as the marked option, as in the following (note the absence of a comma):

that you look so tired worries me

it worries me that you look so tired

The marked forms, 'it collapsed, what he was sitting on' and 'that you look so tired worries me', are both quite acceptable, but there has to be 'good reason' for their selection. So, other things being equal, we usually interpret on the assumption of the unmarked form; that is, we would interpret

what she kept in the cupboard	*terrified*	*him*
Phenomenon (thing)	Process	Senser

as 'the thing that ...' (relative), but

it	*terrified*	*him*	*what she kept in the cupboard*
	Process	Senser.	Phenomenon (fact)

as 'the fact of what ...' (interrogative).

3.2.4

The characteristic feature of a mental process, then, in English, is that it is a process involving a Senser, who must be a conscious being, and a Phenomenon, which may be a phenomenon of experience, a 'thing', but may also be a 'metaphenomenon', a fact or a report.

Usually both of these participants are present in the structure of the clause, but under certain conditions there may be only one, and here it will be helpful to return to the notion of 'inherent' and 'actual' participants, which came up in relation to action clauses (see discussion in the chapter on *Experiential meaning*, #22–23).

In mental process clauses of the 'please' type, Senser and Phenomenon are both inherent participants. This type thus resembles the 'transitive' type of action clause in being 'non-middle' (two inherent participants); and in the same way the actual number of participants may be only one, since either Senser or Phenomenon may be omitted. Thus:

transitive (two inherent participants, one or two actual)

the gift	*pleased*		*Jane*	*the gift*	*pleased*
Phenomenon	Process		Senser	Phenomenon	Process
Jane	*was pleased*	*by*	*the gift*	*Jane*	*was pleased*
Senser	Process		Phenomenon	Senser	Process

representing the system

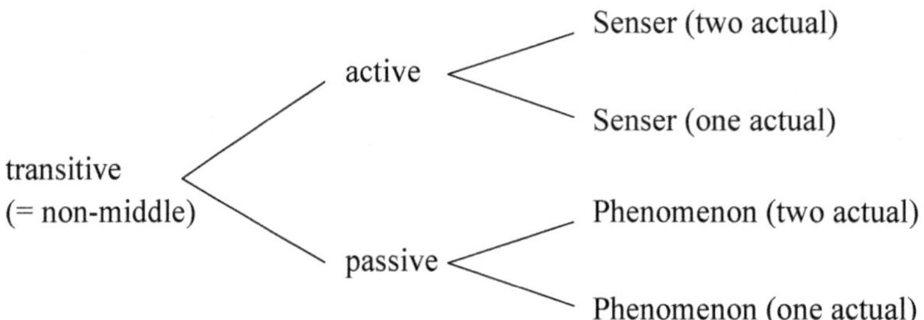

In clauses of the 'like' type, the proposition is more complex. There is one kind in which there is only one participant, the Senser, for example 'be afraid', 'enjoy oneself', 'watch', 'listen', 'think' (= 'cogitate'), 'wonder'. These resemble the intransitive type of action clause; they can be regarded as 'middle' forms. Probably we should include among them the involuntary manifestations of mental processes, sometimes referred to as behavioural processes, such as 'laugh', 'smile', 'cry'; moreover it is likely that a number of mental process clauses which are passive in form, such as 'be amazed', 'be surprised', 'be pleased', are also middle (that is, just one inherent participant, rather than passive, with two inherent and one actual) – there is no special middle form of the verb, and the passive is actually a more likely choice for the expression of the 'middle' sense in this context. With most processes of this type, however, both Senser and Phenomenon are inherent in the process.

With most processes of this type, such as 'like', 'see', 'believe', both Senser and Phenomenon are inherent in the process; but the voice potentialities are rather different. One of the 'active' forms – that with only one actual participant – is impossible (indicated by ^{xx}); and both passives are much rarer (indicated by ^{x}) than other passives in English:

Jane	*liked*	*the gift*	
Senser	Process	Phenomenon	
the gift	*was liked*	*by*	*Jane*^{x}
Phenomenon	Process		Senser

Jane	*liked*^{xx}
Senser	Process
the gift	*was liked*^{x}
Phenomenon	Process

This type does not obviously resemble any of the 'action' – types.

Before representing this as a system, let us briefly reconsider the relation between mental processes and actions. We saw earlier that an analysis in terms of Actor and Goal would not work for mental processes; but it was not entirely successful with action clauses either, and we needed a more abstract concept of the participant roles involved. This was provided by an interpretation in terms of cause and effect; we identified one central participant role, the Medium, as obligatory in all actions, and another, the Agent, which was present just in those instances where the cause was external to the actualization of the process.

It is noteworthy that the Senser is inherent in all mental processes; and this provides the clue to its interpretation. The 'Senser' is, in fact, the 'Medium' participant in the context of a mental process. Hence mental process clauses of the 'please' type are straightforwardly relatable to action clauses – they are those in which the Senser engages in a mental process (no matter whether reaction, perception or cognition) which is brought about by an external agency, namely the Phenomenon – the difference being that a mental process can be brought about not only by experiential phenomena but also by the linguistic representation of these phenomena, by facts and reports. So the 'please' type is the non-middle (two participant) form of a mental process clause.

But the 'like' type does not fit into the existing picture. It is certainly not transitive; this would imply that the gift was involved in a liking process brought about by Jane, which is no better than the 'Actor-Goal' interpretation. Moreover if it was transitive, the passive should be unrestricted; there is a long and technical argument here, involving questions of theme and information structures, but the upshot of it is that forms such as 'the gift was liked (by Jane)', although modelled on the active/passive system, are not true passives in the usual sense. Actually, 'like'-type clauses are all middle; there is no Agent in them. The Phenomenon is in fact functioning as an element of a different kind, related to the traditional notion of a 'cognate object' and circumstantial in character. Hence 'Jane liked the gift', meaning 'Jane was pleased', is a way of describing the situation as 'Jane was pleased, and the circumstance defining her pleasure was the gift'. The reason why 'the gift was liked by Jane' is odd is that a circumstantial element is occupying a role usually reserved for the central participant in the process.

This is also the reason why there are no 'passivals' with clauses of the like type. Transitive clauses, both those of action and please type mental process, have an additional potentiality in the voice system which Sweet referred to as 'passival', defined as 'active in form but passive in meaning', for example:

the door won't open (= 'can't be made to open')

the woodwork polishes beautifully (= 'can be polished')

Jane pleases very easily (= 'can easily be pleased')

But there is no form 'the gift likes easily' [xx]. Such a statement would make no sense, because it would purport to describe something which is not in fact an element in the process at all, but merely the domain or limiting circumstance of it; it is like saying 'tennis plays easily'[xx] or 'that song won't sing'[xx].

The network for mental processes of the 'like' type is:

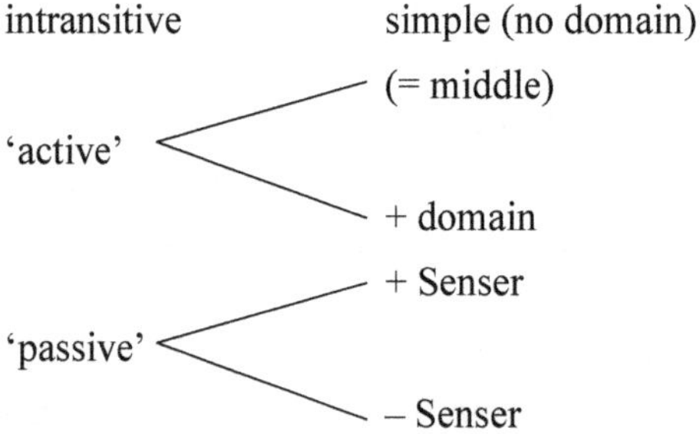

exemplified by 'Jane enjoyed herself' (simple), 'Jane liked the gift'('active'), the gift was liked (by Jane)' ('passive', +/- Senser).

Mental processes also differ from material processes in how the unmarked present tense is realized. For material processes, the unmarked form is be V-ing (e.g. 'I am washing the car'), but for mental processes, the unmarked form is the simple present (e.g. 'I know that …', not 'I am knowing that …'). When the simple present is used for material processes, it implies general or habitual activity.

EXAMPLES OF MATERIAL AND MENTAL PROCESS CLAUSES

	VOICE	MIDDLE (one participant)	NON-MIDDLE (AGENTIVE) (two participants)			
	PROCESS TYPE		active:		passive:	
			+ Goal	- Goal	- Agent	(+ Agent)
MATERIAL	most "transitive"	–	Jim threw the stone	Jim threw	the stone was thrown	(by Jim)
		[the string tied]	Jim tied the string	Jim tied	the string was tied	(by Jim)
		the car started	Jim started the car	[Jim started]	the car was started	(by Jim)
	most "intransitive"	the ball bounced	Jim bounced the ball	–	the ball was bounced	(by Jim)
		the clock struck	–	–	–	
MENTAL	reaction	Ann smiled / enjoyed herself				
		Ann liked the idea	the gift pleased Ann	–	Ann was please	(by the gift)
	perception	Tom listened				
		Tom heard the rumour	The noise assailed Tom	–	Tom was assailed	(by the noise)
	cognition	Joy pondered				
		Joy considered	The book puzzled Joy	[the book puzzled]	Joy was puzzled	(by the book)

3.3 Verbal Processes

3.3.1 Elements of verbal processes

A verbal process is traditionally interpreted as a structure of three elements. One is the process itself, most typically expressed by 'say'; the others are the 'verbalizer' and the 'verbalization', which are treated as Subject and Object respectively:

Brutus	*said*	*Caesar was ambitious*
Subject	Predicator	Object

Interpreting this, we can see that it is equivalent to an analysis in terms of Actor + Process + Goal; or, if we assume a distinction into different process types, where the nearest analogy would be that with mental process clauses, then into Senser + Process + Phenomenon.

However, there are strong reasons for considering that expressions of verbal processes are not single clauses but clause-complexes. Our analysis of this sentence would be:

Brutus	*said*
α: verbalizing	
Sayer	Process

Caesar	*was*	*ambitious*
β: verbalized		

This sentence is analysed as two clauses, the first a verbalizing clause with the structure Sayer + Process as the main clause (indicated by the Greek letter α) plus the second, a verbalized clause (which may be of any process type; here it is a relational clause) as the dependent clause (indicated by the Greek letter β). In other words, the two clauses, one main, the other dependent, form a hypotactic clause complex.

In other words, the verbalization does not enter into the structure of the verbalizing clause, at least not in the normal case. The only cases where the element expressing the verbalization would actually enter into the structure of the verbalizing clause would be (i) where it is the 'name' of a report, as in 'he spoke only two words', 'don't talk nonsense'; (ii) where it is deictic, as in 'he said that', 'he said so', 'what did he say? he told them all the particulars'; (iii) where it is not a report at all but a fact.

The other element that is specific to verbalizing clauses is the Addressee: 'the owl' in 'Pussy said to the owl: "You elegant fowl!"'. In terms of the generalized functions, both Sayer and Addressee are readily identifiable; the Sayer is the Medium, the Addressee the Beneficiary. In clauses such as 'he spoke only two words', where 'two words' is an element in the verbalizing clause, it has the function of Range, in the sense that it indicates the scope of the saying; and the same applies to 'English' in 'she spoke English.'

he	*spoke*	*only two words*
Sayer	Process	Range

she	*spoke*	*English*
Sayer	Process	Range

Let us start from the notion of quotation. Quotation is the expression of a verbal process by paratactic means; the two parts are structurally independent, as in other paratactic constructions:

Said the Piggy:		*'I will'*
1 : verbalizing		2 : verbalized

So far we have slightly oversimplified the nature of a report by saying that it is a 'wording', which is equivalent to saying that it is language at the lexicogrammatical level. More precisely, however, a report is language at any level below that of meaning; we can have quotation which is not only wording but 'sounding', at the phonological or phonetic levels, e.g. 'Say: "Ah"', 'you say "either" [iiðə] and I say "either" [aiðə]'. This pattern includes those statements about the writing system which are so confusing to young children who are trying to master it (and they would still be confusing even if they were accurate), such as 'the letter "a" says [a]'. [There is a parallel to this in referring to the written medium, e.g. 'I can't quite make it out'; I think it says '4 N X 7'. These are different from 'the letter "a" says [a]', which is a phonic interpretation of the written medium.]

A 'sounding', of course, can only be quoted, not reported; we cannot say 'he said that ah'. But wherever the verbalized element is at the level of wording, it can, in principle, be either quoted or reported:

Quoting (paratactic) Reporting (hypotactic)

Said the Piggy:		*'I will'*		*The Piggy said*		*he would*
1 : verbalizing		2 : verbalized		α: verbalizing		β: verbalized

Thus in the typical case the process of verbalization is treated as a logical relation between two elements, the verbalizing and the verbalized, which may, like other logical relations, take either a paratactic or a hypotactic form.

The two parts of a sentence such as 'Brutus said Caesar was ambitious' are from one point of view quite unequal; there are not two distinct processes, with the meaning of 'Brutus said [something] and Caesar was ambitious'. From another point of view, however, the sentence does consist of two parts in equilibrium. 'Caesar was ambitious' is speech, or verbalization as we are calling it; in other words, someone said it, namely Brutus. But 'Brutus said [something]' is also speech; again, someone said it – in this case, Mark Antony, if not quite in those words. But 'Caesar was ambitious' is at one step further away from the level of experience. The relation is a recursive one; we can have an indefinite series 'A said B said C said ...', subject only to general restrictions on the extension of hypotactic structures.

It can be seen that this differs substantially from the pattern of a mental process involving a fact, as in 'Brutus regretted that Caesar was ambitious'. Here, the 'fact' is rank-shifted – that is, it is embedded in the clause in which it functions as Phenomenon:

	Brutus	*regretted*	[[*that Caesar*	*was*	*ambitious*]]
Clause	Senser	Process	Phenomenon : fact		
		[[Clause]]	Carrier	Process	Attribute

3.3.2

At this point, we need to focus on the **similarity** between mental and verbal processes. If we switch our attention, within the mental, from processes of perception and affection-volition (seeing, liking and wanting) to those of cognition (thinking and knowing), we see that these latter share the critical feature of verbal processes: both of them can change the status of a piece of wording, from a (direct) representation of experience to a representation of a representation. In other words, they can ***project***.

We have seen that projection may be done by a verbal process; this is what is called 'reported speech', and what is projected is typically a **wording**, as in *John said "it's too late"*. But it may also be done by a mental process; here what is projected is a **meaning**, as in *Mary thought, "it's too late"*. This has sometimes been called 'reported thought'. In fact both speech and thought can be projected either as quote ('direct') or as report ('indirect'), giving four possibilities as in the table below:

projecting process: / type of projection:	verbal process + locution	mental process + idea
quoting	*John said "it's too late"*	*Mary thought "it's too late"*
reporting	*John said it was too late*	*Mary thought it was too late*

Furthermore, projection preserves the full range of options in mood as set out:

		verbal process + locution	mental process + idea
quoting	declarative	*John said "it's too late"*	*Mary thought "it's too late"*
	interrogative	*John said "is it too late?"*	*Mary thought "is it too late?"*
	imperative	*John said "don't be too late"*	*Mary thought "don't be too late"*
reporting	declarative	*John said that it was too late*	*Mary thought that it was too late*
	interrogative	*John asked whether it is too late*	*Mary wondered whether it was too late*
	imperative	*John ordered (them) not to be too late*	*Mary wanted (them) not to be too late"*

The equivalence between quoting and reporting is less exact in the imperative than in the indicative (declarative/interrogative); but it is still recognizable enough to be seen as systemic, as shown by the fact that learners are expected to convert one to the other ('direct to indirect speech', and vice versa).

We can now go on to reconsider the difference between reports and facts. Like a report, a fact is also the outcome of projection – with the distinctive property that it is not introduced by any projecting process. A fact comes, so to speak, ready processed, packaged as a piece of projection – which is why it is 'embedded' (downranked to become an element in a clause, instead of retaining its status as a ranking clause as do reports and quotes. As we have seen, a fact can participate in a mental process (*Peter accepted (the fact) that it was too late*), and even in a verbal process (*John emphasized (the fact) that it was too late*); but it is not the emphasizing, or the accepting, that gives it the status of a fact – it has no mode of existence as anything else.

Hence a fact has no equivalent quoted form: we wouldn't say *"it's too late," accepted Peter*; and it does not admit of any options in mood. Facts do not select for interrogative or imperative. They can be turned into questions or commands by being added as Qualifiers to an appropriate noun: *the boss raised the issue (of) whether I should retire, the troops disobeyed the order to attack*, and here they can often be nominalized, as in *apologized for the lateness of the application, ordered the withdrawal of the troops*.

3.3.3

Quotes, reports and facts form a kind of continuum, from the most direct to the most indirect manifestations of projection. There are significant and recognizable differences among the three types; there are also many borderline cases and blends.

The indeterminate boundary between quoting and reporting appears clearly in the familiar patterns of what is known as 'free indirect speech'. This refers to a mixed variety of projection where, for example, the direct form of the interrogative is transferred into the reported structure, as in 'she asked could she see the picture'. This does differ in meaning from the paradigm form 'she asked if she could see the picture', but not as question to statement; the following pairs are not proportional:

(i)	(ii)
(a) *she can see the picture*	*she asked if she could see the picture*
(b) *can she see the picture?*	*she asked could she see the picture*

The use of the direct interrogative form as in (b ii) reduces the distance between the event (her asking) and the meta-event (the report of it).

- The version in (ii) is a 'direct interrogative' in the sense that its own structure is interrogative; it has 'could she …', not 'she could …'. But it is not the equivalent quoted form, which would be 'can I …?'. In other words it is a hybrid form, with the structure of the direct interrogative but the pronouns and tenses of the indirect one. This hybrid pattern is a mixture of the paratactic (quoting) and the hypotactic (reporting) versions of verbal and mental projection, and it is exploited in narrative in forms like 'Was she being unjust, she wondered?' Again, the effect is to collapse the two levels of meaning into one so that the listener (or, usually, reader) is both witnessing events and being told about them at the same time.
- This in turn relates to the phenomenon of 'style indirect libre', in which an entire narrative is given in 'indirect speech' with the implication that it has the status of a report. The classical context for this is the description of someone's thoughts, in which we overhear him talking to himself, for example 'But nothing of what Anne had heard that day could really help them. She had taken a decision, and would have to accept its consequences.'
- Instances of this kind can be said to have an equivalent in direct (quoted) speech. For example, '"But", said Anne to herself, "nothing of what I have heard today can really help us. I took a decision, and must accept its consequences"'. But here, the 'verbalized' passage can extend indefinitely – the pattern belongs to written and not to spoken English, and is found only in certain literary genres, within which its limits are set stylistically; and either there is no verbalizing element,

as in the instance in 14.3, or, if there is, as in the instance in 14.4, it is an interpolation in the structure and functions not structurally but cohesively. Although it has the form of a quoting clause, 'said Anne to herself' actually resembles rather a 'discourse adjunct', and serves to relate the 'quoted' text to what has gone before.

- One sign of this is its phonological status: if it is read aloud, it has the intonation of a 'tail' – it is post-tonic to what has gone before. This is characteristic of a whole class of quoting expressions which follow the quoted element; again, this pattern is largely restricted to written English, but such forms are often read aloud – they are common in stories told to children – and they never become tonic, however long. For example, '"I didn't!", protested Peter with an expression of mock dismay:'

// I / **didn't** pro/tested / Peter with an ex/pression of / mock dis/may //

This example illustrates a verbalization structure in which the quoted element is a complete clause. Hence these have, in general, a reported equivalent: 'Peter [with an expression of mock dismay] protested that he hadn't'. This type represents perhaps the limiting case of a verbal process. Very many verbs occur in this pattern, having the sense of 'say' plus some added component of attitude or rhetorical flavour, e.g. 'insist', 'explain', 'object', 'argue', 'complain', 'urge', 'disclaim'. But, in general, these verbs are not found when the quoting clause precedes the quoted, which is its usual position in spoken English; we do not expect 'Peter disclaimed: "But I didn't"'.

Finally, in certain types of narrative fiction, verbs which themselves contain no component 'say' at all are used in a quoting sense following direct speech, e.g. 'shrug', 'demur', 'persist', 'twinkle', 'beam': '"I wish you luck", twinkled the old man'. These, naturally, have no reporting equivalent; we cannot say 'The old man twinkled that he wished them luck'. But there is often a very similar form with the verbalizing component made explicit: 'the old man said with a twinkle ...'.

Verbalization is clearly identified in English as a distinct type of process falling within our experience; but its mode of expression is different from that of other process types. On the one hand, if it is expressed structurally it takes forms that are characteristic of the logical rather than the experiential component: it comes out not as a configuration of elements (process and participants) within the clause, but as a (paratactic or hypotactic) relation between clauses. On the other hand, it may be expressed in a way that is not structural at all, as a text-forming relation that should rather be classed as cohesive. What this means is that when we talk about talking we recognize that this is a different thing from talking about other processes, precisely because of its circularity; the forms of expression take account of this circularity by giving to the verbalized element a free-standing status, so that it is on a par with the verbalizing one. What is said to have been said (i.e. what is reported or quoted) is treated as an act of speech of the same order as what is said. And this extends to what is said to have been known, thought or believed.

3.3.4

We have seen that the verbalized element cannot be a 'thing' – unlike the Phenomenon in a mental process: we can *like* things, *see* things and *think* of things, but we cannot *say* things. This further confirms our structural analysis; if the verbalized element ever had the status of a thing it would function within the verbalizing clause, but without this possibility there is no feeling of its being a participant, and so no reason for analysing it as an element within the verbalizing clause.

Similarly, there are no two-participant forms of verbalization corresponding to those of mental process expressed by 'please', 'frighten' and the like. These, it was pointed out, are typically associated with instances where the Phenomenon is a 'thing', e.g. 'the noise frightened him'; but they are also used with facts, and hence we find pairs in the expression of mental processes to which there is no parallel in verbalization:

	mental process			verbalization	
(i)	*he*	*hated*	*that she looked sad*	*he said*	*that she looked sad*
	Senser	Process	Phenomenon: fact	Verbalizing	Verbalized
(ii)	*That she looked sad*	*distressed*	*him*	——	
	Phenomenon: fact	Process	Senser		

There are two situations in which a nominal element (noun, pronoun, nominal group) does enter as a participant in a verbal process. One is with verbs such as *praise*, *accuse*, *flatter*, *criticize*, where its function is analogous to that of Goal in a transitive material process; for example *you flatter me!*, *everyone was blaming the referee*. The specific term used for this function is Target.

The other is with verbs like *describe*, *outline*, *explain*, as in *can you describe the whole scene?* This function is called the Verbiage; it is either the content of what is said, as in this example, or else the name of some type or class of saying, as in *you're telling me a lie*. The Verbiage corresponds to the Phenomenon in a mental process of the like type; in general ergative terms it is a kind of Range.

Both verbal and mental (especially cognitive) processes admit **nominalization**, like *he announced his intention to take part, I don't recall the reason for that decision*. These are metaphoric nominalizations; they are grammatical metaphors, related to some congruent (non-metaphoric) clausal equivalent: *he announced that he would / intended to take part, I don't recall why it was decided that way*. In the metaphoric version, the nominalization is functioning as Verbiage (verbal process) or as Phenomenon (mental process).

The difference between a mental process and a verbal process is also very marked in the nature of the central participant. In the verbalizing clause, the Sayer is the Medium, the one through whom the process is actualized. It thus corresponds to the Senser in a mental process. The Sayer might therefore be expected to be restricted, like the Senser, to a person, or personalized entity. But it is not. We find verbalizing entities which, although they might be regarded as personalized, are really very different from those found in mental processes as in 'this plant likes the shade'. For example, 'my watch said it was 10 o'clock' does not involve any personalizing of the watch; it is quite unlike, say, 'my watch thought it was 10 o'clock' which could be explained only as a (humorous) personalization. Note however, that there is no quoted equivalent; we do not say '"It's ten o'clock", said my watch'.

Actually the process of verbalization, in English, does not imply a human participant as Sayer at all. We can have either non-personal elements, as in 'the book says', 'the notice said'; or 'impersonal' (i.e. non-specific) ones as in 'it says'. It does not matter that, in something like 'the book says ...', some human being must have written the book – or, if it comes to that, that others must have printed it. The Sayer in this pattern is the book and not the author.

This must be taken in conjunction with the different media of verbalization. The simplest and most direct is spoken language. Second, there is written language; and here, as we have seen, the verbalizing element is as likely to be the channel (e.g. 'the book says') as the source (e.g. 'the author says'). So we have examples like 'the notice says: "keep off the grass"', 'the form asks whether you wear glasses'; and, as a special case, again when children are learning to read, 'the writing says ...'. But third, the medium may not be language at all; it may be some other symbolic system. Most typical are those involving some kind of measurement, like the watch example above, or 'the thermometer says you have a temperature of 102°'; but note also 'the lights say "go"' (i.e. 'they are green'), 'the arrow says it's to the right'.

The nature of the medium also determines in principle certain restrictions on the nature of the verbalization as quoting or reporting. Basically, if it is language it is quotable, e.g. 'it says on page 3: "Supplements will be issued at half-yearly intervals"'; and there will normally be a reported equivalent, 'it says on page 3 that supplements will be issued at half-yearly intervals', 'the notice tells you to keep off the grass'. Where the verbalization is non-linguistic, however, it tends to have only a reported form, as we noted in the case of the example 'my watch said it was 10 o'clock'; the exceptions to this seem to be imperatives like 'the lights say "go"', where the reporting form 'the lights are telling you to go' is perhaps felt to be too personalized.

Such non-linguistic reports provide the limiting case of the principle that a report is a 'wording', since there is no wording against which to set them. They are thus approaching the borderline of facts, which they resemble in some ways (e.g. not being quotable), though in other respects, they fall on the 'reported' side of the line.

Any pair of ranking clauses may be related to one another grammatically; if they are, they form what is called a **clause nexus**. This may occur in two ways, either (1) by expansion or (2) by projection; and in either case the relationship may be either (a) paratactic or (b) hypotactic. Expansion is of three types: (i) the 'that is' type, elaborating, (ii) the 'and' type, extending, (iii) the 'if' type, enhancing; these are discussed in Chapter…

Projection has been introduced in the present chapter. Projection may take the form of (a) quoting (paratactic) or (b) reporting (hypotactic); in either case, what is projected may be either (1) locution (with verbal process) or (2) idea (with mental process). Note that a 'fact' cannot enter into a clause nexus, because it does not occur as a ranking clause*.

Verbal processes project freely in all moods, both paratactically by quoting, and hypotactically, by reporting. Quotes of any mood can be introduced by *say*, whereas in reports the mood is expressed in the reporting verb (e.g. *say*, *state* for declarative; *ask*, *enquire* for interrogative; *ask*, *implore* for imperative). A large number of verbs can be used to project locutions, but many favour just one or other of the logical relations: those which are basically 'saying' verbs, but have other semantic features in addition, tend to favour reporting, while those that are not really 'saying' verbs at all tend to favour quoting, e.g.

* It can, of course, embody a clause nexus in its own make-up, as in *not to mention (the fact) that it won't happen unless you do it.*

boast [either]	*John boasted, "I'm tough!"*	*John boasted that he was tough*
maintain [report]	–	*Henry maintained that he was innocent*
splutter [quote]	*Fred spluttered, "that's an insult!"*	–
	paratactic (quoting)	hypotactic (reporting)

As we noted earlier, the 'splutter' type tend to occur in certain varieties of written narrative fiction – but also in narratives embedded in casual conversation.

The following is a summary of the options for verbal processes. We represent here just those types where the verbalized element is a quote or a report; if it is a fact, or the name of a report, the structure is a single clause and these options do not apply.

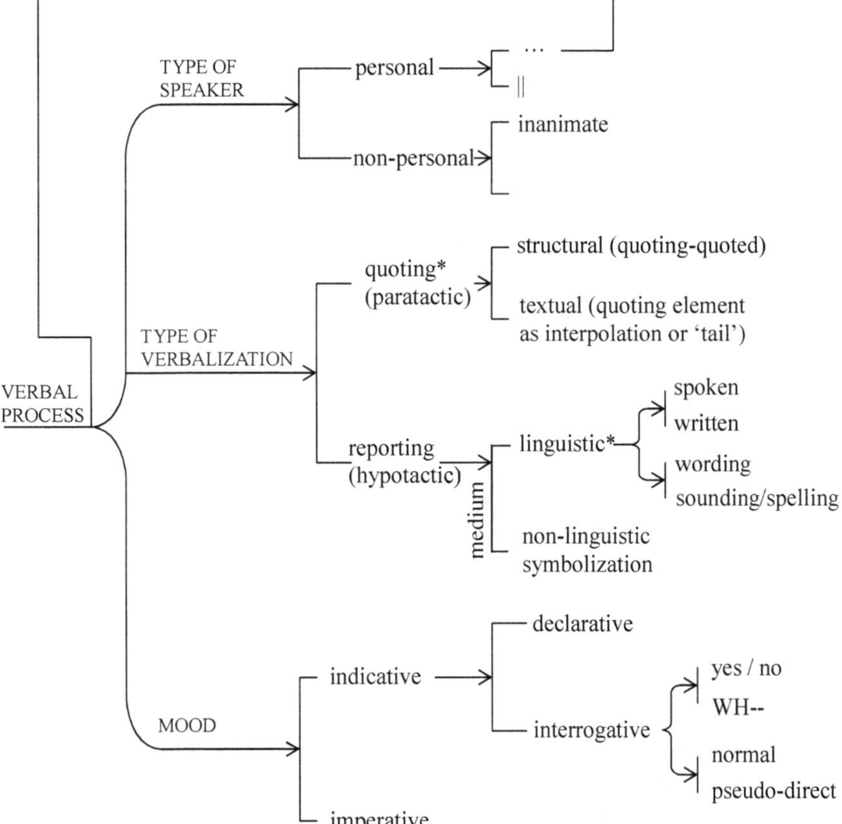

Figure 3.1: Network of verbal processes

4 Relational processes

4.1 Ascriptive

In some ways, relational clauses are the most difficult to interpret of all the English process types. Here, the 'process' takes the form of a relation between two entities – between two roles in the structural configuration; with, as a limiting case, the 'process' of existence, in which only one entity is involved.

Where there are two entities involved, the relation may be either 'ascriptive' or 'equative'; and, cutting across this, it may be 'intensive', 'circumstantial' or 'possessive'. This gives six main types in all. Most of the discussion will centre around the intensive type, since it is here that the ascriptive and equative relations are most clearly displayed; it will then be possible to deal with the other two types much more briefly at the end. It may be helpful at this point to give examples of all six:

	ascriptive (middle)	equative (non-middle)
intensive	*Paula is pretty*	*Rex is the treasurer*
circumstantial	*the cat's on the roof*	*the bridge spans the gorge*
possessive	*Tony has a tortoise*	*the house belongs to Madge*

Let us now add further examples of the intensive type:

(ascription) *Paula is pretty; Piers is a poet; she seems in pain*

(equation) *Rex is the treasurer; Tony is the tallest; the tallest is Tony; that's me;* $x = 2$

Since both these relations are, or may be, expressed by the verb *be*, they are not at first sight easy to distinguish. But the two relations, and the two sets of roles involved, are somewhat different.

In ascription, there is one element, 'Paula' or 'Piers' in the above examples, that is having some attribute ascribed to it, and another element, 'pretty' or 'a poet', that represents the attribute in question. This is not an exclusive relation; 'pretty' describes 'Paula', but there is no implication that she is the only one that can be so described, so the attribute does not serve to identify her. Likewise Piers is describable by the attribute of being a poet; but it is not suggested that this sets him apart from all others. The ascriptive relation is one of membership, or class inclusion: Paula belongs to the class of pretty ones, Piers belongs to the class of poets. Let us refer to these two roles as the Carrier and the Attribute:

Paula	*is*	*pretty*	*Piers*	*is*	*a poet*
Carrier	Process	Attribute	Carrier	Process	Attribute

Note that the only role of 'Paula' and 'Piers' in these structures is as carriers of the attributes in question.

The Attribute may be either a noun or an adjective. More accurately, it is a nominal group having either a noun or an adjective as its Head, since at a more abstract level an adjective is a kind of noun; 'Paula is pretty' is equivalent to 'Paula is a pretty one'. The Attribute cannot however be a personal pronoun; a personal pronoun is a reference word, and an item which has the function of referring cannot be used to describe. In general, as follows from the nature of the ascriptive relation, the Attribute will be indefinite; but this is not an absolute restriction – it is possible to have definite forms in this function, e.g. 'Paula is the prettiest you ever saw', 'Jasper is the perfect host'.

The form of 'probe' in an ascriptive relation is typically 'what?' or 'how?' ('like what?'): 'what is Piers?', 'what is Paula like?', 'how is your father?' The order of the elements cannot be reversed; we cannot say 'pretty is Paula', 'a poet is Piers', 'very well is my father', in unselfconscious English. This reflects the asymmetrical nature of the notion of 'membership'; it is possible to describe Paula by reference to her membership of the class of pretty ones, but we cannot describe the class of pretty ones by reference to Paula's membership of it.

Other than 'be', verbs expressing the relation of ascription include:

(being) *be; keep, remain, stay; become, get, turn; turn out*

(seeming) *seem, look, sound, appear, feel*

These verbs regularly occur unstressed. This is a distinctive characteristic of verbs expressing these relations, that they may be either weak or salient, whereas all other verbs in the language are salient; and it serves to distinguish many pairs of homonyms, e.g. *sound* in 'George sounded delighted' and 'George sounded his horn':

// George sounded de/lighted // *// George / sounded his / horn //*

Other such pairs would be (using a material process clause for contrast):

relational (ascriptive)	material
Jenny kept quiet	*Jenny kept chickens*
the driver turned pale	*the driver turned the corner*
the course turned out a disaster	*the course turned out some good students*
the material felt silky	*Sally felt the material*

4.2 Equative

4.2.1

In the equative we are not describing but identifying; one element is being identified by reference to another. Here the relation is an exclusive one: in 'Rex is the treasurer', the status of being 'the treasurer' uniquely identifies 'Rex'. This does not mean that there are no other treasurers in the real world, of course; but that in the context of the utterance the designation is being offered as unique – there is only one meaning 'the treasurer' that is available. The relation is not one of membership but of equivalence: 'Rex' = 'the treasurer'.

However, the relation is not a tautological one; we do not usually say 'Rex is Rex'. The equivalence is one between different levels of existence; it is a relation of realization, meaning, for example, that Rex fulfils the function of, plays the role of, treasurer. This is not a simple notion, and we shall return to it in more detail below.

Structurally, there is one element that is to be identified, and another which serves to identify it; we shall use the terms Identified and Identifier (abbreviated to Id. and Ir.):

Rex	is	the treasurer	Tony	is	the tallest	that	's	me
Id.	Proc	Ir.	Id.	Proc	Ir.	Id.	Proc	Ir.

Because of the different type of relation involved, these clauses differ in significant ways from those of the ascription type. Here, the Identifier may be a noun or pronoun; but is cannot be an adjective other than a superlative. Normally it is definite, although this is not necessarily the case; we find instances, such as 'the teachers' strike is a good example', where the Identifier has an indefinite form – meaning, as it were, 'this uniquely identifies "the teachers' strike" for the purpose of the discussion, even if other examples are conceivable'. The usual probe, for similar reasons, is 'which?' or 'who?': 'who / which is Rex?', 'which is Tony?', 'who is it?'.

The most significant distinction, however, between the equative and the ascriptive is that equative clauses are reversible; we can say either 'Rex is the treasurer' or 'the treasurer is Rex', 'Tony is the tallest' or 'the tallest is Tony'. This reflects the fact that the relation is one of equivalence. But since the equivalence is directional, the two members of such a pair are not identical in meaning. They differ, in fact, as active and passive. The distinction is a distinction of voice; it is the same as that between the active and the passive in material processes. There is a proportion

Rex is the treasurer	:	*the dog chased the cat*
the treasurer is Rex	:	*the cat was chased by the dog*

Although the verb *be* is common to both ascriptive and equative clauses, the other verbs used are different. Those which are common in equative clauses include 'become', 'spell', 'mean', 'express', 'act as', 'stand for', 'represent', 'play (the part of)', 'resemble', 'equal'; together with a large number of periphrastic expressions such as 'take the form of', 'have the function of', 'be identified with'. Not all of these allow a reversal of the sequence of the two elements; those that do usually become passive, e.g. 'Olivier played Othello', 'Othello was played by Olivier'. These verbs also typically occur unstressed. Again, this is not unexpected; here, as in ascription, the 'process' is simply a relation between two terms which have, moreover, the same referent. The verbs are often designated 'linking verb', or 'copulas'; many of them also function in material processes, so that once again what would otherwise be homonyms may be distinguished by the stress pattern:

relational (equative)	material
Smith stands for progress	*Smith stands for parliament*
$2^9 = 512$	*England equals Australia's 512*
Tom acted as our guide	*Tom acted as a fool*

The following is a summary of the differences between ascriptive and equative clauses:

Ascriptive	Equative
meaning: inclusion ('is a member of the class of') structure: Carrier + Attribute	meaning: equivalence ('is identical with, at another level') structure: Identified + Identifier
non-reversible *Paula is pretty* *Pretty is Paula**	reversible (system of 'voice') Rex is the treasurer the treasurer is Rex
Attribute is noun or adjective, not pronoun (typic. Indefinite) *Piers is a poet* *Paula is pretty*	Identifier is noun or pronoun, not adjective (typic. Definite) *Rex is the treasurer* *Tony is the tallest (one)* *it's me*
probed by: 'what?' 'how?' 'what… like?' *what is Piers?* *what is Paula like?* *how is your father?*	probed by: 'which?' 'who?' *which / who is Rex?* *which is Tony?* *who is it?*
class of verb (may be unstressed) 'be', 'become'; 'keep'; 'get'; 'seem' *Paula is / became a poet* *Jenny kept quiet* *the clothes got wet* *Smith seems suitable*	class of verb (may be unstressed) 'be', 'become'; 'resemble'; 'equal'; 'stand for' *Rex is / became the treasurer* *Peter resembles his father* $x = 2$ *Smith stands for progress*

4.2.2 The verb *be*

There has been lengthy discussion of the verb *be* by linguists, including arguments about whether it is a verb at all. There is of course no 'right answer' to this last question; it depends on the definition of a verb. In the terms of the present description, 'be' is a verb; it has much in common with other verbs, and is no 'more unique' than, say, 'have', or 'do', but it occurs in the expression of a number of different semantic features – that is, it has more than one meaning.

First we need to make a clear distinction between 'be' as an auxiliary verb and 'be' as a lexical verb. The auxiliary verb 'be' is a tense- and voice-forming element. It is quite distinct from lexical 'be' except at one point, where the boundary becomes blurred, namely when it is followed by a form which could be either a participle or an adjective, e.g.

Their coats were brushed, their faces washed,

Their shoes were clean and neat –

These can be resolved by reference to the tense: if 'brushed' had been a passive verb the tense form would have had to be 'had been brushed', so 'were brushed' must be lexical 'be' + adjective. In other words it is the same structure as 'their shoes were clean and neat'; all three clauses are ascriptive.

The lexical verb 'be' is that which functions as a main verb in clauses such as 'that is the question', 'you're hopeless', 'the cat's on the roof', 'there's that cat on the roof', 'there was an earthquake', 'that book is mine', and the rather rare type 'to be or not to be'. The first two of these are relational clauses of the types just introduced: 'that is the question' is equative, 'you're hopeless' is ascriptive. The remainder are either existential, possessive or circumstantial.

If we say that 'be' is a verb, this is not merely because it has the complete range of tenses that is characteristic of lexical verbs in English – though this is a significant fact in itself – but because it enters into various contrasts in meaning of which all the other terms are expressed by lexical means. It contrasts with 'get' and 'keep' (neutral vs. perfective vs. imperfective), with 'seem' (real vs. apparent), with 'resemble' (identical vs. similar), and so on. We are not treating these in detail here. Of course, we shall not find one single lexical meaning to cover all instances of the verb 'be'; but in that respect it is no different from any one of the more frequent lexical items in the language.

4.2.3 Intonation and relational clauses

In ascriptive clauses the typical intonation pattern is that with tonic prominence on the Attribute: // *Paula is* ***pretty*** //. This means that the Attribute carries the 'unmarked focus of information'. This pattern can then be reversed with 'good reason': // ***Paula*** *is pretty* //; either given the probe 'who is pretty?', or in a context where the sense is either ('in addition to someone else' (e.g. 'Paula's pretty, too' with 'Paula' (and, 'too') on a falling tone) or 'in contrast to someone else' ('but Paula's pretty', with a falling-rising tone). However, because this structure is non-reversible, it is impossible to keep the tonic prominence in the unmarked (final) position in the sequence. With all other types of clause where there are two participants, there is a system of 'voice' which provides for reversing the sequence; e.g. ('what happened to the cat?') // the cat was chased by the dog //. But there is no corresponding form ('who is pretty?') // *pretty is been by* ***Paula*** //. [Note: this does not apply to expressions of verbal processes; verbalization, as was pointed out, is not a clause type but a type of relation between clauses.]

Ascriptive clauses have no system of voice; hence there is no unmarked pattern whereby this clause can be given the status of a message about prettiness, in the way that 'the dog chased the cat' can be turned into a message about the cat without involving any 'marking' in the information structure. This relates to what was said above; we do not describe a class by one of its members, even if the class is given to us (as in 'who is pretty?') and the member is to be supplied.

With equative clauses, however, the situation is different. Because these are reversible, we can always keep the tonic prominence at the end, in its unmarked position, if we want to. So

which is Rex?	// *Rex is the* ***treasurer*** //
which is the treasurer?	// *the treasurer is* ***Rex*** //

In both cases the tonic falls on the item that answers the probe, supplying the information that is new; but there is no perturbation in the message, which retains its typical form of 'given' followed by 'new'.

The difference between 'Rex is the treasurer' and 'the treasurer is Rex' is actually one of voice; they are related to each other as active to passive, like 'the dog chased the cat' and 'the cat was chased by the dog'.

4.2.4 Active and passive in equative

In this section we shall explore some of the complexities of the equative relation – hoping to show, however, that it is not as complex as it appears when one first begins to go into it. As in so many areas of language, the complexity is the product of the interaction of a number of essentially very simple variables. Let us return first of all to the pair 'Rex is the treasurer' and 'the treasurer is Rex'. These, it was suggested, are actually an active / passive pair; and this is borne out by the fact that with other verbs of the equative class the passive form does occur. We have a proportion:

the scales represent justice : *justice is represented by the scales* ::
Rex is the treasurer : *the treasurer is Rex*

The second one is really 'the treasurer is been by Rex': this passive form of 'be' is one that is sometimes used by young children in a role-playing situation, e.g. 'well then the doctor won't be be'd by anyone' (= 'there's nobody to play the part of the doctor'), and if the sentence is given a dramatic interpretation we shall find an active / passive pair of this kind, 'Rex plays the treasurer', 'the treasurer is played by Rex'. So the 'identifying' relation exists in both active and passive; it is merely that the verb 'be' has no passive in its morphology. [It is sometimes said that the same is true of 'resemble' and 'equal', though for the present writer both these verbs have a passive formed in the usual way, e.g. 'she wasn't resembled by any of her offspring'. The ones that have no passive are those like 'act as' and 'stand for', but this is because of their own internal makeup, consisting of verb plus preposition.]

If the passive is chosen, the reason is the usual one of keeping the information structure unmarked. If we say 'justice is represented by the scales' it is because we want 'the scales' to come in what is the typical position for new information, at the end; in other words we want to say // *justice is represented by* ***the scales*** // rather than // ***the scales*** *represent justice* //, which would be a marked message form. For the same reason if the probe is 'who built this gazebo?' we are likely to say // *this gazebo was built by* ***Sir Christopher Wren*** // in order to avoid the marking that is present in // ***Sir Christopher Wren*** *built this gazebo* //.

But, of course, it is perfectly possible to select a marked form, under 'good reason' conditions; so that in a material process clause we have the four possibilities:

'what did Sir Christopher Wren build?'	'who built this gazebo?'
unmarked *Sir Christopher Wren built this gazebo*	unmarked *this gazebo was built by Sir Christopher Wren*
marked *this gazebo was built by Sir Christopher Wren*	marked *Sir Christopher Wren built this gazebo*

Exactly the same four exist in an equative clause, but if the verb is 'be' its form will not change and there will be no 'by':

'who did Olivier play?'	'who played Othello?'
unmarked *Olivier played / was* <u>*Othello*</u> Id. Ir.	unmarked *Othello was played by / was* <u>*Olivier*</u> Id. Ir.
marked <u>*Othello*</u> *was played by / was Olivier* Ir. Id.	marked <u>*Olivier*</u> *played / was Othello* Ir. Id.

If we analyse these structurally, in terms of the Identified and the Identifier, we see that the Identified is always the one that is named in the probe, while the Identifier corresponds to the WH-element. Thus if the probe is 'who was Olivier?', then whatever the sequence of elements in the answer, 'Olivier' will be Identified and 'Othello' Identifier.

We shall assume for this discussion that the Identifier always carries the tonic prominence. As a matter of fact this is not always true; there is yet another condition of 'good reason' under which the tonic can fall on the Identified. This is why we cannot simply equate the functions Identified and Identifier with the Given and New of the information structure; they are merely in unmarked association with each other. So for example:

Which is Jane? – Jane is Harry's sister. – Well which is Sarah? –

// <u>*Sarah*</u>	*is*	*Harry's sister //* <u>*too*</u> *//*
Id. / New		Ir. / Given

4.2.5 Value and Token

We saw that the ascriptive relation was one of class inclusion: 'Paula is pretty' means 'Paula is a member of the class of pretty ones'. For a member *a* to be included in a class *x*, *a* and *x* must be of the same order of existence. 'Paula is a pretty girl' can be true or false only if Paula is a girl; 'Paula is happy' only if Paula is of the same order of being as 'the happy ones'. We cannot have 'Patsy is a triangle', 'the running is a teacher', 'the fact that you agreed to it is early', in an ascriptive sense.

With the equative relation the requirements are different. Here the two entities are coextensive, the one being identified precisely through its being coextensive with the other. So in 'Rex is the treasurer', 'Rex' is specified uniquely by virtue of this identity. For the two things to be coextensive and yet not the same, such that to identify one with the other is not a tautology, they must differ in their order of existence. The one must be a meaning, or a value, of the other. The reason we can say 'Olivier is (represents) Othello', 'justice is (is represented by) the scales', is that in each case the two are identical except in this respect. The equative relation is a relation between two entities that are 'equivalent' in the sense of being identical but at different levels of abstraction.

A clear example is the clause '$x = 2$'. This is an equative clause in which a variable x represents a value '2'. We could use this terminology for the structural analysis:

X	*is / equals*	2
Variable	Process	Value

However, as we explain below, the term 'Variable' is problematic; so we have opted for the term 'Token' instead.

Now consider the following two conversations:

(i) There are only two men on the committee: Mr Norwall and my husband. – *Which is your husband?* – *My husband is the chairman.*			(ii) There are only two men on the platform: Mr Norwall and my husband. – *Which is your husband?* – *My husband is the chairman.*		
Identified	Process	Identifier	Identified	Process	Identifier
Token		Value	Value		Token
My husband	is	the chairman	my husband	is	the chairman

In (i), the last sentence means 'my husband takes the function of, holds the office of, chairman'; that is, 'the chairman' in this instance is a value. In (ii), the last sentence means 'my husband takes the form of, can be recognized by being, chairman'; that is, 'the chairman' is the Token by which he is represented. We could express this in the terminology of linguistics by rewriting the former as 'my husband realizes the chairman' and the latter as 'my husband is realized by the chairman'.

Taken by itself, the sentence // *my husband is the chairman* // is ambiguous. Either it is a statement about the role my husband occupies, or it is a statement about how he can be recognized on the platform. Every equative clause with 'be' is potentially ambiguous in just this way, although we are usually unaware of it because in the majority of instances only one interpretation is possible. For example, 'Susan is the daughter of the governor' is almost certainly a 'role' statement, whereas 'Susan is the plump one in the front row' is presumably a 'recognition' statement. But ambiguous instances are not uncommon; for example:

	my bank manager	*is*	***my best friend***	
	Identified		Identifier	
(i)	Token		Value	= 'my bank manager behaves in the most friendly way toward me'
(ii)	Value		Token	= "it's my best friend who manages the local bank"

It was difficult to find a suitable pair of terms with which to label these elements in the equative structure. This is because the relation between them appears in so many specific guises: of function vs. form, content vs. expression, meaning vs. name, message vs. code, referent vs. symbol, role vs. occupant or actor. In its most general sense it is very close to the realization, or 'coding', relation that exists within language between meaning at one end and sound at the other, although in language there are intermediate levels as well. The terms 'Value' and 'Token' have been chosen, because they are abstract and on the whole neutral as regards the more specific interpretations. We shall adopt these terms to describe this dimension in the structure of relational clauses.

The essential point here is that equative clauses display two simultaneous dimensions of structure which vary independently of one another: Value-Token, and Identified-Identifier. In the examples above, the Identified and Identifier were kept constant, while we switched around the Value and the Token. If we now reverse the Identified-Identifier relation, by changing the location of the tonic (indicated by underlining), we shall get two more interpretations:

	my bank manager	*is*	***my best friend***	
	Identified		Identifier	
(i)	Token		Value	= 'it's my bank manager who is the most helpful to me'
(ii)	Value		Token	= 'he manages the local bank, my best friend does'

– of which the last is very unlikely since it is hard to find a motive for expressing it in this sequence; it is rather like saying // ***the cat*** *was chased by the dog* //, which is not impossible but expresses a very rare combination of meaning selections.

4.2.6 Encoding and decoding

We can see from the foregoing that the equative relation is not symmetrical. Like other relations in language, it differs in certain respects from any logical relations, including that by which it is most nearly resembled, namely 'equals'. In mathematics, 2 × 17 = 34 and 34 = 2 × 17 are equivalent; in language, 'twice seventeen is / are thirty-four' and 'thirty-four is twice seventeen' are not.

It is especially in instances of this kind that the term Variable would have been misleading, since the analysis of these two sentences is:

twice seventeen is / are	***thirty-four***	*thirty-four is*	***twice seventeen***
Id. / Tk.	Ir. / Vl.	Id. / Vl.	Ir. / Tk.

– i.e. 'twice seventeen' would be a Variable. But any pair of terms seems likely to be misleading in some instances; the technical terms in grammar, as in other science, are defined by their relation to the theoretical framework within which they achieve their explanatory force.

In its most clearcut form, the distinction we are concerned with is as follows. Either something is identified by reference to its inner meaning or function, by a process of interpretation, e.g. 'Jill's husband is the president of the bank'; or it is identified by reference to its outer form, by some criterion of recognition, as in 'Jill's husband is the tall one'. In the former, Identified = Token and Identifier = Value; in the latter, it is the other way round:

Jill's husband	is	***the president of the bank***	*Jill's husband*	is	***the tall one***
Identified Token	[decode to identify:]	Identifier Value	Identified Value	[encode to identify:]	Identifier Token

It is useful to be able to name these two directions of the equative relation, and we shall take the terms 'encoding' and 'decoding' from stratification theory, since this is what in linguistics would be a 'stratal' relation. If Identifier = Value, we are decoding in order to identify; this is a 'decoding equative'. If Identifier = Token, we are encoding in order to identify; this is an 'encoding equative'.

It is not, therefore, the sequence in which the elements occur that determines the meaning of the equative relation. It is the combination of Identified-Identifier with Value-Token. Since the Identifier is typically tonic prominent, this can be expressed in terms of the location of the tonic with respect to the Value and the Token: tonic on Value = decoding, tonic on Token = encoding.

Here are some further examples. All are in principle ambiguous, so that one may, at first, seize on the wrong interpretation – that is, the one that does not correspond to the description given; but in some cases only one interpretation is actually conceivable, and these are left unglossed.

Sarah is the fat one	Id/Vl + Ir/Tk	(enc.)	so now you recognize her
Sarah is the clever one	Id/Tk + Ir/Vl	(dec.)	she has the brains
the first to arrive will be Fred	Id/Vl + Ir/Tk	(enc.)	Fred will get here first
the first to arrive will be the lucky one	Id/Tk + Ir/Vl	(dec.)	whoever comes first will get a prize
let your conscience be your guide	Ir/Tk + Id/Vl	(enc.)	if you need a guide, use your conscience
the hive bees are the ones that sting	Ir/Tk + Id/Vl	(enc.)	I'll tell you how to recognize the ones that sting
	Id/Vl + Ir/Tk		
the ones that sting are the hive bees	Id/Vl + Ir/Vl	(dec.)	those ones that sting live in the hive
the last piece was the Bach quintet	Id/Vl + Ir/Tk	(enc.)	that's what they played last of all
	Id/Tk + Ir/Vl	(dec.)	that's what that one was
the last piece was the climax of the evening	Id/Tk + Ir/Vl	(dec.)	
the question is this	Id/Tk + Ir/Vl	(dec.)	the real issue is
	Id/Vl + Ir/Tk	(enc.)	what I said I was going to ask you is: …
twice two is four	Id/Tk + Ir/Vl	(dec.)	

The dual structure of equatives imposes a restriction on co-ordination: two items cannot be co-ordinated if they have different functions in respect of Value and Token. So, for example, we cannot say 'the first to arrive will be Fred or the lucky one'. It would be just possible to say 'the last piece was the Bach quintet and the climax of the evening', but only if we interpret 'the Bach quintet' as Value – it could be said to someone who had not been present but knew more or less what was being played, but not to one's companion wanting to know the identity of the piece he had just heard.

The ambiguity that is characteristic of English proverbs is an ambiguity between encoding and decoding. 'An Englishman's home is his castle': does this mean 'where do Englishmen live? They live in castles' (encoding), or 'how does an Englishman value his home? As a stronghold of privacy, like a castle' (decoding)? The second, of course, is the 'intended' sense. Compare 'necessity is the mother of invention', 'home is where your heart is'. The same ambiguity is evident in 'But the real reason for Mr Gulbrandian's coming here was the most likely reason' (Agatha Christie); and in the following sentence from a linguistic essay: 'The theme of a clause is the element that is put in first position'.

Let us look more closely at the last. Is it telling us how to recognize a theme: 'you can tell the theme – it's the thing that comes first' (encoding)? Or what to do with an element that we want to make thematic: 'you know what to do with the theme – put it first' (decoding)? Theoretically we can resolve the ambiguity by the use of 'if', since 'if' is attached to the Token:

> if it comes first, it's the theme (encoding)
>
> if it's the theme, it goes first (decoding)

Unfortunately, 'if' is itself ambiguous in precisely the same way. In addition to the 'true' 'if' of implication, 'if "a", then (that implies) "b"', we have the 'logical' 'if' of deduction, 'if "b", then (it can be deduced that) "a"' – which reverses the direction of the coding. So with 'home is where your heart is', the encoding sense can be expressed in either way:

home	*is*	*where your heart is*	= 'that's how you recognize your home'
Id / Vl		Ir / Tk	

implication: if your heart is in a certain place, then (that implies) you're at home there
deduction: if you're at home in a certain place, then (it can be deduced that) your heart is there

Similarly with the decoding sense:

home	*is*	*where your heart is*	= 'that's what your home means to you'
Id / Vl		Ir / Tk	

implication: if your live in a certain place, then (that implies) your heart is there
deduction: if your heart is in a certain place, then (it can be deduced that) you live there

Hence reversing the direction of coding, in an equative structure, is equivalent to reversing the direction of implication in an 'if'-relation; and there is the same ambiguity of expression in both types.

Many aphorisms and slogans are like proverbs in having this equative structure. What do we understand by 'the medium is the message', 'our roots are our branches', 'time is money?'
The ambiguity may be made explicit in poetry. From Tennyson:

Death	*is*	*the end of life – ah, why Should*	*life all*	*labour be?*
Id / Vl		Ir / Tk	Carrier	Attr
Id / Tk		Ir / Vl		

The first clause has both an encoding interpretation 'we die because life is finished' and a decoding interpretation 'when death comes, life will be over'; its meaning derives from the co-occurrence of the two. The second clause is ascriptive; this is shown by the fact that we could not reverse the order of the elements in it.

4.2.7 Voice; 'it's me'

We noted that many verbs in the equative class have both active and passive forms. Under what conditions is the particular 'voice' selected? As a general rule, verbs of this class have the active form when the order of elements is Token-Value, i.e. when the Variable is Subject:

the scales	*represent*	*justice*	*justice is represented by the scales*
Olivier	*plays*	*Othello*	*Othello is played by Olivier*
Tk / Subj	Vl	Vl / Subj	Tk

This means that, in terms of the two dimensions which make up the equative relationship, that of identifying and that of coding, the active is used (i) in decoding when the identification is progressive (Identified followed by Identifier), and (ii) in encoding when the identification is regressive (Identifier followed by Identified):

	Identified–Identifier	Identifier–Identified
	active	passive
decoding	*Olivier plays Othello*	*Othello is played by Olivier*
	Sarah is the clever one	*the clever one is Sarah*
	Id / Tk Ir /Vl	Ir /Vl Id / Tk
	passive	active
encoding	*Othello is played by Olivier*	*Olivier plays Othello*
	Sarah is the fat one	*The fat one is Sarah*
	Id /Vl Ir / Tk	Ir /Tk Id / Vl

Of these four, the one that is unfavoured is the passive form of the decoding relation, and it is not difficult to see why: it has the regressive sequence Identifier–Identified, which is what the passive is designed to avoid. In the same way, in a material process it would be unusual to say // ***Fred** was beaten by Bill* //; if 'Fred' is the 'new' information, why not say // *Bill beat **Fred*** //? It requires a very good reason to select the passive here.

Exactly the same restriction applies when the verb is *be*; this is explainable provided we interpret clauses with *be* as active or passive in the same way. This interpretation is further borne out by the pattern of concord, which also confirms that the Token is the Subject. This pattern appears both in a WH-question, where the order of elements does not vary since the WH-element comes at the beginning, and in the corresponding answer. We will fill in just the active forms:

	Identified–Identifier	Identifier–Identified
decoding *which am I?*	*I am the clever one*	
Tk	Id / Tk Ir /Vl	
Subj	Subj	
encoding *which is me?*		*The fat one is me*
Subj Vl		Ir / Tk Id / Vl
		Subj

The one form which seems to have no justification is '(it) is I'. This form appeared in Early Modern English (after the disappearance of the Middle English 'it am I') side by side with the more usual, and more grammatical, 'it is me'. The patterns of contemporary English clearly demand 'it is me': in this structure 'me' is the Value, and therefore the Complement of an active verb – a direct object, in traditional terms. The notion of a 'nominative complement' is quite foreign to English; we do not say, in looking at a photograph, 'the fat one is I', 'the fat one represents I'. Those who urge us to write, and even to say, 'it is I' have from the grammatical point of view a very tenuous case.

4.2.8 Definitions; the non-discontinuity of equative and ascriptive

A definition is an equative clause which identifies by decoding. For example:

a gazebo is a pavilion or summerhouse on an eminence, open for the view

Id / Tk Ir / Vl

For reasons given above we would expect the passive of this, // ***a pavilion on an eminence*** *is a gazebo* //, to be rare; and so it is. On the other hand the encoding equivalent, // *a pavilion on an eminence is* ***a gazebo*** //, is very common; this is a naming statement.

Naming and defining are simply the encoding and decoding relations as these apply to language itself. To name is to encode meanings into words; to define is to decode words into meanings. For example:

		Id–Ir	Ir–Id
		active	passive
decoding (defining)	*what is (the meaning of) gazebo?*	*A gazebo is* (means) Id / Tk *a pavilion on an eminence* Ir / Vl	*a pavilion on an eminence* Ir /Vl is (meant by) a gazebo Id / Tk
		passive	active
encoding (naming)	*what is (the word for) a pavilion on an eminence?*	*a pavilion on an eminence* Id / Vl *Is (called) a gazebo* Ir / Tk	*a gazebo is (names)* Ir / Tk *a pavilion on an eminence* Id / Vl

With definitions we come back to a consideration of the relation between equative and ascriptive clauses. In making a distinction between the two, we have been adopting the usual strategy of imposing discontinuity as a means of ordering and interpreting the phenomena under scrutiny. But the phenomena themselves are not so discontinuous, and we should not lose sight of the continuity altogether – where the facts are messy, as they tend to be, their interpretation cannot be wholly tidy.

In the present instance we can see that there is a basic continuity, or 'cline', between the ascriptive and the equative types. The decoding form of the equative, as represented by definitions for example, is actually intermediate between the ascriptive and the encoding form of the equative:

ascriptive	*my bank manager is a good friend* Carr = Tk	 Attr = Vl	(non-reversible)
decoding equative	*my bank manager is my best friend* Tk	 Vl	(= 'behaves as'; reversible with good reason)
encoding equative	*my bank manager is my best friend* Vl	 Tk	(= 'is none other than'; freely reversible)

In ascription, some entity is being said to have an attribute; this means, effectively, assigning it to a class, so that the two elements in this relation, the attribute and the entity that 'carries' it, differ in generality – the one includes the other. Approached from this end, the 'decoding' relation, including definition as an instance of it, is a means of identifying something by assigning it to a class. But as the class tends towards a class of one member, which it must in order to identify that member as distinct from merely describing it, so it comes to be of a higher order of abstraction; otherwise one would have a tautology. The consequence of this is that the relationship becomes reversible. It can be switched to an 'encoding' relation in which the identification proceeds the other way round, with the element that is at a lower level becoming the identifier. If we look back at ascription from this end, the ascriptive relation is seen as one which interprets a class as the 'value' of its members, rather than simply as a list. So from 'John is tall' ('a member of the class "tall ones"', ascriptive) we come via 'John is the tallest' ('boy in the school', decoding) to 'John is the tallest one' ('of those on that photograph'; encoding); and this enables us to see that there is a component of value also in 'John is tall'.

4.3 Relational processes and other process types

We can now attempt to relate ascription and equation to the other process types, in terms of the generalized structural function of 'Medium'. This was the function underlying the Goal (transitive) or Actor (intransitive) in a material process, and the Senser in a mental process. Does the same function underlie any of the elements in a process of the relational type?

There is one feature of material and mental processes which is suggestive. In these clauses the Medium element, and only this element, can have an Attribute assigned to it within the structure of the clause. The Medium, in other words, has the property that it can combine with the role of Carrier. For example:

the plane Med / Carr	*took off*	*empty* Attr		*the water* Med / Carr	*ran*	*cold* Attr	
she Ag	*takes*	*her coffee* Med / Carr	*sweet* Attr	*she* Ag	*boiled*	*the kettle* Med / Carr	*dry* Attr
he Sen/Carr	*watched*	*the scene* Phen	*fascinated* Attr				

This as a matter of fact is further evidence of the notion of 'Medium': in any process, there is just one participant which can be shown as having an attribute that defines, or results from, its participation.

Another feature of ascriptive clauses is that they can have an Agent, as in 'the teacher kept the children quiet'; and here again we find a parallel with other processes. There is a proportion

material process:	*The kettle* Med / Carr	*boiled*	*dry* Attr	:	*she* Ag	*boiled*	*the kettle* Med / Carr	*dry* Attr
ascription:	*the children* Med / Carr	*kept*	*quiet* Attr	:	*she* Ag	*kept*	*the children* Med / Carr	*quiet* Attr

the difference being simply that in the second pair there is no process other than the ascriptive relation, which is here expressed by 'keep'. Compare 'she got angry', 'his remarks got her angry'; and other examples particularly with 'make' and 'leave', 'nothing ever made him serious', 'the news left her despondent'.

It seems therefore that the Carrier in an ascriptive relation is another specific instance of the general function of Medium, and this is how we interpret it. The question whether this extends also into the equative type is more problematical, but there is some evidence for it. We can say 'they made Olivier Othello', but not 'they made Othello Olivier'. Similarly the sentence

something has made my bank manager my best friend

Ag Tk / Attd Vl

is acceptable only in this interpretation, with 'my bank manager' as Token: 'something has made him behave well towards me'; it could not have the sense 'the bank manager's job is held by an acquaintance of mine', which must be expressed as 'they made my best friend my bank manager'. In other words only the Token can act as the element on which the external agency operates; this suggests that the Token is the central element in the equative relation and that we can extend the concept of 'Medium' to refer to it also. If this is so then the notion of Medium is valid for all process types.

The interpretation must remain tentative; but if it is valid it is significant. It means that, having separated out the various types of process in Modern English in order to understand more clearly how they are represented in the language, we have been able to bring them together again at a higher level of generality by showing that there is one thread running throughout them all. This is the concept that, for every process, there is one key function through which that process is brought into being; one element in the semantic configuration which must be present if a process is to be recognized at all. Again, by postulating an intermediate level of analysis that is discontinuous, we reveal the essential continuity that lies behind it.

4.4 Existential, circumstantial and possessive processes

4.4.1 Existentials

So far we have considered just the 'intensive' type of relational process, in which the two elements that are related to one another are identical in reference. In 'Paula is pretty' there is only one referent involved, which has both the (defining) property of being Paula and the (non-defining) property of being pretty; and similarly with 'Rex is the treasurer' (where however both properties are defining).

Much of what was said about these intensive relations applies to the other types also, in which the two elements that are related do not have identity of reference. There are two further types of relational process, circumstantials and possessives; together with a fourth type, the existential, which has only one entity in it and which we shall treat as the limiting case of a relational process.

Let us consider the last of these first. The existential 'process' involves only one participating entity, the 'Existent'; the process is simply a statement of its existence, together with the usual obligatory indication of time. The nature of an existential clause depends on the nature of the element in question – that is, on its linguistic nature, its value in the semantic system.

We think first of existential clauses as expressing the existence of something that is participant-like, e.g. 'there's a wasp', 'there's just a chance', 'these things just are':

there's	*a wasp*	*these things just are*	
Process	Existent	Existent	Process

This type includes 'to be or not to be', in which the Existent is still inherent, though since the clauses are non-finite it is not expressed. The typical verb in such existential clauses is 'be', but we also find 'exist' and some others like 'come into being'.

However, the element which 'exists' may be an event, as in 'there's been an earthquake'; this is typically, as here, a natural phenomenon, and is thus similar to 'it's raining', 'the wind's blowing'. Since to say that the event 'existed' is the same thing as saying that it took place, these clauses could be considered either as relational or as material processes; there is an overlap at this point, due to the dual significance of the notion of 'process', which is at the same time both the total experiential complex and an element within that complex. Previously we presented these as material processes without participants; but this leaves them as the sole exception to the general principle that every clause in English contains Medium element, and they could instead be analysed as existential clauses, containing the element Existent which in this instance represents an event. The process would then be one of simple existence in time, expressed again by 'be', general verbs like 'happen', 'take place', and certain specific verbs referring to natural phenomena:

there's been	*an earthquake*	*the wind's*	*blowing*	*it's raining*
Process	Existent	Existent	Process	Process+Existent

In 'it's raining', Process and Existent are fused in a single element.

Whether or not events are included among them, existential clauses display the Medium in the specific guise of 'that which exists'. Since the 'process' is simply a predication of its existence, this gives the Medium its paradigm sense of 'that through which the process is actualized'.

4.4.2 Circumstantials

The two remaining types are possessives and circumstantials. These, like the intensives, involve two elements, though not two elements which share a common referent. Possessives involve a possession and a possessor; circumstantials a phenomenon of some kind and a circumstance associated with it. However, these turn out to be not distinct elements of structure, but other instances of the elements which we have already recognized in relational clauses of the intensive type: they are either Carrier and Attribute, or Identified and Identifier. In other words possessives and circumstantials also appear in both ascriptive and equative forms.

In a circumstantial clause, something – which may again be a phenomenon of any kind, including an event – is combined with a circumstantial element such as extent, location or manner. This takes either of two forms. Either the circumstance functions as an attribute of the entity in question, in which case the relation is ascriptive; or it serves to link it with another entity, in which case the relation is equative.

In the ascriptive type, the verb is either 'be' or one which expresses a more specific circumstantial relation, e.g. 'stretch' (Extent), 'be situated' (Location), 'happen' (Location, etc., of event). The circumstance is typically expressed in the usual way, as a minor process, by means of a preposition; while the circumstantial feature itself (e.g. Location) is a feature of the whole clause, it combines structurally with the function of Attribute:

the cat's	*on the roof*	
Carr+Pro	Attr / Loc : Loc	
dinner's	*at eight*	
Carr+Pro	Attr / Loc : Temp	
Pat's	*with the doctor*	
Carr+Pro	Attr / Acc	
the fault	*lay*	*in the wiring*
Carr	Pro	Attr / Cause: Reason
the property	*stretches*	*from here to the river*
Carr	Pro	Attr / Ext : Ext
the earthquake	*took place*	*in Peru*
Carr	Pro	Attr / Loc: Loc

[Note: That the circumstance is a feature of the clause as a whole is in fact true of all clauses; there is no difference in this respect between a relational process such as **'the cat is on the roof'** and a material process such as **'the cat is walking on the roof'**. In both, 'location' is a clause feature which is expressed by the presence of an element with the function Location in the clause structure.]

The distinction between a circumstantial Attribute and an ordinary descriptive Attribute (intensive) does not depend on the presence of a preposition; a clause such as ‘she was in pain’ is intensive, whereas on the other hand ‘it cost five pounds’ is circumstantial. In principle, a circumstantial attribute is one which is interpretable independently of being an attribute of anything, and thus can function in processes of other types; but the line between the two is not a very sharp one.

Also ascriptive are those instances which are really a combination of circumstantial and existential, such as:

there's	*a man*	*with her*
Pro	Ex / Carr	Attr / Acc

there was	*an earthquake*	*last night*
Pro	Ex / Carr	Attr / Loc: Temp

there's	*that cat*	*on the roof*
Pro	Ex / Carr	Attr / Loc : Loc

it's raining	*in the mountains*
Pro / Ex / Carr	Attr / Loc: Loc

In the equative type one entity is related to another by means of one of the circumstantial relations. Here the circumstance becomes a (major) process and combines with the Process element in the structure; it is expressed, therefore, in the verb, with verbs such as ‘cause’, ‘accompany’, ‘follow’, ‘span’:

the bridge	*spans the*	*river*
Id	Pro / Ext : Ext	Ir

Fred	*accompanied*	*his wife*
Id	Pro / Acc	Ir

what	*caused the*	*breakdown?*
Id	Pro / Cau : Rea	Ir

his speech	*was followed by a*	*heated argument*
Id	Pro / Loc : Temp	Ir

These clauses have active and passive forms, and are reversible: ‘the river was spanned by the bridge’, ‘a heated argument followed his speech’; and the Identifier is, as always, the element that is expressed by tonic prominence (in the unmarked case). They also have a structure in terms of Value and Token; the Token is the element which is Subject in the active:

	Id–Ir		Ir–Id	
	active		passive	
decoding	*Fred accompanied*	*his wife*	*Fred's wife was accompanied by*	*him*
	Id / Tk	Ir / Vl	Ir / Vl	Id / Tk
	passive		active	
encoding	*Fred was accompanied by*	*his wife*	*Fred's wife accompanied*	*him*
	Id / Vl	Ir / Tk	Ir / Tk	Id / Vl

As usual, therefore, the decoding form of the passive is rare.

There is one other type of relation which should be mentioned here, although strictly speaking it is intensive rather than circumstantial, since the two halves are co-referential. This is the type in which it is the elements that are being related to each other that are circumstantial, for example ‘the distance was from here to the summit’. In ‘the bridge spans the river’, ‘the bridge’ and ‘the river’ are things, related by the circumstantial relation of extent; whereas here both ‘the distance’ and ‘from here to the summit’ are themselves circumstantial elements, and are related simply by identity. One element is the general name for the type of circumstance, e.g. ‘time’, ‘place’, ‘cause’, ‘aim’; it is often accompanied by a modifying expression, as in ‘the only occasion’, ‘the main reason’, ‘his favourite place’. The other is a specific circumstance of the type named.

the distance	*was*	*from here to the summit*
Id	Pro	Ir / Ext : Ext

the time	*is*	*half past two*
Id	Pro	Ir / Loc : Temp

his favourite place	*is*	*(at) the bottom of the garden*
Id	Pro	Ir / Loc : Loc

the aim	*is*	*to please everybody*
Id	Pro	Ir / Cause : Purpose

the main similarity	*is*	*with Ancient Rome*
Id	Pro	Ir / Manner : Comp

the last occasion	*was*	*when the twins were born*
Id	Pro	Ir / Loc : Temp

The verb is typically ‘be’, and the clauses are reversible except when the general element is expressed by ‘it’ as in ‘it’s half past two’. Either the general or the specific term may be the Identifier; but the general element is always the Value; so the pattern is again as in the equatives discussed earlier, of the intensive type:

	Id–Ir		Ir–Id		
	active		passive		
decoding	London’s	the best place	the best place	is	London
	that’s	the main reason	the main reason	is	that
	Id / Tk	Ir / Vl	Ir / Vl		Id / Tk
	passive		active		
encoding	the best place is London		London’s		the best place
	the main reason is that		that’s		the main reason
	Id / VlIr / Tk		Ir / Tk		Id / Vl

4.4.3 Possessives

The same distinction between ascriptive and equative appears again in the possessive relation. We find an ascriptive type, represented by ‘I’ve got a book’, and an equative type, represented by ‘this book is mine’. In both, there is a possessor and a possession. But in the former, which as usual are irreversible, the possession is an Attribute by which the possessor is described.

This, no doubt, has facilitated the development of quasi-possessive forms which in fact simply express attribution: 'Robin has a book' is a description of Robin and so leads easily on to 'Robin has a cold', 'Charles has a long nose'. The verbs typically include 'have' or 'have got', or 'own' (neutral), 'get' (perfective), 'keep' (imperfective). The feature 'possessive' is a feature of the whole clause, but we can as usual express it in the structural analysis:

Robin has a book	*Nora got the biggest helping*
Carr Pro Attr / Possn	Carr Pro Attr / Possn

In the equative type, the possessor appears in a special form that is marked for ownership: 'mine', 'Stephen's', 'the government's'. This is then identified with the possession by means of the verb 'be', the order of elements being, as always, reversible: 'Stephen's is the Jaguar', 'the Jaguar is Stephen's'. Either possession or possessor can be the Identifier; but in the normal type of possessive relation the possessor is always the Value, so that here again we have the active / passive pairs:

	Id–Ir		Ir–Id	
	active		passive	
decoding	*the Jaguar is Stephen's*		*Stephen's is the Jaguar*	
	Id / Tk	Ir / Vl	Ir / Vl	Id / Tk
	passive		active	
encoding	*Stephen's is the Jaguar*		*the Jaguar is Stephen's*	
	Id / Vl	Ir / Tk	Ir / Tk	Id / Vl

The verb 'belongs to' occurs as an alternative in the active only. There is also a rather curious secondary type of equative exemplified by 'Martin's is the main fault', 'the main fault is Martin's', in which the coding is reversed: this is equivalent to 'Martin (Token) is the one mainly at fault (Value)', and the result is a mixed pattern in which 'the main fault belongs to Martin' is therefore slightly odd.

The possessor is not necessarily human; it can be object, institution, even circumstance, as in 'all that land belongs to the college', 'this paper is the day before yesterday's'. The limits of the possessive relation as a semantic category are set by the equative type. The relation of whole to separable part, as in 'the jug has a lid', can in general be considered as possessive; we do say 'the lid belongs to the jug'. But this is not true of inseparable parts, kinship or the various states and conditions regularly expressed by 'have'; we do not say 'the long nose is Charles's', 'that uncle is Jane's', or 'measles belong to Robin'. In these instances the possessive structure with 'have' is being transferred to the representation of types of process which are not, in fact, interpreted as possessive in the linguistic system. In other words, the speaker of English will admit that 'the college possesses land' and 'the jug possesses a lid', but not that 'Charles possesses a nose', 'Jane possesses an uncle' or 'Robin possesses measles'.

4.5 Summary of relational processes

The distinction of ascriptive and equative thus runs through all three types of relational processes, the intensive, the circumstantial and the possessive. In all of them, either an entity is being described, through the ascribing to it of some attribute, or it is being identified, by being equated with something else. The first is an open type of relation, in which there is no suggestion that other entities do not carry the same attribute; the second is in principle closed – the identification is unique, and no other entity available in the context would match the specified condition of equivalence. Hence the attribute tends to be an indefinite form, the identifier a definite one. At the same time there is a continuity between the two types; and the 'decoding' form of the equative is less closed than the 'encoding' form. We can see this, for example, in the possessive, if we contrast decoding // *the black briefcase is* ***mine*** // with encoding // ***the black briefcase*** *is mine* //; presumably I have other possessions, even though they are irrelevant to the point at issue, but the briefcase belongs to nobody but me.

We have been considering these relations as types of process; but they are also represented in the language as types of modification in the nominal group. Here each of the three is associated with a different nominal function. Typically, the possessive element functions as deictic, the attribute as epithet and the circumstance as qualifier:

nominal group				ascriptive clause
my	*verdant*	*couch*	*beneath the stars*	*I have a couch* (possessive)
deictic	epithet		qualifier	*the couch is verdant* (intensive)
(poss.)	(ate.)		(circ.)	*the couch is beneath the stars* (circumstantial)

It is not that there are two forms of expression one of which is derived from the other. There are two alternative patterns of combination. Each of these relations may combine either with that of 'process' or with that of 'modification'. If the former, they are expressed in the clause, as patterns of transitivity; if the latter, they are expressed in the structure of the nominal group.

4.6 Some general observations on transitivity

4.6.1 Summary of participant functions

Here we have sketched the types of process that are recognized by Modern English and which are incorporated into its meaning system. This is the area – the grammar of processes – that we have been referring to under the general heading of 'transitivity'. Transitivity makes up a significant part of the experiential component of the grammar, the component which has the function of encoding into language the total range of our experience.

We have suggested that there are four basic types of process, material, mental, verbal and relational; and that each of these is expressed through configurations of structural functions which are, in fact, specific to that process type. At the same time, underlying these specific functions is a very general pattern whereby every process of whatever type, has associated with it one essential element as a participant; an element which is inherent in the structure and is the condition of there being a process at all. This was the Medium. The following table shows the functions that are inherent in each process type, and which of these represents the Medium.

Process type	Inherent functions (specific)	Affected element is
material:		
intransitive (middle)	Actor	Actor
transitive (non-middle)	Actor, Goal	Goal
mental:		
like-type (middle)	Senser	Senser
please-type (non-middle)	Senser, Phenomenon	Senser
verbal	Sayer	Sayer
relational:		
existential (middle)	Existent	Existent
ascriptive (middle)	Carrier, Attribute	Carrier
equative (non-middle)	Identified, Identifier;	
	Value, Token	Token

We have also made some partial identification of other participant functions, using the general notions of Agent, Beneficiary and Range: Agent as the external source of the process, Beneficiary as the receiver, Range as the limitation of its scope:

Process type	Agent is	Beneficiary is	Range is
material	Actor (if transitive)	Client / Recipient	Range (scope)
mental	Phenomenon (if transitive)	–	Phenomenon (if transitive)
verbal	–	Receiver	Verbalization (if name or fact)

Note: 'verbalization' has since been renamed 'Verbiage'.

We have not attempted to extend these into relational processes, although the same principle could probably be shown to be valid there also.

On the whole, the different types of process are fairly clearly distinct. Not only are they expressed through different structural configurations; they are realized by different classes of verb. This in fact is how verb classes in English are defined: not as 'transitive or intransitive', which, as we saw, have largely ceased to be relevant as categories of the verb, but as expressing material, mental, verbal or relational process, and their various subdivisions.

4.6.2 Indeterminacy

However, it would be wrong to give the impression that these categories are fully discrete and determinate. There is indeterminacy at a number of points, which can in general be resolved into three kinds: overlap, deflection, and uncertainty.

There is overlap in the sense that two different process types may cover processes that are very similar in real life. For example, 'the prospect pleased her' (mental) and 'the prospect made her happy' (relational). Here the boundaries of mental and relational processes overlap one another, if we approach them from a vantage point that is outside language. It would be possible to push the analysis to the point where these two were treated as identical; but this would tend to become a logical, not a linguistic, operation. (Similarly we do not analyse 'give' as 'make ... have', or reduce all processes to propositions about existence.) As far as the English language is concerned, 'please' and 'make ... happy' represent different types of process; they are different interpretations of experience – even if it is in some (undefined) sense 'the same experience' that is being interpreted in two the instances.

Secondly, there is deflection, in which one type of process is as it were dressed up in the form of another; for example, instead of the ascriptive 'his nose is long' we tend to select the possessive 'he has a long nose'; instead of the equative 'the person I was talking to was Richard' the speaker may use a material process structure 'I was talking to Richard', which really answers 'who were you talking to?' instead of 'what was the identity of that person you were talking to?'; instead of the intensive 'Stephen is the one responsible' we use a possessive 'the responsibility is Stephen's', and so on. When this sort of thing happens on a large scale the 'deflected' form may become the norm for the expression of processes of a particular category, and this may lead to a significant shift in the semantic structure of the language. An example of this in English is the representation of material processes as (generalized) Process plus (specific element as) Range: 'have a bath', 'take a nap', 'make a decision', 'get a cold', 'do a jump', 'give a shout', and so on.

The notions of deflection and overlap are themselves not sharply distinct; the difference is that in cases of deflection there is really only one interpretation of the process, and hence one representation, that can be regarded, at the particular stage in the history of the language, as the norm to which the other is referred. The normal, or typical, form of expression is not necessarily the more frequent, either as type or as token, though frequency is one symptom of the position. The example, 'dinner of roast beef was followed by a swim', is of this kind; the 'typical' representation of this would be as two material processes related to each other in time, but instead of this we have an equative clause of the circumstantial kind with 'follow' as a temporal relation (see above on relational processes #4.5).

Finally there are the uncertainties, the types of clause which could be analysed in more than one way. We met one type of example in 'it's raining'; an example of a more complex kind is 'the teacher taught the student English', which could be analysed in (at least) the following ways:

	the teacher	*taught*	*the student*	*English*
material	Actor	Process	Beneficiary	Goal
material	Actor	Process	Goal	Range
mental	(Agent)	Process	Senser	Phenomenon
verbal	(Agent)	Process	Sayer	Range

The last two involve the introduction of an Agent into mental and verbal processes, which we did not cover in our account of these clause types; but the possibility is not excluded. Essentially this is a type of clause that is capable of more than one interpretation, as is reflected in the fact that it has a number of paraphrases which are themselves of different types: 'the teacher imparted English to the student', 'the teacher instructed the student in English', 'the teacher got the student to know English', 'the teacher enabled the student to speak English'. There are likely to be a number of such uneasy process types in the grammar of every language, representing phenomena whose place in the total categorization of experience is shifting and uncertain.

Such indeterminacy as we find is partly a feature of the analysis: it reflects the level at which we are trying to interpret – in this study, an abstract grammar that is language-specific, as distinct from a structural description on the one hand and a logical analysis that is language-universal on the other. But it is partly a feature of language itself, a consequence of the fact that language is constantly changing and that any particular 'état de langue' is inherently unstable and transitional. While it is important to recognize and stress persistence, we cannot maintain, as some linguists have wished to do, that (say) Old English and Modern English are identical underneath and differ only on the surface. There is much that has remained constant; nevertheless there have also been some very fundamental changes in the semantic structure, and these have taken place at varying rates over different periods of time. We sustain the fiction of an internally consistent and stable system for purposes of analysis; but language does not stand still while we describe it.

4.6.3 Orientation to different process types

By comparison with many grammars, we have devoted a large amount of space to the expression of non-material processes, giving at least as much weight to the mental, verbal and relational types. We have done this in order to try and reflect something of the nature of educated adult English, as currently spoken and written.

The proportion of clauses of different types which will be found in any particular text is a function of its register. We cannot make overall statements about their relative prominence in 'the language as a whole'. But we can say that many of the register varieties that are culturally significant display a strikingly high proportion of clauses other than those of material process. For example, in scientific and technical writing, where the subject-matter is largely concerned with material processes in the real world, there is a strong tendency to encode linguistically in the form of relational processes. Here is a typical passage of popular semi-technical English (clause boundaries marked ||; [ ] enclose embedded clauses; – indicates a discontinuous clause, i.e. a clause interrupted by one that is not embedded):

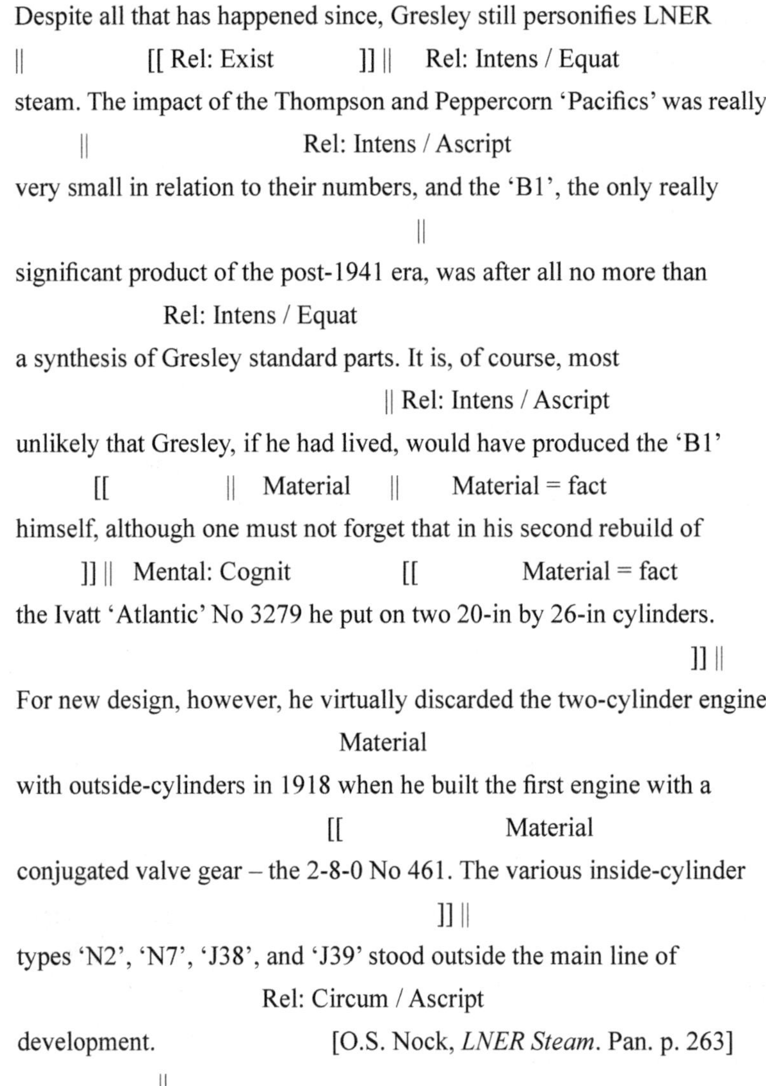

Despite all that has happened since, Gresley still personifies LNER
|| [[Rel: Exist]] || Rel: Intens / Equat
steam. The impact of the Thompson and Peppercorn 'Pacifics' was really
|| Rel: Intens / Ascript
very small in relation to their numbers, and the 'B1', the only really
||
significant product of the post-1941 era, was after all no more than
Rel: Intens / Equat
a synthesis of Gresley standard parts. It is, of course, most
|| Rel: Intens / Ascript
unlikely that Gresley, if he had lived, would have produced the 'B1'
[[|| Material || Material = fact
himself, although one must not forget that in his second rebuild of
]] || Mental: Cognit [[Material = fact
the Ivatt 'Atlantic' No 3279 he put on two 20-in by 26-in cylinders.
]] ||
For new design, however, he virtually discarded the two-cylinder engine
Material
with outside-cylinders in 1918 when he built the first engine with a
[[Material
conjugated valve gear – the 2-8-0 No 461. The various inside-cylinder
]] ||
types 'N2', 'N7', 'J38', and 'J39' stood outside the main line of
Rel: Circum / Ascript
development. [O.S. Nock, *LNER Steam*. Pan. p. 263]
||

A number of factors have contributed to present tendencies. In certain respects, the modern language reveals an orientation away from the nature and structure of processes towards the nature and structure of the act of communication; we have referred to this once or twice, and it will figure more largely in our discussion of the textual function under the heading of 'theme'. Considerations of theme have become more important, relative to considerations of transitivity.

As a corollary to this, within the realm of transitivity itself there has been an orientation away from the direct representation of material processes towards a representation of them in relational terms, the material aspect being as it were subordinated to the relational. Examples:

> Another version of the same approach was the labeling of DNA in bean plant chromosomes with tritium (radioactive hydrogen-3) by the American cytologist J. Herbert Taylor and his associates.
> George and Muriel Beadle (1967) *The Language of Life*. Doubleday. pp. 183

> The precise form which any given analysis will take is intimately connected with the structure of the investigation from which the data are obtained.
> M. J. Moroney (1990) *Facts from Figures*. Pelican. pp. 203

> Another application of geometrical series is for the study of air resistance.
> W. W. Sawyer (1943) *Mathematician's Delight*. Pelican. pp. 203

There are two aspects to this, two distinct trends which reinforce each other. One is that in many contemporary uses of language we are often in fact concerned as much with relations between things as with what happens to them. The other is that, where there are alternative possibilities, such that we can select either type of representation, either 'thing in process' or 'thing = thing', the latter allows for considerably greater variety in the structure of the communication. A sentence such as 'we also study air resistance by means of geometrical series' simply does not give the required pattern of emphasis, especially in written English where intonation is not shown. For this reason, even if we are using a clause of material process, we still often borrow the equative types of structure for the purpose of introducing varieties of emphasis, different 'textual' meanings: instead of 'John kissed Mary', we can say 'it was Mary John kissed', 'the one who kissed Mary was John', and so on. This is not just verbal perversity, or a refusal to face facts. Compared with 'John kissed Mary' with its very limited range of variation in word sequence and intonation pattern, these structures yield a vast number of different messages. Not only do the systems of Identified-Identifier, and Value-Token, come into play, but also a wide range of thematic variation.

There is rather an important distinction here. 'the one who kissed Mary was John' is still an expression of a material process; the structural mechanism of the equative relation has been combined with it in order to produce a particular form of message. It is not the same as, for example, 'The last stage of book production is the Book-jacket.', which is the representation of a relational process; this is an equative clause, not a material process clause in the identifying form. It therefore differs from the 'Book-jacket is produced last' in transitivity as well as in thematic selections.

In stressing the changes that have taken place in the orientation of Modern English we are not suggesting that speakers of Old English confined themselves to the discussion of material processes. (It may be helpful to insert here a reminder that material processes include those of an abstract nature, anything in fact that need not inherently involve a human participant, e.g. 'the government's economic measures put and end to industrial hopes.') Nor are we implying that changes in patterns of culture have had some direct effect on the semantic structure of the language; there is no evidence of this whatever. But it would be difficult to deny that they have had an effect on the uses of language. A thousand years ago there was little scientific or technical discourse and there were no mass media; and these and other developments are reflected in the range of linguistic contexts with which adult members of the community are concerned. It is very probably this effect, of different subject-matters and different media, that we are witnessing in such things as the increased preoccupation with the structure of the message, and the greater tendency towards a representation of experience in the relational mode.

There is nothing absurd in the suggestion that these essentially quantitative changes in orientation, a greater emphasis on the use of certain types of pattern, may lead to some restructuring of the linguistic system. We would rather say, in fact, that they **are** changes in the system, since the system is merely the potential for use. In other words, we do not wish to draw a line between language and the use of language, other than that which separates the potential from the actual. Language is a meaning potential that is actualized in use; and since the system itself is functional in origin, there is no *a priori* reason for assuming that it cannot be affected by major trends in the conditions of use. Only, as we hope to show in the total perspective of our sketch of English, the relation between the functions of language and its underlying organization is a very indirect one.

We see this at its most abstract in the 'meta-functions' of the grammatical system; but the facts that we have been discussing – the systematic representation, in the grammar, of the processes within our experience – are also highly abstract, and not subject to any sudden or immediate effects of changes in the environment. Changes in vocabulary are at the other extreme in the same spectrum. The general rule is that the more specific a category is, the more immediately it is affected by extra-linguistic factors. Lexical items are the most specific categories of linguistic form, and change very readily in response to patterns of culture; we create new lexical items, and patterns of collocation, all the time. The major grammatical categories, like those of transitivity, lie towards the other end of the scale; they are of much greater generality, and respond only very slowly and indirectly, via patterns of language use, to changes in the environment. The most fundamental distinctions of all, like that of the experiential, logical, interpersonal and textual components, would seem to be stable properties of human language as such, reflecting the functions that language serves for us as a consequence of our biological nature.

If we examine varieties of contemporary English, we find in some registers a high proportion not only of relational clauses but also of those of mental and verbal processes; this especially in informal conversation, where, it appears, we are much concerned with likes and dislikes, with thoughts and with perceptions. Again we should be careful here; the large number of mental process clauses in informal speech is partly accounted for by the tendency, which has been shown (by Turner and Pickvance) to be a function of the social structure, to couch many of our statements as expressions of opinion. But it may also reflect something of the turning inward that has often been remarked on as a feature of contemporary culture. Scratch a speaker of English and you find a psycho-analyst – it may not be necessary even to scratch him, as he may already be 'doing his thing' (a clause which is itself of great interest, since it must be analysed as the generalized expression of a material process). Another feature which is linked to this is the prevalence of facts and reports; much of our talk is about talk – it is 'meta-communication' in which the elements that are involved are insulated from reality by being verbalized. They are meanings, or even wordings. Meanings and wordings cannot enter into material processes; but they enter readily into processes of all other kinds, mental, verbal and relational.

Such patterns are thought of by many people, especially teachers of English, as being inimical to poetry and imaginative literature. Perhaps the contemporary modes of discourse do not lend themselves well to the traditional subject-matter of poetry. But the fact that English-language poets of this century have broken away so radically from the traditional preoccupations of the verse form suggests that they also are concerned with new meanings; and while some, notably Yeats, have expressed new meanings though traditional forms, the majority have found it necessary to develop new modes of poetic expression. This is a familiar phenomenon in the history of literature; perhaps the major source of radical breaks in the continuity of literary forms. Its relevance here is that the writer who wishes to reach today's speakers of English has to build in to his work a consideration of what those speakers have internalized about the nature, and the uses, of the English language. Not that he must necessarily copy the current patterns – he may succeed by doing just the opposite; but it is these that will determine the impact of what he writes. But it is not, in fact, impossible to write poetry which does follow contemporary patterns, including those of transitivity.

5 Participants and circumstances

5.1 Group classes and transitivity functions

5.1.1

Up to now we have confined our attention to the participant roles that are inherently associated with material and mental processes: Actor and Goal, Senser and Phenomenon. The roles of Medium and Agent were brought in order to represent these in a more generalized form. Other elements in the clause have so far been left aside.

The components of the clause may be divided into the three basic classes of verbal, nominal and adverbial, corresponding in principle to the distinction, in transitivity, into processes, participants and circumstances. Typically, the verbal group expresses processes, the nominal group participants and the adverbial group circumstances; and the word classes of verb, noun and adverb are just the classes that operate as 'head' words in the groups concerned. For example:

The yellow birds	*were preening*	*their tail feathers*	*very busily*
noun	verb	noun	adverb
nominal group	verbal gp.	nominal gp.	adverbial gp.
participant	process	participant	circumstance

There is one further type of group that enters into the structure of the clause; this is the prepositional phrase. A prepositional phrase is made up of a preposition plus a nominal group, the nominal group being 'rank-shifted', for example 'on' + 'the sea', 'with' + 'all his might':

the sun	*was shining*	*on the sea*	*with all his might*
noun	verb	noun	noun
nominal group	verbal gp.	nom. gp.	nom. gp.
		prepositional phrase	prepositional phrase
participant	process	circumstance	circumstance

5.1.2 Prepositions and prepositional phrase

What is the function in transitivity of the prepositional phrase? In this example, both instances are clearly circumstantial; and this might serve as a first approximation – prepositional phrase, like adverbial groups, express circumstances attendant on the process. But this generalization will not carry us very far before it begins to break down. The prepositional group does not fit neatly into the scheme; but it provides the key to the understanding of developments that have been, and are still, taking place in the language, and for this reason we will first discuss it in more detail.

A preposition represents a kind of non-finite process: that is, a process that does not by itself constitute a message but is ancillary to a main process that does, and therefore derives its time reference and other relevant categories from the main process. A preposition can be said to express a 'minor process', by contrast with the 'major' process represented by the verb. A number of prepositions have, in fact, the form of a non-finite verb, e.g. 'concerning', 'following'.

With this minor process is associated a nominal element, which is a sort of 'inherent participant' in it, not unlike the Medium in a major process. Hence we interpret 'on the sea' as (in this instance) 'reaching the sea', 'with all his might' as 'using all his might'. In many languages the nearest equivalent to an English preposition is in fact a class of verb.

There are two means whereby a nominal element can come to operate in a clause: either directly, or as what we shall call the 'Complement' of a preposition. In the last example, 'the sun' enters directly into the clause structure, and is immediately related to the process 'was shining', whereas 'the sea' is related to it only indirectly, through the mediation of the minor process 'on'.

A natural interpretation of this would be that a nominal element entering into the clause as Complement of a preposition could not be a participant in the major process. For example in 'the sun was shining on the sea' we might reason that the sea does not participate in the shining process but only in the 'on' relation which specifies the circumstance of the shining. This would be tantamount to making the generalization that any prepositional structure expresses a circumstance. Prepositional phrase would be a variant of adverbial groups, which are clearly qualifications on the major process and can in no sense be thought of as 'participants' in it (e.g. 'very busily'). Such a generalization would match the patterns found in the expression of mood. In the modal structure of the clause, verbal groups function as Predicator, nominal groups as Subject or Complement, and adverbial groups as Adjunct:

the moon	*was shining*	*sulkily*
nominal group	verbal group	adverbial group
Subject	Predicator	Adjunct

Prepositional phrase also function in the modal structure as adjuncts, and are in this respect indistinguishable from adverbial groups. So if the prepositional phrase functioned as a circumstance in transitivity there would be a typical pattern of correspondence as follows:

	verbal group	nominal gp.	adverbial gp./prepositional phr.
TRANSITIVITY:	process	participant	circumstance
MOOD:	Predicator	Subject or Complement	Adjunct

as in

John	*kissed*	*Mary*	*tenderly*	*in the park*	
nominal	verbal	nominal	adverbial	prepositional	(group/phrase)
participant	process	participant	circumstance	circumstance	[TRANS.]
Subject	Predicator	Complement	Adjunct	Adjunct	[MOOD]

5.3.1 Subject and Actor

The Subject is a modal function, not a transitivity one; that is to say, it is defined by reference to mood. A nominal group is, in principle, anything that can be a Subject. In any given clause, one nominal group functions as Subject and the remainder are Complements; but a Complement, in turn, is anything that could be a Subject without altering the transitivity structure of the clause. So in the example below, 'Bill' could become Subject ('Bill was stung smartly on the nose by a wasp'); but 'the nose' could not, since it is within an Adjunct; we cannot say 'the nose was stung Bill smartly on by a wasp'.

A wasp	*stung*	*Bill*	*smartly*	*on the nose*
nominal	verbal	nominal	adverbial	prepositional
Subject	Predicator	Complement	Adjunct	Adjunct

So if the pattern of correspondence between transitivity and mood held good, it would be equivalent to saying that a participant was a potential Subject while a circumstance was not. 'A wasp' and 'Bill' are participants; but, if prepositional phrase are circumstantial, 'the nose' is not a participant, and it would follow from this that it cannot be Subject. Similarly we could have 'Mary was kissed by John …' but not 'the park was kissed Mary tenderly in by John'.

5.1.4 Actor-Goal and Subject-Object

In the paradigm form of a 'transitive' representation of processes, there are only two elements that can stand in an immediate relation to the process:

the Actor and the Goal. This yields a clear distinction between participants and circumstances; the Actor and the Goal are the only participants, all other elements being circumstantial. This corresponds to a 'Subject and Object' form of organization of the modal structure. There is one Subject, corresponding to the Actor (if the clause is active), and just one Object, corresponding to the Goal. All other elements are neither Subject nor Object; for them the term 'Adjunct' is appropriate, since they are what are treated as the inessentials, as non-obligatory accessories to the process. For example:

	John (he)	*kissed*	*Mary (her)*	*lovingly with affection*	*here in the garden*	*yesterday after dinner*
	nominal	verbal	nominal	adverb/prep.	advb./prep.	advb./prep.
[MOOD]	Subject	Predicator	Object	Adjunct	Adjunct	Adjunct
[TRANS]	Actor (part.)	Process	Goal (part.)	Manner (circ.)	Time (circ.)	Place (circ.)

Here Predicator = Process = verbal group; Subject and Object = participant = nominal group; and Adjunct = circumstance = adverbial group or prepositional phrase – the last showing pairs which match each other closely in meaning and are thus readily interpretable as having the same function in the clause:

	transitivity functions			
	Actor	Goal	Circumstance	
modal functions				expressed by:
Subject	+ if active	+ if passive	–	nominal group
Object	+ if passive	+ if active	–	
Adjunct	–	–	+	adverbial group or prepositional phrase

5.2 'Participants' in the English clause

5.2.1 Departures from the pattern: The Actor

English does not follow a 'transitive' pattern in the representation of processes; and we shall not be surprised to find that it also departs very markedly from the regular pattern of participants and circumstances as just described. The language never did follow this pattern entirely – we set it up as a hypothetical model – but Modern English has moved much more radically away from it, towards a pattern of a totally different kind.

One example has already illustrated one point of non-correspondence. In 'Bill was stung smartly on the nose by a wasp', 'a wasp', although a potential Subject, and therefore presumably a participant, is introduced into the structure through the mediation of a preposition, 'by', as if it was no more than a circumstantial element in the process. This then is one very general class of instances which run counter to the clear separation of participants and circumstances in the clause. There is an imbalance between the two roles of Actor and Goal; whereas the Goal is Subject or Object, both of which are typically combined with participant roles, the Actor is Subject or Adjunct. The Actor, in other words, is slightly less unambiguously treated as a participant than the Goal is.

If this was the only departure, such that in all other instances a participant was Subject or Object and a circumstance Adjunct, with no overlap, we could treat the 'by' form of the Actor as a special case – or even as an irregularity at the morphological level, like the past tense forms of 'strong' verbs – and retain the basic Subject-Object model. But it is, of course, not the only departure. The language has moved so far from the 'paradigm' form that the distinction between participants and circumstances has been largely reinterpreted. This has to do in general terms with the shift of orientation from transitive to ergative; but it is also rather more than that. It is an example of something that has been happening in a number of aspects of Modern English: of a shift in the focus of attention away from the experiential to the textual component – a greater interest in the structure of the information as distinct from the structure of the content that is being expressed. What were originally distinguished as 'participants' and 'circumstances' now tend to differ in their information potential, rather than in their function relative to the process; and the use of 'by' with the Actor in a passive clause turns out to be a part of the general pattern. But, at the same time, as with most of the changing scene in Modern English, this is not a complete or accomplished transition; it is, rather, a tendency, a partial shift in orientation, and the present state of the language is extraordinarily mixed.

5.2.2 Further departures: Beneficiary and Range

In 'Bill was stung by a wasp' we have an example of what is essentially a participant, the Actor, disguised as a circumstance by being dressed up in a prepositional form. If we insisted that any nominal that was related directly to the major process was a participant, while any one that was related to it only through the mediation of a preposition was circumstantial, we should be forced to conclude that a wasp had a different function in the passive form than which it has in the active. Now in a sense this is true; it has a different function in the information structure (see below). But it does not have a different function in transitivity: its role in the process is unchanged – it is still the Actor. Consider the following examples where again we have both 'Steve' and 'to Steve', both 'Robert' and 'for Robert'. These, however, are not Actor or Goal; they lie outside the basic list of participants, and therefore, if anything, would be circumstantial elements capable of being disguised as participants rather than the other way round.

Peter lent Steve the car	Mary bought Robert a tie
Peter lent the car to Steve	Mary bought a tie for Robert

However, they have no obvious adverbial correspondents. Unlike 'with affection in the garden after dinner', we could not find adverbial groups with equivalent functions in place of '(to) Steve' and '(for) Robert'; this suggests that the nominal element plays an essential part in their function. 'Steve' and 'Robert' have the function of 'Beneficiary'. This has two subdivisions: 'recipient', usually with the preposition 'to', meaning the one to whom something is given – who receives goods; and 'client', usually with 'for', meaning the one for whom something is done – who receives services. Both may be present in association with the same process, as in:

Reginald	threw	breadcrumbs	to the blackbirds	for his sister
			Ben. (recipient)	Ben. (client)

Although the prepositions 'to' and 'for' are not required with a Beneficiary, they have not disappeared, nor are they in process of disappearing. Both forms of expression exist side by side.

In the examples that follow, we have a different element in the structure, one that defines the scope or range of the process; we shall refer to it as the 'Range'.

Sue played (at) tennis

Paul spoke (in) French

Fred waited (for) three months

Here again this may enter into the clause either with or without a preposition; the actual choice of preposition is varied, since it depends on the type of process and on whether the Range is in terms of quality – what kind, e.g. 'what game', 'what language' – or in terms of quantity – 'how much', 'how far', 'how long', etc. Both forms, with and without preposition, occur regularly.

The examples given of the Beneficiary suggest that the presence or absence of the preposition is tied up with the position of this element in the clause, and this is in fact true: in general, the prepositional form is used if the Beneficiary occurs at the end, and the nominal form otherwise. Since there are almost always two other inherent participants in a clause having a Beneficiary in it there is usually some choice of ordering in the active; and either Goal or Beneficiary can become Subject in the passive:

Steve was lent the car	Robert was bought a tie
the car was lent to Steve	a tie was bought for Robert

There is less choice of ordering with the Range, since Range elements are more common with clauses having only one inherent participant; but there is the same tendency for the prepositional form to be associated with final position. The Range can also be Subject in the passive, as in:

tennis was played

French is spoken

three months were spent (in) waiting

where, of course, it cannot have a preposition; but the following set of examples show the general tendency, sometimes with a different verb in the two instances:

Sue played (at) tennis with Mary	*Jim fed some hay to the donkey*
Sue played (with) Mary at tennis	*Jim fed the donkey (with) some hay*
Paul spoke French to his colleagues	*Fred waited half and hour for Jill*
Paul spoke to / addressed his colleagues in French.	*Fred waited for Jill for half an hour*

5.2.3 Is there such a thing as a participant?

The distinction between participants and circumstances no longer exists in anything approaching the 'paradigm' form. Our hypothetical model of

participants	circumstances
Actor & Goal (only)	all others
no preposition	+ preposition (or adverbial)
can be Subject	cannot be Subject

has to be abandoned. But this does not necessarily mean that the concepts of participant and circumstance have to be abandoned. The distinction does correspond to something in our experience; nor is it totally absent from the language. The point is rather that it has been combined with, and to a certain extent overlaid by, a distinction of a different kind.

Let us assume that, at any rate, Actor and Beneficiary are both types of participant. It is characteristic of both that they are expressed as nominal elements, never adverbially; so although they may occur as complement to a preposition, and in this respect are not distinguishable from circumstances, they also – unlike circumstantial elements – have the potentiality of standing in an immediate structural relation to the process.

Moreover, both Actor and Beneficiary are 'probed' (asked for in a WH-type question) by

what (...)? which...? who? whose...?

whereas circumstances are normally probed by

when? where? why? how?

to which correspond the traditional circumstantial categories of time, place, cause and manner.

Third, the concept of 'inherent' applies to participants but not, in general, to circumstances. There are a few instances of inherent circumstances, e.g. the Place element is inherent with the process of placing, with verbs such as 'put', 'leave', 'go' ('leave the pad by the telephone', 'where does the carving knife go?'); but these can be seen to be special cases, whereas it is true of almost all processes that they have at least one participant inherently associated with them.

So the notion 'participant' is reflected in certain features of the clause:

Participants	Circumstances
nominal group or	adverbial group or
prepositional phrase	prepositional phrase
'what' 'which' 'who' 'whose'	'when' 'where' 'why' 'how'
can be inherent	not inherent

At the same time there is considerable indeterminacy, not only in ways that we have already noted but in others also. For example circumstances that are typically expressed with a preposition are usually in fact probed in the same way; so the probe corresponding to 'I came with Peter' is 'who did you come with?' rather than 'how did you come?'; and functions such as 'instrument' and 'accompaniment', though usually considered as types of Manner circumstantial, are very participant-like. Note also pairs like

the boy was throwing stones on the bridge (where was he throwing stones?)

the boy was throwing stones at the bridge (what was he throwing stones at?)

where the bridge in the second example might also be regarded as a participant, perhaps a type of Beneficiary (a Beneficiary does not necessarily enjoy the benefit he receives; cf. 'she gave him a dose of poison'). But such elements need a preposition, and may even be expressed adverbially, so their appearance is more like circumstances.

The function of Range, on the other hand, is rather the other way round. It fulfils all the criteria suggested above for a participant – it regularly has no preposition, is probed by what ('What was she playing? – Tennis.'), and is often inherent; but if we consider its meaning it does not really suggest a participant. Not because it is often abstract; all participants can be abstract. But it seems to be neither a separate entity nor an attendant circumstance; it seems rather to be part of the process itself. There is no tennis other than the act of playing it. The English language, however, treats tennis here firmly as an entity, as if it was a participant in the playing process; and though it has not yet gone so far as to allow 'what she does to tennis is play it', we can say 'what she's doing to that song is not singing it (but murdering it)', as if the song was a thing with its own mode of existence. (There is again the influence of the ergative pattern here; if a process is thought of as being 'actualized' by its participant, then there is little difference between the throwing of a ball, where the ball actualizes the process of throwing, and the singing of a song, where song 'means' the actualization of the process of singing.)

It is not surprising therefore that the term 'Object' was extended by grammarians to cover not only the Beneficiary ('indirect object') but also (some instances of) the Range ('cognate object') as well; things that were not at all like the (direct) object in its original sense but were being treated by the language as participants rather than as circumstances. We could retain the term 'object', interpreting it in the specific sense of 'anything that could be (but is not) a Subject'. But the range of functions covered by this definition is now so wide that it bears little relation to the original notion of an Object, as conceived of in a simple 'transitive' model of processes; and for this reason we use the more general term 'Complement' instead. The Complement, like the Subject, is a modal function; that is, it forms a part of the structural mechanism for expressing mood. It includes whatever is typically noun-like in the clause, other than the Subject; not only direct object, indirect object and cognate object but also the elements that have usually been referred to as complements, such as 'happy' in 'Jane sounded happy' and 'their spokesman' in 'they elected Jones their spokesman'.

5.2.4 Summary of participant functions

The following are the functions, or roles, that we have recognized under the heading of 'participants', showing the preposition that may be used with each:

Role	Preposition	
Actor (transitive)	by	
Actor (intransitive)	–	
Goal	–	
Beneficiary: recipient	to	
Beneficiary: client	for	Note that all can also occur without preposition
Range: quality	at, in &c.	
Range: quantity	for	

All of these can be expressed 'immediately', by a nominal element; and also through the mediation of a preposition – except the Actor in an intransitive process, and the Goal. But this combination – Goal in a transitive clause, Actor in an intransitive – corresponds exactly to the participant function of 'Medium' which we identified as the key function in the ergative interpretation. This is another sign of the orientation towards the ergative pattern. The one participant role which cannot be expressed as if it was a circumstance (i.e. prepositionally) is one that cannot be identified in any simple way so long as we attempt to define it transitively, but which stands out clearly as the central function in an ergative-type configuration.

There is one context in which the Medium can be expressed by means of a preposition, namely if the process is nominalized, as in 'the flowing of the water' (intransitive Actor), 'the pouring of the water' (Goal). But this involves precisely the generalized 'neutral' preposition 'of', which does not express any specific kind of 'minor process' – it is merely a structure marker; and again it is only the Medium that can be expressed in this way, not the Actor in a transitive clause, which may have 'by' or ''s' but not 'of' ('the pouring of the water by Polly', 'Polly's pouring of the water' but not 'the pouring of Polly').

The ergative configuration is nuclear rather than linear. There is one central role, the Medium, through which the process is actualized; this is fused with the Process into a nuclear element, with other roles clustering around. To give a somewhat implausible example, containing the Affected and three other participant functions:

Robert is feeding Jenny her donkey with hay

Agent (*by*) *Robert*

Beneficiary (*for*) *Jenny*

Process *feed* + Medium *donkey*

Range (*with*) *hay*

It is rare to have Agent, Beneficiary and Range all in one clause – and interestingly enough there is another possible representation of this process with the hay as Medium and the donkey as recipient, 'Robert is feeding Jenny hay to her donkey'. Normally there are not more than two others from the list of participants above, though the cluster often includes circumstantial elements as well. But whatever the number of participants, there is a typical pattern in the way they are expressed, with a preposition or without. This is because of the contrast in meaning which now exists between the different implications of these two forms of expression for the total meaning of the clause.

The typical pattern is one in which all participants except the last are expressed without a preposition. The one that occurs in final position is accompanied by a preposition – unless, of course, this happens to be the Medium, which as we have seen is closely bonded with the Process and does not take a preposition whatever its place in the clause.

In other words, the '+ or – preposition' is bound up with the order in which the elements occur. But this has to do, not with transitivity, but with the informational structure of the clause, its meanings as a message. As far as transitivity is concerned, the elements are free to occur in any order; it is the information structure that determines the arrangements of the elements in a particular sequence, and thus supplies the 'linear' aspect of the organization of the clause.

5.3 Participant functions and information structure

5.3.1 Position in the clause – final and non-final

If we keep within the more usual limits of just three participants, the Medium and two others, the typical clause patterns are:

George Agent	*gave*	*Anne* Recipient	*the flowers* Medium
George Agent	*gave*	*the flowers* Medium	*to Anne* to + Recipient
Anne Recipient	*was given*	*the flowers* Medium	*by George* by + Agent

In other words, any of the three participants can come in final position; and if any other than the Medium occurs finally, it takes a preposition. There are two separate questions here: why the variation in sequence, and why is the presence of a preposition associated with it?

To get the clue to the variation in sequence, try reading the above examples aloud. The natural way of speaking them is with the 'tonic' (that is, the part that is prominent in intonation, the main pitch movement – the biggest fall in pitch, if you are using a falling tone) on the final element. We represent this as follows:

*// George gave Anne **the flowers** //*

*// George gave the flowers to **Anne** //*

*// Anne was given the flowers by **George** //*

This is not the only possible pattern; we could have for example:

*// George gave **Anne** the flowers //*

But that is a 'marked' form, one which would be used only with good reason; in writing it would have to be signalled by italics or some other form of typographical prominence, without which the reader would not interpret in this way.

The reason for this is that tonic prominence signals 'information focus': it expresses 'what's new' in the clause. More exactly, it expresses what the speaker decides to treat as being information that the hearer could not recover from the context. In English, the normal place for new information is at the end – this is so in many languages but not all. Since in any actual context of speaking, as distinct from artificial uses of language such as citation in a book on linguistics, there is always some distribution of the information in the clause, it is necessary to be able to vary the sequence so that any element can come in the position typically associated with what is new, namely the end position. The variation in sequence allows us to put any element in give any element the status of 'new' information without drawing special attention to it – to give it 'unmarked information focus', in technical terminology.

Another way of appreciating this is to consider the probes to which the various forms would stand in answer:

George gave Anne the flowers ('What did George give to Anne?')

George gave the flowers to Anne ('Who did George give the flowers to?')

It is for exactly the same reason that the Agent can also occur at the end; this is one part of the reason for using a passive:

Anne was given the flowers by George ('Who gave Anne the flowers?')

Note that the analysis by probe does not imply that this question has actually been asked; if it has we are much more likely to get an elliptical answer, simply 'George' or 'the flowers'. It means that the way the speaker distributes the information is not random, but represents his choice in the light of the current stage of the discourse. If he wishes to treat the Agent as information that is not recoverable by the hearer, and the rest as recoverable, this is equivalent to supplying the information that would be called for by asking 'who gave Anne the flowers?'; and he achieves this effect by putting the Agent at the end unless there is good reason to do otherwise.

There is always one form of the clause which is unmarked as regards the distribution of information, and which is the typical form out of context – for example at the beginning of a discourse, or in citations. Here it is the one with the Medium at the end: 'George gave Anne the flowers'.

5.3.2 Structural form – with and without preposition

The variation in the order permits any participant to come in final position, and thus to function as the 'new' information without being 'marked'. The second question is: why is there a tendency to associate the prepositional form with final position – to put the preposition in with just that element that occurs at the end and leave it out otherwise?

We can give an explanation of this, too. It is the preposition which makes the function of the participant explicit. The form 'Anne' by itself gives no indication of what Anne's role in the process is; but once we use the form 'to Anne', it is clear that she comes in as a Beneficiary, more specifically a Recipient. So if the notion of 'Anne-in-the-role-of-Recipient' is already there – the speaker is treating it as what we called 'recoverable' information – the natural form to choose is simply 'Anne'; whereas if she is being introduced as 'new' information, we need to show what her role in the process is, by using the explicit form 'to Anne'. We have already noted that the typical place for an element that is new information is at the end of the clause; therefore, the final element is the one that will have the preposition accompanying it.

For the same reason it is less usual to have prepositions with third person pronouns. A third person pronoun refers to something that has been being talked about already, or is in some other way recoverable, so there is usually no reason to specify the participant role. So 'nobody gave him a ticket' is much more likely that 'nobody gave a ticket to him'.

Note that we are not here offering an explanation of particular instances; other factors also enter into the picture. We are explaining the principle that lies behind the structural variation that occurs in the expression of participant functions, by linking these patterns up with other patterns in the language, those of the distribution of information into what is new and what is not new, or 'given'. In general, a participant can be expressed in two ways, one of which makes its role explicit while the other does not; the former is typically used when the participant in question is in the position that is typically associated with 'new' information, i.e. at the end. Either of these 'typical' patterns may be overridden – for good reason. At the same time, most instances do follow the general principle; and we can see it at work in the resolution of ambiguity. For example, 'I posted Jean a letter' is ambiguous, whereas 'I posted a letter to Jean' and 'I posted a letter for Jean' both make Jean's role clear.

The function of the prepositional group, therefore, as far as the expression of participant roles is concerned, is based on the principle of information structure. An information unit is a block of message, and contains only so much that the speaker encodes as 'new'; the remainder is 'given', in the sense that it is being treated by the speaker as information that is in principle recoverable by the hearer. The new information needs to have its role in the process made clear, so it is accompanied by a preposition which expresses that role. With what is 'given', the role is already known or at least knowable, and so it is not stated over again; instead the participant is put into 'direct' relation with the process, without the mediation of a preposition.

Hence the existence of choice between the two forms of representation of participants in the clause, one with and one without preposition, does not reflect their role in transitivity – their function relative to the process – but rather their role in the structure of information.

The difference between them has ceased to be experiential and has become textual. It is in fact a matter of voice; the distinction between 'Peter lent his car to Steve' and 'Peter lent Steve his car' is of exactly the same type as that between 'a wasp stung Bill' and 'Bill was stung by a wasp'. Both are concerned with the distribution of elements of transitivity structure (participants) into various patterns having typical values in the structure of information. We add a final note to end this subsection. There will be a little more to say about information structure and the concept of 'Given and New" in Chapter 8 below. There we also introduce another dimension of textual meaning, that of **thematic** structure, with the elements 'Theme and Rheme'; this involves not what comes at the end of the clause but what comes at the beginning. We shall not discuss this here, except to note that the same principle, that of 'dressing up' a participant as a circumstance (i.e. in a prepositional phrase), is also a feature of clause-initial position. If any element other than the Subject occurs as the first content element in the clause, then it is introduced by a preposition; for example, with Beneficiary and Agent:

George gave Anne flowers → { *to Anna, George gave flowers* / *by George, Anna was given flowers* }

The same may be found even with a Range element:

Sue plays tennis outstandingly *at tennis Sue plays outstandingly*

5.3.3

The principle that a preposition is used to make explicit the function that an element has with respect to the process expressed in the clause is nothing new; this is the usual function of prepositions. What is new in Modern English is the emergence, with many certain functions, of an option 'plus or minus preposition' meaning, roughly, 'the function of this element is part of what I'm telling you about' or 'you know the function of this element already'.

This option does not extend to all functions, for very good reasons: presumably we cannot leave out 'on' in 'on the table' if we are also going to leave out 'under', 'by', 'near' and all the other place prepositions. But the limitations of this option serve to define the notion of a participant. The pattern that has emerged in Modern English is roughly as follows:

'Medium' participant:	always nominal (i.e. without preposition)
Other participants:	either nominal or prepositional
Circumstances:	always prepositional

On the one hand, the Medium is singled out as inherently associated with all processes and, as it were, part of the process itself; it is never mediated by a preposition. The Medium, in a material process, is the Goal of a transitive and the Actor in an intransitive; it is also the Senser in a mental process and it is also the key role in the remaining process types. It is the one participant that is never treated as anything else, and this of course is an aspect of the ergative orientation in the representation of processes in English. On the other hand, among the remaining elements the distinction between participants and circumstances, although weakened, has by no means disappeared altogether: not only do we identify specific circumstantial elements such as those of place and time but, in general, we can still say that circumstances must be expressed prepositionally and cannot become Subjects.

Our hypothetical account of the situation can be summarized as follows: first, we postulate a 'transitive' stage in which there are two participants, Actor and Goal, expressed nominally and clearly distinct from all other elements, which are circumstantial and expressed prepositionally. Secondly, other elements are brought in as participants, being expressed in either of these two ways; a form with preposition can now be interpreted as a 'participant' and the line between participants and circumstances is blurred. Thirdly, and simultaneously, one element comes to be separated off as the essential element in processes of all types; this is never expressed prepositionally, but is closely bonded with the process itself. The clause then consists of a nucleus, formed of the process together with this central participant, with other elements clustering around it; some of these must be joined through the medium of a preposition, while others – those that are more 'participant'-like – may or may not be, according to their status in the message.

Perhaps the clearest symptom of this partial, but progressive, neutralization of the difference between participants and circumstances is the spread of the potentiality for occurring as Subject. The potential for functioning as Subject is important in its own right, since the Subject is the unmarked theme of the clause; it is also, however, a measure of the range of possible variation in order of the other elements in the clause, and therefore in the distribution of these elements into the values of 'given' and 'new'. We have seen that it is quite normal for the Beneficiary – both Client and Recipient – to function as Subject, as in 'the dog was given a bone', 'the cat was poured some milk'; and likewise also the Range, whether quality or quantity, as in 'tennis was played', 'six months were wasted'. But in contemporary language, even elements which have to have a preposition are made to function as Subject with the preposition still hanging round their necks, for example

I don't like being sat next to by small boys

he just stood there and let himself be hurled insults at

this hook's been hung far too many coats on

he's not used to being gone for a walk with by quite so many people

And even if we should not yet quite accept 'look at all these people we've been come in after by', or 'carelessness was lost an awful lot of marks through', we have no trouble in understanding them – or the following cry of exasperation overheard on a tennis court:

this court simply will not serve from

No doubt the tendency to allow as Subjects elements that are introduced by a preposition is strengthened by the fact that Agent, Beneficiary and Range can occur in the clause with a preposition as well as without, so that the potential of being 'prepositionalized' is not felt as a disqualification for the Subject role. A further factor would be the emergence of a class of process-expressions where the boundaries between the transitivity structure and the modal structure do not coincide, for example

	listen	*to the rain*
TRANSITIVITY	Process	Participant
MOOD	Predicator	Adjunct

Here 'the rain' is a participant (a Phenomenon, in this instance); the process is 'listen to', and this regularly occurs in the passive: 'he's never listened to'. This in turn is related to the development of 'phrasal verbs' which incorporate an adverb into the process, where the modal and the transitivity structures follow suit, both drawing the boundaries at the same place:

	Put	*the light*	*out*
TRANSITIVITY	Process	Participant	
MOOD	Predicator		Complement

Forms such as 'the light was put out', and even more 'the light was put on' (since 'on' is preposition as well as adverb) smooth the way to 'he was listened to', 'don't get run over' and eventually to 'why must you let yourself be put everyone else before?'

5.4 'Circumstances' in the English clause

5.4.1 Certain elements are clearly circumstantial

We started with the assumption that there was such a thing as a 'participant', and that it could be defined as anything which could be Subject in the clause. On this hypothesis, the category of participant would be very broad, since it would include not only Actor and Goal and Beneficiary and Range but also items occurring as Complement to the preposition in expressions of place, and so on (e.g. 'the flowers have been trodden on') – the participants in minor processes which are themselves circumstantial to the main process.

If we wanted a narrower definition of 'participant' in terms of its potential, we could refer to the potentiality of functioning as the Medium in a process – perhaps specifically in a material process. This of course is a different kind of potential; Medium is a transitivity function and therefore alternative to – not combinable with – functions such as Beneficiary and Range. But the actual linguistic items that have this potentiality correspond fairly well to our notions of what a 'participant' ought to be.

There is nothing wrong with extending the notion of participant in this way; it makes very good sense. Although up to a point it does blur the distinction between participants and circumstances, this simply brings it closer to the facts; the distinction is not a sharp one, and in any case it does not eliminate it. There are still elements which are clearly at the 'circumstantial' end of the scale.

In the examples

the last owner drove this car in bottom gear for fifty miles

this car was driven fifty miles in bottom gear by the last owner

both 'the last owner' and 'fifty miles' occur both with and without a preposition; but it would probably be agreed that the former is a participant and the latter a circumstance. There is no mystery about this; 'the last owner' is a human being whereas 'fifty miles' is an abstract measure of distance. And this is borne out by the Subject criterion; we can hardly make 'fifty miles' the Subject:

fifty miles was driven the car by the last owner in bottom gear

It should be noted that any nominal or adverbial element can be the Subject in a relational clause in which the Complement is, or includes, the 'general' term for the function in question, e.g. 'fifty miles is a long way to go', 'after dinner would be best' ('the best time'), 'five shillings was the cheapest price'; but these are special cases.

What characterizes the elements that are clearly circumstantial to the process is that they are not simple, undifferentiated functions like Actor but need to be further specified. They involve what we referred to earlier as a 'minor process', expressed in the form of a preposition. It is enough for an Actor to be identifiable just as an Actor; the question 'what kind of Actor?' does not arise (or, if it does, it is fully determined by the nature of the process). But it is not enough for a place element to be identified just as Place. We might have 'the mountain' labelled as having a Place function, but this would not tell us whether the reference was on, round, under, through, on top of the mountain or what. Specifically, for a Place element we need to know:

i. the nature of the minor process (i.e. whether rest: at, near, round, etc.; or motion: to, from around, etc.)
ii. the location relative to the item in question (i.e. whether front, back, top, bottom, side, inside, etc.)

and the same applies, *mutatis mutandis*, to Time elements as well. So in 'the car was driven through the field before lunch' there is no question of leaving out 'through' and 'before' and having 'the field' and 'lunch' related directly as participants to the main process, the driving of the car.

There is an apparent exception, in that one particular time/place relation tends to be left unspecified; this is 'rest at an unspecific location relative to' as in 'at home', 'on Tuesday'. Probably on the analogy of time and place adverbs like 'tomorrow', 'here', 'nearby', we often treat such terms as if they were direct elements in the clause, e.g. 'he stayed home Wednesday'. But most speakers would probably agree in regarding these as interchangeable with the prepositional forms (and perhaps as 'standing for') 'at home', 'on Wednesday'. The crucial point is that their occurrence with or without preposition has nothing to do with their informational status; it is not a meaningful option, as with the participant functions, but merely free variation taking advantage of the fact that in a system you can always leave one alternative inexplicit provided you make explicit all the others.

The position is quite different with measure elements such as the '(for) fifty miles' above. These are not Time or Place elements, even though they may be measurements of time or space; they are examples of the function of Extent, which is closely related to Range. Note that, unlike 'Wednesday' and 'home' which can be Subject only under the restricted condition stated earlier (generic relational clauses such as 'home is (the place) where your heart is', 'Wednesday was (a) fine (day)'), 'fifty miles' can be Subject in a material process clause like the one above provided we sacrifice 'the car': 'fifty miles was driven in bottom gear'. Here it is being treated by the grammar as a Range element, intermediate between the clearly participant functions, such as Actor, and the clearly circumstantial such as Time and Place, hence somewhere on the borderline between the two.

5.4.2 The circumstantial elements in the English clause

The circumstantial elements in the English clause can be classified in a number of different ways. One classification that is familiar is that into Time, Place, Cause and Manner, referred to above, based on the four items 'when?' 'where?' 'why?' and 'how?'. This rests on the notion of a probe, i.e. a classification according to the (implied) question that is being 'answered'. But when one comes to examine it in more detail this is in some ways unsatisfactory as a general framework; where, for example, does it accommodate elements that 'answer' questions such as 'how long?' 'how far?' and 'how many?' We shall modify this framework slightly and adopt the headings: ***Extent, Location, Cause, Manner, Matter, Accompaniment*** (see also Section 5.5.1 below).

Let us first go back to the participant function of ***Range***, which we said was on the borderline of participant and circumstance. The Range element is one which expresses the limitation on or definition of the scope of the process, a limitation which may be either in terms of quality or in terms of quantity. The former defines the scope of the process qualitatively: 'play tennis', 'speak French', 'like music' – where 'tennis' specifies the kind of game, 'French' the kind of speech and 'music' the kind of enjoyment. In Quantity Range on the other hand its scope is defined in terms of how much or how many: 'play five games', 'speak five languages', 'pay five shillings'. The function of Quantity Range is, naturally, more bounded, in the sense that numerical systems are 'closed' as far as language is concerned.

There is a 'limiting case' of the Range function, whereby a process itself may be dressed up in the form of Process + Range, e.g. 'play games', 'sing a song'. This is extremely common in Modern English, particularly with neutral verbs such as 'make', 'do' and 'have' which do no more than signal that there is a process involved; the nature of the process is entirely contained in the Range element, e.g. 'make a mistake', 'do a dive', 'have dinner', 'take care'. These structures are often used as a means of further specifying the process in terms of quality or quantity, e.g. 'make two mistakes', 'have a good dinner'. If these were the only type of 'Range'-like element that occurred in English, there would be no need to recognize Range as a distinct function, because these could be regarded as a form of composite representation of the process. But in fact they are closely related to, and in the last resort indistinguishable from, combinations of the type of 'play tennis', 'speak French' where the nominal element does constitute a substantive limitation on the process – one can play other 'things' (i.e. in other ways) than tennis; and hence there are good grounds for identifying the function of Range as common to all these types of expression.

In Modern English the Range has taken on many of the features of a participant. Not only does it occur regularly without preposition, but it also frequently functions as Subject in the clause. This is a corollary of the ergative tendency where by the major distinction arises between the Medium and all other elements; this then allows the participant-circumstance distinction within the other elements to become blurred. But the effect in this instance has been to emphasize the boundary between the functions of Range and Extent: both lie as it were on the borderline of participants and circumstances, but because the Range function has become somewhat participant-like, to that degree it becomes necessary to separate it from what we are calling 'Extent', which remains just to the 'circumstance' side of the line.

The function of ***Extent*** is like that of Quantity Range except that it involves the measure of actual units of time and space; it answers the question 'how long?' or 'how far?', for example:

we drove fifty miles	*shorten it five inches*	*I'll come all the way*
it keeps for ages	*write for half an hour*	*she stayed the whole night*

Such items can occur without a preposition, and can also function as Subject, as we have already noticed; but in both these respects they are much more restricted than items having the status or Range. There is obviously a 'cline' here:

Quality Range	Quantity Range	Extent
play tennis	*play five games*	*play (for) five hours*

but because of the facts as we find them in the contemporary language it is convenient to draw a boundary at the place we have done, between what are specifically measures of time (duration) and space, and all other expressions of the scope of the process whether in quantitative or in qualitative terms.

On the other side of the Extent function, but related to it through the fact that both are concerned with time and space, are the circumstantial functions usually classified as 'Time' and 'Place' (or 'Temporal' and 'Locative') which 'answer' the questions 'when?' and 'where?', for example: 'on Tuesday', 'since Tuesday', 'on the table', 'from behind the table'. These have generally been treated as distinct functions, no doubt in part at least because of the existence of the two distinct *wh-* words; but in fact English handles time to a large extent as one-dimensional space, and the two can be regarded as constituting a single function. We refer to this as 'Location'. Just as Extent includes both extent in time and extent in space, so also ***Location*** may be location in time or in space:

Realm:		
time	space	
Function:		
Extent	(duration)	(extent)
Location	(time, temporal)	(place, locative)

It would be possible to recognize four distinct functions, corresponding to the four cells; or just the two functions 'time' and 'space' corresponding to the columns. But the cut that is most significant for English seems to be that corresponding to the rows, into Extent and Location, and that is the one we are adopting here.

We should not exaggerate the degree to which time and space are identified in the language, and there may be some signs that English is actually moving away from this perspective; nevertheless it is the predominant orientation that the grammar reveals. The representation of time in measures on the analogy of space – not merely abstract units like minutes, on the analogy of inches, but also containerized time as in 'a summer of happiness' like 'a yard of cloth' – was brilliantly interpreted by Whorf, who showed how very differently the concept of time could be handled in other languages and suggested certain aspects of the structure of western thought that might be linked to our linguistic interpretation of the experience of time. Certainly there are enough parallels between time and space as we talk about them for them to be analysed as together constituting a single type of circumstantial function in the grammar of processes.

The most far-reaching of the similarities between time and space in English is the one that we have already built in to the analysis, namely the fact that both incorporate the notions of extent and of location. We also noted that, in both time and space, the extent is measurable in standard units, such as 'minute', 'hour', 'year', 'inch', 'mile', 'acre', 'cubic foot'. Here are some further parallels between them:

iii. in both time and space, the extent, and the location may be either definite or indefinite;
iv. in both, the location may be relative (to the 'here and now') or absolute, and, if relative, either near or remote – i.e. there is a scale of distance from the 'here and now'.
v. both recognize the distinction between rest and motion, and, within motion, between motion towards and motion away from.

Examples:

		Time	Space
(1)	Definite / Indef.		
(a)	Extent		
	Definite	*five minutes*	*five inches*
	Indefinite	*a long time*	*a long way*
(b)	Location		
	Definite	*at 12 o'clock*	*at Charing Cross*
	Indefinite	*soon*	*near*
(2)	Relative / Absolute		
	Relative	[to 'now'] *yesterday*	[to 'here'] *a mile away*
	(Distance:	*now* —— then	*here* —— *there*)
	Near	*recently*	*nearby*
	Remote	*a long time ago*	*a long way away*
	Absolute	*in 1972*	*in London*
(3)	Rest / Motion		
	Rest	*on Tuesday, at noon*	*at Charing Cross, in London*
	Motion towards	*till Tuesday*	*to London*
	Motion away from	*since Tuesday*	*from London*

Moreover location in time (an expression which is itself worth noting in this connection; cf. 'in a short space of time') looks very much like location in space if one subtracts the additional dimensions that we recognize for the latter: in space we have above and below, in front of and behind, to the left of and to the right of, whereas in time there is only before and after. And in some instances the same prepositions occur in both time and space expressions, e.g. 'on', 'at', 'in'. This is no proof that pairs such as 'at 12 o'clock' and 'at Charing Cross' are conceived of as similar in meaning – there are plenty of examples in all languages of quite different meanings sharing the same mode of expression – but it is a further reflection of the semantic parallelism that can be shown to exist on other grounds.

At the same time there are some significant differences, and these may be increasing. It is significant, for example, that time is thought of as unidimensional – we do not take an Ouspenskian, 3-D view of time – and that we think of time as moving, and carrying the observer along with it, in the current, whereas space is three-dimensional and static, with the observer moving freely within it. This is reflected in the fact that the prepositions for expressing 'motion' are in general not the same for time as for space: 'till Tuesday', 'since Tuesday' suggest that Tuesday comes and goes, by contrast with 'to London', 'from London', with London staying where it is. And 'before' and 'after' are not identified, as they were at an earlier stage of the language, with 'in front of' and 'behind'; the time dimension is no longer equated with the observer-centred horizontal axis, or indeed with any one of the dimensions of space. Then, we have somewhat distinct metaphorical extensions of the two concepts; in particular, there is a well-developed notion of abstract space (e.g. 'he stands somewhere between the radicals and the socialists') which is not paralleled in the time function. And finally – an important point – there is a close interconnection between time as embodied in the circumstantial function of Location and time as embodied in the tense system of the verb. Modern English has developed a remarkable system of time reference which is inherent in all expressions of processes, and this has had a considerable effect in dissociating the concepts of time and space from one another and linking the notion of time more closely with the logical component in the grammar of the language.

The two other categories that are usually recognized are Cause and Manner. Both of these subsume a number of more specific meanings. The ***Cause*** element answers 'why?', which includes ***reason***, ***purpose*** and ***behalf***; for example:

vi. reason, 'out of fear', 'in the light of what was said',
vii. purpose, 'in the hope of promotion', 'for victory',

viii. behalf or 'sake', related to the function of client (within Beneficiary), 'for John', 'for the sake of his reputation'.

Many of the prepositional forms used here are composite expressions of the type just illustrated; and this is related to the fact that the expression of cause, and particularly of purpose, tends to be treated as logical rather than experiential and expressed by means of hypotaxis ('in order to ...', 'in order that ...', etc.).

The ***Manner*** element answers 'how?' This is also a miscellany, but basically resolvable into three headings, ***means***, ***quality*** and ***comparison***. The category of (i) means includes instrument; examples are 'by force', 'by train', 'with scissors'. That of (ii) quality covers the expression of qualities, states and conditions, typically by '–ly' adverbs such as 'quickly', 'uneasily', 'well'. That of (iii) comparison refers to similarity or dissimilarity with something else, e.g. 'like this', 'in accordance with your instructions', 'very differently'. The instrument has sometimes been considered to be a participant function, on the assumption that 'he cut the string with the scissors' is structurally the same as 'the scissors cut the string'. But this view is based on too sharp a division between animate and inanimate, it being assumed that inanimate elements cannot function as Agent. In fact, in 'the scissors cut the string' the scissors is a participant (Agent), but in 'he cut the string with the scissors' the Agent is now 'he' and 'the scissors' becomes a circumstantial element of Manner.

The scissors	*cut*	*the string.*	*He*	*cut*	*the string*	*with the scissors.*
Agent	Proc.	Medium	Ag.	Proc.	Medium	Manner

Most of the circumstantial elements in the clause are covered by the functions Extent, Location, Cause and Manner provided they are defined in sufficiently broad and abstract terms. But there are two remaining functions which are not catered for, and which are in one way or another on the fringe of what we think of as circumstances, namely ***Matter*** and ***Accompaniment***. Accompaniment is really a form of joint participation in the process, but expressed circumstantially; it answers the question 'and who?' or 'what else?', but is typically expressed by 'with' and hence often treated as if it was a kind of Manner. But there is a difference between 'I opened the door without my key' (Manner) and 'I came out without my key' (Accompaniment), as is shown up by the zeugmatic effect of coordinating pairs of this kind, e.g. 'he walked by with a gorgeous blonde and a broad grin'.

Finally the function which we are calling 'Matter' is on the borderline of the experiential component; it is an internal textual relation answering 'what about?' and expressed by prepositional forms such as 'about', 'concerning', 'with reference to'. Matter elements often occur in verbalization clauses or as elliptical forms of these, e.g. 'talking about dogs ...' They are on the borderline of 'comment' expressions, which are not circumstantial because they lie outside the grammar of processes altogether; but they do occur regularly as circumstantial to a process and therefore need to be included.

5.5 Summary of participants and circumstances

5.5.1 Table of Functions

The Table 5.1 shows the total set of functions that we have identified in the experiential component of English clause structure; the 'transitivity functions', in other words. These include the process and the various participant and circumstantial roles. The participant functions are shown here in their generalized, ergative form; that is, as Medium, Agent and so on.

Table 5.1

		Function
	1	Process: material, mental, verbal, relational
	2	Medium
most	3	Agent
participant	4	Beneficiary: Recipient, Client
like	5	Range: Quality, Quantity
	6	Extent: Duration (time), Extension (space)
	7	Location: Temporal (time), Locative (space), Rest, Motion; Relative Location
	8	Cause: Reason, Purpose, Behalf
most	9	Manner: Means, Quality, Comparison
circumstance	10	Contingency
like	11	Accompaniment
	12	Matter
	13	Angle
	14	Role
		(functions outside experiential component, e.g. comments, conjunctions)

i. ***Process***. Always present; often not thought of as a grammatical function, but it is. Basic types of process in English (as listed) have specific participant roles associated with them, but underlying these are a small set of generalized functions of which the nuclear one is:
ii. ***Medium***. Always present whenever there is a process, except in a few natural phenomena. The Medium is that whereby the process is actualized, whether or not the process is also bought about by it. Note reflexives: in, e.g., 'pussy is washing' (= herself), one entity, 'pussy', has two roles, but structurally is Medium (only) – this is an option within the 'middle' voice.

iii. ***Agent***. That which causes the process if it is not brought about by the Medium. This is a simple opposition, of '+ / - Agent'; if there is an Agent, the voice is non-middle, and if not, the voice is middle. Modally the Agent is Subject in active, Adjunct in passive, usually with 'by' but also 'through', 'with' and others.

iv. ***Beneficiary***. Subdivides according to nature of benefit: goods ('Recipient') or services ('Client'). The former is more fully a participant, and functions frequently and unrestrictedly as Subject. The latter is more restricted; we can say 'John was painted a picture' but not 'the one who was painted the picture was John', still less 'what John was painted was the picture' (contrast 'what John was lent was the picture', where 'John' is Recipient). Some processes have inherent Beneficiary, e.g. 'lend'. (We exclude the 'ethic dative' as in 'but me no buts', which is hardly ever used outside this quotation and could scarcely be other than 'me'.)

v. ***Range***. Scope or extent of process, defined in terms of quality or quantity (other than actual measures of time and space), treated in Modern English more as a type of participant; regularly functions as Subject. Includes what are no more than nominalized expressions of the process itself, as in 'do a jump', especially common with modification as in 'he did three big jumps'.

vi. ***Extent***. Like Range except that it involves the actual measure of time or space (hence the two subcategories of duration and extension). Expressions of Extent do function as Subject, but very restrictedly; they are significantly less participant-like in their treatment than those of Range.

vii. ***Location***. Location, like Extent, is either in time or in space; it is also either relative (to the 'here and now') or absolute. It may express rest or motion, the latter including motion towards, motion away from, or more complex types such as motion 'along', 'around', 'against', 'athwart', etc.; and different locations relative to some point of reference, e.g. top, bottom, back, front, left, right, before, after, and also inside, outside, between, touching or not touching and so on. These are based on a unidimensional concept of time and a three-dimensional concept of space, with abstract space based on the three-dimensional model. Location in time is closely tied to the system of tense.

viii. ***Cause***. Cause may be subcategorized into reason, purpose and behalf. Reason answers 'why?', or sometimes 'how?' ('because of', 'as a result of'; also as negative 'for lack of'); purpose answers 'what for?' ('for', 'with a view to'); behalf answers 'who for?' ('for', 'on behalf of'). Both reason and purpose are closely related to a hypotactic clause nexus, introduced by a conjunction such as 'because', 'since', '(in order) to'; e.g. *I'm going for the sake of my health / in order to get better.*

ix. ***Manner***. Manner also comprises three subcategories: means, quality and comparison. Means answers 'how?', 'what with?' ('with', 'by (mean of)'), often specifying the instrument as in *hit it with a hammer*, or agency as in *send it by courier*. Quality answers 'how?', 'in what manner?', usually with an adverb as in *come quickly!* Comparison answers 'what like?', typically in a prepositional phrase with *like*; many are fixed expressions, such as *spread like wildfire*.

These last four are the circumstances that typically serve to answer the basic questions of where when why and how. There are then five more circumstantial elements that we can recognize in the grammar of English: contingency, accompaniment, matter, angle and role.

x. ***Contingency***. These elements are often introduced under the heading of cause, but they are rather different: the contingency is an element on which the actualization of the process depends. There are three types: condition, in the sense of 'if', e.g. *in the event of rain* (this is the original sense of *in case of*, which now means 'because there is a possibility of'); concession, e.g. 'despite, in spite of' as in *despite the rain*; default, e.g. 'in the absence of' as in *in the absence of further evidence*. These also relate to hypotactic clause nexuses, with conjunctions such as 'if', 'although', 'unless'.

xi. ***Accompaniment***. This may be either positive, 'with', 'as well as', or negative, 'without', 'instead of'; the underlying question is 'and who/ what else?', 'but not who/what?'. These phrases are often attached to participants, as in *she came with a friend, instead of coal they use oil*, where they express joint or alternative participation in the process; but they may relate to any element in the clause, and are treated as circumstantial to the process as a whole; c.f. *you must not travel without a ticket, move along quickly but not too noisily*. They relate to clause nexuses such as 'without', 'besides', 'instead of'; e.g. *he left without apologizing for his mistake*.

xiii. ***Matter***. These elements answer the question 'what about?' and are typically attached to verbal or mental processes, e.g. *I can't stop thinking about the problem*. This is the one context in which 'of' functions as a preposition, as in *they talked of nothing else*. The Matter element may be foregrounded by being placed in first position in the clause, as Theme (see Chapter 8 below), and introduced by 'as for'; e.g.

for the ghost, it hasn't been seen since. Matter is related to Verbiage in a verbal process: *can you describe / tell us about the scene?*

xiii. ***Angle.*** This corresponds either to the role of Sayer in a verbal process, indicating the source of a piece of wording; or to the Senser in a mental process, showing the holder of a viewpoint or opinion: 'according to', 'in the opinion of'. For example, *according to the record she was entirely cured, to me it seems quite impossible.* The related clause nexus is a projection: *the record states that she was entirely cured, I think it's quite impossible.* The question being answered is 'who/what says this?', 'who thinks so?'

xiv. ***Role.*** There are two subcategories of Role: guise and product. Guise answers the question 'what as?'; it corresponds to an attribute, or the identity in a relational process, as in *he was employed as a hairdresser, she acted as Joan of Arc.* There are many expanded expressions of Guise, such as 'in the capacity of'. Product answers 'what into?'; it also corresponds to an attribute or identity, but with the sense of becoming instead of being, for example *she developed into a real leader, it froze into a solid black of ice.* But often the sense of becoming is incorporated in the verb, so the product appears as a guise: *he ended up as a recluse.*

5.5.2 Concluding remarks on participants and circumstances

Not everything in the clause is accounted for as process, participant or circumstance. These account for everything that enters into the expression of processes – everything in transitivity; but some elements in the clause, such as conjunctions and comment adjuncts, lie outside transitivity altogether and have no place in a transitivity structure. In an example such as 'frankly I don't know' the word 'frankly' has no function in the expression of any process; it expresses the speaker's comment on the process, his personal angle on it. It fulfils an interpersonal role but no experiential role.

We have seen that there is no hard and fast line between participants and circumstances. There is really a cline, from 'most participant-like' at one end to 'most circumstance-like' at the other. We make a more or less arbitrary cut somewhere between the two related functions of Range and Extent, on various grounds such as the ability to function fairly unrestrictedly as Subject; but, as so often happens in language, while the distinction we are recognizing is a real one, it does not occur at any very clearly defined place; there is, rather, a gradation, a shading of one type into the other with multiple criteria which are often indeterminate and do not all correspond.

The participant is fundamentally a noun-like entity – that is, a phenomenon of a type that is typically expressed in nominal form (person, other animate object, inanimate object, institution or abstraction); hence it characteristically takes on a nominal role in the modal (interpersonal) structure, either Complement or Subject. For this reason, we have been able to use the 'potential of being Subject' as a major criterion in recognizing participant-like functions. Circumstances are typically expressed in adverbial or prepositional form, and hence are characteristically Adjuncts in the modal structure. The system which maps transitivity and modal functions on to one another is that of voice.

But, as we noted, a new distinction has arisen such that the presence or absence of a preposition is no longer a signal of function in transitivity. Whereas earlier a nominal group entering directly into the clause was typically a participant and one dependent on a preposition was typically a circumstance, in contemporary English all the more participant-like functions can occur either with or without preposition, the difference being nothing to do with their role in transitivity (which does not change) but with their role in the information structure. The preposition occurs where the item in question is in the position associated with new information, i.e. in clause-final position. This is because the preposition indicates explicitly what the transitivity function of the element is. Elsewhere, where the item occurs in a position that is typically reserved for information that is not new, it is not accompanied by a preposition, since there is no need to spell out the role that it is occupying.

The exception is the Medium element, which never takes a preposition; this is because the Medium is closely bonded together with the Process into a 'clause nucleus' – it is not so much a distinct function relative to the process as the element through which the process is actualized, an inherent part of the process without which there can be no process at all. Thus the 'cline' from circumstance to participant really extends right through into the Process itself. The Process is very much a function in the expression of processes; and the Medium, though we can call it a participant, is 'process-like' in a very real sense, so that there is no clear boundary between the process and the participants that are 'involved' in it. Hence we have processes expressed as nouns, and the whole nominalizing tendency of Modern English is closely linked to the concept of the 'Medium' as the actualizing element in the process.

The Medium, as already noted, is common to all process types; it is Goal or Actor in a material process (depending on the number of inherent participants), Senser in a mental process, Sayer or Target in a verbal process; in a relational process it is Carrier (ascriptive), Token (equative) or Existent (existential). On the whole, each process type has its own set of participants; whereas the same set of circumstances is relevant for processes of all kinds.

6 Things and 'meta-things'

6.1 Things in the lexicogrammar

6.1.1 Categorizing human experience

When we start to think about what are the things that take part in the processes construed by the lexicogrammar, we are likely to think first of the concrete phenomena of our ordinary everyday experience: the persons and other living creatures, and the inanimate objects, that present themselves as 'real' to our senses. These are the prototypical 'things' that we first learnt to talk about.

From the grammar's point of view, however, the category of 'things' is a broad, very general category that embraces the imaginary as well as the real, the abstract as well as the concrete, the dynamic (or 'happening') as well as the static (or 'existing') – all the various modes of being that can be construed as taking on some role or other in some describable process. Here *light* is as much a 'thing' as *a lamp*; *a phoenix* as much as *a fox*; *growth*, or *growing*, as much a 'thing' as *grass*.

This does not mean, of course, that there are no grammatical distinctions setting these up as different modes of being. Probably every language categorizes phenomena in some manner or other, into some such schema as that which lies behind a word class system of verbs, nouns, and the rest: things that are seen as essentially processes, like *grow* (verb), or as participants, like *grass* (noun), or as circumstantial features, like *everywhere* (adverb) or *on the plains* (prepositional phrase). This is the basic pattern that we find in a language such as English.

The prototypical kind of **participant** is an entity of some kind, concrete or abstract, real or imagined. Entities are things which, in English and also in many other languages, are construed in their own right as nouns (as opposed to being construed as something else and then turned into nouns). Even within this category, of course, many further distinctions are made; but these do tend to vary somewhat from one language to another: in English, we distinguish between entities that typically appear bounded ('count nouns'), which require deixis, and those that typically appear unbounded ('mass nouns'), which do not require deixis (e.g. *wine*), though they may get it either instantially (*the wine's been chilled*) or in the sense of 'a kind of' (*I want a drier wine*). Abstract entities are treated as unbounded: *wit* is like *wine* in not requiring dexis, not like *wife*, which does (*the farmer takes a wife*). (Count nouns in the indefinite plural (e.g. *husbands and wives*) appear to have no deixis, but in fact they have; it just happens that the feature 'indefinite plural' is realized in English as zero.) But the grammar has no special treatment for entities which are imaginary: a unicorn is just another (presumably mammalian?) quadruped.

So how do 'things' get incorporated into the lexicogrammar? Typically, as lexical items. If we are thinking of entities, these may be simple words, like *light* and *house* and *moon*; compound words, like *lighthouse* and *moonlight*; or word groups, like *landing lights* and *light in the sky*. These are all **lexical items**, made up largely of 'content words' (in contrast to 'function words,' which are those like *and* and *if* and *what* that express terms and relations in the grammar). The lexical items of a language can be compiled into a **thesaurus**; this is an ordered list of thing-names, processes and circumstances as well as entities, arranged according to their semantic relations in terms of synonymy, antonymy, hyponymy and meronymy ('similar to', 'opposite to', 'a kind of', 'a part of'). The classic example of a thesaurus in English is *Roget's Thesaurus*, compiled by Peter Mark Roget between 1800 and 1850, and reprinted, revised and imitated in countless incarnations ever since.

Things of every other kind, whether quality, process or circumstance (and even some semantic elements that are not things at all), can be disguised as entities by the application of **grammatical metaphor** (see section 6.6 below). But these other things are shown to be essentially distinct, in that they are construed first of all – in the history of the language, and also in the history of each individual mother tongue speaker of the language – not as nouns but as other classes of words: as verbs, adjectives and adverbs. The universe of 'things', as construed in English, consists of: (1) processes, which typically function as the Process element in the clause (which is why we call them by the same name); (2) entities and qualities of entities, which together function as participants in the clause – as Actor, Goal, Beneficiary and so on; and (3) circumstantial elements, often deriving from qualities but functioning as characteristics of the process as a whole. Simple configurations of these elements make up the typical English major clause.

6.1.2 Names and naming

Things have names. We shall make a distinction below (sections 6.5.1–6.5.3) between 'things', which are referred to by name, and 'meta-things', which are not – they have class names, like *idea* and *fact*, but in themselves they are constructions in the language (wordings and meanings), not names.

If we think of a word in isolation (as when it occurs as entry in a dictionary), we get a sense of its function as a name. This naming function includes both its ideational meaning, or 'denotation', and its interpersonal meaning or 'connotation'. Some words may seem to have little or no connotative meaning, for example names of inanimate objects like *steel* or *brush*, or names of institutions like *office*; but for a speaker of the language, if they are familiar terms, they will often have associations (like *tough as steel, a brushoff, tax office*) which give them a subtle, or sometimes not so subtle, interpersonal flavouring.

As an example, think of the complex meaning of the verb *claim*, with its interpersonal loading of 'implausible' as in *he claimed he was only wanting to help*. We would not expect to hear *I asked him the time and he claimed it was 3 o'clock*. But with a first person subject, as in *I shall be claiming that these results prove ...*, the interpersonal meaning is 'you will consider it implausible, so I am undertaking to convince you'. Contrast the closely agnate verb *pretend*, which means 'known to be untrue'; here the first person *I shall pretend that ...* does not override that particular interpersonal feature. Hence the difference between *she pretended to be a witch*, which might be said of an actor playing a part, and *she claimed to be a witch* – a different matter altogether. (Note that French *prétendre* is closer to English *claim* that to English *pretend* – one of the wellknown 'false friends' of the teacher and translator.)

This example also brings out the fact that the line between denotative and connotative meaning, in lexical items, is really rather fuzzy. We certainly cannot exclude the interpersonal meaning from the way a word functions as a name. (The expression *calling people names*, in the sense of 'insulting' them, makes this point very clearly!)

A name will often be used as a form of address. This may be a **common name** (name of a class), such as we expect to find in certain poetic and public speaking registers: *Dearest child*!, *My fellow citizens*!, *O wild west wind!* and so on. But it happens in daily life also, that we address someone by some common noun, especially when we get impatient with them: *mind where you're going, idiot!,* and we may address animals and even inanimate objects this way: *hullo, dog!* to an unfamiliar but friendly beast (my 20-month-old son once climbed on his high chair for breakfast and greeted the teacosy: *hullo, teacosy!*). But the more usual form of address is a **proper name**; and in ordinary English usage the word *name* means, first and foremost, 'proper name'.

A proper name refers to an individual; so it is readily available as a form of individual address: if you are 'called' (i.e. 'named') *Bill*, you can also be 'called' (i.e. 'addressed as') *Bill!*. This may in fact be the usual form of address among family, friends and colleagues; different cultures and sub-cultures vary in this regard. Some favour kinship terms within the family, with expressions of 'younger sister', 'maternal aunt', etc.; or a combination of kinship term and name (*Uncle John, Cousin Mary*); likewise with colleagues (we may find *John, Professor Smith* or simply *Professor*). The individualizing of such 'common' names as terms of address occurs in all institutional contexts (*Captain, Mr Chairman* and so on); in this way any common name designating status can be turned into a proper name by being used as a form of address. The limiting case is that of a second person pronoun, when we address someone as *Hey, you! You in the back row!*

To return for a moment to the word *name*: in English this is usually used to mean 'proper name'. It may refer to a common name, for example if we are seeking a term for some particular object: 'What's the name of that little locking device that restricts access to the control panel?'. But common nouns are not usually thought of as names, and English tends to use other terms to refer to their naming function: 'What do you call that …?', 'I can't remember the word for …' and so on. This is reflected in (and perhaps reinforced by) the terminological distinction between *name* and *noun*; English does not use *name* as a technical term in grammar. The Roman grammarians, following the practice of the Greeks, took the Latin word *nomen* 'name' for 'noun', so that the word meaning 'name' also referred to a class of words – the class whose members were proper names and common names and names of states and qualities ('nouns substantive' and 'nouns adjective'); and this practice is followed in a number of modern European languages (except that adjectives have been detached to form a separate class). But it was not followed in English, where *name* does not equate with noun; if it is used as a common term it can just as well refer to verbs ('names of processes') and other word classes besides.

Thus written English marks off proper names, by giving them a capital letter; but it does not give any special marking to nouns in general – in contrast to German, where every noun requires a capital letter to start with. English gives more prominence to the distinction between nouns and everything else. But there is, nevertheless, a sense in which the noun has special status as a 'naming' word: it is the only class of word that can, in fact, be 'proper'. In the grammar, proper names are always nouns.

6.1.3 Proper nouns, common nouns and pronouns

The nouns is the only word class a member of which may be inherently particular, in the sense that it can refer to some individual person or other entity without further specification. Thus proper names are always, grammatically, nouns, and nouns alone exhibit the proper/common distinction. There are no 'proper verbs', 'proper adjectives' or 'proper adverbs'. As soon as a proper noun is turned into another class of word it thereby ceases to be proper. The words *pasteurize*, *machiavellian*, are derived from the proper names *Pasteur*, *Macchiavelli*; but they are no different from other verbs and adjectives – they refer to classes of processes and qualities, not to individuals (and hence they normally lose their capital letter in written English).

The difference between *Blue Lake* and *blue lake* is that the former uniquely specifies an individual member of the class of lakes, whereas the latter does not. The second can be made specific, by the use of deixis: either alone, e.g. *the blue lake*, or *that blue lake*, where it is obvious from the context, or has been referred to before, or with a modifier, like *the blue lake we saw from the air*. The proper name *Blue Lake* needs no deixis, and its specificity is independent of any context.

Proper names in English for topographical features, and for institutions, do often include the 'definite article' *the*, which is of course itself a deictic word. Examples are *the Yellow River*, *the River Nile*, *the University of Sydney* – but not, for example with *Mount Everest*: here you do not add *the*. This seems somewhat perverse, though there is a principle behind it: *river* and *university* are common nouns, whereas *mount* is not – it only occurs in proper names, the equivalent common noun being *mountain*. It cannot be claimed that that principle operates with one hundred per cent consistency, but it does hold in the majority of cases. What is more consistent is that no other deictic can replace the *the* when it is functioning as part of a proper name.

On the other hand, *the* figures in many proper names where it signals that the common term is being transferred to another category. Thus *the Daily Mirror* is the name of a newspaper; *the Black Swan* is the name of a public house – not of an individual mirror, or an individual swan. The original source may itself be a proper name, as in *the William Shakespeare* (also the name of a pub), or *the Queen Elizabeth* (name of a ship). Here also *the* does not alternate with any other deictic term.

There is a set of instances in which a proper name does occur accompanied by a deictic, usually *this* or *that*: these are expressions such as *this John Smith you were talking about*. Here however the deictic is not specifying one *John Smith* among many; it is functioning as a textual signal, relating to some previous moment within the text. The answer, on the other hand, might well be a deictic in its typically 'phoric' function, most probably *the*: for example, *the John Smith who used to live next door*. Here there is a class of John Smiths (or perhaps we should write 'john smiths'), of which one member is being identified.

Other than in instances such as these, proper names, since they are themselves inherently specific, are not subject to further specification in the form of deixis. There is one other type of noun that shares this property, namely personal pronouns. A personal pronoun is a reference item which is interpreted in terms of the roles in verbal interaction: basically, those of speaker, addressee(s), and 'other person(s)' – everybody and everything else. These identify interactants by reference to the speech situation: the word *I* means 'the person now using the word *I*', and this is quite sufficient to identify the person concerned. *you* means 'the person(s)that this *I* is talking to'. Everyone and everything else is *he/she/it/they*, and these entities are identified either in the previous text or in the context of situation. Different languages combine and carve up these interactant roles in a variety of different ways, but all relate to the basic system known in our grammatical tradition as 'first, second and third person'. Since they are in their own way fully specific, like proper names they are not accompanied by a deictic.

As a tailpiece to this sub-section: it is this particularizing function of pronouns, whereby they specify an individual without naming a class, that lies behind the interesting observation by Willard V. Quine, that nouns are words that stand for pronouns rather than the other way round. The pronoun identifies the individual entity that is being talked about; and the noun may be called in as a substitute for it, so to speak, in situations where a pronoun is not adequate for the purpose. The noun helps by indicating the relevant class. Notice, however, that pronouns have a wider scope: they can refer to 'meta-things' (facts and reports) as well as things.

Proper nouns, common nouns and pronouns all belong to the general class of nouns. We have discussed proper nouns and pronouns; but a few more words are needed about the very broad category of 'common nouns'.

Common nouns, in English as in many other languages, express a very wide range of meanings. Every language, in its experiential function (that of construing human experience), has names for persons, other living beings, objects, institutions, abstractions, processes, qualities, states and relations. Every one of these types of phenomenon can be expressed, in English, by a noun (the names of the categories themselves are also nouns). But the noun is the 'congruent' category (for this see Section 6.4 below) for just the first five of these (persons, other living beings, objects, institutions and abstractions); the others (processes, qualities, states and relations) can all be turned into nouns (by 'grammatical metaphor'), but congruently they are expressed by other word classes. Let us say a few more words first about the categories that are congruently construed as nouns.

We tend to regard the first three – persons, animals and concrete objects – as representing the 'core' meaning of the noun as a class – possibly because these are the ones that figure in our earliest experience of language as small children. But institutions and abstractions are just as 'congruently' nouns (that is, their inherent status in the grammar is that of a noun).

All except abstractions display the distinction we have been discussing, between 'common noun' and 'proper noun'. This is not to say that all are equally likely to be particularized by being given a proper name; we do not normally give proper names to concrete objects or small creatures, such as telephones or spiders. But even among concrete objects, buildings and means of transport (aircraft, ships, locomotives) are often named; and we can attach a proper name to any favourite or intimate possession, giving it a special value in our personal scheme of things. We do give proper names to topographical features, whether natural (like mountains) or man-made (like cities); and there is no very clear line between man-made features and institutions – in fact there is often some ambiguity, since the same name may designate either. For example, an institution may be known as *Regent College*, so we can say *she's in her final year at Regent College*; but the name might also refer to the building, as in *Regent College is on fire*.

The one type of noun that differs somewhat is the abstraction. Abstract nouns do not display any clear distinction into common and proper; every abstract noun is essentially a common noun, even one formed by derivation from a proper name, such as *marxism* (often written *Marxism*). But although, like other common nouns, abstract nouns refer to classes, an abstract noun typically designates a class that has only one member. Abstract nouns are thus in a sense intermediate between common and proper, and more or less neutralize the distinction between the two. The fact that we can say *there is only one truth* (that is, we accept it as making good sense) is evidence that *truth* is a common noun; while the fact that we might actually say it (that is, we accept it as arguable) shows that, like a proper name, truth is fully specified and needs no further qualification.

Because abstract nouns are felt to resemble proper nouns, there is a tradition, now appearing somewhat quaint, of giving them capital letters, whether or not they derive from proper names: to write *Bereavement* with a capital B endows it with both the uniqueness of an individual occasion and the weight and durability of an institution. There is no definite article or other deictic, because they are 'mass' nouns; at the same time they form a distinct sub-class of mass noun, since what they name cannot be cut up into portions. So although up to a point *truth* is grammatically like, say, *bread* (we can *cover up the truth* as we can *cover up the bread*; *truth* can *prevail*, *bread* can *sustain*, and so on), *truth* is not readily quantifiable like *a slice* or *a loaf of bread*.

6.2 Word classes and their meanings

6.2.1 Word classes

The principal word classes of a language are characteristically associated with the naming of phenomena of different types. At the same time, what we perceive as different types of phenomena are not just given to us by our senses. They are constructed, or **construed**, by our language. All of us human beings live on the same planet, and all of us have the same brains; so there is going to be a lot in common in the way we interact with our environment. But there is also quite a lot of 'play' in the way language has evolved; so the boundaries between categories, and the categories themselves, will not exactly correspond from one language to another. In any case, the categories and their boundaries are inherently fuzzy, as they always tend to be in a system that is not designed but has evolved.

So the classification of experiential phenomena into the categories enumerated above – persons, other living beings, objects, institutions, abstractions, processes, qualities, states and relations – is a linguistic classification: these are the categories, in the world of our experience, which resonate with the lexicogrammar – in this case, the lexicogrammar of English and many other languages like it. The categories themselves are **semantic**: they lie at the interface between the lexicogrammar and the 'outside world' (which includes, of course, the 'inside world' of our own evolving consciousness).

This sort of classification arose from the attempts of grammarians in the classical traditions to explain why their languages had words of different classes. It was a reasonable question to ask, especially in languages like Greek and Sanskrit where the different word classes took different forms and behaved in different ways in the construction of sentences. English words often belong to more than one class; but the classes are still there, and can be seen in their different functions in higher units (groups and clauses). In this section we make a few very general observations about the English word classes and the phenomena with which they are typically associated.

Word classes used to be known as 'parts of speech'. This mysterious term arose out of a mistranslation of the original Greek expression meaning 'parts of a sentence'. The ancient grammarians realized that a sentence was made up of different kinds of words, and that these stood for different kinds of phenomena. Following this principle, the set of most general word classes in Modern English would be:

Word Class	Kind of Phenomenon
noun (noun substantive)	entity
adjective (noun adjective)	quality (of an entity)
adverb	quality (of a process)
verb	process
conjunction	relation (between processes)
preposition	relation (of entity to process)

The older terms for noun and adjective (noun substantive, noun adjective) were more satisfactory: the adjective, in some languages including English, is in effect a sub-type of noun (whereas in some other languages, including Chinese, it is a sub-type of verb).

All these classes can be subdivided into various sub-classes, like count and mass nouns, intransitive and transitive verbs, paratactic and hypotactic conjunctions. Some of these are particularly significant for the analysis of discourse as we are presenting it in this book, and have already arisen in preceding chapters; here we shall just run through the word classes in a summary fashion, and then we shall go into more detail in the discussion of nouns, to round off these excursions into regions of the lexicogrammar.

We talked about verbs in some detail in Chapter 4, pointing out that the verb is the key element in expressing the process which is at the heart of each clause, and that the system of process types is therefore fundamental to the construction and understanding of discourse. Children are taught early in their schooling that verbs express actions and events; it might be more helpful to summarize the class meaning of verbs by saying that they denote processes of doing and happening, sensing and saying, being and having. These appear in the grammar of English as material and behavioural processes (collectively – not one to one – doing and happening), mental and verbal processes (sensing and saying), relational and existential processes (collectively – again, not one to one – being and having). Many languages show grammatical distinctions broadly along these same lines.

Adjectives express qualities, more specifically the quality of some entity or class of entities; hence their syntactic domain is a noun (noun substantive). The adjective (noun adjective) occurs either inside the nominal group (as Epithet, e.g. *a red sweater*, or as Classifier, e.g. *red wine*) or in an ascriptive clause (as Attribute, e.g. *your eyes look red*).

Adverbs also express qualities, in this case the quality of the process. They were traditionally thought of as being attached to verbs – hence the name; but their domain is the clause, not the verb as such, and they move around the clause according to their news value (compare *hurriedly they were released / they were hurriedly released / they were released hurriedly*). Qualities of processes are also expressed as prepositional phrases, consisting of a preposition plus a nominal group (e.g. *in a hurry*, *up the hill*); these also move between the beginning and the end of the clause.

A preposition sets up the relationship between some entity and the process in which that entity is involved (e.g. *up* in *up the hill*); the preposition together with the nominal group denoting this entity form a prepositional phrase. This is like a subsidiary or minor clause; the preposition is really a restricted kind of non-finite verb (compare *can you open it with/without a knife*, *can you open it using / not using a knife*).

A conjunction also sets up a relationship, in this case between one process and another. The two processes may be given equal standing (e.g. *pay the bill, then you can leave*, or unequal standing, one being dependent on the other (e.g. *you can leave once you've paid the bill*). Any sequence of clauses linked by conjunctions forms a clause complex; this is the origin of what we recognize in writing as a sentence.

The remaining word class is that of the noun, which is the class of 'things' – or 'entities', if we want to refer to just those things in reference to which the class of noun evolved. This is a huge open class of words, which also combine in compounds and in word groups (the 'nominal group'); over the course of time, the class has extended, by grammatical metaphor, to including 'nominalizations', the transformation of almost anything else into the grammatical status of a noun. The nominal group is, in effect, anything that can serve as participant in a process construed as a clause.

A set of word classes such as outlined here is typical of very many languages the world over; even where there are other variants, every language has some analogous strategy for categorizing the elements of human experience – of ourselves, of our environment, and of the interaction between the two. It is in this sense that we can characterize grammar as a theory of human experience. It is a theory which has proved fundamental to our survival, up to now, as a species.

6.2.2 Grammatical metaphor

The pattern just outlined, of the distribution of word classes in the naming of various phenomena, is that which evolved as the typical pattern in the grammar of English. But at the same time, many of these types of phenomena may be named by words of more than one class; it is a feature of modern English, and again of many other modern languages, that there is great diversity in the relation of word class to phenomenal type. Take for example the sentence 'The brilliance of his performance was followed by general applause.' Here we find the word classes distributed as follows:

	Phenomenal type:	Typical class	Here named by:
brilliance	quality	adjective	noun
performance	process	verb	noun
followed	relation (between processes)	conjunction	verb
general	entity (persons)	noun	adjective
applause	process	verb	noun

If we 'translate' this, rewriting each word in its typical word class, we would have instead 'he performed brilliantly, then everyone applauded'. We shall refer to this as the most 'congruent' pattern, meaning the version in which each word is functioning as far as possible in the class in which it first evolved. For example, 'applaud' is a process, so its congruent form is that of a verb; 'follow' is a relation between two processes, so its congruent form is that of a conjunction.

There are various reasons for moving away from the congruent towards more 'metaphorical' variants; without exploring these further here, we can summarize one effect they have had on the language: there is a general tendency in modern English (with parallels in some other languages) for the grammatical shape of the clause to be determined by its structure as a message rather than by its experiential content. This tendency shows up most prominently in the case of nouns, because the noun has a unique capacity for distilling information, and certain kinds of status in the message strongly favour the nominal group. Here is a headline from an international newspaper: 'Outdated stadiums and poor attendance blight Italian football's top clubs'. We can notice how much information is packed into that first nominal group complex 'outdated stadiums and poor attendance': '(the fact that) the stadiums are out of date and few people have been attending'. The first paragraph contains the sentence 'The latest departure of the best players smacks of lowering standards', where the nominal groups again predominate; a more congruent version would have to say something like 'most recently the best players have departed, and from this we can tell that affairs are being less well managed'.

The core meaning of the noun, as we saw, is that of a person, other creature, or concrete object: something which has extension in space-time, and which can be particularized, since it displays the contrast between a class and a class member in its clearest form. Nouns which name abstractions, and then qualities, processes and relations, are modelled on those for persons and objects, and display the categories which are appropriate for persons and objects such as count / mass and singular / plural. It was pointed out many years ago by Benjamin Lee Whorf that such categories are not necessarily appropriate to abstractions and other extended domains of the noun, like *time*, *dawn*, *summer*, *absence*, *departure*, *cause*, *aim*; and that when we categorize words like these in terms that evolved as properties of persons and objects, this may affect the way we conceptualize our experience of the world.

But this 'nominalization' – rewording processes, qualities and inter-process relations into nouns, as if they were entities – is not the only way in which meanings get switched from one grammatical category to another. Another very productive pattern is that whereby a relation between processes is reworded as if it was itself a process. We saw an example of this with the word *follow* above ('*a* happened, then *b* happened'); compare also *smacks of* ('*x* happened, so we know that *y* happened'). In principle, any phenomenon can be worded as if it was something **more concrete** than it actually is; the ordering of phenomena works out as follows:

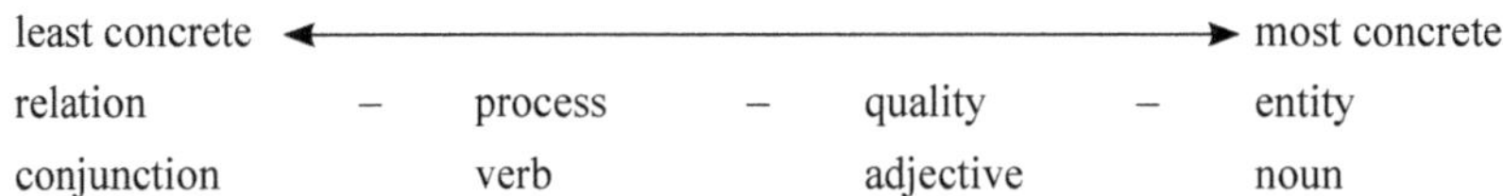

This 'rewording' is in fact a form of metaphor. But whereas metaphor in its usual sense is a lexical relationship (one lexical item takes over from another), here the relationship is grammatical: one grammatical class takes over from another. So we call it grammatical metaphor: it is a metaphoric process, but one that is taking place in the grammar, not in the vocabulary.

In this sense of metaphor, a great deal of modern discourse is highly metaphorical. The impetus towards grammatical metaphor seems to have come originally from the sciences – or rather, from the evolution of systematic scientific knowledge; it can be traced, as far as the west is concerned, to its origins in ancient Greek and Latin, but similar effects were found in ancient Chinese. It was only with the Renaissance, however, that scientific discourse came to be largely taken over by grammatical metaphor, in the sense that the most favoured clause type is one such as the following: *high blood pressure is probably caused by excess consumption of salt*, where two phenomena of either process or quality (congruently verb or adjective) are both realized as nouns, and then linked by a logical-semantic relation (congruently a conjunction) which is realized as a verb. The conjunctive relation itself may also be nominalized, if we reword this as *a likely cause of high blood pressure is excess consumption of salt*. In other words, instead of presenting the argument as '*a* happens, so *b* happens', in scientific discourse the norm has become 'happening *a* causes (or "is the cause of") happening *b*'.

Such forms of wording are clearly motivated in the discourses of science, because they make it much easier to build up a structured argument and in so doing to work towards a coherent and powerful theory. When processes and qualities are transformed into virtual 'things', they persist, with extension in time. The grammar is working in harmony with the principles of Newtonian physics: when you are studying any complex phenomenon, it is helpful if it stays as it is while you are observing it.

But because this elaborated kind of discourse gained a high prestige, it has penetrated far beyond the discourses of learning to other varieties of the language, especially where there is some hierarchy of power. We are all familiar with bureaucratic formulations such as 'Failure to reconfirm will result in cancellation of your reservation', where the grammatical metaphor has no other function than to create an impression of authority. The movement towards 'plain English' has had some success in countering this kind of pomposity; but we should still be surprised if we were told 'if you don't reconfirm, your reservation will be cancelled'.

6.3 How nouns are organized

6.3.1 The taxonomic principle

Leaving aside metaphoric nominalizations such as discussed in the last section, we can see that much of the repertory of names of entities, in English as in every language, is organized taxonomically: that is, in hierarchies of classes, such that one class includes other classes, each of which may include further classes, and so on. For example, the class of *clothes* includes *coats*, *hats*, *dresses*, *boots*, *shoes* and so on; the class of *coats* includes *jackets*, *raincoats*, *overcoats* ...; and there are various kinds of *jackets* according to function, shape, and material. The class of *games* includes *ball games*, *board games*, *card games*, etc.; *card games* includes *rummy*, *whist*, *pontoon*, *bridge* ...; *bridge* includes *auction bridge*, *contract bridge*; and now *contract bridge* has further sub-classes of its own.

Not every level in a taxonomy will have a name. For example, there is a general term *way* in English, but no intermediate term for 'man-made way' covering *track*, *path*, *pavement*, *road* and *railway*. The class of *books* includes two major sub-classes neither of which (in English, unlike some other languages) has a name: 'books for reading', like *textbook*, *novel*, *poetry book*, and 'books for writing in', such as *notebook*, *exercise book*, *account book*. Sometimes there is a superordinate term but from a more formal or specialized register, like *vehicle* for *car*, *train*, *truck*, *bus*, *bicycle* – anything with wheels; or *sibling* including *brother* and *sister*. Often a new term may be introduced, perhaps for official or commercial purposes, like *footwear* for *boot*, *shoe*, *sandal*, *slipper*; such terms may remain restricted, or they may spread into the everyday language, if people start saying things like *Just wait while I put my footwear on; then I'll be ready*.

This kind of taxonomy is based on the relationship 'is a kind of': a jacket is a kind of coat, bridge is a kind of card game and so on. The technical term for this relationship is **hyponymy**: *jacket* is a hyponym of *coat*. There is one other type of taxonomy, one that is based on the relationship 'is a part of', technically known as **meronymy**. It is easy to switch from one to the other by choosing a different superordinate term: *jacket*, *trousers* are **hyponyms** of *garment* but **meronyms** of *suit*. The combination of hyponymy and meronymy provides a grid for the systematic organization of the constantly growing number of nouns that form a major part of the vocabulary.

Sometimes different taxonomies covering the same domain may coexist side by side. An obvious example of this is provided by scientific and everyday taxonomies: in zoology, *vertebrates* includes *fishes*, *amphibia*, *reptiles*, *birds* and *mammals*; *mammals* includes *marsupials* and *placentals*; the latter includes (among others) *carnivores*, *ungulates* and *primates*; *primates* includes *lemurs*, *monkeys*, *apes*, *chimpanzees* and so on. Popular, commonsense taxonomies do not match these: some terms are missing, others occur in different locations, and some have no natural counterparts. For example, for many speakers *fishes* includes sea mammals such as *whales* and *dolphins*; among the invertebrates, *insects* includes *spiders*; and there is no zoological class corresponding to *pets* or *vermin*. Sometimes, as among bird-watchers for example, there is a third, **expert** taxonomy which is in some ways intermediate between the scientific and the popular; this will contain categories such as *waders* and *birds of prey*.

As the above discussion brings out, naming hierarchies show considerable interplay between more and less familiar, everyday words; this may happen in any language, but it is a particularly noticeable feature of modern English. This has happened because, while the commonsense terms come typically from the native, Anglo-Saxon word stock, new names are generally derived from the 'borrowed' lexicon of Latin and Greek. This often makes it harder to see exactly where some class actually belongs: how do *cats* and *dogs* fit in, what are *animals*, how far does the class of *shellfish* actually extend? As in all use of language, uncertainty is typically resolved, as far as it needs to be, by the context; you do not mix up the categories in use in a restaurant with those that are applied in a zoo. But compared with Chinese, where the taxonomic organization of thing names is notably transparent, that of English is relatively irregular and opaque.

6.3.2 Noun compounding

Noun compounding is one strategy for extending the scope of the vocabulary while maintaining some kind of taxonomic order. Old English compounds like *doorknob*, *doorsill*, *doorpost* show clearly their relationship to the superordinate term *door*; whether this is a relationship of hyponymy or of meronymy is not entirely clear, but for most purposes it does not matter which. The principle is that one element of the compound is the more general term, while the other gives a more specific reference; the exact semantic relationship between the two is extremely variable. Thus a *compound noun* is a particular kind of noun, one that is made up of two (or more) parts; a *charter flight* is a particular kind of air journey, arranged for by special charter; a *wristwatch* is a particular kind of watch, one that is worn on the wrist. Ambiguity can arise, of course: is a *paper bag* a bag that is made of paper, or is it a bag for putting paper in (but even here the two are clearly differentiated in speech, if not in writing)? And is *type face* really a kind of face – or how would we define *face* to ensure that it was?

Compounding is a name-forming process which does show the location of the name in some kind of taxonomic hierarchy. But the last example brings out a significant feature of such structures: that the exact nature of the hierarchic relation may be far from clear – to the extent that we have to invoke the concept of 'metaphoric compounding' to account for many instances that we encounter. For example, it is quite clear that *gravyboat* consists of the two elements *gravy* and *boat*; but we can hardly classify a gravyboat as a kind of boat – nor a *gravy train* as a kind of train. In fact we might formulate the general question 'is the compound formed of $a + b$ a kind of b, or is it not?' – and if the answer is 'no', we have what we may call a metaphoric compound. In many cases, we will be uncertain, but that is no more than a general feature of language: we can establish clearcut categories on explicit criteria, but assigning each instance to one category or the other will always show up cases of indeterminacy. Take the word *firework*, as in *firework display*: is it or is it not a kind of *work*? Originally, it was – it was like *needlework* and *waxwork* and *patchwork*, with *work* meaning 'artefact' (as in 'the work of van Gogh', 'works by modern composers'); but *firework* is no longer recognized as a compound of this type, or thought of as being a compound at all.

Compounding of the non-metaphoric kind plays a part in the taxonomic organization of nouns, as can be seen from the wording of familiar classes like trees and fishes. Some nouns, like *halibut* and *sycamore*, contain no general term as indication of their taxonomic status – you have to know that one is a fish, the other a tree. On the other hand, with nouns like *catfish*, *peartree*, the general term has to be included in the name: a *catfish* is not the same thing as a *cat*, a *peartree* is not the same thing as a *pear*. Compounds like *raincoat*, *teacup*, *football* are all of this type. Then there are intermediate cases like *cod/codfish*, *oak/oaktree*, where the general term may or may not be added, according to whether or not the category is already in the air, or perhaps largely for their different effect on the rhythm. Metaphoric compounds lie outside the taxonomic order in which the general term occurs: a *spoonbill* has no place in the hierarchy of *bills* – though it belongs in another hierarchy, that of *birds*. In any case there is no very clear line between the two; does *eyelid* figure in the general class of *lids*? in what sense is a *flying boat* a *boat*, rather than a kind of aeroplane?

As a typological variable, however, we can notice that languages differ in their preference for one type or the other. For example, Chinese tends to favour explicit, non-metaphoric taxonomies: there is a general term, used on its own, like *che* 'wheeled vehicle', *yu* 'fish', *jiqi* 'machine', and every member of the class consists of this general element preceded by a specific term, e.g. *mache* '(horse) cart', *dianche* 'tram', *qiche* 'motor car' and so on; and this pattern prevails throughout the noun component of the vocabulary. By comparison, Malay-Indonesian tends to favour metaphoric compounds, like the well-known 'day-eye' *matahari*, meaning 'sun'; compare *matatong* 'barrel eye', meaning 'bung', 'breast-eye' *mata susu* 'nipple' and numerous others. These are all variants within the general principle of compounding as a resource for constructing names.

6.3.3 Technical and brand names

Many technical terms are everyday words that have been transferred into specialized contexts, like *population* and *universe* in statistics, or *capital* and *interest* in finance, or *commitment* and *role* in sociology. The implication is that we can use our everyday experience in constructing a model for explaining the phenomena under investigation; not unreasonably, since in the social sciences at least the phenomena being investigated are often drawn from areas of everyday experience. But the technical term that is created in this way is a new name; it is not the same name as the original. Thus for example *group* in its non-technical sense is related to *crowd*, *gathering* and so on, in a general class of which perhaps there is only a more formal name such as *collective*. But as a technical term in mathematics *group* has quite a different status; there is no *crowd* in mathematical group theory, and the superordinate term is not *collective* but *set*.

The distinguishing feature of a technical term is that it functions as part of a theory. It can be defined only in conjunction with other technical terms and in relation to the theory as a whole. So technical terms in linguistics, many of which are taken from everyday language, like *active* and *subject*, or *onset* and *stress* in phonology, are redefined in relation to a general theory of language. Since linguistics is one of the oldest of the sciences, many of its technical terms evolved originally in Greek, or even in Sanskrit, and the terms used in modern languages such as English came in as translations, usually from Greek via Latin; but this does make any difference to their theoretical status.

Other technical terms are specially created, or 'coined', so as to serve in the construction of a theory. In English, this process normally takes place through grammatical metaphor; and especially through nominalization, since technical terms are typically nouns, although other word classes will often be derived from them. So in English we have terms like *nominalization* itself (the name of a process 'is turned into a noun'), *dependency* (name of a relation 'depends on'), *dissimilation* (name of a quality '(makes or becomes) not alike'). Usually such terms are created as they are needed, by a particular researcher or research team; but sometimes the process gets institutionalized, in contexts where it is felt necessary to develop a technical vocabulary rather quickly for educational, scientific and administrative purposes; a commission on terminology is set up and charged with creating a slate of new vocabulary in a single operation. Such vocabulary is more likely to be taken up if it is based on principles that already underlie the natural naming processes of the language in question.

A brand name has something in common with a technical term; but it is not coined for the purpose of classifying or explaining any objective phenomenon. What it names is not a natural class, or even a hypothetical class set up as part of a theory, but a class that has been artificially created with a particular economic purpose. The name is as essential element in this process. Brand names, therefore, have their status defined in the legal system; they can be owned, and bought and sold, as property. But although the law may draw a clear line between brand names and common names, the language does not; to take one example, the class of breakfast cereals includes a number of intermediate instances which one would be uncertain whether to regard as brand names or not. Firms other than Kellogg's, for example, can market *corn flakes*.

Brand names themselves have a somewhat indeterminate linguistic status. In general, they resemble common nouns, but they have some features of proper nouns also; Geoffrey Leech, in one of the earliest studies of the language of advertising, referred to them as having an 'unstable' syntactic function. And while many of them may persist over a long period, and even settle in as ordinary words of the language, others fall away as the commodity they name goes out of use. But while they are around, they accommodate to the patterns of the everyday language; M. A. K. Halliday, in a paper written in the 1960s, cites an example of an utterance he heard in which every common term, noun and verb, was a brand name: 'The dripolator needs brilloing; let's just have some nescafe in the denby' – which passed unnoticed in the ordinary course of the conversation.

Brand names that are newly coined, especially with certain types of product, tend to exploit the associative potentialities of naming, through resemblance to existing common names; sometimes they recall the sound of some particular word, like *soov* for an ointment that relieves the discomfort caused by rashes and stings (cf. *soothe*); sometimes they incorporate **phonaesthetic** features – sounds, or sound combinations, that are regularly associated with certain areas of meaning, such as the 'glowing' sense of words beginning with gl- (*glow*, *glimmer*, *glint*, *gleam*, *glisten*, etc.).

These phonaesthetic effects lie on the borderline of ideational and interpersonal meaning; they tend to connote well-being, sympathy, or some positive feature (or sometimes negative, if the product is designed to eliminate dirt or decay) that will have the desired impact on the consumer.

6.4 Increasing our naming power

6.4.1 Defining names

If we think about the meaning of a name, we usually think first (and sometimes think only) of its ideational meaning: we assume that the term denotes some particular class of referents in the real (or imaginary) world. The types of taxonomic organization we described in the last section (hyponymy, meronymy) were based on ideational meaning – what lexicographers call the 'denotation' of a word. But words may also carry interpersonal meaning (a word also has a 'connotation'). Interpersonal meanings are not organized taxonomically; the connotation is typically in terms of the simple opposition of 'desirable' ('purr words') and 'undesirable' ('snarl words') – although this may combine with other variables; for example *pride* is 'self-esteem / justifiable', in contrast to *arrogance*, which is 'self-esteem / unjustifiable'; compare *soil* 'earth / in the right place' versus *dirt* 'earth / in the wrong place'. As a simple opposition between 'purr' and 'snarl', or at least 'purr' and 'non-purr', we might think of *scent* 'odour / pleasant', *smell* 'odour / neutral or unpleasant'.

Interpersonal meanings are not, of course, confined to nouns; they are a feature of all lexical items, and many such pairs are found with adjectives and verbs – sometimes in two or all three forms of the same lexeme, e.g. *shine shiny to shine* 'give off light / pleasant', *glare glary to glare* 'give off light / unpleasant'. Such interpersonal features are a part of the meaning of the word, and although groups of speakers may differ in their assessment a little more than they do with ideational meanings, there is an overall consensus – otherwise the words would lose their effectiveness in the discourse.

So when we define a word, we include an indication of its interpersonal meaning, if it is anything other than purely neutral, or 'unloaded'. Definition is a way of encoding the meaning of a word within a particular grammatical format: a relational process of the intensive / identifying type (see Chapter 5 above). The verb is one of the identifying (or 'equative') class, most commonly the verb *be*; the word to be defined usually serves as the (element to be) 'Identified', the definition as the 'Identifier' (abbreviated as Id, Ir):

(1) A *gazebo* (Id) is ('names') a pavilion or summerhouse on an eminence, open to the view (Ir)

Alternatively, the definition may be introduced as the 'Identified' element:

(2) A pavilion or summerhouse on an eminence, open to the view (Id), is ('is named') a *gazebo* (Ir)

But we can see that this does not give a full account of the structure of the definition, because it does not show which is Token and which is Value (cf. Chapter 5 above). Since a name stands for, or represents, an entity and not the other way round, in a definition the naming is the Token and the definition is the Value; the structure is therefore

(3) A gazebo (Id/Tk) is a pavilion on an eminence (Ir/Vl)

(4) A pavilion on an eminence (Ir/Vl) is a gazebo (Id/Tk)

Here we are using *gazebo* in its normal function as a name. We could instead frame it as a citation form, or 'lemma', as in

(5) The word 'gazebo' means a pavilion on an eminence

(6) A pavilion on an eminence is called a gazebo

This makes it possible to add an Assigner (grammatically a type of Agent) which assigns the Token to the Value:

(7) We (Ag) call a pavilion on an eminence (Id/Vl) a gazebo (Ir/Tk)

We are assuming here that the term *gazebo* has no interpersonal loading. Where there is, this can be incorporated into the gloss; we might think of a gazebo as being ornate and attractive to look at, say 'a decorative pavilion'. Some such loading may be built into the definition through the denotation of one of the key terms:

(8) A refugee is a person fleeing from injustice

(9) A renegade is a person fleeing from justice

6.4.2 Uses and limitations of definitions

Definitions are familiar in educational contexts, especially school textbooks in mathematics and the sciences, where they are often used to test the students' knowledge of technical terms. The problem is that in a definition each term is treated in isolation, whereas a scientific theory is a system of related terms which need to be understood as a collective, since ultimately they all define each other. So at a more advanced stage groups of terms may be defined together, with the aid of cross-reference; perhaps with one or two picked out as 'primitive', whose definition can be given independently so that these serve as anchorage for all the rest.

A definition can never tell the whole of a word's story. Typically it will include one or two synonyms plus a short passage of explanation setting out some features or functions of the thing being defined, like the gazebo definition quoted above. The lemma is a word that has been taken out of its context (it is 'decontextualized'); the definition makes a move towards recontextualizing it, through its synonyms and explanatory glosses. Dictionaries often have a set of categories indicating the domain in which the word is likely to occur – its registerial address, so to speak; with headings such as nautical, diplomacy, chemistry and so on. These also serve as contextualizing devices.

When children encounter unfamiliar words, they ask for a definition: 'what does ___ mean?' Here defining becomes part of casual conversation; and the parent, or whoever is being appealed to as the knower, will typically add some further information about the context. For example:

(10) What is an alibi?

– It's saying you were somewhere else. Suppose the teacher said to you, 'Did you start that fight this morning in the gym?', and you answered 'No, I wasn't there. I was out with the nature class.' You'd be saying you have an alibi – you were somewhere else when it happened.

At any time in our lives we are always likely to encounter new names. This may be, just as it often is with growing children, in the ordinary cause of events as we are listening or reading in any of the modalities that technology has made available to us. Asking for definition is a useful tactic, but under many circumstances we can't do that, or at least we can't expect an answer, because there is no interlocutor there to respond; so we depend on the context for help in understanding – as we are often forced to do in a language that we don't know very well. People are very skilled – some, no doubt, more than others – at picking up clues in the meaning of a name from evidence in the surrounding context, both the verbal context and the context of situation.

One thing that may help us to acquire and keep up this ability is that we often play naming games, starting quite early in life. These often depend on other aspects of a name than just its meaning, like 'I'm thinking of a word that rhymes with …', or 'I spy with my little eye something beginning with …' which are based on the sound or the spelling. A little later, we may take up the game of 'coffee pot', which depends on working out sets of homonyms; and as adults some of us are addicted to cryptic crosswords, which exploit all the aspects of a name – its sound, its spelling, its meaning, its synonyms and homonyms – in order the better to disguise it. So called 'quick' or 'plain' crosswords, on the other hand, depend exclusively on finding a name to fit a meaning – an equally valuable if less contorted exercise. These examples are all taken from English, where the hybrid spelling system strongly favours games played with writing (witness the commercial success of the game of Scrabble); but speakers of probably all languages play some kind of naming games.

6.4.3 Children learning names

Infants starting to speak typically begin with a 'protolanguage': a meaningful array of sounds and gestures through which they interact with a little group of intimates. This 'language' is not based on reference – it doesn't name. They abandon this when they take up the mother tongue, which is language in the usual sense, some time in their second year. Naming begins when some vocal signs come to be associated with some particular entity typically starting with the name for mother; these are 'proper names', referring to individuals, and they are transitional between protolanguage and language.

To move into language, the child has to generalize: to learn to use names that are the name of classes, or 'common names'. These are usually nouns, to start with – words like *baby*, or *dog*, or *bus*, which refer not to an individual thing but to a class of things. Once they have recognized this principle, the gateway into language is open, and they can race ahead. They soon learn that not only entities can be learned but also qualities and processes: a light may be *green* or *red*, the cat may *run* or *jump*. Here all names are common: there are 'proper nouns', but no 'proper adjectives' or 'proper verbs'.

Children also recognize, at the same time, that some classes include other classes: they hear 'let's put your clothes on', where *clothes* includes *vest* and *shirt* and *shorts* and *socks* and *cardigan*. In other words, names form into taxonomies, based on the principle of generalization, or 'is a kind of': *poodles* and *terriers* are kinds of *dogs*, *red* and *green* are kinds of *colour*, *fry* and *boil* are kinds of *cook*. Of course they 'make mistakes' in building up the classes, and classes of classes; but someone – parent, elder sibling, uncle or aunt – is always around and ready to correct them, to say 'That's not a bus, it's a van', 'No that's not green, it's blue'. Most of the categories construed by our language, whatever language it is, are inherently indeterminate, or 'fuzzy'; our eco-social environment is so complex that such compromises are necessary for our survival, and this indeterminacy is itself something that children have to learn in the course of their learning how to mean.

More problematic is the move from general to abstract names. The abstract is different from the general, a further step away from direct experience. A *bird* is a more general category than a *parrot* or a *crow*; but it is no more abstract – you can see a bird flying just as well as you can see a crow flying. On the other hand, you can't see a *habit* or a *lie*; these are abstract names, as in 'That's a good habit' or 'You mustn't ever tell a lie', and they can be difficult for children before the age of about four. It seems likely that the way they progress to the abstract is through names of observable processes, like *run*, *wash*, *cry*, and then qualities of observable phenomena, such as *narrow*, *heavy*; with help especially from words that have a strong element of appraisal, like *clever*, *cross*, *unfair*, where there are clear perceptible clues and the meaning often impacts directly on themselves.

One way or another, we expect children to be familiar with abstract names by the time they come into primary school, because that is when we teach them to read and write. Writing depends entirely on abstractions: not just single terms like *sentence* or *letter* or (most exclusive of all!) 'complete idea', 'complete thought', but the entire notion that you can 'write down' what you say, and that a piece of written matter 'says' something – these require a considerable degree of understanding of the abstract. So of course does citation, where a name refers not to an entity but to itself, as in 'How do you spell *antelope*?' Since young children work hard at learning language, another way in which they get into abstract meanings is through the names of linguistic categories, already familiar in everyday talk and in their games;

so if you ask 'How do you spell the word *antelope*?' you are building on what they already understand.

Most difficult at this stage are probably the names of variables, like *size*, *weight*, or *difficulty*. A four-year-old knows perfectly well what is meant by *big*, *small*, *heavy*, *light*, *hard*, *easy*; but words like *size*, *weight*, are abstractions which correspond variously to statements, as in 'collapsed under the weight' (it was heavy), to questions as in 'guess the weight of it' (how heavy is it?), or to exclamations as in 'what a weight!' (how heavy it is!), and these will often be unfamiliar until introduced in the primary school classroom. It is sometimes assumed that if a child has problems with the abstract concepts of mathematics, such as *volume*, this is because he hasn't grasped the qualities they reflect; but it may be that the difficulty lies more in the language, in having names for abstract 'things'.

6.4.3 Glossary of some technical terms

Citing	the use of a word to denote itself.
Coining	the process of synthesizing names
Common name	name of a class of phenomenon of any type (person, other living being, object, abstraction, institution, process, quality, state or relation)
Count noun	noun displaying option of singular and plural; typically, naming phenomenon regarded as discrete
Mass noun	noun not displaying option of singular and plural; typically, naming phenomenon regarded as continuous, or requiring quantification
Naming	meaning function of a word as isolate (more accurately, of a lexical item, or 'lexeme'); using a word, phrase, etc. to denote that which it names.
Proper name	name of an individual person or object
Taxonomy	hierarchical organization of classes

6.5 'Meta-things': Facts and reports

6.5.1 The distinction between things and 'meta-things'

In general, words – or, more strictly speaking, lexical items, the elements of the vocabulary – are the names of things. It is things that have names. Facts and reports are expressed but, as a rule, they are not named; that is, they require a grammatical structure, typically a clause structure, for their encoding – though there are some exceptions to this which we shall note below. Of course a 'thing' may be complex – that is, analysed by the language as consisting of more than one element, e.g. a process plus a participant – in which case it too requires a structure to represent it. But in principle things can be named, whereas facts and reports are not.

It is this distinction, between things and 'meta-things', rather than the distinction within things into persons and objects versus processes, etc., that affects the function of naming in the discourse. We tend to think of names as somehow restricted to nouns, perhaps because only nouns can be 'proper' (and in some languages the word for 'noun' is the same as the word for 'name'). But, as we saw, this concept of a name is too narrow. What is sometimes expressed as a noun may at other times be expressed as a verb; and the same phenomenon may be represented now as a process (alone), now as a process with one or more participants, now as a participant (alone). So the naming function is not the function of encoding persons, objects, etc. as distinct from processes; it is the much more general function of encoding things – whether these are persons, objects, processes, qualities or circumstances – as distinct from what we are calling 'meta-things', i.e. facts and reports.

In discussing the nature of processes, and the elements that are involved in their linguistic expression (i.e. in 'transitivity'), we identified the process itself, and the participants and circumstances. But we also saw that this classification into process, participant and circumstance, while valuable as a general guide, is by no means rigid. The basic notion was rather than of an element in a process, which might enter in a number of specific functions such as Process, Agent, Medium and the like. Now we assumed, in the discussion of these functions, that the elements of a process were things – the phenomena of experience, which could be named. This is in fact the typical case. Typically, the entities that figure in the processes of our experience are the phenomena of our experience themselves; this seems natural and almost tautological. But, as had been noted in the discussion of types of process, this is really true only of material processes. In material processes the elements are all 'things' in this sense: the process itself, and entities, qualities and circumstances. But in the representation of mental processes this restriction does not hold, since there is one function in a mental process which may be taken on either by a thing or by a fact or report – a 'meta-thing' as we have labelled it. This is in fact one of the fundamental differences between material processes and mental processes: the latter are not tied to the phenomena of experience, but admit experience as filtered through language – facts and reports – as one of their component elements.

Let us recapitulate a little on the difference between things and 'meta-things'. Consider the examples

I watched the tide coming in

you were surprised that the tide was coming in

he said that the tide was coming in

The first of these has a 'thing' as complement of 'watch', namely 'the tide coming in'. It happens to be encoded as a complex process involving the movement of some object as participant – rather an odd way of looking at it, perhaps, but that is how English sees it. Anyway it is a thing, a phenomenon of our experience, and it can enter into other processes e.g. 'he was left stranded by the tide coming in (the incoming tide)', and so on. However the other two examples are not wholly concerned with things. The 'you' and the 'he', the 'surprised' and the 'said', are all things; but the 'that the tide was coming in' is not a thing. It is a thing that has been encoded in language, and thus becomes what we call a 'meta-thing'. Either it is a fact, a piece of semantic structure, as in 'you were surprised that the tide was coming in'; or it is a report, a piece of text, as in 'he said / she knew that the tide was coming in'. It relates only indirectly to a phenomenon of experience.

Facts and reports cannot enter into material processes. We can say 'he was astounded by the fact that the tide was coming in', but not 'he was stranded by the fact that the tide was coming in'. We saw that this distinction between material and mental processes was a very fundamental one in language. Material processes can have any kind of thing as participant but cannot have a fact or a report; whereas on the other hand mental processes, which must involve an animate, typically human, participant as Senser (or, in metaphorical and other figurative language, an inanimate entity which by virtue of taking on this function becomes thereby 'personified'), in their other key function, that of Phenomenon, accept facts as well as things. And some mental processes (those of cognition, like *think*, *believe*, *knew*) are like verbal processes in that they can 'project': they can bestow on another clause the status of a report.

6.5.2 The nature of facts and reports

We have used the term 'thing' as a generalized label to refer to the phenomena of experience. It contrasts with 'fact' and 'report', which are our 'meta-things': phenomena which have been 'treated' linguistically, in the sense of being encoded in language. Facts and reports are, essentially, linguistic phenomena; they 'exist' at certain levels, or strata, in the linguistic coding system. Hence both are different from things; but they also differ from each other, because a ***fact*** has been encoded only as far as the semantic level – it exists linguistically as a meaning; whereas a ***report*** has been encoded one stage further, at the lexicogrammatical level (the 'syntactic' level, in one sense of the term) – in words and structures, and hence exists linguistically as a wording. A fact is (a phenomenon that has become) a meaning; a report is (a phenomenon that has become (not only a meaning but)) a wording.

There is an important linguistic point to be made here, which is that meaning is already within language. The semantic level (referred to in some earlier writings before about 1960 as the 'contextual level') is within the linguistic system; it is one level, or stratum, within the systematic organization of language, that which serves as the interface between language and the rest of reality. A 'fact' is true (or false) at this level; that is to say, 'truth', in relation to a fact, means being true to the meaning. A 'report', on the other hand, is true (or false) at the lexicogrammatical level; to be 'true', it should be true to the wording. This has consequences for the practical everyday use of language, and especially for language in a court of law. We accept that there are two kinds of truth here, as the following shows:

i. *What did he say? –*

ii. *He said that the tide was coming in. –*

iii. *Where those his very words? –*

iv. *Well, no; what the actually said was that the waves were coming further up the beach.*

As it turns out, (ii) was 'untrue'; it is dressed up as a report, being introduced by the verb 'say', but it is not true to the wording, as (iv) shows. A report has a 'quoted' (direct speech) equivalent – as sometimes built on in English language textbooks in the form of exercises for turning the one into the other, which is a clearly defined grammatical operation.

But projection, as we saw, can be done by thinking as well as by saying; and here it is difficult to make an appeal to the truth value, since we don't know what someone is thinking until they've said it. If I say 'she thought that the tide was coming in', this is a report; and like a verbal report, it can be turned from indirect to direct: 'she thought, "the tide's coming in"'. We often use this kind of 'direct thought' in informal personal narrative, for example '... and the tide's coming in, I thought, so I'd better get moving...'. This gives us four options:

type of projection nature of report	paratactic ('direct')	hypotactic ('indirect')
('speech') locution	She said, 'You're too late.'	She said I was too late.
('thought') idea	'I'm too early,' he thought.	He thought he was too early.

We introduced the new terms 'locution' and 'idea', to make it clear that this is a systemic option within the grammar, and to avoid other issues concerning the relation between speech and thought.

Facts are different from reports. They have no quoted equivalents: we can say 'he was alarmed that the tide was coming in', but not '"the tide's coming in", he was alarmed'. On the other hand, we can say 'that the tide was coming in alarmed him'; and this shows that a fact is actually an element inside the outer clause, not a **projection** beyond it.

Grammatically a fact is **embedded**, and functions as Phenomenon – just like a nominal group as in 'the flow of the tide alarmed him'. The Phenomenon, as we know, may be (in ergative terms) a Range, as in 'he dreaded the oncoming waters', or an Agent, as in 'the oncoming waters alarmed him'; a fact is likely to be an Agent, as we can see if we add the words *the fact* in front of it:

> the fact that the tide was coming in alarmed him
>
> he was alarmed by the fact that the tide was coming in

– where there is the usual mark of an Agent in the passive, the preposition *by*. Of course we can say:

> he dreaded (the fact) that the tide was coming in

where the fact is functioning ergatively as Range. But this is where we find an interesting ambiguity, or perhaps even a blend: if we say 'he feared that the tide was coming in', this might mean that the incoming tide was a fact, and he was alarmed by the fact; but more commonly it would mean he thought that the tide was coming in, and he was alarmed of the possibility. In that case, it could be a report, with *fear* as a process of cognition, rather than a fact, with *fear* as a process of reaction. Some speakers of English see this clearly as an ambiguity, while others see it as a blend between the two. (In other words, it is a typical example of the duplicitous ways in which languages create new meanings!)

6.5.3 Facts, reports and names

We have made a series of distinctions: between things and 'meta-things', within meta-things, between facts and reports; within reports, between ideas and locutions.

Any expression of a process – congruently any clause – may be captured by another clause, to become either a participant in the other process (a fact) or a projection of it (a report); and if it is a report; it may be presented as a meaning (an idea) or as a wording (a locution). The latter distinction corresponds to the stratum at which the report is being projected: either at the semantic stratum (by a cognitive process) or at the lexicogrammatical stratum (by a verbal process).

We often attach a 'key signature' to facts and reports by using a noun of the relevant class to introduce them: the fact that, the idea that, the report that; or else some other term within these last two categories:

(idea) thought, opinion, belief, suggestion, knowledge, suspicion …

(locution) statement, information, news, announcement, story, assertion …

There are many terms that may be used in this way, some with additional features like *insinuation* or *pretence*; and they are often indeterminate as between the cognitive and the verbal, such as *rumour*: *they told me the rumour that …, I didn't believe the rumour that …* The word *report* itself is of this kind. It is difficult on the other hand to find a near-synonym of *fact*, since a 'fact' is being represented not as anyone's thinking or saying but as something that has already hardened into reality. A fact is intermediate between a thing and a report.

These terms occur as Head nouns, with the projection embedded as Qualifier; they also occur by themselves with the same status – namely as Phenomenon in the mental or verbal process clause. This gives a set of three related possible structures:

he was bothered by	(a) *the thought*
	(b) *what might happen*
	(c) *the thought of what might happen*
he didn't believe	(a) *the rumour*
	(b) *that they were bankrupt*
	(c) *the rumour that they were bankrupt*

It is in this special sense, then, that facts and reports are named: that is, there is a name for the general concepts 'a fact' and 'a report', just as there is a name for the general concept 'a thing' (i.e. thing) and for the principal classes of things (*person*, *creature*, etc.). These names for fact and report participate in processes in the same way that facts and reports themselves do. Unlike the latter, however, they can also participate in material processes, at least within certain limits: 'the rumour damaged his reputation', 'the news convulsed her'; these are perhaps to be interpreted as more complex patterns in which 'the rumour' means 'the spreading of the rumour', 'the news' means 'the receipt of the news'.

The other case where facts and reports are named is that where the name is not the general class of 'fact' or 'report' but the nominalization of some specific instance. This is seen in examples such as

his hope encouraged her (ct. his hope came true)

their departure was announced (ct. their departure was delayed)

he admitted her beauty (ct. he admired her beauty)

where those on the left are 'meta-things', meaning 'the report that he had hope encouraged her', 'the fact that they were departing was announced', 'he admitted the fact that she was beautiful' – contrasting with those on the right which are things, meaning 'that (occurrence) which he hoped for came true', 'their (process of) departing was delayed', 'he admired her (quality of) beauty'. These are abstract nouns which are essentially the names of processes or qualifiers, and therefore they resemble nominalizations of the type of '(she was amazed at) their departing so suddenly' which also regularly occur as facts.

In other instances the presence of a fact is obscured by particular locutions which are actually complex, for example 'I believe in God'. Here 'God' is presented as if it was a 'thing', as in 'God will save you'; but actually it means 'in (the fact of) God's existence' and is a representation of a fact. Contrast 'I trust in God' which does not mean 'I trust in the fact of God's existence', and which therefore cannot be expressed as a fact.

6.5.4 A note on nominalization

The typical way of expressing a specific fact or report is, as we should expect, in the form that is usual for the expression of processes, namely as a clause. In the case of facts, this clause is embedded in functions with the same potential as a nominal group. In the case of reports, it is a ranking (non-embedded) clause. Either type, however, may be embedded as Qualifier to a nominal group with fact noun or report noun as Head.

We noted earlier that the mere presence of a nominalized clause is not automatically a sign of a 'meta-thing'; things also can be expressed as nominalizations. This arises initially as a result of the use of 'what' as a portmanteau form of 'that which', as in 'what he was sitting on collapsed' (i.e. 'the thing that he was sitting on'); and hence we get ambiguities such as 'I couldn't see what she was wearing', meaning either 'I couldn't see her dress' (thing), parallel to 'I couldn't see the boy who was climbing the tree', or 'I couldn't see which dress she was wearing' (fact, i.e. find out the answer to the question 'which dress was she wearing?'), parallel to 'I couldn't see who the boy was who was climbing the tree'. But, no doubt by extension from this, the ambiguity is carried over to the analytic forms 'the thing that', 'the one that', which are used, conversely and rather oddly, to mean 'the answer to the question "what?"'. For example, 'I know the thing you want', meaning not 'I am acquainted with the object' but 'I can answer the question'.

Then by a further extension the same thing occurs with persons. The form *who* is not used as a portmanteau for *he who*, so in principle there is a clear distinction between 'I can't see who (it is that)'s batting' (fact) and 'I can't see the man who's batting' (thing). However the latter form is used in the former sense, so that 'I know the man you want' can mean, likewise, either 'I am acquainted with him' or 'I can answer the question "who do you want?"'. Here, what is actually a fact is expressed as if it was a thing, by means of a general noun such as 'one', 'thing', 'man', 'person', etc., plus a qualifying relative clause.

6.5.5 Talking about things

Let us return finally to the general notion of things and 'meta-things', beginning with a reminder that by a 'thing' we understand the semantic representation of a phenomenon of experience. We have been using the term 'thing', as well as the more specific terms 'process', 'person', 'living being', 'object', 'event', etc.; in various expressions like 'talking about things', in ways which might suggest that a 'thing' was equivalent to 'referent'; but this use is an abbreviation – the terms refer to elements of meaning, not to their extra-linguistic counterparts. They refer to the phenomena of experience as these are encoded in the semantic system of a language. This is why we are able to talk of 'things' entering into material and mental processes, where these latter – material and mental processes – are themselves semantic categories; it is obvious that no referent can enter into a linguistic relation, an idea that is made fun of in a famous passage by Swift: in Lagado, on his voyage to Laputa, Gulliver visits the School of Languages, where

> The three Professors sat in Consultation upon improving the Language of their own Country. The first Project was to shorten Discourse by cutting Polysyllables into one, and leaving out Verbs and Participles; because in Reality all things imaginable are but Nouns. The other, was a Scheme for entirely abolishing all Words whatsoever: And this was urged as a great Advantage in Point of Health as well as Brevity. For, it is plain, that every word we speak is in some Degree a Diminution of our Lungs by Corrosion; and consequently contributes to the shortening of our Lives. An Expedient was therefore offered, that since Words are only Names for Things, it would be more convenient for all Men to carry about them, such Things as were necessary to express the particular Business they are to discourse on. And this Invention would certainly have taken Place, to the great Ease as well as Health of the Subject, if the Women in conjunction with the Vulgar and Illiterate had not threatened to raise a Rebellion, unless they might be allowed the Liberty to speak with their Tongues, after the manner of their Forefathers: Such constant irreconcilable Enemies to Science are the common People. (*Gulliver's Travels*, Collins ed. 1953: 203–204)

A 'thing', as we are using the term, is not something that can be carried about; but since it would not be feasible to repeat the formulation 'semantic representation of our experience of ...' each time we mention the term 'thing', or 'process', or 'person, object', etc., these terms are used by themselves to refer to elements in the semantic system of language.

7 Modality in English: 'Modals and pseudo-modals'

7.1 Modality in the grammar

Modality refers to a particular region of the interpersonal component in the semantics and grammar of a language. It is the speaker's (or writer's) angle on what he is saying. More specifically, it is the speaker's assessment either (i) of the probability of the thesis – how likely, or how usual, it is:

she may be busy /	*he can be late /*
perhaps she's busy	*sometimes he's late*

or (ii) of the desirability of the thesis – what degree of obligation, or of inclination, the speaker is attaching to it:

he should know /	*she would tell you /*
he's supposed to know	*she's willing to tell you*

All kinds of nuances can be attached to expressions of modality, especially with the aid of the intonation pattern; for example, *surely you can't still be hungry*

// 5 **surely** you / can't // 4 still be / **hungry** //

Where the modals *surely* and *can't*, with the rise-fall tone followed by the fall-rise, signal the speaker's attitude of 'I refuse to believe it – it's absurd!', all fully integrated into the grammatical structure of the clause.

These two types of modality are known in formal grammars as 'epistemic' and 'deontic'. We shall refer to them, instead, as 'indicative' and 'imperative', using these grammatical terms in their congruent semantic senses: indicative meaning 'this is how things are' and imperative meaning 'this is how things should be' – all from the speaker's point of view, of course. In these terms, type (i) is indicative modality, type (ii) is imperative modality. In their own grammar, of course, they are all indicative, and hence either declarative or interrogative. If declarative, they express the speaker's point of view; if interrogative, they ask for the listener's view. If my wife hears my mobile phone ringing, and I appear to be ignoring it, she will say 'shouldn't you answer that?'; in other words, 'don't you think it's your obligation to answer it?' [Note also the *will* in *she will say*: 'she generally says' something of that sort.]

The grammar of English has a variety of resources for expressing modality; but they boil down to two basic devices. One involves the use of one or other of a fairly large set of lexical items. Those in indicative modality usually take the form of adverbs ('modal Adjuncts', like *probably, always, perhaps*); but they also appear as adjectives, as in *he is certain to be late*; and as adjective or noun forming a separate proposition: *it's possible that she's busy, there's a chance that he's away*. Those in imperative modality are typically adjectives or passive participles, *keen to, able to, supposed to*; again, some occur as separate propositions, like *it is necessary that, there is no need to.*

The other device is to use one of a small class of finite verbs known as 'modal auxiliaries': *can could will would shall should may might must ought to need dare.* Of these, *will would shall should* also function as markers of future tense, as in *I shall be back within the week / I told them I should be back within the week.* Of the others, *need* and *dare* also occur as full verbs in a verbal group complex; we can say either *no-one dare do that* or *no-one dares to do that.* And the two verbal expressions *is to* and *has to* are on the borderline of the 'modal auxiliary' class; of the two, *is to* is more like the others, *has to* is more like a full verb. (But it doesn't really matter – they are both modal expressions anyway.)

These two devices for expressing modality, one lexical the other grammatical, are closely related in meaning, and they very commonly co-occur; for example, *perhaps she may still be busy, you certainly ought to check all the figures.* Here the two are simply reinforcing one another. On occasions they may be pulling in opposite directions; if I say *she certainly might not have known*, I am asserting that there is definitely a possibility that she didn't know. In any such combination, whether reinforcing or supplementing, only one of the expressions of modality can take the form of an auxiliary (this is one of their defining characteristics, as outlined in the next paragraph).

The modal auxiliaries are distinct in a number of ways: (i) they do not add *–s* in third person singular (*s/he can*, not **s/he cans*); (ii) they form negative and interrogative directly (*he cannot/can't, can he?*, not **he doesn't can, does he?*); (iii) they have no non-finite forms (**to can*, **canning*); (iv) they do not occur as imperatives. All of these are related to the fact that they do not form part of the thesis; rather, as we have said, they are the speaker's stake in it, his assessment of its likelihood or concern to bring it about (or prevent it). Hence also they have no tenses. Some occur in two forms, 'direct' and 'oblique': the oblique forms, *would*, *should*, *could* and *might*, were originally past tense forms, and some traces of that can sometimes be seen in their usage; but now they are oblique variants (e.g. *could you do this for me*? as against *can you do this for me*?), and occur as the 'sequent' form in the context of indirect projection (*he said 'I can do it' / he said he could do it*) and hypothesis (*if I knew, I would tell you*). If past tense is required, it is formed lexically (*I used to be able to do it*, rather than *I could do it earlier*).

And (v) the modal auxiliaries do not normally combine; if there are two modalities, at least one of them will be expressed lexically. Informal speech is very creative, so we do hear exchanges such as:

> You ought to have given a hand. – I might ought to have, but I didn't feel like it.

But it is precisely because such combinations break the rules that they are perceived as jokey; if we reword as *maybe I ought to have*, there would be no humorous or any other special effect.

7.2 The meaning of 'modality' in English

Semantically, modal expressions open up the realm of meaning intermediate between positive and negative – between the two poles of 'yes' and 'no'. In the case of indicative modality, this means the space between 'it is' and 'it isn't'; in imperative modality, it means the space between 'do!' and 'don't!'.

In both types, this space is organized into three sectors: a 'median' value, which is roughly half way between the two poles, and two outer values, 'low' and 'high'. We can represent these schematically as:

	[low]	[median]	[high]
[indicative]	(it) may be	(it) will be	(it) must be
[imperative]	(you) may do	(you) will do	(you) must do

These can be seen as describing a trajectory from a negative pole to a positive pole; e.g. (i) *that isn't right – that may be right – that will be right – that must be right – that is right;* (ii) *don't go! – you may go – you will go – you must go – go!*

In principle, *may might can could* are low value, *will would shall should* are median value, and *must ought to need have to* are high value. Once we recognize this we can match them up with the other types of modality:

	may	will	must
[indicative]	possibly sometimes	probably usually	certainly always
[imperative]	allowed to willing to	supposed to anxious to	required to determined to

Here 'willing' stands for 'willing or able', since it includes the familiar sense of *can* as marker of ability.

We need to expand on the meanings of 'indicative modality' and 'imperative modality' a little further. The indicative is the characteristic mood of statements and questions; these have to select between positive and negative polarity. The space between these two poles is the relative **likelihood** of the thesis, defined in terms of its relative probability or frequency. Probability and frequency are fairly clearly distinguished lexically: *possible probable certain* as against *sometimes usually always*; the modal auxiliaries cover both these senses, sometimes clearly one or the other but sometimes in a kind of blend between the two.

The imperative is the characteristic mood of commands and offers. Its typical context is that of a second person: *go* 'you go!', in the sense of conferring **obligation**; with modality this can be predicated of any subject person, the scale of low to high being that of the degree or strength of the obligation. The minor motif is that of **inclination**, again with three degrees but with the 'low' value extended to include the sense of **ability** (hence 'able and willing' above). The modal auxiliaries occur in all these four senses, probability, frequency, obligation and inclination (plus a fifth, ability, in the case of *can, could*): *it can kill you* 'possibly', *it can snow here* 'sometimes'; *you can sit down* 'are allowed to'; *we can help* 'are willing to'; *I can understand* 'am able to'. In principle this means that there is a great deal of indeterminacy; this is usually unnoticed, because it is resolved one way or another by the context: *she must be happy* is likely to be high probability, while *she must apologize* is likely to be high obligation; *she must be thoughtful* could be either, but there is almost certain to be a wider context of discourse in which this too would be resolved. Misunderstandings do happen, of course; but they are often noticed and put right: 'no I meant ...'.

We have introduced the categories of modality, and illustrated them, as attached to a thesis that is itself positive. But a negative thesis may also be modalized: we can have *probably not, not supposed to* and so on. Here a further complication ensues, because the negative may be attached either to the modality as in *not required to* or to the thesis as in *required not to.* Clearly the two are complementary, at least at the outer values: *not required to* means the same as *allowed not to*, while *not allowed to* means the same as *required not to*. With the median value, on the other hand, the meaning remains the same: *not supposed to* is the same as *supposed not to* (compare *you're not supposed to look at that, you're supposed not to look at that*). We can also set these out in tabular form.

Negative modality				
		low value	median value	high value
indica- tive	thesis negative	that may not be right possibly isn't sometimes isn't	that will not be right probably isn't usually isn't (I think that's not right)	that must not be right certainly isn't always isn't [never is]
	modality negative	that needn't/ mightn't be right isn't certain to be isn't always	that won't be right isn't likely to be isn't usually (I don't think that's right)	that can't be right isn't possibly isn't ever
impera- tive	thesis negative	you can not go you're allowed not to I'd rather not/prefer not to	you will not go you're supposed not to I'm anxious not to	you must not go you're required not to I'm determined not to
	modality negative	you needn't go you're not required to I'm not determined to	you won't go you're not supposed to I'm not anxious to	you can't go you're not allowed to I'm not able/willing to

We have set these out as paradigms to show how the modality system works, with the wordings given in a prototypical form. As will be obvious, some of the wordings are not the most frequent or most likely in actual speech. For example, in the 'modality negative' corner, rather than the forms with *required* and *determined* we are more likely to come across expressions such as *you're not forced to go, I'm not set on going*. We have chosen forms which could be retained consistently throughout, and which are as semantically neutral as possible – that is, not encumbered with special prosodies such as marks of authority or impatience. There is a broad range of expressions, especially in informal spoken language, which function in the construal of modality, both the indicative and the imperative type.

7.3 Defining the domain of modality

In section 7.2, we set out the semantic framework underlying the various systems of modality. Now, interpersonal systems tend to be fuzzy, and modality more so than most, because it involves the complex and shifting relationship of the speaker to what he is saying and to the listener(s) he is addressing. The grammatical patterns – both the options available and their realizations – vary considerably across space and across time (dialectally and diachronically). They also get mixed up with a number of other variables, such as degrees of familiarity and distance, and of politeness, prosodies of sarcasm and irony – all the features of smaller speech fellowships like families, workplaces, congregations or social clubs.

So how far do we extend the systemic domain of modality? Essentially it is the domain that is defined by the modal auxiliaries. (Remember: these are descriptive categories, not 'universals'; we are talking about the grammar of contemporary English.) The modal auxiliaries (or 'finite operators' as they are sometimes called) mark out certain dimensions of meaning as systems of the verbal group and specifically as 'deictic' systems, those which anchor the process in a particular moment of space and time – realized grammatically as a finite clause. This 'moment' is defined by the here-&-now of the speech event; but it is distinguished from the purely temporal (past / present / future) by being grounded in the speaker's assessment of likelihood or desirability. This then becomes the issue at stake, as shown by the associated question tag: if I say *they could be wrong, couldn't they*?, I am asking 'do you agree that that is a possibility?.

But the boundaries of modality are fuzzy, because of the bundles of semantic features that are typically implicated in the speaker's judgement and attitude. For example: it is clear that *I think* usually functions as modality, in an instance such as *I think that's all*; partly because it combines with other modalities, like *I think that'll probably be all*, but more because of the choice of question tag: *I think that's all, isn't it?* (not *I think that's all, don't I?* as it would be if *I think* was a part of the thesis of the clause). Similarly with expressions such as *I'm sure, I believe*. But with others such as *I'm afraid, I fear, I would imagine, I dare say*, the speaker is moving slightly towards projection (reported speech and thought), as in *I said I'd be back today*, with question tag *didn't I?* (not *wouldn't I?*).

Note that it is only in first person present tense (or second person if interrogative) that expressions of this kind function as modality. As soon as we move to past tense, as in *I thought ...*, or another person, as in *she thinks ...*, the thinking becomes part of the thesis; and again this can be shown by the tag. For example, *she thinks it's finished, does she?*; here the tag shows that the thesis is 'she thinks' – otherwise the tag would be *has it?* Since the modality is the speaker's angle, then if it is expressed as a mental process it can only be what the speaker is thinking at the present moment. Notice that here too the negative may be attached to the modality, as in *I don't think it's finished yet, is it?*, on the model of *she doesn't think it's finished yet, does she?* where there is no modality and the negative is on the thesis, where it belongs.

We have illustrated these variant forms from the indicative modals because there the match between the modal auxiliaries and other forms stands out more clearly than with the imperatives. Also it is only in the indicative sense that the auxiliaries combine with all the tenses of the non-finite verb:

to take, taking	can take (may take, might take, etc.)
to have taken, having taken	can have taken
to be taking, (being taking)	can be taking
to be / being about to take	can be about to take
to be / being about to have taken	can be about to have taken
to have / having been taking	can have been taking
to be / being about to be taking	can be about to be taking
to have / having been about to take	can have been about to take

Set out like this in a paradigm, these might seem artificial; but in fact they figure quite naturally in informal spontaneous speech, though *going to* is more likely than *about to* in a modalized future tense. With imperative modality, only the oblique ones occur (*could, would, should, ought to* and *might*).

The oblique modals combine with non-finite past to confer past unfulfilled obligation, as in *they ought to have known, you might have told me!* As soon as we use a 'direct' modal, as in *you may have told me*, the meaning shifts to the indicative, as in *you may have told me* 'it is possible that you did tell me'. But here there has been a recent change in the language: people, or at least young people, use *may have* in the sense of earlier *might have*: where older folk would say *if I had known I might have told him*, younger folk will say *if I knew I may have told him*. Thus *may have*, which used to mean 'it is possible that I did', now means (also) 'I might have done (but didn't)'.

There are a few modal expressions analogous to *I think* in the imperative sense, like *I wish*, as in *I wish you'd keep quiet*, with tag *won't you?*, or *will you?*; also *I hope*, as in *I hope it's not too late*, tag *is it?* There is also an adverb analogous to *possibly*, namely *hopefully* in the sense of 'I hope', as in *hopefully they're still open*. But the most common of the expanded forms are passive verbs in the sense of obligation, and adjectives (some passive in form) in the sense of inclination or ability: *they're supposed to ask permission, she's happy to help*. These give the impression of being more ideational in meaning, as if *she's expected to win* or *we are resolved to track them down* are closer to being direct representations of the situation rather than the speaker's comment on it (this is what led Halliday to use the term 'pseudo-modals' in an earlier study (1970)). But these are also construed by the grammar as modal auxiliaries: *she must win* 'she is determined to win', *others may leave* 'others are allowed to leave'; they are common both in interrogative mood (*why must they make all that noise?*) and in negative polarity (*nobody is to know about this, beggars can't be choosers*). If we judge by the scope of the modal auxiliaries, then on that criterion imperative modality is closely parallel to the indicative type.

There is a difference, however, in the way the two combine with the system of voice. If I say *he may be frightened by the dogs*, or *by the noise*, this can only be indicative; I am not suggesting that the dogs are allowed to frighten him. But if I use the passive, in the imperative type, the obligation is shifted on to the Agent, as in *these drugs may be sold by any registered pharmacist, can't this be handled by the committee?*; and this holds good even where the Agent is not made explicit, as in *dogs must be kept on a leash, Smith ought to be persuaded to resign*, where it is left to the listener to infer where the obligation falls.

7.4 Variant realizations of modality

We have been treating the various realizations of the modality system as semantically equivalent; and in terms of the general range of meanings that they cover, they are. But within that range of meanings there are more delicate distinctions, which appear when we examine the way these variants are used in discourse. Again we will illustrate from the indicative modals, where the differences are perhaps more easily perceived.

If my doorbell sounds, I could say, to whoever is with me:

> that'll be Fred
>
> I think that's Fred
>
> that's probably Fred
>
> it's likely that that's Fred

Let me consider each of these in turn.

The version *that'll be Fred* is the simplest way of expressing my opinion, as an assessment of the probabilities in the situation. Since for much of the time in our daily lives we are facing that kind of situation, which calls for some assessment of the chances however trivial, this is the default choice, selected unless there is 'good reason' for selecting something else.

But this formulation doesn't proclaim explicitly that it's my opinion. Alternatively, I may make that clear by formulating the modality as a mental process with myself as Subject: *I think that's Fred*. Similarly, if I am asking your opinion, I can say just *will that be Fred?*, or I can make the request explicit by saying *d'you think that's Fred?* In other words, the fact that it is a subjective judgement can be left unsaid, by the use of a modal auxiliary, or it can be built in to the expression of the modality.

Suppose however that I am presenting my assessment as an objective feature of the situation. In that case I will say *that's probably Fred* – or, with the assessment as Theme in the clause, *probably that's Fred.* This is less likely to occur in the interrogative, except in the form of a tag: *that's probably Fred, isn't it?* 'do you agree?'.

Hence again however the source of judgement has been left implicit. I could say, on the other hand, *it's likely that that's Fred,* where the formulation as an impersonal proposition makes the objectivity claim explicit. The listener can of course question it, or counter it, with *do you think so?* or *I don't think so,* making it clear that he has a different view by switching over to the explicit subjective mode.

These examples were all of the median degree of probability, where the location of the negative can be switched without change of meaning (*that's not likely to be Fred* or *that's probably not Fred*); they can be matched in the other variants, e.g. ('high' degree) *that must be Fred, I'm sure that's Fred, that's bound to be Fred, it's certain that that's Fred,* though there are several gaps and inconsistencies. We find a comparable range of options in the imperative modals: for example, in the 'median' degree of obligation:

[subjective implicit]	they should go now
[subjective explicit]	I want them to go now
[objective implicit]	they'd better go now
[objective explicit]	it's better for them to go now

Again, these can be matched in the 'high' and the 'low' degrees of obligation; but with some lexical variation, e.g. (high) *they must go now, I order them to go now, they're required to go now, it's essential for them to go now.* In the sense of inclination and ability, the options are fewer, since here there is no opposition of implicit / explicit; the 'low' degree forms are (subjective) *she can read, he'll help you,* (objective) *she's able to read, he's willing to help.* The sense of 'ability' comes in as a special case of the 'low' degree; at the other values, we find both 'median' and 'high' degrees of inclination, but these are often coloured by particular prosodies of disapproval (e.g. *he must interfere, she insists on taking charge*), and the modal *will* may mean either 'is willing to' or 'insists on' according to the pattern of intonation.

The imperative modals in particular display a great deal of variation and indeterminacy, and instances will always be interpreted with reference to their relevant context. But while instances may be indeterminate – there are ambiguities and borderlines and blends – and there is a great deal of variation in the lexicogrammatical expression, the underlying systemic pattern is clear. Modality is a powerful meaning-making resource; the distinctions that can be made are subtle, as are many of the shades of meaning that colour our everyday conversations. They are exploited by poets, dramatists and novelists; and also by public speakers – everywhere in the spoken language, with all its additional resources of intonation and rhythm. Some of the effects will be apparent in the texts analysed in Part III of the present book.

Part Two

Text and texture

8 Textual meaning

8.1 Grammatical texture

One of the requirements every language has to meet is that of ***texture***. The internal organization of a language, its grammar, vocabulary and sound system provides, among other things, the means whereby the speaker or writer can create ***texts*** – coherent and interconnected pieces of language, as distinct from unorganized strings of sentences.

There are two aspects to texture. One is what we have called ***cohesion***: this refers to the way in which successive sentences are integrated to form a whole. Cohesion is, as it were, 'inter-sentence texture'. The second is related to organization within the sentence, the 'intra-sentence texture'.

Intra-sentence texture is the structuring of the sentence itself as an act of communication. The speaker has a message to convey, and (s)he selects the patterns which will convey this message in a form that is appropriate, to the particular linguistic and situational context. The 'message' has no meaning or existence except as part of a text, and the specific form of 'fit' to the context is an integral part of the message itself.

This fit to the context comprises two aspects: the organizing of the message so that it correctly represents what the speaker wants to say, and the organizing of it so that it ties up with the preceding text. There is thus, as it were, a 'speaker angle' and a 'hearer angle', and both are reflected in the construction of any sentence.

The terms ***thematic structure*** and ***information structure***, more briefly ***Theme*** and ***Information***, refer respectively to these two aspects. The thematic structure of a sentence is, basically, its organization as a move, within the speaker's perspective something as a point of departure (the ***Theme***) and an observation relating to it. A model for this might be a definition: in a sentence such as 'A dado is a skirting of wood along the lower part of the walls of a room', the Theme is *a dado*. The remainder of the message is called the ***Rheme***. The thematic structure also includes various special treatments of the Theme, by which the speaker may express more specific meanings such as 'this **and this alone** is what my message is about'.

Information structure is, basically, the organization of discourse into **message blocks**, each of which adds something new: that is to say, each of which expresses some content that the speaker decides to treat as not being recoverable from elsewhere. It also specifies the **domain** of a large number of items in the language whose range of relevance is potentially very variable:

an example of such an item is *too*, as in 'Mary shops in London too', the domain of which may be *Mary* (i.e. 'as well as Jane'), *shops* ('as well as working there') or *in London* ('as well as in Hong Kong').

Information structure comprises both an optional element functioning as ***Given*** accompanied by an element functioning as ***New***. This distinction between Given and New has to do with whether the information presented by the speaker is recoverable (i.e. Given), or not recoverable (i.e. New). Given refers to something locatable, or already present in the verbal or non-verbal context.

In speech, new information typically receives topic prominence or focus. In writing, information units usually correspond to the clause, unless otherwise indicated by punctuation. There is then usually overlap between Theme-Rheme and information structures, such that the Theme is typically given information, while the Rheme offers new information.

8.2 Thematic structure

8.2.1 Meaning and choice of Theme

In English the general principle of thematic structure is very simple indeed: the Theme is put first. Thus in 'My love is like a red, red rose', the Theme is *my love*. The Theme, in other words, is normally the first grammatical element in the structure of the clause. The Theme is underlined in each of the following examples: '*John's* already left', '*I* don't know', '*yesterday* we discussed the financial arrangements', '*his spirit* they could not kill', '*with trembling hands* he unties the ropes that bound her' and '*people who live in glasshouses* shouldn't throw stones'.

Which element in the clause is selected as Theme, and thus put in first position, is meaningful for the very reason that it is a matter of choice. Of the three major lexical classes of English, both nominals and adverbials are regularly thematic; verbs as themes are more restricted, and rather rare. Note that the Theme is the whole of the first element in the structure of the clause (with exceptions explained below), whatever its internal make-up: it may be a simple nominal or adverbial consisting of one noun, pronoun or adverb only (*John, I, yesterday*), or a longer nominal or adverbial group (*his spirit, with trembling hands*; including any clauses embedded in the group, as in *people who live in glasshouses*).

As far as function in the clause is concerned, the Theme may have any of the transitivity functions, participants or circumstances, taken on by nominals and adverbials. It may be Actor, Goal, Beneficiary, etc.; or any of the 'circumstantial' functions of time, place, manner, etc. Not all of these are equally likely; there is a tendency for the Theme to be a nominal and to be associated with the Actor rather than with other participant functions. This association, however, is actually an indirect one; the direct association is that of Theme with Subject – there is an unmarked relation between Theme and Subject such that the Theme of a clause will also be the Subject of that clause unless there is 'good reason' for it not to be.

In older English, the Subject of the clause was more closely tied to the (ideational) function of 'Actor' than to the (textual) function of 'Theme', and thematic structure was differently expressed. In the modern language, however, while there is still some degree of association between Subject and Actor, that between Subject and Theme is stronger; hence, although active clauses are still much more frequent than passive ones, passive clauses (whose Subject is not Actor) are much more frequent than they used to be. The passive is used in Modern English precisely in order to maintain the identity of Subject and Theme, at the cost of that of Subject and Actor: in 'this gazebo was built by Sir Christopher Wren', where *Sir Christopher* is Actor and *the gazebo* is Theme, it is the Theme that is expressed as the Subject. In the majority of passive clauses in English, in fact, there is no Actor: the most frequent use is that illustrated by 'this practice has now been discontinued'.

The unmarked association of Theme with Subject is a feature of declarative clauses. In interrogatives, the pattern is different. In yes/no questions, the unmarked Theme is the finite element of the verb: e.g. '*Did* John come?' '*Has* John come?' '*Can* John come?' '*Is* John coming?' The reason for this is that the Theme of a yes/no question is simply the request for an answer 'yes' or 'no': automatically therefore the normal Theme is that element in the verb that carries the polarity (*did/didn't*, etc.). Likewise, in a *wh*-question, the unmarked Theme is the interrogative word (the '*wh*- element': *what, who, how, why*, etc.): the Theme of such a question is the request for information on just this point. Languages, which, like English, favour the inverted order for yes/no questions, and the initial position for interrogative words, are those with a strong feeling for initial position as thematic.

The Theme is the starting point for saying anything at all; it provides the foundation for the message – hence in many languages the use of initial position in the clause to express this function. What the theme does is to locate the message in its place within the discourse. It must therefore be interpretable by the hearer; and this accounts for the very frequent occurrence of reference items as Themes: they are interpretable by reference to what has gone before.

The choice of a Theme is thus the basic decision about the structure of the message, as the speaker conceives it. And it is a choice that is an inherent part of the message itself. If we want to model the speaker's planning procedures, he does not, as it were, first decide to state a thesis 'Wren built this gazebo' and then decide whether this is to be a message about Wren or about the gazebo. Communication involves a thesis which is also and simultaneously a message, and it is more helpful to think of the decisions as simultaneous and interdependent; neither can be carried out (expressed in speech or writing) independently of the other.

8.2.2 Possible Themes

The Theme, however, may include elements which lie outside the thesis proper: that is, elements from the textual and interpersonal components. Consider an example such as *'in that case perhaps **I**'d better depart'*. Here there are no less than three elements with thematic function: a conjunctive *in that case*, a modal *perhaps*, and a Theme of the kind we have been talking about so far, namely *I*, which belongs to the thesis and has a notional function. Complex themes of this kind, with a discourse (cohesive) or a modal element, or both, being selected as point of departure, as well as the Theme drawn from the ideational material, are extremely common, especially in spoken English.

Elements which are obligatorily in first position in the clause might not be considered thematic because there is no choice involved: this applies to subordinating conjunctions like *if, because, when*. Actually, however, there is a gradation here, in the tendency of different elements to occur as theme: we could express this as follows, showing, at one end, the 'marked themes' – the elements less likely to be thematic, such as verbs, and then nominals other than the Subject – and at the other, the elements which have to come first:

Elements Obligatorily first		Subordinating conjunctions (hypotactic clauses)	e.g. *if*
	more likely ('unmarked themes')	Conjunctives; modal adjuncts	e.g. *however; perhaps*
		Interrogative words (in *wh*-interrogative clauses)	e.g. *what ...?*
		Finite verbal element (in *wh*-interrogative clauses)	e.g. *did ...?*
Elements Optionally first		Subject (in declarative clauses)	e.g. *he, John*
		Adverbials of time, place, manner, etc.	e.g. *yesterday*
		Nominals other than subject	e.g. *him, John (... I like)*
	('marked themes') less likely	Verbs (in declarative clauses)	e.g. *resign (... he did)*

While Subject as Theme of a declarative clause is typical and unmarked, a circumstantial adjunct as Theme is marked. But a complement as Theme, e.g. '*Me*, they blame for it' is even more marked because a complement is least likely to be made thematic.

Just as, in interrogatives, the fact that the finite element of the verb, or the *wh*-element, usually comes first in the clause is attributable to their being the normal themes of such clauses, so the obligatory first position of *if, when,* etc. can be explained by the fact that if they are present at all they must be thematic – since if one clause is related to another as a condition, cause, etc., then that relationship is, automatically, its theme. So *if, when,* etc. could be regarded as being thematic: but if so, they are always thematic wherever they occur, which means that there is no need to show this as a property of the particular sentence.

The co-ordinating conjunctions are, however, a different matter. The 'pure' co-ordinators *and* and *or* are structure markers; they do not enter into the structure of the clause and thus lie outside consideration of theme. The 'mixed' co-ordinators *but, yet, so* and *then* contain a conjunctive element and thus, when occurring initially, come under the heading of 'discourse' (cohesive) themes.

Two types of clause need to be specially mentioned: imperatives, and clauses beginning with 'dummy' Subject *it* and *there*. Imperatives have as their normal Theme the person or persons enjoined: either addressee(s) only, as in '(you) go away!', or addressee(s) and speaker, as in 'let's go away!'; note that this is true even if the 'you' is not expressed. In *it*[1] and *there* clauses, like 'it's raining', 'there's a cat on the lawn', the words *it* and *there* are introduced simply to fulfil the requirement that indicative clauses must have a Subject; these clauses have no theme – the message is not something 'about' something. For the related forms 'it's John I want', 'there's John (who) might know', see below.

8.2.3 Extensions of thematic structure

There are three special structures in English which have the function of organizing the clause as a message in ways that are related to, and in fact extensions of, the Theme-Rheme structure. We deal briefly with each in turn.

1 Not the personal pronoun *it*. There are two words *it*, one belonging to the set of personal forms *I you he she it we they one*, the other belonging to the small set of 'dummy' forms *it* and *there*. In the latter pair, *it* corresponds to the (definite) and *there* corresponds to *a, an* (indefinite).

IDENTIFICATION. Here the clause is structured into two parts, joined by the verb *to be*, as in 'what I need is a new car' (related to 'I need a new car'). This is, in fact, an 'equative' clause (e.g. 'the winner was John') with a ***nominalization*** in it; the nominalization, in almost all instances, takes in every element in the clause except one. The message thus takes the form of a two-part relational structure, one part being the 'thing to be identified', the other the 'identifier'. The nominalization always represents the 'thing to be identified'. Either part may come first, however, and whichever comes first is the Theme. If the 'thing to be identified' is in initial position the whole if it, however long, is thematic. Halliday calls this a ***thematic equative***, i.e. an identifying clause with a thematic nominalization in it. Thematic equatives have two distinct semantic features: (i) a thematic equative identifies what the Theme is and then equates it with the Rheme; and (ii) a thematic equative adds a notion of exclusiveness, i.e. this and this alone.

For example, in 'the one who could really tell you everything you need to know with absolute assurance is John', the theme is *the one who could really tell you everything you need to know with absolute assurance*. This, in fact, is one of the reasons for selecting this structure: it is the only means whereby the speaker can organize the message so as to have more than one of the clause elements as his theme: the meaning is 'as far as there being someone able to tell you everything you need to know with complete assurance is concerned…'. The effectiveness of this form of communication is due to the fact that **the relation between Identified and Identifier is an exclusive one**. Whereas 'I need a new car' is expressed in such a way as to leave open the possibility that I may also need other things, 'what I need is a new car' is expressed in such a way as to imply that is all I need.

In the example, 'The duke gave my aunt that teapot', we can create a nominalization, 'what the duke gave my aunt', which contains several elements from the clause, such as the Subject (*the duke*), Finite + Predicator (*gave*), Indirect Object (*my aunt*). By putting this nominalization in thematic position before the verb 'to be', as in '*What the duke gave my aunt* was that teapot', we equate the thematic nominalization with what follows, *that teapot*. This will be interepreted to mean that 'it was the teapot, and nothing else, that the duke gave to my aunt'.

PREDICATION. This structure is also built around the verb to be; but here the Theme itself (only) occurs as Complement, the Subject being the dummy *it* (occasionally also *there*), with the rest of the message expressed as a discontinuous qualifier to it. For example, 'it's John I want', 'there's John (who) might know' (related to 'I want John', 'John might know'). The question which arises here is whether as a result of appearing in a predication of this type the 'Theme' is in fact no longer thematic: in other words, in 'it's John I want' is *John* the Theme, or is the Theme now *it* ... *I want* (i.e. 'the one I want') as in the 'identification' form 'the one I want is John'? A full discussion of this would involve also a consideration of information structure, because the two are in association here: in the unmarked case, the 'predicated Theme' is also 'new information'.[2] But this is, as it happens, the reason why it **seems** not to be a Theme; in fact *John* still is the Theme here, and this structure is used as a means of expressing this rather unexpected combination of the Thematic with the new. The meaning is 'I'm talking about John; but at the same time you (the hearer) cannot be expected to know that'. A predicated Theme signals that the normal expectations for overlap between Theme-Rheme and Given-New do not apply. As in the identification type, the use of the equative structure implies exclusiveness: 'John and no-one else', although here there is a less common alternative with *there* which is not exclusive. In *there's John (who) might know*, the meaning is 'John, possibly among others'.

The sentence 'The queen sent my uncle that hatstand' might be re-stated several different ways, each with a different predicated Theme, as in the following: (bold type indicating tonic prominence)

- It was the **queen** who sent my uncle that hatstand.
- It was my **uncle** the queen sent that hatstand to.
- It was that **hatstand** the queen sent my uncle.

Each re-statement carries the meaning that there was something about this event which was other than the listener expected, either that it was someone other than *the queen* who did the sending, or someone other than *my uncle* who was the recipient, or something other than *the hatstand* which the queen sent. Thanks to predication (*It is/was* ...), this new and unexpected information suitably occurs in the unmarked position of Rheme of the predicated clause.

SUBSTITUTION. Here the Theme is displaced to end of the clause, being introduced first by a personal pronoun in initial position, as in 'he's very friendly, that dog'. The Theme is *that dog*, but the speaker wishes to encode the message into a particular information structure in which, while the Rheme *is very friendly* is the major point of new information, *that dog* is to be presented as a minor, or subsidiary, piece of new information in its

2 i.e. // it's **John** I want //. Note however that this is not obligatory; a context such as: the only one who's here is John. - // it's John I **want** // shows that the two selections are partially independent of one another. A predicated theme, in other words, is also 'new information' unless there is good reason for it to be otherwise.

own right – e.g. because, although the dog is clearly visible, the message does not obviously apply to it. This always requires the order: major followed by minor. The minor element forming the minor information point, however, in order to function also as Theme is anticipated by the appropriate personal pronoun at the beginning of the clause (note that when *it* occurs in this structure, it is the personal pronoun *it*, not the dummy *it* as in the previous type). This is sometimes regarded as a casual and rather lazy type of locution, but it is a highly structured form of message, without any hesitation pauses or other marks of incomplete planning. It has a regular intonation pattern and a stable construction (found not infrequently in Shakespeare). Moreover, in one type of clause it is the unmarked form: this is the 'mental process' clause with a fact or a report as the Subject, as in 'it worried me that you look so tired'. Here the Theme is *that you look so tired*; and the substitution structure is the normal form for this type of message, selected unless there is good reason to do otherwise, because the idea of a fact or a report being actor or 'causer' in the clause is a slightly complex and unexpected one, more easily encoded in this displaced form.[3]

All the variations in thematic structure discussed here are significant and meaningful variations. They are not introduced into speech or writing simply for the sake of variety, nor are they used any less consistently by speakers and writers than are other kinds of grammatical resources. It is easy to show the meaning of a choice of Theme by changing it around; the result will be to turn a coherent text into a strangely scrambled piece of communication. This is not to say that the speaker has no freedom of choice; he is selecting the thematic structure he wants to express but, like all linguistic options, thematic options are exercised within contexts and in conjunction with other options. The surrounding context imposes special interpretations and, in some cases, limitations on what is appropriate.

8.2.4 Thematic progression

Thematic progression, i.e. the successive choices of what to make thematic, relates both to the flow of information, and the rhetorical development of the text. Three typical patterns of thematic progression identified by Daneš (1974) include: linear, continuous, and derived.

3. This point is worth stressing. It is the **function** of the thematic element, its status as fact or report, not its superficial structural complexity or its length, that determines its tendency to substitution. With any element that is not fact or report, even a long nominalization, the non-substitute form is the normal one, e.g. *what he doesn't know about teams and players and who beat who in the championship every year since the year dot could go on the back of a postage-stamp.*

Linear thematic progression occurs when the new information found in the Rheme of one clause next occurs as Theme in the subsequent clause. The flow of information is New→Given. In the following example, describing the birth of City Polytechnic of Hong Kong, notice how the Themes of the second and third clauses refer back to what was just mentioned in the Rheme of the immediately preceding clause:

> [1] ***The genesis of the City Polytechnic of Hong Kong*** *lay in the report of a committee appointed by the Governor in November 1980 to review the scope of post-secondary and technical education in Hong Kong.* [2a] ***In its report of June 1981*** *it recommended that there should be a general and substantial increase in the provision of places for tertiary education;* [2b] ***one of the measures recommended for achieving this*** *was the establishment of a second polytechnic.*

The Theme of [2a] refers back to the report just mentioned in the Rheme of the preceding clause [1], while the *this* in the Theme of [2b] refers back to the Rheme of [2a], i.e. 'a general and substantial increase in the provision of places for tertiary education'.

In continuous thematic progression, the same Theme is repeated over subsequent clauses. This is illustrated in the follow paragraph from a magazine article in which the author compares two English language dictionaries ('Look it up' by James Nation in *Asia Magazine*):

> *The two* are the Collins Cobuild English Dictionary and the Longman Dictionary of Contemporary English. *Both* are third editions. *Both* have been published in 1995, so they are uptodate. *Both* are designed for people learning the language and, *although neither* include the etymology of words listed, *both* offer other information not usually contained in such works, such as word frequency. *Both dictionaries* also give examples or sentence parts using the words in question.

Derived Themes are Themes of successive clauses which may be regarded as related to some superordinate topic or ***Hypertheme***. In the case of the piece about the birth of City Polytechnic of Hong Kong, one notices repeated thematic references to the main players and points in time when they were involved in the establishment of the institution.

8.2.5 What a difference the choice of theme makes!

To demonstrate the significance of thematic structure in the development of a text, we present below two versions of the same passage, the first with its original Theme-Rheme structure, the second with a 'scrambled' thematic structure.

The sun's shining; it's a perfect day. Here come the astronauts. They're just passing the great hall; perhaps the president will come out to greet them. No, it's the admiral who's taking the ceremony. He has great dignity, the admiral. He's shaking hands with them now. What puzzles me is why there are only two of them. The ones that are in view are the two navy men; the space doctor I can't see anywhere. It was the space doctor who aroused most of the excitement. It must be him the crowds are welcoming now with all those cheers.

Cl #	Theme				Clause
	Text-ual	Inter-personal	Ideational	Displaced	
1a			The sun		The sun's shining;
1b			It		it's a perfect day.
2			Here		Here come the astronauts.
3a			They		They're just passing the great hall;
3b		perhaps	the president		perhaps the president will come out to greet them.
4		No	it's the admiral (predicated)		No, it's the admiral who's taking the ceremony.
5			He	the admiral.	He has great dignity, the admiral.
6			He		He's shaking hands with them now.
7			What puzzles me		What puzzles me is why there are only two of them.
8a			The ones that are in view		The ones that are in view are the two navy men;
8b			the space doctor		the space doctor I can't see anywhere.
9			It was the space doctor (predicated)		It was the space doctor who aroused most of the excitement.
10			It must be him (predicated)		It must be him the crowds are welcoming now with all those cheers.

It's the sun that's shining; the day is perfect. The astronauts come here. The great hall they're just passing; he'll perhaps come out to great them, the president. No, it's the ceremony that the admiral's taking. The admiral has great dignity. What he's shaking with them now is hands. Why there are only two of them puzzles me. The two navy men are in view; anywhere I can't see the space doctor. What the space doctor aroused was most of the excitement. With all those cheers the crowd must be welcoming him now.

Cl #	Theme				Clause
	Text-ual	Inter-personal	Ideational	Displaced	
1a			It's the sun (predicated)		It's the sun that's shining;
1b			the day		the day is perfect.
2			The astronauts		The astronauts come here.
3a			The great hall	they	The great hall they're just passing;
3b			he	the president	he'll perhaps come out to great them, the president.
4		No	it's the ceremony (predicated)		No, it's the ceremony that the admiral's taking.
5			The admiral		The admiral has great dignity.
6			What he's shaking with them now (thematic equative)		What he's shaking with them now is hands.
7			Why there are only two of them		Why there are only two of them puzzles me.
8a			The two navy men		The two navy men are in view;
8b			anywhere	I	anywhere I can't see the space doctor.
9			What the space doctor aroused (thematic equative)		What the space doctor aroused was most of the excitement.
10			With all those cheers	the crowd	With all those cheers the crowd must be welcoming him now.

There are several noticeable variations on thematic structure between these two versions.

Whereas the first version of this passage starts off with a definite ***given***, namely, *The sun,* the second version employs a predicated theme at the outset, presenting *the sun* in the Rheme as ***new*** information, suggesting the unlikely possibility that the reader may have been thinking it was something other than the sun which was shining.

Continuing on in version 1, immediately at the outset of <2>, the fronted *Here come ...* announces the introduction of the ***New-as-Rheme***, i.e. *the astronauts.* Illustrating linear thematic progression, the New-as-Rheme in <2> then becomes the ***Given-as-Theme*** in <3a>. In the second version, not only is the sense of introducing the arrival of *the astronauts* lost by putting *here* in the Rheme of <2>, but also its placement at the end of clause <2> just preceding the marked fronting of the complement in <3a>, *The great hall,* risks misleading the listener/reader into thinking that the adverbial *here* in the Rheme of <2> is a reference to *The great hall* mentioned in the Theme of <3a>. In fact, what at first appears to be a case of linear thematic progression, i.e. the Rheme of the preceding clause becomes the Theme of the next, is not. In other words, the New-as-Rheme of <2>, i.e. *here*, is not a reference to the Given-as-Theme of <3a>, i.e. *The great hall.* Rather, *The great hall* is just what they are passing at that moment on their way to *here.*

Both <3b> and <4> of version 1 begin with an interpersonal element as Theme, followed by a topical Theme. *Perhaps* as interpersonal Theme in <3b> indicates that what follows is the speaker's supposition about who will come out to greet the astronauts. The speaker supposes it will be *the president*, who is thematically mentioned just after the disjunct at the beginning of <3b>. That the speaker's supposition turns out to be incorrect, and it was *the admiral* instead of *the president* who came out to greet *the astronauts* is highlighted by not only the thematic positioning of the negative reply, *No,* but also by putting *the admiral* in a predicated theme. It is as though the speaker were saying, 'It isn't who I expected to come out and greet the astronauts, instead it is the admiral who is doing so'.

In the second version of this passage, there is an apparently unmotivated displacement of *the president* as Theme, which is relegated to a minor position at the end of the clause. Though, as in the first version, the negative reply, *No,* is in thematic position at the beginning of <4>, and there is still a predicated Theme, nevertheless, what is predicated is not *the admiral,* but *the ceremony.* This makes no sense at all, however, as there was never any other expectation for what the admiral would be taking.

Continuous thematic progression is maintained across clauses <5> and <6> in the first version, by repeating the pronoun *He* as the grammatical Subject in clause initial position. In <5> the pronoun substitutes for the displaced Theme, *the admiral.* This smooth thematic progression in the first version contrasts with the awkward wording of the second version, which verges on the laughable. The thematic equative in <6>, *What he's shaking with them now is hands,* begs the question, 'What else could he be possibly shaking?' Moreover, since the New-as-Rheme in <6> is *hands,* what is the reader/listener to suppose is being referred to by the pronoun in the next clause: *Why there are only two of them puzzles me* <7>. Given the reader's/listener's expectations for linear thematic progression, might this be misunderstood to mean, 'Why there are only two **hands** puzzles me'.

Beginning with <8b> through to the end of the first version, whether as marked topical Theme or predicated Theme, *the space doctor* continues to be selected as Theme. Like the crowd attending the ceremony, our attention is focused on *the space doctor*. In contrast to this consistency in Theme choice, the corresponding clauses in the second version appear haphazard and unmotivated. Whereas in version one, *the space doctor* as predicated Theme <9> communicates the idea of it being exclusively *the space doctor who aroused most of the excitement,* the thematic equative <9> in version two suggests it was exclusively *most of the excitement* which *the space doctor aroused.* In version two attention is focused on **what** *the space doctor aroused* rather than on **who** *aroused the most excitement.*

What our analysis of these two passages demonstrates is how meaningful is the choice of Theme from one clause to the next, and how thematic progression contributes to the coherent development of the text.

8.7 Thematic structure of the clause complex

At the level of the clause complex, the initiating clause is topical or ideational Theme, the continuing clause is the Rheme. In the following example, the conjunction *But* is textual Theme for the whole clause complex, not just the initial dependent clause, which is itself clause-as-Theme: ***But when you have the right connections****, everything can be tailor-made to suit your needs.* Turning our attention to each of the constituent clauses of this clause complex, the initiating dependent clause has its own textual Theme, *when,* and topical Theme, *you*; while the starting point for the main clause is the topical Theme, *everything.*

Appendix: Terms

Theme:	(1) speaker's point of departure for the clause considered as a message: the element or elements that are 'what the clause is about'. (2) = thematic structure
Rheme:	That part of the clause that is not Theme; the remainder of the message, constituting the observation relating to the Theme.
Thematic structure:	The organization of the clause into a message consisting of (in the usual case) Theme followed by Rheme.
Identification:	The organization of the clause into a two-part equative structure, one element (usually a participant or circumstance) serving to identify the others, e.g. *John was the one who broke the window.*
Predication:	(short for 'Theme predication') the predication of the Theme to bring it into prominence as what the message is about, e.g. *it was John who broke the window*.
Substitution:	Displacement of the Theme to the end of the clause as minor information point, e.g. *he's very reliable, the director.*

THE TEXTUAL COMPONENT: principal categories

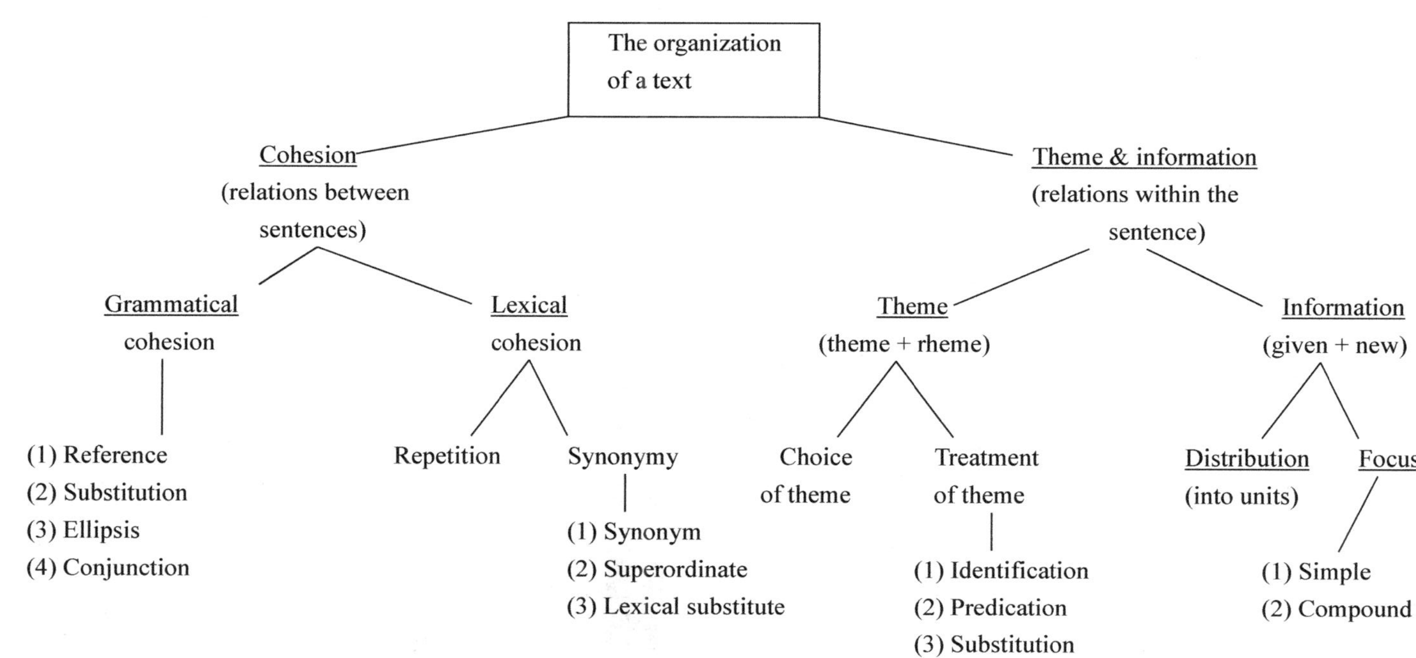

9 Rhetorical structure of texts

9.1 Introduction

Texture is also evident in the grammatical realization of relations occurring between functionally-significant text spans. A functionally-significant text span ranges in size anywhere from the text as a whole down to each individual constituent clause. Between the text as a whole at one end and its constituent clauses on the other end is a hierarchical organization of spans of text, each span related to another as intended by the writer or speaker.

Based on their investigation into the rhetorical structure of texts, William C. Mann, Sandra Thompson and Christian Matthiessen concluded that text structure may best be understood as pairs of regions of text, which are related in some way. Their approach, known as Rhetorical Structure Theory (RST), complements the clausal orientation of systemic-functional grammar by investigating the relations that occur between functionally-significant text spans at clause level and above.

The underlying assumptions of RST are as follows (Mann *et al.* 1992a: 43–46):

Underlying assumptions of Rhetorical Structure Theory:	
Organization	Texts consist of functionally significant text spans
Unity and coherence	A sense of unity to which each part/span contributes. Derives from the writer's purpose.
Hierarchy	Elementary parts composed into larger parts. The same functional description applies at all levels.
Relational composition	Finite set of relations holds between pairs of parts/spans of text
Asymmetry of relations	One member of the pair may be more nuclear/core, the other more peripheral.

Relations between spans are the glue that holds the text together. Among the finite set of relations are 'elaboration', 'concession', 'antithesis', etc. Each relation is defined in terms of constraints on a span's nucleus and satellite(s), individually and in combination; and by the likely intended effect the writer wished to have upon his/her readers by employing that relation. The relations apply between text parts or spans. The relation may be either asymmetrical or symmetrical. In an asymmetrical relation, one span is considered more peripheral to the overall meaning of the text (i.e. the 'Satellite'), while the other plays a more significant role as part of the core meaning of the text (i.e the 'Nucleus'). A symmetrical relation, on the other hand, is multinuclear, N+N. Current RST lists seven multi-nuclear relations: 'conjunction', 'contrast', 'disjunction', 'joint', 'list', and 'multinuclear restatement'. (The definitions of all the RST relations are available at www.sfu.ca/rst/01intro/definitions.html – see also Appendix 9.1.)

We observe something of the hierarchical organization of a text in the letter to the editor shown below. In this letter to the editor of a university's student newspaper, the writer takes issue with what appeared in 'Megan's column' under the headline: 'Job Seekers Beware: Scams Target Rookies'. The text clearly demonstrates a hierarchical structuring of the text into functionally-significant text spans. Boxes have been drawn around the introductory statement and the body, which in turn is partitioned into three parts.

Dear Editor,

Regarding Megan Durham's April 30 column, "Job Seekers Beware: Scams Target Rookies":

Though **I found Megan's column informative and topical,** a few aspects troubled me.

First, **Megan says, "It doesn't hurt to keep your Social Security number and date of birth off your resume."** Megan is drastically understating her point: Jobseekers should under no circumstances include their Social Security number on their resume. To do so is to invite identity theft.

Secondly, **Megan advises, "... be careful of any job opportunity that requires you to give money; you're only interested in jobs that give you money, after all."** I cannot think of any reason why a reputable employer would ask for money. Jobseekers should not only "be careful" of such an inquiry; they should report the scam.

In addition, **I felt Megan neglected to mention the jobseeker's best friend: UCSD's own Alumni Association, which gives UCSD students and alumni access to job postings, networking events and other invaluable resources targeted to UCSD students.** The leads you will generate through the Alumni Association are much more reputable - and valuable - than the mixed bag of scammers, temp agencies and others you will find on Web sites such as Monster.com.

After an introductory statement conceding Megan's column was 'informative and topical', the writer comments that 'a few aspects troubled me.' Then, over the next three paragraphs, the writer elaborates on what exactly troubled her. Each of the three paragraphs, in what we might refer to as the body of the letter, begins by signalling the sequence of arguments: 'First … Secondly … In addition'.

One considers the letter to be coherent because each span of text contributes to the overall meaning of the text as intended by the writer. There is a sense of unity to which each span of text contributes. In a way, a text is like a picture puzzle. Each piece of the puzzle contributes to the full picture. Suppose you were assembling the pieces of a puzzle depicting a landscape painting. You might begin by putting all the 'sky' pieces together, followed by the 'ground' pieces. The picture may be seen to be structured into 'functionally significant' blocks, which when finally assembled, display a complete picture. A text may be viewed similarly as being composed of functionally significant blocks or spans of text, not just as single pieces.

The initial introductory statement is a clause complex which is composed of two clauses. The first clause begins with the subordinate conjunction, 'though', which signals a relationship of ***concession*** between this clause and the next. In Rhetorical Structure Theory (RST), concession is described as an asymmetrical relation, where, as noted above, one of the spans is more core (the 'Nucleus'), and other more peripheral (the 'Satellite'). The Nucleus and the Satellite are distinguishable on the following basis. First, as regards the N(ucleus): 'Writer has positive regard for the situation presented in the Nucleus'; and as for the S(atellite): 'Writer is not claiming that the situation presented in Satellite does not hold'. In addition to stating the constraints on the N and S, the definition of each relation also states the intended (by W) effect this relation is expected to have on the Reader: 'Reader's positive regard for the situation presented in Nucleus is increased.'

Concession

N (nucleus):	Writer has positive regard for the situation presented in Nucleus;
S (satellite):	Writer is not claiming that the situation presented in Satellite does not hold;
the effect:	Reader's positive regard for the situation presented in Nucleus is increased

Rhetorical Structure Theory also employs a notation for graphically representing the relations between spans. For example, we represent the concession relation between the two clauses that make up the initial introductory statement as shown below:

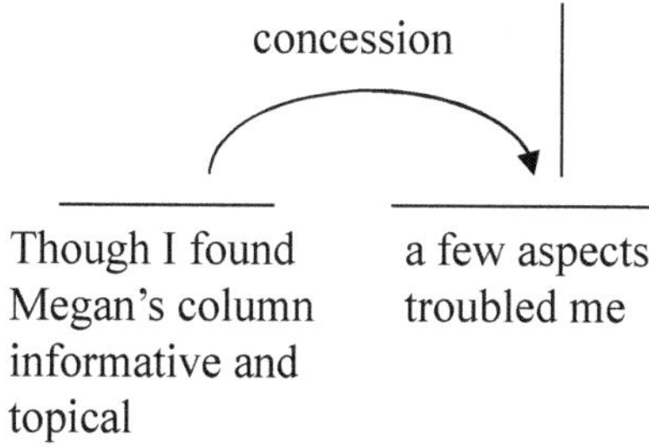

The Nucleus is shown with a vertical bar above it. An arc points from the Satellite to the Nucleus. Above the arc is the name of the relation, which here is 'concession'.

What follows this introductory statement is the body of the letter which elaborates on those aspects that troubled the writer. The relation, ***elaboration***, is defined in Rhetorical Structure Theory as follows:

Elaboration

Satellite presents additional detail about the situation or some element of subject matter which is presented in Nucleus in one or more of the ways listed below. 1. set: member / 4.process: step 2. abstract: instance / 5.object: attribute 3. whole: part / 6.generalization: specific	
the effect:	Reader recognizes the situation presented in Satellite as providing additional detail for Nucleus.

That elaboration may be further subdivided into three spans, each of which details a particular aspect of what it was that troubled the writer.

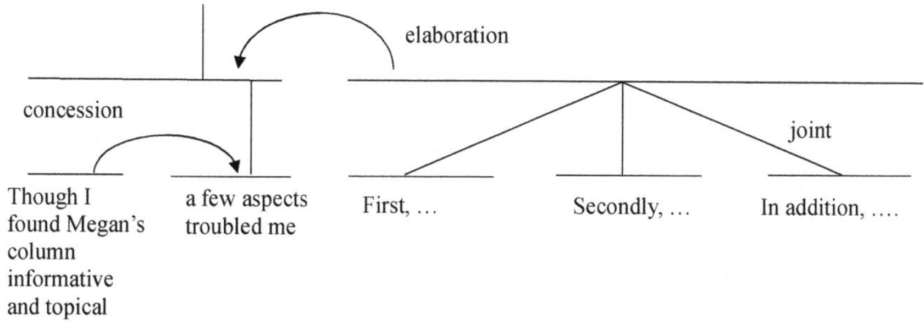

The relationship between the three spans is symmetrical, or, in other words, multi-nuclear. Looking at each of these three jointly-related spans, one notices how the writer similarly structures her argument, first by reporting what 'Megan says' or 'Megan advises', then by presenting her counterpoint. Though the writer's idea contrasts with Megan's, nevertheless, the writer clearly favours her own point of view over Megan's. This being the case, the two spans are not simply related in terms of contrast (a multinuclear relation), but instead related in terms of ***antithesis***. In antithesis, though the N and S are in contrast, nevertheless, 'W has positive regard for the situation presented in N', and the intended outcome is 'Reader's positive regard for N is increased'. The goal of the writer, i.e. the function of the relation, is to persuade the reader to accept the writer's point of view.

Antithesis

N (nucleus):	W has positive regard for the situation presented in N
N + S	The situations presented in N and S are in contrast
the effect:	Reader's positive regard for N is increased

We can represent the first span graphically as pictured below

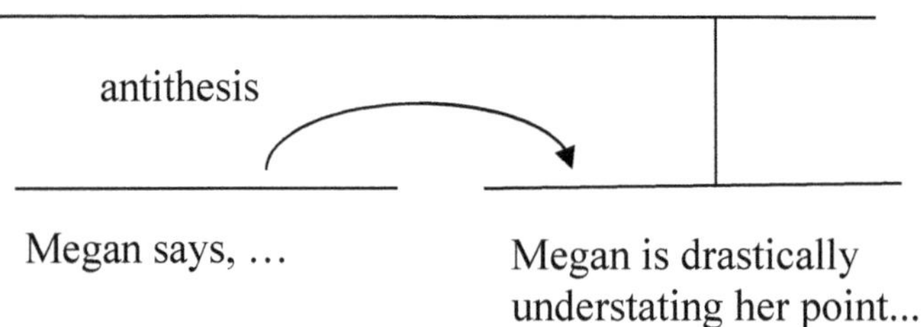

A full RST analysis would continue down to the clause level for the whole text, revealing the analyst's interpretation of the text, in particular the relations between spans as functionally-significant constituents of the text. Since a text may be interpreted differently, it follows then that there may be more than one possible analysis of the same text. Some relations, e.g. motivation, can only be inferred on the basis of an implicit understanding of the writer's intention and the effect upon the reader(s). Other relations, however, are more obviously signalled through certain linguistic devices. Certain conjunctions signal potential relations between spans, e.g. 'although' signals concession; 'but' or 'however' may signal either contrast or concession.

9.2 ZPG letter

In the book *Discourse Description: Diverse Linguistic Analyses of a Fund-raising Text* (Mann and Thompson, 1992), the Zero Population Growth fund-raising letter (see Appendix 9.2) was analysed by a variety of methods, including both a systemic analysis by M. A. K. Halliday and an RST analysis by Mann, Matthiessen and Thompson.

Here I will take several examples from Mann and Thompson's analysis of this letter to illustrate the application of RST to text analysis. The letter begins with a simple narrative account of a day in the life of ZPG staffers, progressing ***sequentially***, beginning in the morning <4>, continuing all day <5>, and lasting late into the night <6a–c>. The two *-ing* clauses, <6b> and <6c>, elaborate on what these staffers were busy doing.

> [4]*At 7.00 a.m. on October 25, our phones started to ring.* [5] *Calls jammed our switchboard all day.* [6a] *Staffers stayed late into the night,* [6b] *answering questions* [6c] *and talking with reporters from newspapers, radio stations, wire services and TV stations in every part of the country.*

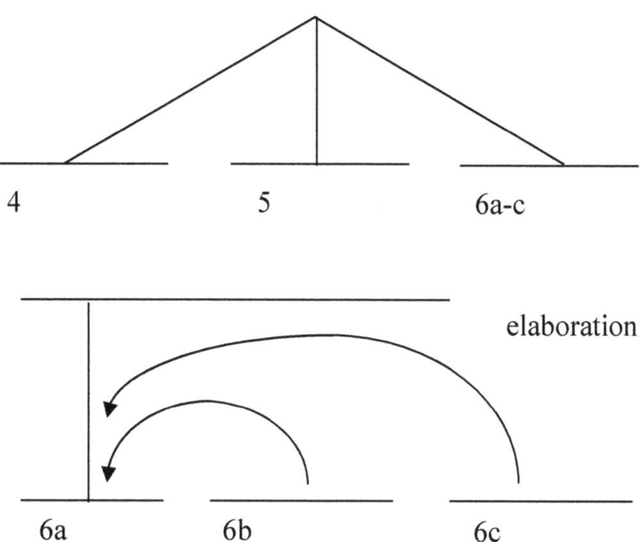

Contrast is signalled between clauses <9> and <10> by the thematic expressions of time 'At first' <9> and 'Now' <10> which compare the earlier response with the current one.

Contrast

N + S	No more than two nuclei; the situations in these two nuclei are compared with respect to one or more differences
the effect:	Reader recognizes the comparability and the difference(s) yielded by the comparison being made

[9] At first, the deluge of calls came mostly from reporters eager to tell the public about Urban Stress Test results and from outraged public officials who were furious that we had 'blown the whistle' on conditions in their cities.

[10] Now we are hearing from concerned citizens in all parts of the country who want to know what they can do to hold local officials accountable for tackling population-related problems that threaten public health and well-being.

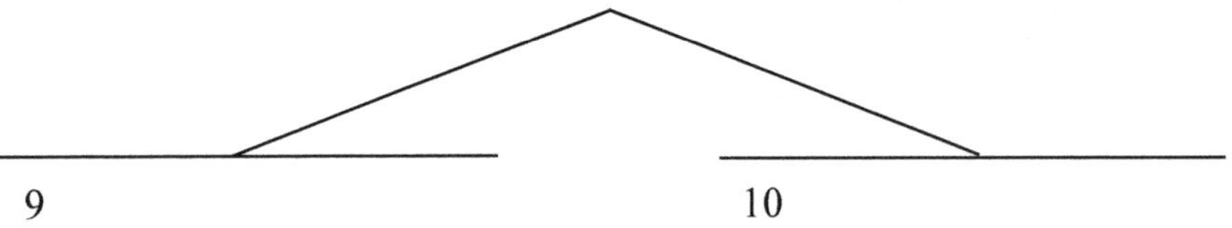

9 10

Thematic progression over the span of text between <11> to <13> is continuous with repeated references to ZPG's Urban Stress Test. In fact, continuous thematic progression is certainly a positive indicator of continuity across clauses, and thus a contributing factor when it comes to identifying those clauses which together form a complete span of text.

[11a] ZPG's 1985 Urban Stress Test, [11b] created after months of persistent and exhaustive research, ... [11a] is the nation's first survey ... [12] It ranks 184 urban areas ....

[13] The Urban Stress Test translates complex, technical data into an easy-to-use action tool for concerned citizens, elected officials and opinion leaders.

What follows this span of text between <11> and <13> is the conjunction 'But' in clause 14. Here 'But' signals ***concession*** between not just two clauses, but rather between two spans of text. Whereas clauses <11–13>

describe the positive features of the Urban Stress Test, clauses <14–16> emphasize that readers' donations are necessary to make good use of the test. Clearly conjunctions signal relations not only between clauses but also between spans of text of varying size throughout the hierarchical structure of the text.

Finally, this letter is all about asking readers to donate money to support the efforts of Zero Population Growth. The actual request comes in clause <22> – 'Please make a special contribution ot Zero Population Growth today.' Whatever precedes this request is there to motivate the reader to act on this request. Likewise the final clause gives the double punch of motivation, telling the reader that whatever they give 'will be used immediately to put the Urban Stress Test in the hands of those who need it most.'

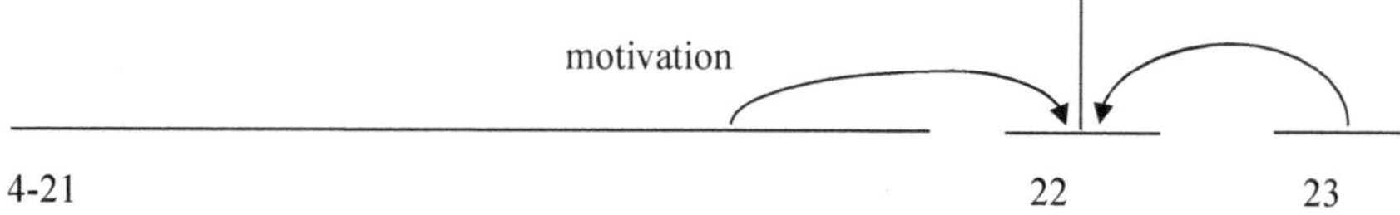

9.3 Barack Obama's email

Paying particular attention to the grammatical signalling of relations, note the following example extracted from an email received during the US primary season when Barack Obama and Hilary Clinton were both campaigning to be the Democratic Party's candidate to become the US President. (See the full text of the email in Appendix 9.3 with indication of clause breaks.)

This extract is the second of three sections, all of which end with a very similar request to make an online donation, followed by a web link to donate. The purpose of the email was to motivate readers to donate money to help Barack Obama win his party's nomination to run for president. When this email was sent, Barack Obama and Hilary Clinton were the two main contenders for the nomination. Although Barack Obama was leading in delegates, Hilary Clinton refused to call it quits and continued her fight for the nomination.

The extract below is already analysed into its constituent clauses, and the clauses are numbered.

> [16a] *The chatter among pundits may have gotten better for the Clinton campaign after last night,* [16b] *but by failing to cut into our lead,* [16c] *the math – and their chances of winning – got considerably worse.*

> [17a] *Today, we still have a lead of more than 150 delegates,* [17b] *and there are only 611 pledged delegates left to win in the upcoming contests.*

[18] *By a week from today, we will have competed in Wyoming and Mississippi.*

[19] *Two more states and 45 more delegates will be off the table.*

[20a] *But if Senator Clinton wants* [20b] *to continue this,* [20c] *let's show* [20d] *that we're ready.*

[21a] ***Make an online donation of $25 now*** [21b] ***to show*** [21c] ***you're willing to fight for this:*** **https://donate.barackobama.com/math**

The span of text from <16a-20d> is intended to ***motivate*** the Reader to act on the imperative <21> to 'Make an online donation of $25 now …'. The *to*-infinitive clause <21b–c>, 'to show you're willing to fight for this:' presents the ***purpose*** for making the donation.

The conjunction 'But' at the beginning of <20>, 'But if Senator Clinton wants … we're ready' signals a ***concession*** relation between <20> on the one hand, and the preceding span of clauses <16–19>. Within <20> the reference to 'this' ('But if Senator Clinton wants to continue ***this***') also refers back to what was being talked about in the previous span between <16> and <19>, i.e. the competition for delegates. What is being conceded is the fact, as explained by the writer, that Clinton's chances of winning had gotten considerably worse, but even so, she may still wish to continue the fight.

Clauses <17–19> ***elaborate*** on the statement in clause <16> that 'the math – and their chances of winning – got considerably worse.'

Another 'but' in <16b> signals ***concession*** between <16a> ('The chatter among pundits may have gotten better for the Clinton campaign last night') and what follows in <16b–c> where the writer argues that their chances actually just got worse.

The conjunction 'if' in <20a> signals a ***condition*** between <20a–b> and <20c–d>.

The reference to time – 'Today' <17> and 'By a week from today' <18> – signals the multinuclear relation of ***sequence*** between these two spans.

<17a> and <17b> are linked by the conjunction 'and', so we use the multinuclear relation by the same name, ***conjunction***.

Clauses <18> and <19> are two separate statements. There are no conjunctions to signal the relation between them, but clearly they are related. In the absence of any specific grammatical signal, it is left to the analyst to interpret according to his/her understanding of how these two spans are indeed related. In this instance, I interpret <19> to be the outcome of what has taken place in <18>. In other words, once the primaries in Wyoming and Mississippi have taken place, this will result in two more states and 45 more delegates being 'off the table'. <19> is the result/outcome of <18>, or more precisely, the ***non-volitional result*** of what has taken place in <18>.

Non-volitional result

N (nucleus):	N caused S. Presentation of N is more central to W's purpose than the presentation of S.
S (satellite):	S is not a volitional action.
the effect:	Reader recognizes that N could have caused the situation in S.

We have now mapped the rhetorical structure for this text. Based on our analysis, if we follow the path of nuclear spans from top to bottom, then <21a> may be considered the core clause of the whole text: '**Make an online donation of $25 now**'.

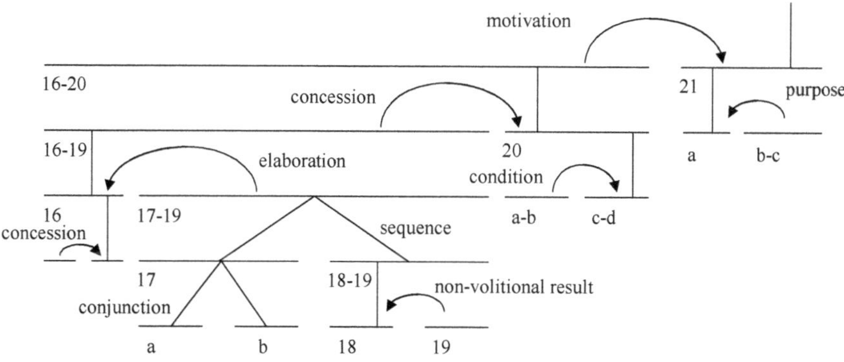

9.4 A theory of the text

A text is organized into functionally significant parts, or spans, which together assemble what Mann and Thompson (1986) refer to as the 'rhetorical structure' of the text. Each span contributes some meaning to the text as a whole. Together these spans combine to form larger units in a hierarchical organization with simple clauses at the bottom of the hierarchy, and the whole text at the top. If clauses are the most basic lexico-grammatical unit, and the text as a whole is a semantic unit, then how do we deal with those functionally-significant spans in between? What role does the lexico-grammar play in signalling relations between pairs of spans above the clause?

The lexico-grammatical signals of clause expansion (elaboration, extension, enhancement) and projection are also at work between spans across the hierarchy, contributing to the overall coherence of the text. Likewise, parataxis and hypotaxis not only describe relations between clauses at the level of clause-complex, but also apply to functionally significant spans further up the hierarchy. Relations between spans are asymmetric (hypotactic) or symmetric (paratactic).

Not all relations will be grammatically obvious, however, leaving the reader to infer on the basis of what the writer/speaker has communicated. Thus, an RST representation of a text requires some subjective interpretation on the part of the analyst. In Mann and Thompson's definitive work on RST, 'Rhetorical Structure Theory: A Theory of Text Organization', published in *Text* volume 8, number 3 (originally based in a research report from USC Information Sciences Institute, ISI/RS-87-190, http://www.sfu.ca/rst/05bibliographies/report.html), they comment about the potential for different RST analyses of the same text:

> An analysis always involves three elements: the text, the structure, and the analyst. An analysis is a statement that a particular analyst finds a certain collection of propositions plausible. Differences between analysts, based on genuine differences in their reactions to the text are to be expected. Such differences occur, but we find them infrequent. More often we find that when two analysts' analyses differ, each will accept the structures that the other posits, and so they will come to agree that a particular ambiguity exists.

An RST analysis is a theory about the text, specifically about how it is structured in such a way as to be accepted and understood as a text by its readers/listeners.

Appendix 9.1

RST relations (http://www.sfu.ca/rst/01intro/definitions.html)

Definitions of Presentational Relations			
Relation Name	**Constraints on either S or N individually**	**Constraints on N + S**	**Intention of W**
Antithesis	on N: W has positive regard for N	N and S are in contrast (see the Contrast relation); because of the incompatibility that arises from the contrast, one cannot have positive regard for both of those situations; comprehending S and the incompatibility between the situations increases R's positive regard for N	R's positive regard for N is increased
Background	on N: R won't comprehend N sufficiently before reading text of S	S increases the ability of R to comprehend an element in N	R's ability to comprehend N increases
Concession	on N: W has positive regard for N on S: W is not claiming that S does not hold;	W acknowledges a potential or apparent incompatibility between N and S; recognizing the compatibility between N and S increases R's positive regard for N	R's positive regard for N is increased
Enablement	on N: presents an action by R (including accepting an offer), unrealized with respect to the content of N	R comprehending S increases R's potential ability to perform the action in N	R's potential ability to perform the action in N increases
Evidence	on N: R might not believe N to a degree satisfactory to W on S: R believes S or will find it credible	R's comprehending S increases R's belief of N	R's belief of N is increased
Justify	none	R's comprehending S increases R's readiness to accept W's right to present N	R's readiness to accept W's right to present N is increased
Motivation	on N: N is an action in which R is the actor (including accepting an offer), unrealized with respect to the content of N	Comprehending S increases R's desire to perform action in N	R's desire to perform action in N is increased
Preparation	none	S precedes N in the text; S tends to make R more ready, interested or oriented for reading N	R is more ready, interested or oriented for reading N

Definitions of Subject Matter Relations			
Relation Name	**Constraints on either S or N individually**	**Constraints on N + S**	**Intention of W**
Circum-stance	on S: S is not unrealized	S sets a framework in the subject matter within which R is intended to interpret N	R recognizes that S provides the framework for interpreting N
Condition	on S: S presents a hypothetical, future, or otherwise unrealized situation (relative to the situational context of S)	Realization of N depends on realization of S	R recognizes how the realization of N depends on the realization of S
Elabora-tion	none	S presents additional detail about the situation or some element of subject matter which is presented in N or inferentially accessible in N in one or more of the ways listed below. In the list, if N presents the first member of any pair, then S includes the second: • set :: member • abstraction :: instance • whole :: part • process :: step • object :: attribute • generalization :: specific	R recognizes S as providing additional detail for N. R identifies the element of subject matter for which detail is provided.
Evaluation	none	on N + S: S relates N to degree of W's positive regard toward N.	R recognizes that S assesses N and recognizes the value it assigns
Interpret-ation	none	on N + S: S relates N to a framework of ideas not involved in N itself and not concerned with W's positive regard	R recognizes that S relates N to a framework of ideas not involved in the knowledge presented in N itself
Means	on N: an activity	S presents a method or instrument which tends to make realization of N more likely	R recognizes that the method or instrument in S tends to make realization of N more likely
Non-volitional Cause	on N: N is not a volitional action	S, by means other than motivating a volitional action, caused N; without the presentation of S, R might not know the particular cause of the situation; a presentation of N is more central than S to W's purposes in putting forth the N-S combination.	R recognizes S as a cause of N

Relation Name	**Constraints on either S or N individually**	**Constraints on N + S**	**Intention of W**
Non-volitional Result	on S: S is not a volitional action	N caused S; presentation of N is more central to W's purposes in putting forth the N-S combination than is the presentation of S.	R recognizes that N could have caused the situation in S
Otherwise	on N: N is an unrealized situation on S: S is an unrealized situation	realization of N prevents realization of S	R recognizes the dependency relation of prevention between the realization of N and the realization of S
Purpose	on N: N is an activity; on S: S is a situation that is unrealized	S is to be realized through the activity in N	R recognizes that the activity in N is initiated in order to realize S
Restate-ment	none	on N + S: S restates N, where S and N are of comparable bulk; N is more central to W's purposes than S is.	R recognizes S as a restatement of N
Solution-hood	on S: S presents a problem	N is a solution to the problem presented in S;	R recognizes N as a solution to the problem presented in S
Summary	on N: N must be more than one unit	S presents a restatement of the content of N, that is shorter in bulk	R recognizes S as a shorter restatement of N
Uncondi-tional	on S: S conceivably could affect the realization of N	N does not depend on S	R recognizes that N does not depend on S
Unless	none	S affects the realization of N; N is realized provided that S is not realized	R recognizes that N is realized provided that S is not realized
Volitional Cause	on N: N is a volitional action or else a situation that could have arisen from a volitional action	S could have caused the agent of the volitional action in N to perform that action; without the presentation of S, R might not regard the action as motivated or know the particular motivation; N is more central to W's purposes in putting forth the N-S combination than S is.	R recognizes S as a cause for the volitional action in N
Volitional Result	on S: S is a volitional action or a situation that could have arisen from a volitional action	N could have caused S; presentation of N is more central to W's purposes than is presentation of S;	R recognizes that N could be a cause for the action or situation in S

Definitions of Multinuclear Relations		
Relation Name	**Constraints on each pair of N**	**Intention of W**
Conjunction	The items are conjoined to form a unit in which each item plays a comparable role	R recognizes that the linked items are conjoined
Contrast	No more than two nuclei; the situations in these two nuclei are (a) comprehended as the same in many respects (b) comprehended as differing in a few respects and (c) compared with respect to one or more of these differences	R recognizes the comparability and the difference(s) yielded by the comparison is being made
Disjunction	An item presents a (not necessarily exclusive) alternative for the other(s)	R recognizes that the linked items are alternatives
Joint	None	none
List	An item comparable to others linked to it by the List relation	R recognizes the comparability of linked items
Multinuclear Restatement	An item is primarily a reexpression of one linked to it; the items are of comparable importance to the purposes of W	R recognizes the reexpression by the linked items
Sequence	There is a succession relationship between the situations in the nuclei	R recognizes the succession relationships among the nuclei.

Appendix 9.2

The Zero Population Growth fund-raising letter

Dear Friend of ZPG:

At 7.00 a.m. on October 25, our phones started to ring. Calls jammed our switchboard all day. Staffers stayed late into the night, answering questions and talking with reporters from newspapers, radio stations, wire services and TV stations in every part of the country.

When we released the results of ZPG's 1985 Urban Stress Test we had no idea we'd get such an overwhelming response. Media and public reaction has been nothing short of incredible!

At first, the deluge of calls came mostly from reporters eager to tell the public about Urban Stress Test results and from outraged public officials who were furious that we had 'blown the whistle' on conditions in their cities.

Now we are hearing from concerned citizens in all parts of the country who want to know what they can do to hold local officials accountable for tackling population-related problems that threaten public health and well-being.

ZPG's 1985 Urban Stress Test, created after months of persistent and exhaustive research, is the nation's first survey of how population-linked pressures affect U.S. cities. It ranks 184 urban areas on 11 different criteria ranging from crowding and birth rates to air quality and toxic wastes.

The Urban Stress Test translates complex, technical data into an easy-to-use action tool for concerned citizens, elected officials and opinion leaders. But to use it well, we urgently need your help.

Our small staff is being swamped with requests for more information and our modest resources are being stretched to the limit.

Your support now is critical. ZPG's 1985 Urban Stress Test may be our best opportunity ever to get the population message heard.

With your contribution, ZPG can arm our growing network of local activists with the materials they need to warn community leaders about emerging population-linked stresses before they reach the crisis stage.

Even though our national government continues to ignore the consequences of uncontrolled population growth, we can act to take positive action at the local level.

Every day decisions are being made by local officials in our communities that could drastically affect the quality of our lives. To make sound choices in planning for people, both elected officials and the American public need the population-stress data revealed by our study.

Please make a special contribution to Zero Population Growth today. Whatever you give – $25, $50, $100 or as much as you can – will be used immediately to put the Urban Stress Test in the hands of those who need it most.

Sincerely,
Susan Webster

Appendix 9.3

Barack Obama for President email

Jonathan –

[1a] Our projections show [1b] the most likely outcome of yesterday's elections will be that Hillary Clinton gained 187 delegates, and we gained 183.

[2] That's a net gain of 4 delegates out of more than 370 delegates available from all the states that voted.

[3] For comparison, that's less than half our net gain of 9 delegates from the District of Columbia alone. [4] It's also less than our net gain of 8 from Nebraska, or 12 from Washington State. [5] And it's considerably less than our net gain of 33 delegates from Georgia.

[6] The task for the Clinton campaign yesterday was clear. [7a] In order to have a plausible path to the nomination, [7b] they needed to score huge delegate victories and cut into our lead.

[8] They failed.

[9] It's clear, though, that Senator Clinton wants to continue an increasingly desperate, increasingly negative – and increasingly expensive – campaign to tear us down.

[10] That's her decision. [11a] But it's not stopping John McCain, [11b] who clinched the Republican nomination last night, [11a] from going on the offensive. [12a] He's already made news attacking Barack, [12b] and that will only become more frequent in the coming days.

[13a] Right now, it's essential for every single supporter of Barack Obama to step up [13b] and help fight this two-front battle. [14] In the face of attacks from Hillary Clinton and John McCain, we need to be ready to take them on.

[15] **Will you make an online donation of $25 right now?**
https://donate.barackobama.com/math

[16a] The chatter among pundits may have gotten better for the Clinton campaign after last night, [16b] but by failing to cut into our lead, [16c] the math – and their chances of winning – got considerably worse.

[17a] Today, we still have a lead of more than 150 delegates, [17b] and there are only 611 pledged delegates left to win in the upcoming contests.

[18] By a week from today, we will have competed in Wyoming and Mississippi. [19] Two more states and 45 more delegates will be off the table.

[20a] But if Senator Clinton wants [20b] to continue this, [20c] let's show [20d] that we're ready.

[21a] **Make an online donation of $25 now** [21b] **to show** [21c] **you're willing to fight for this: https://donate.barackobama.com/math**

[22] This nomination process is an opportunity to decide what our party needs to stand for in this election.

[23a] We can either take on John McCain with a candidate who's already united Republicans and Independents against us, [23b] or we can do it with a campaign that's united Americans from all parties around a common purpose.

[24a] We can debate John McCain about who can clean up Washington [24b] by nominating a candidate who's taken more money from lobbyists than he has, [24c] or we can do it with a campaign that hasn't taken a dime of their money because we've been funded by you.

[25a] We can present the American people with a candidate who stood shoulder-to-shoulder with McCain on the worst foreign policy disaster of our generation, and agrees with him that George Bush deserves the benefit of the doubt on Iran, [25b] or we can nominate someone who opposed the war in Iraq from the beginning and will not support a march to war with Iran.

[26a] John McCain may have a long history of straight talk and independent thinking, [26b] but he has made the decision in this campaign to offer four more years of the very same policies that have failed us for the last eight.

[27] We need a Democratic candidate who will present the starkest contrast to those failed policies of the past.

[28] And that candidate is Barack Obama.

[29] **Please make a donation of $25 now:**
https://donate.barackobama.com/math

Thank you,
David

Part Three

Case studies in text linguistics

10 Stepping into meaning

A case study of Billy Graham's Address at the National Prayer and Memorial Service at the Episcopal National Cathedral on 14 September 2001

10.1 Introduction

Whatever kind of text we are trying to interpret, it must be understood against the backdrop of the total resources of language available to the user, or, in other words, against 'an infinity of shadow texts' (Halliday, [1992] 2002: 226) that might have been.

Only objective linguistic scholarship using the categories of the description of the language as a whole, not 'ad hoc, personal and arbitrarily selective statements', can contribute to the analysis of literature and allow for 'the comparison of each text with others, by the same and by different authors, in the same and in different genres' (Halliday, [1964] 2002: 5, 6).

As we proceed to look at each of the three kinds of meaning: ideational, interpersonal and textual, and how they are discoverable in a text, I will outline seven steps for doing the analysis. The text we will examine is Billy Graham's address at the National Prayer and Memorial Service at the Episcopal National Cathedral on 14 September 2001. The full text is given at the end of this chapter, tagged by paragraph (e.g. <p 1>, <p 2>... <p n>), and by clause (e.g. <c 1>, <c 2>...<c n>). For the purpose of illustrating the points below, however, we will focus on just the first five paragraphs of this text.

10.2 STEP 1 – Clause analysis: parse the text into it constituent clauses.

The first step is to parse the text into simple, complex and embedded clauses.

> *<p 1> <c1> President and Mrs. Bush, I want to say a personal word on behalf of many people. <c 2> Thank you, Mr. President, for calling this day of prayer and remembrance. <c 3> We needed it at this time.*
>
> *<p 2> <c 4a> We come together today <c 4b> to affirm our conviction [<c 4c> that God cares for us,] <c 4d> whatever our ethnic, religious, or political background may be. <c 5a> The Bible says <c 5b> that He's the God of all comfort, <c 5c> who comforts us in our troubles. <c 6a> No matter how hard we try, <c 6b> words simply cannot express the horror, the shock, and the revulsion [<c 6c> we all feel over [<c 6d> what took place in this nation on Tuesday morning.]] <c 7> September eleven will go down in our history as a day to remember.*

> *<p 3> <c 8a> Today we say to those [<c 8b> who masterminded this cruel plot,] and to those [<c 8c> who carried it out,] <c 8d> that the spirit of this nation will not be defeated by their twisted and diabolical schemes. <c 9a> Someday, those responsible will be brought to justice, <c 9b> as President Bush and our Congress have so forcefully stated. <c 10a> But today we especially come together in this service <c 10b> to confess our need of God.*
>
> *<p 4> <c 11a> We've always needed God from the very beginning of this nation, <c 11b> but today we need Him especially. <c 12> We're facing a new kind of enemy. <c 13> We're involved in a new kind of warfare. <c 14> And we need the help of the Spirit of God. <c 15a> The Bible words are our hope: <c 15b> God is our refuge and strength; an ever present help in trouble. <c 16a> Therefore we will not fear, <c 16b> though the earth give way, <c 16c> and the mountains fall into the heart of the sea.*
>
> *<p 5> <c 17> But how do we understand something like this? <c 18> Why does God allow evil like this to take place? <c 19a> Perhaps that is [<c 19b> what you are asking now.] <c 20> You may even be angry at God. <c 21a> I want to assure you <c 21b> that God understands these feelings [<c 21c> that you may have.] <c 22a> We've seen so much on our television, <c 22b> heard on our radio, stories [<c 22c> that bring tears to our eyes,] <c 22c> and make us <c 22d> all feel a sense of anger. <c 23a> But God can be trusted, <c 23b> even when life seems at its darkest.*

Sentence 4 contains four clauses:

- <c 4a> We come together today
- <c 4b> to affirm our conviction
- [<c 4c> that God cares for us]
- <c 4d> whatever our ethnic, religious, or political background may be.

Clause <c 4c> is an embedded clause – *that God cares for us* – postmodifying 'conviction'. The predicate in 4d includes both a modal auxiliary – *may* – and the main verb – *be*.

Sentence 5 contains three clauses:

- <c 5a> The Bible says
- <c 5b> that He's the God of all comfort,
- <c 5c> who comforts us in our troubles.

Clause <c 5b> is a projected clause and clause <c 5c> is a non-defining relative clause.

In sentence 6, the second simple clause, 6b, illustrates double-embedding. Embedded in a defining relative clause (whose relative pronoun is ellipted) post-modifying 'revulsion' is another nominalization as object of the preposition 'over':

- <c 6a> No matter how hard we try,
- <c 6b> words simply cannot express the horror, the shock, and the revulsion
  [<c 6c> (which) we all feel over
    [<c 6d> what took place in this nation on Tuesday morning]].

10.3 Stepping into ideational meaning

Ideational meaning may be sub-divided into the ***experiential*** and the ***logical***. The experiential refers to our ability to talk about our experience, while the logical deals with the expression of certain logical relations, such as by means of conjunctions like *and, or, if, not*.

10.3.1 Experiential meaning

We talk about our experience of the world in terms of processes (typically verbs), along with those participants (nouns) and circumstances (adjuncts) that accompany them. Each idea corresponds to a clause, which consists of a process, along with possible participants and circumstances.

Processes describe 'happenings', i.e. events or actions (e.g. *Ted's flight* ***arrived*** *early*; *Tom* ***bought*** *the tickets at the reception desk*), states (mental or otherwise) or other abstract relations (e.g. *I* ***feel*** fine; Mary ***is*** *tall; Mary* ***is*** *the tallest girl at her school*), both in the world around us and within our own consciousness. Processes come in different types, including material processes of doing; mental processes of sensing; verbal processes of saying; relational processes of being or having; as well as processes of behaving and existing.

Processes usually include (may even require) mention of participants (e.g. *Ted's flight, Tom, the tickets, Mary, the tallest girl in the class*) and circumstances (e.g. *early, at the reception desk, at her school*). Participants are anything or anyone – typically referred to by nouns, and queried by *who* or *what* – involved in the activity or state described by the Process. Participants can be persons, objects or abstractions. Participants have a role in the process, either as the doer or agent of the process, or as one affected by or benefiting from the process being performed. The circumstances may include expressions of time, place, manner, means, cause, condition, concession – typically queried by *where, when, why,* and *how.*

10.3.1.1 STEP 2 – Transitivity analysis: for each clause identify processes by type, participants by role, and circumstances

The experiential function of language is realized by the semantic system of transitivity. Transitivity analysis is concerned with the semantic configuration of process, participant and circumstance, or in other words the clause as a means of representing the processes of doing, happening, feeling, thinking, being, speaking, etc. (see Table 10.1).

Table 10.1: Process types and participant roles

<table>
<tr><th colspan="2">PARTICIPANT ROLES</th><th colspan="2">PROCESS TYPE</th></tr>
<tr><td>ACTOR/AGENT</td><td>GOAL/AFFECTED</td><td>material</td><td>doing, happening</td></tr>
<tr><td>SENSER</td><td>PHENOMENON</td><td>mental</td><td>sensing, knowing, seeing, feeling</td></tr>
<tr><td>SAYER</td><td>VERBIAGE</td><td>verbal</td><td>saying</td></tr>
<tr><td>BEHAVER</td><td></td><td>behavioral</td><td>behaving, coughing, sleeping,</td></tr>
<tr><td>'There'</td><td>EXISTENT</td><td>existential</td><td>existing</td></tr>
<tr><td>CARRIER</td><td>ATTRIBUTE</td><td rowspan="3">relational</td><td rowspan="3">being, becoming, having</td></tr>
<tr><td>IDENTIFIER</td><td>IDENTIFIED</td></tr>
<tr><td>POSSESSOR</td><td>POSSESSED</td></tr>
</table>

Table 10.2: Transitivity analysis

P#	C#	Transitivity Structure				Clause (Complex)
		Process (type)	Participant(s)		Circumstance(s)	
			X…	Roles		
1	1	want to say (verbal)	I	Sayer	on behalf of many people	<c 1> President and Mrs. Bush, I want to say a personal word on behalf of many people.
			a personal word	Verbiage		
	2	calling (material)	(you)	Actor		<c 2> Thank you, Mr. President, for calling this day of prayer and remembrance.
			this day of prayer and remembrance	Goal		
	3	needed (relational)	we	Possessor	at this time.	<c 3>We needed it at this time.
			it	Possessed		
2	4a	come together (material)	we	Actor	today	<c 4a> We come together today <c 4b> to affirm our conviction [<c 4c> that God cares for us,] <c 4d> whatever our ethnic, religious, or political background may be.
	4b	affirm (mental)	our conviction	Phenomenon		
	4c	cares (mental)	God	Senser	for us	
	4d	be (relational)	whatever	Identifier		
			our ethnic, religious, political background	Identified		
	5a	says (verbal)	The Bible	Sayer		<c 5a> The Bible says <c 5b> that He's the God of all comfort, <c 5c> who comforts us in our troubles.
	5b	is (relational)	He	Identified		
			the God of all comfort	Identifier		
	5c	comforts (material)	who	Actor	in our troubles	
			us	Goal		
	6a	try (material)	we	Actor	hard	<c 6a> No matter how hard we try, <c 6b> words simply cannot express the horror, the shock, and the revulsion [<c 6c> we all feel over [<c 6d> what took place in this nation on Tuesday morning.]]
	6b	express (material)	words	Actor		
			the horror, the shock, and the revulsion [<c 6cd>]	Goal		
	6c	feel (mental)	we all	Senser	over […]	
	6d	took place (material)	what	Affected		
	7	go down (relational)	September eleven	Carrier	in our history	<c 7> September eleven will go down in our history as a day to remember.
			a day to remember	Attribute		

P#	C#	Transitivity Structure				Clause (Complex)
		Process (type)	Participant(s)		Circumstance(s)	
			X...	Roles		
3	8a	say (verbal)	we	Sayer	Today	<c 8a> Today we say to those [<c 8b> who masterminded this cruel plot,] and to those [<c 8c> who carried it out,] <c 8d> that the spirit of this nation will not be defeated by their twisted and diabolical schemes.
			to those [<c 8b>] and to those [<c 8c>]	Receiver		
			<c 8d>	Verbiage		
	8b	masterminded (material)	who	Actor		
			this cruel plot	Goal		
	8c	carried X out (material)	who	Actor		
			it	Goal		
	8d	defeated (material)	the spirit of this nation	Goal		
			by their twisted and diabolical schemes	Actor		
	9a	brought (material)	those responsible	Goal	Someday	<c 9a> Someday, those responsible will be brought to justice, <c 9b> as President Bush and our Congress have so forcefully stated.
	9b	stated (verbal)	President Bush and our Congress	Sayer		
	10a	come together (material)	we	Actor	today … in this service	<c 10> But today we especially come together in this service <c 10b> to confess our need of God.
	10b	confess (verbal)	we	Sayer		
			our need of God	Verbiage		
4	11a	needed (relational)	we	Possessor	from the very beginning of this nation	<c 11a> We've always needed God from the very beginning of this nation, <c 11b> but today we need Him especially.
			God	Possessed		
	11b	need (relational)	we	Possessor	today	
			Him	Possessed		
	12	facing (material)	we	Actor	until the end of the decade	<c 12> We're facing a new kind of enemy.
			a new kind of enemy	Goal		
	13	involved (material)	we	Goal		<c 13> We're involved in a new kind of warfare.
			in a new kind of warfare	Range		
	14	need (relational)	we	Possessor		<c 14> And we need the help of the Spirit of God.
			the help of the Spirit of God	Possessed		
	15a	are (relational)	The Bible words	Carrier		<c 15a> The Bible words are our hope: <c 15b> God is our refuge and
			our hope	Attribute		

P#	C#	Transitivity Structure				Clause (Complex)
		Process (type)	Participant(s)		Circumstance(s)	
			X…	Roles		
	15b	is (relational)	God	Carrier		strength; an ever present help in trouble.
			our refuge	Attribute		
	16a	will not fear (mental)	we	Senser		<c 16a> Therefore we will not fear <c 16b> though the earth give way, <c 16c> and the mountains fall into the heart of the sea.
	16b	give way (material)	the earth	Actor		
	16c	fall (material)	the mountains	Actor	into the heart of the sea	
5	17	understand (mental)	we	Senser		<c 17> But how do we understand something like this?
			something like this	Phenomenon		
	18a	allow (material)	God	Actor		<c 18a> Why does God allow <c 18b> evil like this to take place?
			<c 18b>	Goal		
	18b	take place (material)	evil like this	Actor		
	19a	is (relational)	that	Identified	now	<c 19> Perhaps that is [<c 19b> what you are asking now.]
			[<c 19b>]	Identifier		
	19b	asking (verbal)	you	Sayer		
			what	Verbiage		
	20	be (relational)	you	Carrier		<c 20> You may even be angry with God.
			angry	Attribute		
	21a	want to assure (verbal)	I	Sayer		<c 21a> I want to assure you
			you	Receiver		
			<21b>	Verbiage		
	21b	understands (mental)	God	Senser		<c 21a> I want to assure you <c 21b> that God understands these feelings [<c 21c> that you may have.]
			these feelings [<c 21c>]	Phenomenon		
	21c	have (relational)	you	Possessor		
			these feelings	Possessed		
	22a	seen (mental)	we	Senser	on our television	<c22a> We've seen so much on television,
			so much	Phenomenon		
	22b	heard (mental)	stories that bring tears to our eyes	Phenomenon	on our radio	<c22 b> heard on our radio, stories that bring tears to our eyes
	22c	make (material)	us all	Goal, Senser		<c22c> and make us all feel a sense of anger.
			a sense of anger	Phenomenon		
	23a	trusted (material)	God	Goal		<c23 a> But God can be trusted
	23b	seems (relational)	life	Carrier		<c23 b> even when life seems at its darkest.
			at its hardest	Attribute		

Based on our transitivity analysis of the full text – available at the end of this chapter – we notice that Billy Graham's references to himself emphasize his role as Senser/messenger engaged in verbal (*say, assure, confess, pray*) and mental (*know, think, believe, accept, hope, doubt*) processes. Repeated references to '*we*' (35 times); '*our*' (27 times); and '*us*' (18 times) helps to strengthen this sense of togetherness and unity in the face of tragic circumstances.

That the address is less an exhortation to action, and more concerned with affecting a positive response, is realized in part by the author's preference for attributing other than material processes – relational, mental, behavioural, verbal – to those whom he is addressing – the American people as victims of those described as having masterminded and carried out these 'twisted and diabolical schemes'.

Early on in the address, a distinction is made between 'those who masterminded this cruel plot' and 'those who carried it out' (3.8). They are identified only by their deeds. Elsewhere they are referred to as 'those responsible' (3.9), and 'those perpetrators who took this on to tear us apart' (7.41). The deictic distinguishes them from us. Their actions are described as 'evil'; they are 'a new kind of enemy'.

In paragraph 3, in both instances cited above they are not the actors – other than as part of their defining deeds which are encapsulated within the nominalization itself – instead they are the Recipients of what is being said ('we say to those who … and to those who …'), or they are the Goal to be 'brought to justice' (3.9) Interestingly, in the sentence which follows, the third such nominalization, although thematic, is neither grammatical Subject nor Actor in the clauses which follow: 'So those perpetrators who took this on to tear us apart, it has worked the other way – it's back lashed. It's backfired' (7.41–7.42). The pronoun, 'It', is the grammatical Subject of the next two clauses, and refers back to 'this' (in the post-modifying relative clause of the thematic nominalization), another instance in a chain of repeated anaphoric references to the events of September 11. We infer that, as it has worked out, 'Those perpetrators' are the targets of the resulting backlash, and their plotting has backfired. The point being that those responsible for September 11 were no longer the actors engaged in doing, they instead would be on the receiving end of the actions to follow.

The eleventh paragraph recalls the events of that day in vivid terms:

> *We all watched in horror as* ***planes crashed*** *into the steel and glass of the World Trade Center. Those majestic towers, built on solid foundations, were examples of the prosperity and creativity of America. When damaged, those* ***buildings eventually plummeted*** *to the ground,* ***imploding*** *in upon themselves.* (11.76–11.78)

The planes are not **Actors** in a material process, rather they are the **Medium** in an ergative structure with no mention made of those responsible for initiating these events. The World Trade Center has become a thing of the past, as the deictic element demonstrates: 'Those majestic towers', 'those buildings' – they are gone.

Processes attributed to God are either in the present or future tense: 'God is ...;' '... comforts,' 'allows,' 'understands,' 'can be trusted,' 'declares;' '... will never forsake,' 'is going to give ...'. There is one exception, however, which is sandwiched between two present tense verbs:

> *the cross tells us that **God understands** our sin and our suffering. For **he took upon himself**, in the person of Jesus Christ, our sins and our suffering. And from the cross, **God declares** 'I love you.'* (10.64–10.67)

Calling the attention of his audience to the symbols of the cross '*all around us*' in the National Cathedral, Billy Graham continues:

> *The story does not end with the cross, for Easter points us beyond the tragedy of the cross to the empty tomb. It tells us there is hope for eternal life, for Christ has conquered evil, and death, and hell. Yes there's hope.* (10.69–10.71)

Neither is the tragedy of September 11 the end of the story. Whereas, over subsequent paragraphs, the vivid images of that fateful day are painted in past tense, the struggle to rebuild is described as having only just begun.

Just as the cross is the **Sayer** in a verbal process, so too the Bible 'says', 'speaks' and 'talks'. There is a noticeable contrast established between our words, which fail us, and Bible words, which offer hope:

> *No matter how hard we try, words simply cannot express the horror, the shock, the revulsion we all feel over what took place in this nation on Tuesday morning.* (2.6)

> *The Bible words are our hope* (4.15)

Paragraph 13 ends in the words of the old hymn quoted by Andrew Young, 'How firm a foundation'. It too speaks in the present tense.

10.3.2 Logical meaning

The logical aspect of ideational meaning looks at how clauses expand into and become the text as a whole through ***elaborating*** ('equals'), ***extending*** ('is added to'), and ***enhancing*** ('is multiplied by'). One clause can elaborate on another through exemplification, clarification, or restatement; or a clause can extend the meaning of another by adding some new element, giving an exception, or offering an alternative; or a clause can enhance another through embellishment, or qualification.

Besides clause expansion, a sensing (mental) or saying (verbal) process can ***project*** another clause which can either be what was thought/seen (an idea) or said (a locution). For example, from the Billy Graham address, clause 5a projects the 'that'-clause which follows, 5b–5c.

> *<c 5a> The Bible says <c 5b> that He's the God of all comfort, <c 5c> who comforts us in our troubles.*

The relations between clauses combined through elaboration, extension, enhancement or projection may be symmetrical (***paratactic***) or asymmetrical (***hypotactic***). Parataxis is 'the relationship between two like elements of equal status, one initiating, the other continuing' (Halliday 1994: 218):

> <clauseX>$_1$ <clauseY>$_2$

Projection may be either paratactic or hypotactic. Indirect speech or thought illustrates hypotactic projection. Direct speech, on the other hand, is paratactic projection:

> paratactic projection: < The Bible says >$_1$ < 'He's the God...' >$_{'2}$
>
> hypotactic projection: < The Bible says >$_\alpha$ < that the story was interesting. >$_{'\beta}$

A paratactic relationship between clauses is represented with the notation: 1 =2 (elaboration), 1 +2 (extension), 1 ×2 (enhancement), 1 "2 (projection).

Apposition, or ***paratactic elaboration*** is illustrated in the following example from the Billy Graham text:

> *<The Bible words are our hope:>$_1$ < God is our refuge and strength; an ever present help in trouble. >$_{=2}$* (4.15)

Coordination, which includes both of the categories addition, alternation and variation, is ***paratactic extension***. For example, note the paratactic extension between 16b and 16c:

> *<c 16a> Therefore we will not fear,*
>
> *<16b> though the earth give away,*
>
> *<c 16c> and the mountains fall into the heart of the sea.*

See Table 10.3 for more examples of each category of expansion.

Halliday defines hypotaxis, on the other hand, as 'the relation between a dependent element and its dominant, the element on which it is dependent.' (1984: 218). Here the dependent element is identified as the β-element, and the dominant element as the *a*-element. A hypotactic relationship between clauses is indicated with the notation: α β:

> <clauseX>$_\alpha$ <clauseY>$_\beta$

The combination of elaboration and hypotaxis (***hypotactic elaboration***), for example, may be realized as a non-defining relative clause, as in sentence 5 from the Billy Graham text:

< that He's the God of all comfort, >$_{\alpha}$ *< who comforts us in our troubles.>*$_{\beta}$

Hypotactic enhancement occurs in clauses introduced by a hypotactic conjunction (e.g. *when, since, as soon as, while, as, because, if,* etc.). For example:

< Someday, those responsible will be brought to justice, >$_{\alpha}$ *< as President Bush and our Congress have so forcefully stated. >*$_{x\beta}$ (3.9)

Addition, replacement and alternation, where expressed by a dependent clause, illustrate ***hypotactic extension***.

Table 10.3 show the possibilities for expanding a clause with their corresponding notation. The information in the table may also be represented graphically as shown below, either in (i) a box-like notation, or (ii) with arcs indicating the relations. In a hypotactic relationship, the arc begins on the subordinate clause and points to the main clause. The symbol above the arc indicates whether the relation is elaborating (=), extending (+), enhancing (×), or projecting (″).

As noted in our earlier discussion of the rhetorical structure of texts, parataxis and hypotaxis not only describe relations between clauses at the level of clause-complex, but also apply to functionally significant spans further up the hierarchy. Relations between spans may be asymmetric (hypotactic) or symmetric (paratactic).

Table 10.3: Clausal expansion notation

		Elaborating (=) i.e. exemplification, clarification, restatement	**Extending** (+) i.e. adding some new element, giving an exception, or offering an alternative	**Enhancing** (x) i.e. embellishment, or qualification	**Projecting** (") i.e. locution, or an idea
Paratactic (1 + 2) <clauseX>$_1$ <clauseY>$_2$ 'the relationship between two like elements of equal status, one initiating, the other continuing' (Halliday 1994:218).	+	<There are three components of meaning: >$_1$ <they are ideational, interpersonal and textual.>$_{=2}$	<I will leave soon,>$_1$ <but you can stay.>$_{+2}$	<We saw him off at the airport;>$_1$ <then we returned home.>$_{x2}$	<Tom said,>$_1$ <'I'll be away next week.'>$_{"2}$
Hypotactic (α β) <main clause>$_\alpha$ <dependent clause>$_\beta$ 'the relation between a dependent element and its dominant, the element on which it is dependent.' (Halliday 1994:218).	x	<This is my friend,> $_\alpha$ <who is studying here.>$_{=\beta}$	<He went home> $_\alpha$ <instead of going out with his friends> $_{+\beta}$	<When John arrives>$_{x\beta}$ <we will eat dinner.>$_\alpha$	<Tom said> $_\alpha$ <that he'd be away next week.>$_{"\beta}$

10.3.2.1 STEP 3 – Identify the hypotactic and paratactic relations between clauses

Table 10.4: Logical analysis

P#	Simple Clause	Clause complex											
		Paratactic				Hypotactic							
		Expansion			Projection	Expansion						Projection	
		Elaboration	Extension	Enhancement		Elaboration		Extension		Enhancement			
						α	β	α	β	α	β	α	β
1	1												
	2												
	3												
2						4a-c	4d			4a	4b[c]		
						5b	5c					5a	5b,c
										6b[c[d]]	6a		
	7												
3												8a[b][c]	8d
										9a	9b		
										10a	10b		
4				11a + 11b									
	12												
	13												
	14												
		15a = 15b											
			16b + 16c	16a x 16bc									
5	17												
						18a	18b						
	19												
	20												
												21a	21b[c]
			22a + 22b[cde]										
										23a	23b		

10.3.2.1

STEP 4 – Identify the hypotactic and paratactic relations between functionally significant spans above the level of clause complex.

Beginning with the text as a whole, Figure 10.1 shows our mapping of this text's rhetorical structure down to paragraph level only.

A hypotactic relationship is shown between the span consisting of paragraphs 2 to 4, and another comprising paragraphs 5 to 10.

Note how paragraph 2 begins, 'We come together today to affirm …' Paragraph 3 continues this focus on 'we' and 'today' in the initial clause 'Today we say …'. Similar to how paragraph 2 began, paragraph 3 closes with 'But today we especially come together …'. Paragraph 4 then elaborates on the new information introduced in Paragraph 3, namely, what Billy Graham means by 'our need of God'.

Parataxis between paragraph 5, on the one hand, and paragraphs 6–10, on the other, is signalled by how both similarly begin with the conjunction 'but' followed by a question, which is then addressed in the subsequent clauses that make up that span.

> But how do we understand something like this? (5.17) …
>
> But what are some of the lessons we can learn? (6.24)

The span comprising paragraphs 6–10 (see Figure 10.1) then proceeds over successive paragraphs to **elaborate** a three-part answer to the question raised at the outset of this span. The **paratactic** structure of the three-part answer is signalled by three successively placed thematic conjunctive adjuncts: 'First' (6.25), 'secondly' (7.36), 'Finally' (8.45).

Paragraphs 8 through 10 focus on ***hope*** – of 13 occurrences of the word 'hope' in this text, 11 occur in this span. Both paragraphs 8 and 9 open with a continuous thematic reference to 'this event'. The rheme of the main clause in the first clause complex in paragraph 8 outlines what is addressed in paragraph 8 – 'hope for the present', and paragraphs 9 and 10 – 'hope for the future'.

The second clause in paragraph 8 opens the span with the affirmation: 'Yes, there's hope'; the final clause of paragraph 10 closes with the same affirmation: 'Yes, there's hope.' In fact, this is rather similar to the repetition of the phrase 'We come together today' at the beginning of paragraph 2, and 'today we especially come together' at the end of paragraph 3. In both instances – 'Yes, there's hope' and 'We come together today' – the repetition of the same phrasing at the beginning and closing of a span of text gives the reader the feeling of having come full circle, back to where the discourse (or at least that span of text) began.

In paragraphs 11–14, tense figures prominently in configuring a sequencing of perspectives from the past, the present and the future (see Figure 10.1). In paragraph 11, Billy Graham, reminiscing about his past, recalls a previous occasion when he heard Andrew Young speak at a prayer breakfast. He then goes on to describe the events of September 11 more graphically here than elsewhere in the text.

Paragraphs 12 and 13 deal with how the tragedy of September 11 should be responded to in the present.

> *Yes, our nation has been attacked. Buildings destroyed. Lives lost.* ***But now*** *we have a choice ...* (12.81–12.84)

> *This has been a terrible week with many tears.* ***But*** *also it's been a week of great faith ...* (13.90–13.91)

Paragraphs 12 and 13 sum up a theme that is developed throughout the text and is very much in keeping with the occasion itself. 'This day of prayer and remembrance' was an occasion for not only remembering but also recasting the past; on the one hand, acknowledging the tragic events of September 11, while at the same time affirming a new perspective, a new resolve going forward. Paragraph 14 is noticeably all future tense: 'we **will** feel ... **will** know ... He **will** never forsake us ... God **is going to** give ... this **is going to** be a day that we **will** remember as a day of victory'. The victims become the victorious.

10.4 Stepping into interpersonal meaning

Grammar is a resource not only for talking about our experience of the world around us and what is going on inside us, but also for communicating our attitudes toward and expectations of those with whom we are interacting. This 'interactive' dimension of language is referred to by Halliday as the interpersonal metafunction or component of language. The interpersonal metafunction deals with our use of language to relate to our listeners. When we communicate we deliver more than just content or information, we also communicate our role *vis-à-vis* our partners in the exchange.

In any exchange, there is give and take. When we ask a question – *Is it raining*? – we anticipate an answer. If our communication is successfully comprehended by our listener(s), then they will know what we expect of them, and, depending on their ability and willingness, provide us with the information we have requested. If we want someone to do something for us – *Please turn up the volume on the television* – then we need to use a suitable grammatical pattern for this purpose, and again hopefully elicit our desired response.

Language functions to facilitate exchange, both of information and goods-and-services. The interpersonal function of language addresses this issue of how we communicate our respective roles in this exchange. In English, the interpersonal function is realized in terms of choices involving declarative, interrogative and imperative clause types, or moods. The declarative typically expresses a statement – typically giving information; interrogative expresses a question – typically asking for information; imperative expresses a directive; exclamative, an exclamation. Such choices are realized structurally by what Halliday refers to as mood-residue structure. ***Mood*** consists of the elements Subject and Finite. ***Residue*** consists of Predicator, and possibly Complement and Adjunct.

In English, it is the Mood element – consisting of the ***Subject*** and ***Finite*** – which indicates whether the clause is a statement or a question, whether the speaker is giving or asking for information. The sequence of Subject before Finite realizes a declarative; Finite before Subject realizes a yes/no interrogative. Indeed, the relationship between mood and illocutionary act is not one-to-one but instead many-to-many. While a declarative typically expresses a statement intended to give information, it may also function to make a request of the listener. For example, the statement, 'it sure is cold here' could in fact be a request to someone to turn off the air-conditioner. To understand the speaker's intended meaning, the situation context and the linguistic co-text are essential.

Modality is another aspect of interpersonal meaning related to the expression of the speaker's attitude about what he is saying. In English, modality is expressed by the use of modal adjuncts (possibly by certain adverbs like 'surely', 'possibly', or by various thematic structures such as 'it is possible that', 'there is a possibility that'), or through a small set of verbs known as modal auxiliaries, e.g. 'can', 'may', 'might', etc.

10.4.1 STEP 5 – Identify whether the main clause is interrogative, declarative or imperative

Paragraph 5 in the Billy Graham text begins with two interrogatives:

> *<p 5> <c 17>* ***But how do we understand something like this?*** *<c 18>* ***Why does God allow evil like this to take place?***

10.4.2 STEP 6 – Identify modal adjuncts and modal auxiliaries

Following the two paragraph-initial interrogatives, the next clause (clause 19) begins with a modal adjunct – 'Perhaps'. The next two sentences each contain the modal auxiliary 'may', indicating possibility.

> *<p 5> <c 17>* ***But how do we understand something like this?*** *<c 18>* ***Why does God allow evil like this to take place?*** *<c 19>* ***Perhaps*** *that is what* ***you*** *are asking now. <c 20>* ***You may*** *even be angry at God. <c 21a>* ***I want to assure you*** *<c 21b> that God understands these feelings that* ***you may*** *have. <c 22a> We've seen so much on our television, <c 22b> heard on our radio, stories that bring tears to our eyes, <c 22c> and make us all feel a sense of anger. <c 23a> But God can be trusted, <c 23b> even when life seems at its darkest.*

The use of interrogatives and modal adjuncts and auxiliaries contributes to the highly interpersonal emphasis of this paragraph, which is further strengthened by the repeated references to 'you'.

10.5 Stepping into textual meaning

Textual meaning deals with those structures that give texture to a text. The more cohesive and coherent the text is, the greater is its texture. On the one hand, cohesion deals with how successive sentences are integrated to form a whole, i.e. inter-sentence texture. Cohesion in a text increases as the elements within a text become more mutually dependent on one another for their interpretation. Cohesive ties cross clause and sentence boundaries. Coherence, or intra-sentence texture, on the other hand, has to do with fit to context. The organization of the message to fit the context comprises two aspects: one aspect, which Halliday refers to as the 'hearer angle', relates to the organization of the message so that it ties up with the preceding text, with that which the hearer has already heard about, i.e. the Given; the second aspect, the 'speaker angle', relates to how the message is organized around what the speaker wants to say, or what Halliday calls 'Theme' (see Chapter 8).

By analysing the text for its thematic structure, i.e. identifying the point of departure for each clause, 'we can gain insight into its texture and understand how the writer made clear to us the nature of his underlying concerns' (Halliday, 1985: 67). The point of departure may be related to textual, interpersonal or ideational meaning, or even a combination of meanings. As the writer/speaker launches into a new clause or message unit, he may include in his point of departure some grammatical device to link what he is about to say with what was previously said, i.e. textual meaning; and/or include something which communicates on an interpersonal level. But above all, the writer/speaker will provide an experiential point of reference for the clause contents which follow.

10.5.1 STEP 7 – Identify Theme { -topical | -interpersonal | -textual } in each finite clause

Table 10.5: Theme analysis

P#	C#	Theme				Clause
		Textual	Interpersonal	Topical/ Existential	displaced	
1	1		President and Mrs. Bush	I		<c 1>President and Mrs. Bush, I want to say a personal word on behalf of many people.
	2		Thank you, Mr. President,			<c 2> Thank you, Mr. President, for calling this day of prayer and remembrance.
	3			We		<c 3> We needed it at this time.
2	4a			We		<c 4a> We come together today <c 4b> to affirm our conviction [<c 4c> that God cares for us,] <c 4d> whatever our ethnic, religious, or political background may be.
	4d			whatever our ethnic, religious, or political background		
	5a			The Bible		<c 5a> The Bible says <c 5b> that He's the God of all comfort, <c 5c> who comforts us in our troubles.
	5b	that		He		
	5c	who		who		
	6a			No matter how hard	we	<c 6a> No matter how hard we try, <c 6b> words simply cannot express the horror, the shock, and the revulsion [<c 6c> we all feel over [<c 6d> what took place in this nation on Tuesday morning.]]
	6b			words		
	7			September eleven		<c 7> September eleven will go down in our history as a day to remember.
3	8a			Today	we	<c 8a> Today we say to those [<c 8b> who masterminded this cruel plot,] and to those [<c 8c> who carried it out,] <c 8d> that the spirit of this nation will not be defeated by their twisted and diabolical schemes.
	8d	that		the spirit of this nation		
	9a			Someday	those responsible	<c 9a> Someday, those responsible will be brought to justice, <c 9b> as President Bush and our Congress have so forcefully stated.
	9b	as		President Bush and our Congress		
	10a	But		today	we	<c 10a> But today we especially come together in this service <c 10b> to confess our need of God.

Figure 10.1: Rhetorical structure at top (paragraph) level

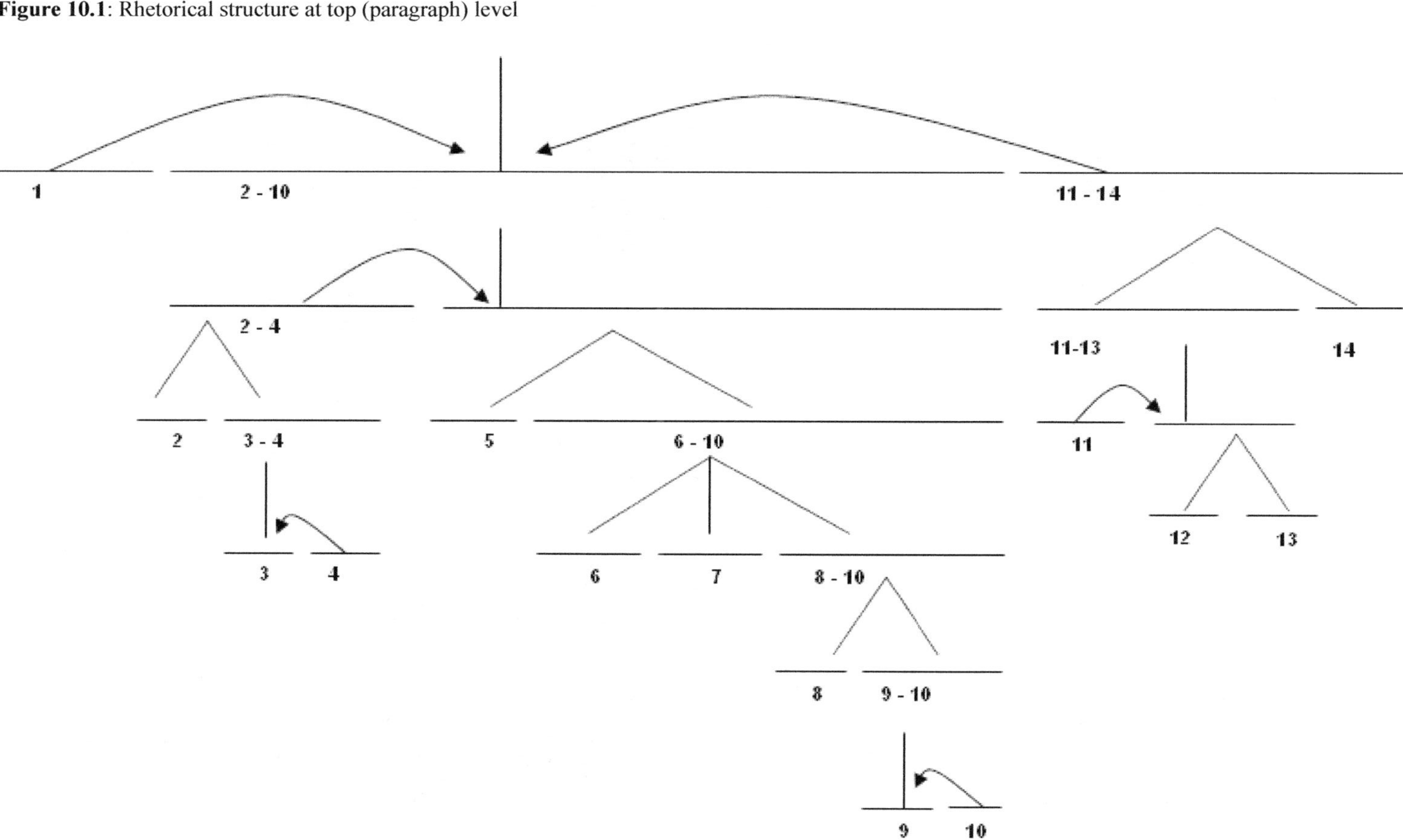

10.6 Motifs in the grammar

This message, like any other, is the outcome of ongoing processes of construing human experience, enacting social relationships, and creating discourse. Choices were made at every turn of phrase with the purpose of creating and imparting meaning on every level.

'September 11 will go down in our history as a day to remember,' states Billy Graham in his address. At the time this address was given by Billy Graham, in the immediate aftermath of the attacks, 'September 11' was only beginning to become cast as the tragic-laden term it is today. Most certainly, September 11 was already etched in the national psyche as a day to remember, but how '*this event*' would be remembered was what mattered. For Billy Graham, this National Prayer and Memorial Service was an occasion for turning a national tragedy into a call for unity and hope.

Coming as it did in the days immediately following the September 11 attacks, and given the prominence of the occasion at which it was spoken, Billy Graham's address at the National Prayer and Memorial Service at the Episcopal National Cathedral on 14 September 2001, can be understood both in terms of how it responded to the immediately preceding events ('the horror, the shock, and the revulsion'), and by how it sought to shape the subsequent public response ('Whether to implode and disintegrate emotionally and spiritually as a people, and a nation, or whether we choose to become stronger …'). In the timeline of events subsequent to 9/11, this occasion and Billy Graham's address preceded President Bush's address to congress and the nation on 20 September.

The text is an instance of meaning which occurs in context of situation. Viewing this address then in the context of this national tragedy, we observe how its lexico-grammatical realization construes a number of motifs, among them: unity in the face of 'a new kind of enemy', and hope 'for the present, … and for the future'.

These motifs are to be found in the grammar. They are realized not just in terms of lexical choice and the repetition of certain terms throughout the text (e.g. the motif of unity is supported by the repeated use of the phrasing 'come together … to V'; and references to 'this nation', 'our nation'), but also grammatically by means of those choices that contribute textual meaning (e.g. the frequency of first person pronouns in thematic position – see Appendix 10.4, *Theme-rheme structure*), interpersonal meaning (i.e. clause type, whether interrogative or declarative), and ideational meaning, including the logical (clause expansion and projection – see Appendix 10.3, *Logical structure*) and the experiential (i.e. process-participant-circumstance: who is doing what to whom – see Appendix 10.2, *Transitivity structure*.

Appendix 10.1

Billy Graham: Address at the Episcopal National Cathedral

<p 1> <c1> President and Mrs. Bush, I want to say a personal word on behalf of many people. <c 2> Thank you, Mr. President, for calling this day of prayer and remembrance. <c 3> We needed it at this time.

<p 2> <c 4a> We come together today <c 4b> to affirm our conviction [<c 4c> that God cares for us,] <c 4d> whatever our ethnic, religious, or political background may be. <c 5a> The Bible says <c 5b> that He's the God of all comfort, <c 5c> who comforts us in our troubles. <c 6a> No matter how hard we try, <c 6b> words simply cannot express the horror, the shock, and the revulsion [<c 6c> we all feel over [<c 6d> what took place in this nation on Tuesday morning.]] <c 7> September eleven will go down in our history as a day to remember.

<p 3> <c 8a> Today we say to those [<c 8b> who masterminded this cruel plot,] and to those [<c 8c> who carried it out,] <c 8d> that the spirit of this nation will not be defeated by their twisted and diabolical schemes. <c 9a> Someday, those responsible will be brought to justice, <c 9b> as President Bush and our Congress have so forcefully stated. <c 10a> But today we especially come together in this service <c 10b> to confess our need of God.

<p 4> <c 11a> We've always needed God from the very beginning of this nation, <c 11b> but today we need Him especially. <c 12> We're facing a new kind of enemy. <c 13> We're involved in a new kind of warfare. <c 14> And we need the help of the Spirit of God. <c 15a> The Bible words are our hope: <c 15b> God is our refuge and strength; an ever present help in trouble. <c 16a> Therefore we will not fear, <c 16b> though the earth give way, <c 16c> and the mountains fall into the heart of the sea.

<p 5> <c 17> But how do we understand something like this? <c 18a> Why does God allow <c 18b>evil like this to take place? <c 19a> Perhaps that is [<c 19b> what you are asking now.] <c 20> You may even be angry at God. <c 21a> I want to assure you <c 21b> that God understands these feelings [<c 21c> that you may have.] <c 22a> We've seen so much on our television, <c 22b> heard on our radio, stories[<c 22c> that bring tears to our eyes, <c 22d> and make us <c 22e> all feel a sense of anger.] <c 23a> But God can be trusted, <c 23b> even when life seems at its darkest.

<p 6> <c 24a> But what are some of the lessons [<c 24b>we can learn]? <c 25> First, we are reminded of the mystery and reality of evil. <c 26a> I've been asked hundreds of times in my life <c 26b> why God allows tragedy

and suffering. <c 27a> I have to confess <c 27b> that I really do not know the answer totally, even to my own satisfaction. <c 28a> I have to accept by faith <c 28b> that God is sovereign, <c 28c> and He's a God of love, and mercy, and compassion in the midst of suffering. <c 29a> The Bible says <c 29b> that God is not the author of evil. <c 30> It speaks of evil as a mystery. <c 31> In 1 Thessalonians 2:7 it talks about the mystery of iniquity. <c 32a> The old testament prophet Jeremiah said <c 32b> 'The heart is deceitful above all things' and beyond cure. <c 33> 'Who can understand it?' <c 34a> He asked that question, <c 34b> 'Who can understand it?' <c 35a> And that's one reason [< 35b> we each need God in our lives].

<p 7> <c 36a> The lesson of this event is not only about the mystery of iniquity and evil, <c 36b> but secondly it's a lesson about our need for each other. <c 37> What an example New York and Washington have been to the world these past few days. <c 38a> None of us will ever forget the pictures of our courageous firefighters and police, <c 38b> many of whom have lost friends and colleagues. <c 38a> Or the hundreds of people attending or standing patiently in line to donate blood. <c 39> A tragedy like this could have torn our country apart. <c 40a> But instead it has united us, <c 40b> and we have become a family. <c 41a> So those perpetrators [<c 41b> who took this on [<c 41c>to tear us apart,]] it has worked the other way – <c 41d> it's back lashed. <c 42> It's backfired. <c 43> We are more united than ever before. <c 44a> I think <c 44b> this was exemplified in a very moving way <c 44c> when the members of our Congress stood shoulder to shoulder the other day <c 44d> and sang 'God Bless America.'

<p 8> <c 45a> Finally, difficult as it may be for us to see right now, <c 45b> this event can give a message of hope – hope for the present, and hope for the future. <c 46> Yes, there is hope. <c 47a> There's hope for the present, <c 47b> because I believe <c 47c> the stage has already been set for a new spirit in our nation. <c 48a>One of the things [<c 48b>we desperately need] is a spiritual renewal in this country. <c 49> We need a spiritual revival in America. <c 50a> And God has told us in His word, time after time, <c 50b> that we are to repent of our sins <c 50c> and return to Him, <c 50d> and He will bless us in a new way. <c 51> But there's also hope for the future because of God's promises. <c 52> As a Christian, I hope not for just this life, but for heaven and the life to come. <c 53a> And many of those people [<c 53b>who died this past week] are in heaven right now. <c 54> And they wouldn't want to come back. <c 55> It's so glorious and so wonderful. <c 56a> And that's the hope for all of us [<c 56b who put our faith in God]. <c 57a> I pray <c 57b> that you will have this hope in your heart.

<p 9> <c 58> This event reminds us of the brevity and the uncertainty of life. <c 59a> We never know <c 59b> when we too will be called into eternity. <c 60a> I doubt <c 60b> if even one those people [<c 60c>who got on those planes, <c 60d> or walked into the World Trade Center or the Pentagon last Tuesday morning] thought <c 60e> it would be the last day of their lives. <c 61> It didn't occur to them. <c 62a> And that's [<c 62b> why each of us needs to face our own spiritual need <c 62c> and commit ourselves to God and His will now.]

<p 10> <c 63> Here in this majestic National Cathedral we see all around us symbols of the cross. <c 64a> For the Christian – <c 65> I'm speaking for the Christian now – <c 64a> the cross tells us <c 64b> that God understands our sin and our suffering. <c 66> For He took upon himself, in the person of Jesus Christ, our sins and our suffering. <c 67a> And from the cross, God declares <c 67b> 'I love you. <c 68a> I know the heart aches, and the sorrows, and the pains that you feel, <c 68b> but I love you.' <c 69a> The story does not end with the cross, <c 69b> for Easter points us beyond the tragedy of the cross to the empty tomb. <c 70a> It tells us <c 70b> that there is hope for eternal life, <c 70c> for Christ has conquered evil, and death, and hell. <c 71> Yes, there's hope.

<p 11> <c 72> I've become an old man now. <c 73> And I've preached all over the world. <c 74a> And the older I get, <c 74b> the more I cling to [<c 74c> that hope that I started with many years ago], <c 74d> and proclaimed it in many languages to many parts of the world. <c 75a> Several years ago at the National Prayer Breakfast here in Washington, Ambassador Andrew Young, <c 75b> who had just gone through the tragic death of his wife, <c 75a> closed his talk with a quote from the old hymn, 'How Firm A Foundation.' <c 76a> We all watched in horror <c 76b> as planes crashed into the steel and glass of the World Trade Center. <c 77a> Those majestic towers, <c 77b> built on solid foundations, <c 77a> were examples of the prosperity and creativity of America. <c 78a> When damaged, <c 78b> those buildings eventually plummeted to the ground, <c 78c> imploding in upon themselves. <c 79> Yet underneath the debris is a foundation [<c 79b> that was not destroyed]. <c 80> Therein lies the truth of that old hymn that Andrew Young quoted: 'How firm a foundation.'

<p 12> <c 81> Yes, our nation has been attacked. <c 82> Buildings destroyed. <c 83> Lives lost. <c 84> But now we have a choice: <c 85a> Whether to implode and disintegrate emotionally and spiritually as a people, and a nation, <c 85b> or, whether we choose to become stronger through all

of the struggle to rebuild on a solid foundation. <c 86a> And I believe <c 86b> that we're in the process of starting to rebuild on that foundation. <c 87> That foundation is our trust in God. <c 88a> That's [<c 88b>what this service is all about.] <c 89a> And in that faith we have the strength [<c 89b> to endure something as difficult and horrendous <c 89c> as what we've experienced this week].

<p 13> <c 90> This has been a terrible week with many tears. <c 91> But also it's been a week of great faith. <c 92> Churches all across the country have called prayer meetings. <c 93a> And today is a day [<c 93b> that they're celebrating not only in this country, but in many parts of the world.] <c 94a> And the words of that familiar hymn [<c 94b>that Andrew Young quoted], it says <c 94c> 'Fear not, <c 94d> I am with thee. <c 95a> Oh be not dismayed <c 95b> for I am thy God <c 95c> and will give thee aid. <c 96a> I'll strengthen thee, <c 96b> help thee, <c 96c> and cause thee to stand upon my righteous, omnipotent hand.'

<p 14> <c 97a> My prayer today is [<c 97b> that we will feel the loving arms of God wrapped around us <c 97c> and will know in our hearts <c 97d> that He will never forsake us <c 97e> as we trust in Him]. <c 98a> We also know <c 98b> that God is going to give wisdom, and courage, and strength to the President, and those around him. <c 99a> And this is going to be a day [<c 99b> that we will remember as a day of victory]. <c 100> May God bless you all.

Appendix 10.2

Transitivity Structure of Billy Graham's Address at the National Prayer and Memorial Service, 14 September 2001.

Para#	Cl#	Transitivity Structure				Clause (Complex)
		Process (type)	Participant(s)		Circumstance(s)	
			X…	Roles		
1	1	want to say (verbal)	I	Sayer	on behalf of many people	<c 1> President and Mrs. Bush, I want to say a personal word on behalf of many people.
			a personal word	Verbiage		
	2	calling (material)	(you)	Actor		<c 2> Thank you, Mr. President, for calling this day of prayer and remembrance.
			this day of prayer and remembrance	Goal		
	3	needed (relational)	we	Possessor	at this time.	<c 3>We needed it at this time.
			it	Possessed		
2	4a	come together (material)	we	Actor	today	<c 4a> We come together today <c 4b> to affirm our conviction [<c 4c> that God cares for us,] <c 4d> whatever our ethnic, religious, or political background may be.
	4b	affirm (mental)	our conviction	Phenomenon		
	4c	cares (mental)	God	Senser	for us	
	4d	be (relational)	whatever	Identifier		
			our ethnic, religious, political background	Identified		
	5a	says (verbal)	The Bible	Sayer		<c 5a> The Bible says <c 5b> that He's the God of all comfort, <c 5c> who comforts us in our troubles.
	5b	is (relational)	He	Identified		
			the God of all comfort	Identifier		
	5c	comforts (material)	who	Actor	in our troubles	
			us	Goal		
	6a	try (material)	we	Actor	hard	<c 6a> No matter how hard we try, <c 6b> words simply cannot express the horror, the shock, and the revulsion [<c 6c> we all feel over [<c 6d> what took place in this nation on
	6b	express (material)	words	Actor	simply	
			the horror, the shock, and the revulsion [<c 6cd>]	Goal		

Transitivity Structure of Billy Graham's Address at the National Prayer and Memorial Service, 14 September 2001.

Para#	Cl#	Transitivity Structure				Clause (Complex)
		Process (type)	Participant(s)		Circumstance(s)	
			X…	Roles		
	6c	feel (mental)	we all	Senser	over [<c 6d>]	Tuesday morning.]]
	6d	took place (material)	what	Affected		
	7	go down (relational)	September eleven	Carrier	in our history	<c 7> September eleven will go down in our history as a day to remember.
			a day to remember	Attribute		
3	8a	say (verbal)	we	Sayer	Today	<c 8a> Today we say to those [<c 8b> who masterminded this cruel plot,] and to those [<c 8c> who carried it out,] <c 8d> that the spirit of this nation will not be defeated by their twisted and diabolical schemes.
			to those [<c 8b>] and to those [<c 8c>]	Receiver		
			<c 8d>	Verbiage		
	8b	masterminded (material)	who	Actor		
			this cruel plot	Goal		
	8c	carried X out (material)	who	Actor		
			it	Goal		
	8d	defeated (material)	the spirit of this nation	Goal		
			by their twisted and diabolical schemes	Actor		
	9a	brought (material)	those responsible	Goal	Someday	<c 9a> Someday, those responsible will be brought to justice, <c 9b> as President Bush and our Congress have so forcefully stated.
	9b	stated (verbal)	President Bush and our Congress	Sayer		
	10a	come together (material)	we	Actor	today … in this service	<c 10a> But today we especially come together in this service <c 10b> to confess our need of God.
	10b	confess (verbal)	we	Sayer		
			our need of God	Verbiage		
4	11a	needed (relational)	we	Possessor	from the very beginning of this nation	<c 11a> We've always needed God from the very beginning of this nation, <c 11b> but today we need Him especially.
			God	Possessed		

Transitivity Structure of Billy Graham's Address at the National Prayer and Memorial Service, 14 September 2001.

Para#	Cl#	Transitivity Structure				Clause (Complex)
		Process (type)	Participant(s)		Circumstance(s)	
			X…	Roles		
	11b	need (relational)	we	Possessor	today	
			Him	Possessed		
	12	facing (material)	we	Actor		<c 12> We're facing a new kind of enemy.
			a new kind of enemy	Goal		
	13	involved (material)	we	Goal		<c 13> We're involved in a new kind of warfare.
			in a new kind of warfare	Range		
	14	need (relational)	we	Possessor		<c 14> And we need the help of the Spirit of God.
			the help of the Spirit of God	Possessed		
	15a	are (relational)	The Bible words	Carrier		<c 15a> The Bible words are our hope: <c 15b> God is our refuge and strength; an ever present help in trouble.
			our hope	Attribute		
	15b	is (relational)	God	Carrier		
			our refuge and strength; an ever present help in trouble	Attribute		
	16a	fear (mental)	we	Senser		<c 16a> Therefore we will not fear <c 16b> though the earth give way, <c 16c> and the mountains fall into the heart of the sea.
	16b	give way (material)	the earth	Actor		
	16c	fall (material)	the mountains	Actor	into the heart of the sea	
5	17	understand (mental)	we	Senser		<c 17> But how do we understand something like this?
			something like this	Phenomenon		
	18a	allow (material)	God	Actor		<c 18a> Why does God allow evil like this <c 18b> to take place?
			evil like this <c 18b>	Goal		
	18b	take place (material)	evil like this	Actor		
	19a	is (relational)	that	Identified	now	<c 19> Perhaps that is [<c 19b> what you are asking now.]
			[<c 19b>]	Identifier		

Transitivity Structure of Billy Graham's Address at the National Prayer and Memorial Service, 14 September 2001.

Para#	Cl#	Transitivity Structure				Clause (Complex)
		Process (type)	Participant(s)		Circumstance(s)	
			X…	Roles		
	19b	asking (verbal)	you	Sayer		
			what	Verbiage		
	20	be (relational)	you	Carrier	with God	<c 20> You may even be angry with God.
			angry	Attribute		
	21a	want to assure (verbal)	I	Sayer		<c 21a> I want to assure you <c 21b> that God understands these feelings [<c 21c> that you may have.]
			you	Receiver		
			<c 21b>	Verbiage		
	21b	understands (mental)	God	Senser		
			these feelings [<c 21c>]	Phenomenon		
	21c	have (relational: possession)	you	Possessor		
			these feeling	Possessed		
	22a	seen (mental)	we	Senser	on our television	<c 22a> We've seen so much on our television, <c 22b> heard on our radio, stories [<c 22c> that bring tears to our eyes <c 22d> and make <c 22e> us all feel a sense of anger.]
			so much	Phenomenon		
	22b	heard (mental)	stories that bring tears to our eyes	Phenomenon	on our radio	
	22c	bring (material)	stories	Actor		
			tears	Goal		
	22d	make (material)	us	Goal		
	22e	feel (mental)	us	Senser		
			a sense of anger	Phenomenon		
	23a	trusted (material)	God	Goal		<c 23a> But God can be trusted <c 23b> even when life seems at its darkest.
	23b	seems (relational)	life	Carrier		
			at its hardest	Attribute		

Transitivity Structure of Billy Graham's Address at the National Prayer and Memorial Service, 14 September 2001.

Para#	Cl#	Transitivity Structure				Clause (Complex)
		Process (type)	Participant(s)		Circumstance(s)	
			X...	Roles		
6	24a	are (relational)	what	Identifier		<c 24a> But what are some of the lessons [<c 24b> we can learn?]
			some of the lessons [<c 24b>]	Identified		
	24b	learn (mental)	we	Senser		
	25	reminded (material)	we	Goal		<c 25> First, we are reminded of the mystery and reality of evil.
			of the mystery and reality of evil	Range		
	26a	asked (material)	I	Goal	hundreds of times in my life	<c 26a> I've been asked hundreds of times in my life <c 26b> why God allows tragedy and suffering.
	26b	allows (material)	God	Actor		
			tragedy and suffering	Goal		
	27a	confess (verbal)	I	Sayer		<c 27a> I have to confess <c 27b> that I really do not know the answer totally, even to my own satisfaction.
			<c 27b>	Verbiage		
	27b	know (mental)	I	Senser	totally, to my own satisfaction	
			the answer	Phenomenon		
	28a	accept (mental)	I	Senser	by faith	<c 28a> I have to accept by faith <c 28b> that God is sovereign, <c 28c> and He's a God of love, and mercy, and compassion in the midst of suffering.
			<c 28bc>	Phenomenon		
	28b	is (relational)	God	Carrier		
			sovereign	Attribute		
	28c	is (relational)	He	Carrier		
			a God of love, and mercy, and compassion in the midst of suffering.	Attribute		
	29a	says (verbal)	The Bible	Sayer		<c 29a> The Bible says <c 29b> that God is not the author of evil.
			<c 29b>	Verbiage		

Transitivity Structure of Billy Graham's Address at the National Prayer and Memorial Service, 14 September 2001.

Para#	Cl#	Transitivity Structure				Clause (Complex)
		Process (type)	Participant(s)		Circumstance(s)	
			X…	Roles		
	29b	is (relational)	God	Identified		
			the author of evil	Identifier		
	30	speaks (material)	It	Actor		<c 30> It speaks of evil as a mystery.
			of evil as a mystery	Range		
	31	talks (material)	it	Actor	In 1 Thessalonians 2:7	<c 31> In 1 Thessalonians 2:7 it talks about the mystery of iniquity.
			about the mystery of iniquity	Range		
	32a	said (verbal)	The old testament prophet Jeremiah	Sayer		<c 32a> The old testament prophet Jeremiah said <c 32b> 'The heart is deceitful above all things' and beyond cure.
			<c 32b>	Verbiage		
	32b	is (relational)	The heart	Carrier		
			deceitful above all things and beyond cure.	Attribute		
	33	understand (mental)	who	Senser		<c 33> 'Who can understand it?'
			it	Phenomenon		
	34a	asked (material)	He	Actor		<c 34a> He asked that question, <c 34b> 'Who can understand it?'
			that question	Goal		
	34b	understand (mental)	Who	Senser		
			it	Phenomenon		
	35a	is (relational)	that	Identifier		<c 35a> And that's one reason [<c 35b> we each need God in our lives]
			one reason [<c 35b>]	Identified		
	35b	need (relational)	we each	Possessor	in our lives	
			God	Possessed		

Transitivity Structure of Billy Graham's Address at the National Prayer and Memorial Service, 14 September 2001.

Para#	Cl#	Transitivity Structure				Clause (Complex)
		Process (type)	Participant(s)		Circumstance(s)	
			X…	Roles		
7	36a	is (relational)	The lesson of this event	Carrier		<c 36a> The lesson of this event is not only about the mystery of iniquity and evil, <c 36b> but secondly it's a lesson about our need for each other.
			not only about the mystery of iniquity and evil	Attribute		
	36b	is (relational)	it	Carrier		
			a lesson about our need for each other	Attribute		
	37	been (relational)	What an example	Attribute	to the world these past few days	<c 37> What an example New York and Washington have been to the world these past few days.
			New York and Washington	Carrier		
	38a	forget (mental)	None of us	Senser		<c 38a> None of us will ever forget the pictures of our courageous firefighters and police, <c 38b> many of whom have lost friends and colleagues. <c 38a (cont.)> Or the hundreds of people [<c 38c> attending or standing patiently in line to donate blood.]
			the pictures of our courageous fire fighters and police … Or the hundreds of people [<c 38c>]	Phenomenon		
	38b	lost (material)	many of whom	Actor		
			friends and colleagues	Goal		
	38c	attending or standing (behavioural)	the hundreds of people	Behaver		
	39	torn (material)	A tragedy like this	Actor	apart	<c 39> A tragedy like this could have torn our country apart.
			our country	Goal		
	40a	united (material)	it	Actor		<c 40a> But instead it has united us, <c 4b> and we have become a family.
			us	Goal		
	40b	become (relational)	we	Carrier		
			a family	Attribute		

Transitivity Structure of Billy Graham's Address at the National Prayer and Memorial Service, 14 September 2001.

Para#	Cl#	Transitivity Structure				Clause (Complex)
		Process (type)	Participant(s)		Circumstance(s)	
			X…	Roles		
	41a	worked (material)	it	Affected	the other way	<c 41a> So those perpetrators [<c 41b>who took this on [<c 41c> to tear us apart,]] it has worked the other way -- <c 41d> it's backlashed.
	41b	took X on (material)	who	Actor		
			this	Goal		
	41c	tear (material)	us	Goal		
	41d	backlashed (material)	it	Affected		
	42	backfired (material)	it	Affected		<c 42> It's backfired.
	43	are (relational)	we	Carrier	than ever before	<c 43> We are more united than ever before.
			united	Attribute		
	44a	think (mental)	I	Senser		<c 44a> I think <c 44b> this was exemplified in a very moving way <c 44c> when the members of our Congress stood shoulder to shoulder the other day <c 44d> and sang 'God Bless America.'
			<c44b-d>	Phenomenon		
		exemplified (material)	This	Goal	in a very moving way <c44 c-d>	
	44c	stood (behavioural)	the members of our Congress	Behaver	shoulder to shoulder the other day	
	44d	sang (material)	'God Bless America'	Goal		
8	45a	be (relational)	it (= for us to see)	Carrier	right now	<c 45a> Finally, difficult as it may be for us to see right now, <c 45b> this event can give a message of hope -- hope for the present, and hope for the future.
			difficult	Attribute		
	45b	give (material)	this event	Actor		
			a message of hope…	Goal		
	46	is (existential)	there			<c 46> Yes, there is hope.
			hope	Existent		
	47a	is (existential)	there		for the present	<c 47a> There's hope for the present, <c 47b> because I believe <c 47c> the stage has already been set for a new spirit in our nation.
			hope	Existent		

Transitivity Structure of Billy Graham's Address at the National Prayer and Memorial Service, 14 September 2001.

Para#	Cl#	Transitivity Structure				Clause (Complex)
		Process (type)	Participant(s)		Circumstance(s)	
			X…	Roles		
	47b	believe (mental)	I	Senser		
	47c	set (material)	the stage	Goal	for a new spirit in our nation	
	48a	is (relational)	One of the things [<c 48b>]	Identified		<c 48a>One of the things [<c 48b> we desperately need] is a spiritual renewal in this country.
			a spiritual renewal in this country	Identifier		
	48b	need (relational)	we	Possessor		
	49	need (relational)	We	Possessor	in America	<c 49> We need a spiritual revival in America.
			a spiritual revival	Possessed		
	50a	told (verbal)	God	Sayer	in His word, time after time	<c 50a> And God has told us in His word, time after time, <c 5b> that we are to repent of our sins <c 5c> and return to Him, <c 5d> and He will bless us in a new way.
			us	Receiver		
			<c 50b-d>	Verbiage		
	50b	repent (material)	we	Actor	of our sins	
	50c	return (material)	(we)	Actor	to Him	
	50d	bless (material)	He	Actor	in a new way	
			us	Goal		
	51	is (existential)	There		for the future because of God's promises	<c 51> But there's also hope for the future because of God's promises.
			hope	Existent		
	52	hope (mental)	I	Senser	As a Christian…	<c 52> As a Christian, I hope not for just this life, but for heaven and the life to come.
			not for just this life, but for heaven and the life to come.	Phenomenon		
	53a	are (relational)	many of those people [<c 54b>]	Carrier	right now	<c 53a> And many of those people [<c 53b> who died this past week] are in heaven right now.
			in heaven	Circumstance		
	53b	died (behavioural)	those people	Behaver		

Transitivity Structure of Billy Graham's Address at the National Prayer and Memorial Service, 14 September 2001.

Para#	Cl#	Transitivity Structure				Clause (Complex)
		Process (type)	Participant(s)		Circumstance(s)	
			X…	Roles		
	54	want to come back (material)	they	Actor		<c 54> And they wouldn't want to come back.
	55	is (relational)	it	Carrier		<c 55> It's so glorious and so wonderful.
			so glorious and so wonderful	Attribute		
	56a	is (relational)	that	Identified	for all of us who put our faith in God	<c 56a> And that's the hope for all of us [<c 56b> who put our faith in God.]
			the hope	Identifier		
	56b	put (material)	who	Actor	in God	
			our faith	Goal		
	57a	pray (verbal)	I	Sayer		<c 57a> I pray <c 57b> that you will have this hope in your heart
			<c 57b>	Verbiage		
	57b	have (relational)	you	Possessor	in your heart	
			this hope	Possessed		
9	58	reminds (mental)	This event	Initiator		<c 58> This event reminds us of the brevity and the uncertainty of life.
			us	Senser		
			of the brevity and the uncertainty of life	Phenomenon		
	59a	know (mental)	we	Senser		<c 59a> We never know <c 59b> when we too will be called into eternity.
			<c 59b>	Phenomenon		
	59b	called (material)	we	Goal	into eternity	
	60a	doubt (mental)	I	Senser		<c 60a> I doubt <c 60b> if even one of those people [<c 60c> who got on those planes, <c 60d>or walked into the World Trade Center or the Pentagon last Tuesday morning] thought <c 60e> it would be the last day of their lives.
			<c 60b>	Phenomenon		
	60b	thought (mental)	one of those people [<c 60c>]	Senser		
			<c 60d>	Phenomenon		
	60c	got on (material)	who	Actor		

Transitivity Structure of Billy Graham's Address at the National Prayer and Memorial Service, 14 September 2001.

Para#	Cl#	Transitivity Structure				Clause (Complex)
		Process (type)	Participant(s)		Circumstance(s)	
			X…	Roles		
	60d	walked (material)				
	60e	would be (relational)	it	Identified		
			the last day of their lives	Identifier		
	61	occur to (mental)	it	Phenomenon		<c 61> It didn't occur to them.
			them	Senser		
	62a	is (relational)	that	Identified		<c 62a> And that's [<c 62b> why each of us needs to face our own spiritual need <c 62c> and commit ourselves to God and His will now.]
			<c 62b>	Identifier		
	62b	need to face (material)	each of us	Actor/Senser		
			our own spiritual need and commit ourselves to God and His will now	Goal		
	62c	commit (verbal)	ourselves	Sayer		
10	63	see (mental)	we	Senser	Here in this majestic National Cathedral… all around us…	<c 63> Here in this majestic National Cathedral we see all around us symbols of the cross.
			symbols of the cross	Phenomenon		
	64a	tells (verbal)	the cross	Sayer	For the Christian	<c 64a> For the Christian -- <c 65> I'm speaking for the Christian now -- <c 64a> the cross tells us <c 64b> that God understands our sin and our suffering.
			us	Receiver		
			<c 64b>	Verbiage		
	64b	understands (mental)	God	Senser		
			our sin and our suffering	Phenomenon		
	65	speaking (material)	I	Actor	for the Christian	<c 65> I'm speaking for the Christian now --
	66	took (material)	he	Actor	upon himself, in the person of Jesus Christ	<c 66> For He took upon himself, in the person of Jesus Christ, our sins and our suffering.
			our sins and our suffering	Goal		
	67a	declares (verbal)	God	Sayer	from the cross	<c 67a> And from the cross, God declares <c 67b> 'I love you.
			<c 67b>	Verbiage		

Transitivity Structure of Billy Graham's Address at the National Prayer and Memorial Service, 14 September 2001.

Para#	Cl#	Transitivity Structure				Clause (Complex)
		Process (type)	Participant(s)		Circumstance(s)	
			X…	Roles		
	67b	love (mental)	I	Senser		
			you	Phenomenon		
	68a	know (mental)	I	Senser		<c 68a> I know the heart aches, and the sorrows, and the pains that you feel,
			the heart aches, and the sorrows, and the pains that you feel	Phenomenon		
	68b	love (mental)	I	Senser		<c 68b> but I love you.'
			you	Phenomenon		
	69a	end (material)	The story	Actor	with the cross	<c 69a> The story does not end with the cross, <c 69b> for Easter points us beyond the tragedy of the cross to the empty tomb.
	69b	points (material)	Easter	Actor	beyond the tragedy of the cross to the empty tomb	
			us	Goal		
	70a	tells (verbal)	It	Sayer		<c 70a> It tells us <c 70b> that there is hope for eternal life, <c 70c> for Christ has conquered evil, and death, and hell.
			us	Receiver		
			<c 70b>	Verbiage		
	70b	is (existential)	there		for eternal life	
			hope	Existent		
	70c	conquered (material)	Christ	Actor		
			evil, and death, and hell.	Goal		
	71	is (existential)	there			<c 71> Yes, there's hope.
			hope	Existent		
11	72	become (relational)	I	Carrier	now	<c 72> I've become an old man now.
			an old man	Attribute		
	73	preached (material)	I	Actor	all over the world	<c 73> And I've preached all over the world.

Transitivity Structure of Billy Graham's Address at the National Prayer and Memorial Service, 14 September 2001.

Para#	Cl#	Transitivity Structure				Clause (Complex)
		Process (type)	Participant(s)		Circumstance(s)	
			X…	Roles		
	74a	get (relational)	I	Carrier		<c 74a> And the older I get, <c 74b>the more I cling to that hope [<c 74c> that I started with many years ago,] <c 74d>and proclaimed it in many languages to many parts of the world.
			older	Attribute		
	74b	cling to (material)	I	Actor		
			that hope [< c 74c>]	Goal		
	74c	started (material)	I	Actor		
			with	Accompaniment		
	74d	proclaimed (material)	it	Goal	in many languages to many parts of the world	
	75a	closed (material)	Ambassador Andrew Young	Actor	Several years ago at the National Prayer Breakfast here in Washington, … with a quote from the old hymn, 'How firm a foundation'	<c 75a> Several years ago at the National Prayer Breakfast here in Washington, Ambassador Andrew Young, <c 75b> who had just gone through the tragic death of his wife, <c 75a> closed his talk with a quote from the old hymn, 'How Firm A Foundation.'
			his talk	Goal		
	75b	gone through (mental)	who	Senser		
			the death of his wife	Phenomenon		
	76a	watched (material)	We all	Actor	in horror	<c 76a> We all watched in horror <c 76b> as planes crashed into the steel and glass of the World Trade Center.
	76b	crashed (material)	planes	Actor	into the steel and glass of the World Trade Center	
	77a	were (relational)	Those majestic towers	Identified		<c 77a> Those majestic towers, <c 77b> built on solid foundations, <c 77a> were examples of the prosperity and creativity of America.
			examples of the prosperity and creativity of America	Identifier		
	77b	built (material)	(Those majestic towers)	Affected	on solid foundations	
	78a	damaged (material)	(those buildings)	Affected		<c 78a> When damaged, <c 78b> those buildings eventually plummeted to the ground, <c 78c> imploding in upon themselves.
	78b	plummeted (material)	those buildings	Affected	to the ground	
	78c	imploding (material)	(those buildings)	Affected	in upon themselves	

Transitivity Structure of Billy Graham's Address at the National Prayer and Memorial Service, 14 September 2001.

Para#	Cl#	Transitivity Structure				Clause (Complex)
		Process (type)	Participant(s)		Circumstance(s)	
			X…	Roles		
	79a	is (relational)	a foundation [<c 79b>]	Carrier	underneath the debris	<c 79> Yet underneath the debris is a foundation [<c 79b> that was not destroyed.]
	79b	destroyed (material)				
	80	lies (relational)	the truth of that old hymn…	Carrier	Therein	<c 80>Therein lies the truth of that old hymn that Andrew Young quoted: 'How firm a foundation.'
12	81	attacked (material)	our nation	Goal		<c 81> Yes, our nation has been attacked.
	82	destroyed (material)	Buildings	Goal		<c 82> Buildings destroyed
	83	lost (material)	Lives	Goal		<c 83> Lives lost.
	84	have (relational)	we	Possessor	now	<c 84> But now we have a choice:
			a choice	Possessed		
	85a	implode and disintegrate (material)				<c 85a> Whether to implode and disintegrate emotionally and spiritually as a people, and a nation, <c 85b> or, whether we choose to become stronger through all of the struggle to rebuild on a solid foundation.
	85b	choose (material)	we	Actor, Carrier	through all of the struggle to rebuild on a solid foundation	
		to become (relational)	stronger	Attribute		
	86a	believe (mental)	I	Senser		<c 86a> And I believe <c 86b> that we're in the process [<c 86c> of starting <c 86d> to rebuild on that foundation.]
			<c 86b>	Phenomenon		
	86b	are (relational)	we	Carrier	in the process of starting to rebuild	
	86c	starting (material)				
	86d	rebuild (material)			on that foundation.	
	87	is (relational)	That foundation	Identified		<c 87> That foundation is our trust in God.
			our trust in God	Identifier		

Transitivity Structure of Billy Graham's Address at the National Prayer and Memorial Service, 14 September 2001.

Para#	Cl#	Transitivity Structure				Clause (Complex)
		Process (type)	Participant(s)		Circumstance(s)	
			X…	Roles		
	88a	is (relational)	That	Identified		<c 88a> That's [<c 88b> what this service is all about.]
			<c 88b>	Identifier		
	88b	is (relational)	all about what	Attribute		
			this service	Carrier		
	89a	have (relational)	we	Possessor	in that faith	<c 89a> And in that faith we have the strength [<c 89b> to endure something as difficult and horrendous <c 89c>as what we've experienced this week.]
			the strength [<c 89b-c>]	Possessed		
	89b	endure (mental)	something	Phenomenon	as difficult and horrendous	
	89c	experienced (mental)	we	Senser	this week	
13	90	been (relational)	This	Carrier	with many tears	<c 90> This has been a terrible week with many tears.
			a terrible week	Attribute		
	91	been (relational)	it	Carrier		<c 91> But also it's been a week of great faith..
			a week of great faith	Attribute		
	92	called (material)	Churches all across the country	Actor		<c 92> Churches all across the country have called prayer meetings.
			prayer meetings	Goal		
	93a	is (relational)	today	Carrier		<c 93a> And today is a day [<c 93b> that they're celebrating not only in this country, but in many parts of the world.
			a day [<c 93b>]	Attribute		
	93b	celebrating (material)	they	Actor	not only in this country, but in many parts of the world	
	94a	says (verbal)	it (familiar hymn that Andrew Young quoted)	Sayer		<c 94a> And the words of that familiar hymn [<c 94b> that Andrew Young quoted,] it says <c 94c> 'Fear not, <c 94d> I am with thee
			<c 94b-96c>	Verbiage		
	94b	quoted (material)	Andrew Young	Actor		
	94c	Fear (mental)				

Transitivity Structure of Billy Graham's Address at the National Prayer and Memorial Service, 14 September 2001.

Para#	Cl#	Transitivity Structure				Clause (Complex)
		Process (type)	Participant(s)		Circumstance(s)	
			X…	Roles		
	94d	am (relational)	I	Carrier	with thee	
	95a	be (relational)	dismayed	Attribute		<c 95a> Oh be not dismayed <c 95b> for I am thy God <c 95c> and will give thee aid.
	95b	am (relational)	I	Identified		
			thy God	Identifier		
	95c	give (material)	(I)	Actor		
			thee	Recipient		
			aid	Goal		
	96a	strengthen (material)	I	Actor		<c 96a> I'll strengthen thee, <c 96b> help thee, <c 96c> and cause thee to stand upon my righteous, omnipotent hand.'
			thee	Goal		
	96b	help (material)	(I)	Actor		
			thee	Goal		
	96c	cause to stand (material)	(I)	Actor	upon my righteous, omnipotent hand	
			thee	Actor, Behaver		
14	97a	is (relational)	My prayer	Identified		<c 97a> My prayer today is [<c 97b>] that we will feel the loving arms of God wrapped around us <c 97c> and will know in our hearts <c 97d> that He will never forsake us <c 97e> as we trust in Him.]
			[<c 97b-e>]	Identifier		
	97b	feel (mental)	we	Senser		
			the loving arms of God wrapped around us	Phenomenon		
	97c	know (mental)	(we)	Senser	in our hearts	
			<c 97cd>	Phenomenon		
	97d	forsake (material)	He	Actor		
			us	Goal		
	97e	trust (material)	we	Actor		
			Him	Goal		

Transitivity Structure of Billy Graham's Address at the National Prayer and Memorial Service, 14 September 2001.

Para#	Cl#	Transitivity Structure				Clause (Complex)
		Process (type)	Participant(s)		Circumstance(s)	
			X…	Roles		
	98a	know (mental)	We	Senser		<c 98a> We also know <c 98b> that God is going to give wisdom, and courage, and strength to the President, and those around him.
			<c 98b>	Phenomenon		
	98b	give (material)	God	Actor		
			wisdom, and courage and strength	Goal		
			to the President, and those around him	Recipient		
	99a	be (relational)	this	Carrier		<c 99a> And this is going to be a day [<c 99b> that we will remember as a day of victory.]
			a day…	Attribute		
	99b	remember (mental)	we	Senser		
			as a day of victory	Phenomenon		
	100	bless (material)	God	Actor		<c 100> May God bless you all.
			you all	Goal		

Appendix 10.3

Logical structure of Billy Graham's Address at the National Prayer and Memorial Service, 14 September 2001.

Paragraph	Simple clause	Clause complex											
		Paratactic				Hypotactic							
		Expansion			Projection	Expansion						Projection	
		Elaboration	Extension	Enhancement		Elaboration		Extension		Enhancement			
						α	β	α	β	α	β	α	β
1	1												
	2												
	3												
2	4					4a-c	4d			4a	4b[c]		
	5					5b	5c					5a	5b,c
	6									6b[c[d]]	6a		
	7												
3	8											8a[b][c]	8d
	9									9a	9b		
	10									10a	10b		
4	11			11a + 11b									
	12												
	13												
	14												
	15	15a = 15b											
	16		16b + 16c	16a x 16bc									
5	17												
	18					18a	18b						
	19												
	20												
	21											21a	21b[c]
	22		22a + 22b[cde]										
	23									23a	23b		
6	24a[b]												
	25												
	26				26a '26b								

Logical structure of Billy Graham's Address at the National Prayer and Memorial Service, 14 September 2001.

Paragraph	Simple clause	Clause complex											
		Paratactic				Hypotactic							
		Expansion			Projection	Expansion						Projection	
		Elaboration	Extension	Enhancement		Elaboration		Extension		Enhancement			
						α	β	α	β	α	β	α	β
	27											27a	27b
	28		28b + 28c									28a	28b,c
	29											29a	29b
	30												
	31												
	32											32a	32b
	33												
	34				34a '34b								
	35a[b]												
7	36		36a + 36b										
	37												
	38					38a	38b						
	39												
	40		40a + 40b										
	41	41a[b[c]] = 41d											
	42												
	43												
	44		44c + 44d							44b	44c,d	44a	44b-d
8	45									45b	45a		
	46												
	47									47a	47b,c	47b	47c
	48a[b]												
	49												
	50		50b + 50c 50b,c + 50d									50a	50b-d
	51												
	52												
	53a[b]												
	54												

Logical structure of Billy Graham's Address at the National Prayer and Memorial Service, 14 September 2001.

Paragraph	Simple clause	Clause complex											
		Paratactic				Hypotactic							
		Expansion			Projection	Expansion						Projection	
		Elaboration	Extension	Enhancement		Elaboration		Extension		Enhancement			
						α	β	α	β	α	β	α	β
	55												
	56												
	57											57a	57b
9	58												
	59											59a	59b
	60											60a	60b[cd]
												60b[cd]	60e
	61												
	62a[bc]												
10	63												
	64											64a	64b
	65												
	66												
	67				67a '67b								
	68			68a x 68b									
	69									69a	69b		
	70									70b	70c	70a	70b,c
	71												
11	72												
	73												
	74		74a[b] + 74c										
	75					75a	75b						
	76									76a	76b		
	77					77a	77b						
	78					78b	78c			78b,c	78a		
	79a[b]												
	80												
12	81												

Logical structure of Billy Graham's Address at the National Prayer and Memorial Service, 14 September 2001.

Paragraph	Simple clause	Clause complex											
		Paratactic				Hypotactic							
		Expansion			Projection	Expansion						Projection	
		Elaboration	Extension	Enhancement		Elaboration		Extension		Enhancement			
						α	β	α	β	α	β	α	β
	82												
	83												
	84												
	85		85a + 85b										
	86											86a	86b
	87												
	88a[b]												
	89a[bc]												
13	90												
	91												
	92												
	93a[b]												
	94			94c x 94d	94a[b] '94c,d								
	95		95b + 95c							95a	95bc		
	96		96a + 96b + 96c										
14	97a[b-d]												
	98											98a	98b
	99a[b]												
	100												

Appendix 10.4

Theme-rheme structure of
Billy Graham's Address at the National Prayer and Memorial Service, 14 September 2001.

Sent#	Cl#	Theme				Clause
		Textual	Inter-personal	Topical/ Existential	displaced	
1	1		President and Mrs. Bush	I		<c 1>President and Mrs. Bush, I want to say a personal word on behalf of many people.
2	2		Thank you, Mr. President,			<c 2> Thank you, Mr. President, for calling this day of prayer and remembrance.
3	3			We		<c 3> We needed it at this time.
4	4a			We		<c 4a> We come together today <c 4b> to affirm our conviction [<c 4c> that God cares for us,] <c 4d> whatever our ethnic, religious, or political background may be.
	4d			whatever our ethnic, religious, or political background		
5	5a			The Bible		<c 5a> The Bible says <c 5b> that He's the God of all comfort, <c 5c> who comforts us in our troubles.
	5b	that		He		
	5c	who		who		
6	6a			No matter how hard	we	<c 6a> No matter how hard we try, <c 6b> words simply cannot express the horror, the shock, and the revulsion [<c 6c> we all feel over [<c 6d> what took place in this nation on Tuesday morning.]]
	6b			words		
7	7			September eleven		<c 7> September eleven will go down in our history as a day to remember.
8	8a			Today	we	<c 8a> Today we say to those [<c 8b> who masterminded this cruel plot,] and to those [<c 8c> who carried it out,] <c 8d> that the spirit of this nation will not be defeated by their twisted and diabolical schemes.
	8d	that		the spirit of this nation		
9	9a			Someday	those responsible	<c 9a> Someday, those responsible will be brought to justice, <c 9b> as President Bush and our Congress have so forcefully stated.
	9b	as		President Bush and our Congress		
10	10a	But		today	we	<c 10a> But today we especially come together in this service <c 10b> to confess our need of God.
	10b					

Theme-rheme structure of
Billy Graham's Address at the National Prayer and Memorial Service, 14 September 2001.

Sent#	Cl#	Theme				Clause
		Textual	Inter-personal	Topical/ Existential	displaced	
11	11a			We		<c 11a> We've always needed God from the very beginning of this nation, <c 11b> but today we need Him especially.
	11b	but		today	we	
12	12			We		<c 12> We're facing a new kind of enemy.
13	13			We		<c 13> We're involved in a new kind of warfare.
14	14	And		We		<c 14> And we need the help of the Spirit of God.
15	15a			The Bible words		<c 15a> The Bible words are our hope: <c 15b> God is our refuge and strength; an ever present help in trouble.
	15b			God		
16	16a	Therefore			we	<c 16a> Therefore we will not fear, <c 16b> though the earth give way, <c 16c> and the mountains fall into the heart of the sea.
	16b	though		the earth		
	16c	and		the mountains		
17	17	But	how do	We		<c 17> But how do we understand something like this?
18	18		Why does	God		<c 18a> Why does God allow <c 18b> evil like this to take place?
19	19		Perhaps	That		<c 19> Perhaps that is [<c 19b> what you are asking now.]
20	20			You		<c 20> You may even be angry at God.
21	21a			I		<c 21a> I want to assure you <c 21b> that God understands these feelings [<c 21b> that you may have.]
	21b	that		God		
22	22a			We		<c 22a> We've seen so much on our television, <c 22b> heard on our radio, stories [<c 22c> that bring tears to our eyes, <c 22d> and make <c 22e> us all feel a sense of anger.]
	22b					
23	23a	But		God		<c 23a> But God can be trusted, <c 23b> even when life seems at its darkest.
	23b	even when		Life		
24	24	But	what are	some of the lessons		<c 24a> But what are some of the lessons [<c 24b> we can learn?]
25	25	First		we		<c 25> First, we are reminded of the mystery and reality of evil.
26	26a			I		<c 26a> I've been asked hundreds of times in my life <c 26b> why God allows tragedy and suffering.
	26b		why	God		
27	27a			I		<c 27a> I have to confess <c 27b>

Theme-rheme structure of
Billy Graham's Address at the National Prayer and Memorial Service, 14 September 2001.

Sent#	Cl#	Theme				Clause
		Textual	Inter-personal	Topical/ Existential	displaced	
	27b	that		I		that I really do not know the answer totally, even to my own satisfaction.
28	28a			I		<c 28a> I have to accept by faith <c 28b> that God is sovereign, <c 28c> and He's a God of love, and mercy, and compassion in the midst of suffering.
	28b	that		God		
	28c	and		He		
29	29a			The Bible		<c 29a> The Bible says <c 29b> that God is not the author of evil.
	29b	that		God		
30	30			It		<c 30> It speaks of evil as a mystery.
31	31			In 1 Thessalonians 2:7	it	<c 31> In 1 Thessalonians 2:7 it talks about the mystery of iniquity.
32	32a			The old testament prophet Jeremiah		<c 32a> The old testament prophet Jeremiah said <c 32b> 'The heart is deceitful above all things' and beyond cure.
	32b			The heart		
33	33		Who can			<c 33> 'Who can understand it?'
34	34a			He		<c 34a> He asked that question, <c 34b> 'Who can understand it?'
	34b		Who can			
35	35	And		that		<c 35a> And that's one reason [<c 35b> we each need God in our lives.]
36	36a			The lesson of this event		<c 36a> The lesson of this event is not only about the mystery of iniquity and evil, <c 36b> but secondly it's a lesson about our need for each other.
	36b	but, secondly		it		
37				What an example		<c 37> What an example New York and Washington have been to the world these past few days.
38	38a			None of us		<c 38a> None of us will ever forget the pictures of our courageous firefighters and police, <c 38b> many of whom have lost friends and colleagues. <c 38a (cont.)> Or the hundreds of people [<c 38c> attending or standing patiently in line to donate blood.]
	38b			many of whom		
39	39			A tragedy like this		<c 39> A tragedy like this could have torn our country apart.
40	40a	But instead		it		<c 40a> But instead it has united us, <c 40b> and we have become a family.
	40b	and		we		

Theme-rheme structure of
Billy Graham's Address at the National Prayer and Memorial Service, 14 September 2001.

Sent#	Cl#	Theme				Clause
		Textual	Inter-personal	Topical/ Existential	displaced	
41	41a	So		those perpetrators who took this on to tear us apart,	it	<c 41a> So those perpetrators [<c 41b>who took this on [<c 41c> to tear us apart,]] it has worked the other way --
	41b			it		<c 41d> it's backlashed.
42	42			It		<c 42> It's backfired.
43	43			We		<c 43> We are more united than ever before.
44	44a			I		<c 44a> I think <c 44b> this was exemplified in a very moving way <c 44c> when the members of our Congress stood shoulder to shoulder the other day <c 44d> and sang 'God Bless America.'
	44b			this		
	44c	when		the members of our Congress		
	44d	and				
45	45a	Finally		difficult		<c 45a> Finally, difficult as it may be for us to see right now, <c 45b> this event can give a message of hope -- hope for the present, and hope for the future.
	45b			This event		
46			Yes	there		<c 46> Yes, there is hope.
47	47a			There		<c 47a> There's hope for the present, <c 47b> because I believe <c 47c> the stage has already been set for a new spirit in our nation.
	47b	because		I		
	47c			the stage		
48	48			One of the things	we	<c 48a>One of the things [<c 48b> we desperately need] is a spiritual renewal in this country.
49	49			We		<c 49> We need a spiritual revival in America.
50	50a	And		God		<c 50a> And God has told us in His word, time after time, <c 50b> that we are to repent of our sins <c 50c> and return to Him, <c 50d> and He will bless us in a new way.
	50b	that		we		
	50c	and				
	50d	and		He		
51	51	But		there		<c 51> But there's also hope for the future because of God's promises.
52	52			As a Christian	I	<c 52> As a Christian, I hope not for just this life, but for heaven and the life to come.
53	53	And		many of those people who died this past week		<c 53a> And many of those people [<c 53b> who died this past week] are in heaven right now.
54	54	And		they		<c 54> And they wouldn't want to come back.
55	55			It		<c 55> It's so glorious and so wonderful.

Theme-rheme structure of
Billy Graham's Address at the National Prayer and Memorial Service, 14 September 2001.

Sent#	Cl#	Theme				Clause
		Textual	Inter-personal	Topical/ Existential	displaced	
56	56	And		that		<c 56a> And that's the hope for all of us [<c 56b> who put our faith in God.]
57	57a			I		<c 57a> I pray <c 57b> that you will have this hope in your heart.
	57b	that		you		
58	58			This event		<c 58> This event reminds us of the brevity and the uncertainty of life.
59	59a			We		<c 59a> We never know <c 59b> when we too will be called into eternity.
	59b	when		we		
60	60a			I		<c 60a> I doubt <c 60b> if even one of those people [<c 60c> who got on those planes, <c 60d> or walked into the World Trade Center or the Pentagon last Tuesday morning] thought <c 60e> it would be the last day of their lives.
	60b	if		even one of those people who got on those planes, or walked into the World Trade Center or the Pentagon last Tuesday morning		
	60d			it		
61	61			It		<c 61> It didn't occur to them.
62	62	And		that		<c 62a> And that's [<c 62b> why each of us needs to face our own spiritual need <c 62 c>and commit ourselves to God and His will now.]
63	63			Here in this majestic National Cathedral	we	<c 63> Here in this majestic National Cathedral we see all around us symbols of the cross.
64	64			For the Christian	the cross	<c 64a> For the Christian -- <c 65> I'm speaking for the Christian now -- <c 64a> the cross tells us <c 64b> that God understands our sin and our suffering.
65	65			I		<c 65> I'm speaking for the Christian now
66	66	For		He		<c 66> For He took upon himself, in the person of Jesus Christ, our sins and our suffering.
67	67a	And		from the cross	God	<c 67a> And from the cross, God declares <c 67b> 'I love you.
	67b			I		
68	68a			I		<c 68a> I know the heart aches, and the sorrows, and the pains that you feel, <c 68b> but I love you.'
	68b	but		I		

Theme-rheme structure of

Billy Graham's Address at the National Prayer and Memorial Service, 14 September 2001.

Sent#	Cl#	Theme				Clause
		Textual	Inter-personal	Topical/ Existential	displaced	
69	69a			The story		<c 69a> The story does not end with the cross, <c 69b> for Easter points us beyond the tragedy of the cross to the empty tomb.
	69b	for		Easter		
70	70a			It		<c 70a> It tells us <c 70b> that there is hope for eternal life, <c 70c> for Christ has conquered evil, and death, and hell.
	70b	that		there		
	70c	for		Christ		
71	71		Yes	there		<c 71> Yes, there's hope.
72	72			I		<c 72> I've become an old man now.
73	73	and		I		<c 73> And I've preached all over the world.
74	74a	And		the older	I	<c 74a> And the older I get, <c 74b> the more I cling to that hope [<c 74c> that I started with many years ago,] <c 74d>and proclaimed it in many languages to many parts of the world.
	74b			the more	I	
	74d	and				
75	75a			Several years ago at the National Prayer Breakfast here in Washington	Ambassador Andrew Young	<c 75a> Several years ago at the National Prayer Breakfast here in Washington, Ambassador Andrew Young, <c 75b> who had just gone through the tragic death of his wife, <c 75a> closed his talk with a quote from the old hymn, 'How Firm A Foundation.'
	75b	who		who		
76	76a			We		<c 76a> We all watched in horror <c 76b> as planes crashed into the steel and glass of the World Trade Center.
	76b	as		planes		
77	77a			Those majestic towers		<c 77a> Those majestic towers, <c 77b> built on solid foundations, <c 77a> were examples of the prosperity and creativity of America.
	77b					
78	78a	When				<c 78a> When damaged, <c 78b> those buildings eventually plummeted to the ground, <c 78c> imploding in upon themselves.
	78b			those buildings		
	78c					
79	79	Yet		underneath the debris		<c 79a> Yet underneath the debris is a foundation [<c 79b> that was not destroyed.
80	80			Therein		<c 80>Therein lies the truth of that old hymn that Andrew Young quoted: 'How firm a foundation.'
81	81		Yes	our nation		<c 81> Yes, our nation has been attacked.
82	51			Buildings		<c 82> Buildings destroyed.
83	83			Lives		<c 83> Lives lost.
84	84	But		now	we	<c 84> But now we have a choice:

Theme-rheme structure of
Billy Graham's Address at the National Prayer and Memorial Service, 14 September 2001.

Sent#	Cl#	Theme				Clause
		Textual	Inter-personal	Topical/ Existential	displaced	
85	85a	Whether				<c 85a> Whether to implode and disintegrate emotionally and spiritually as a people, and a nation, <c 85b> or, whether we choose to become stronger through all of the struggle to rebuild on a solid foundation.
	85b	or whether		we		
86	86a	And		I		<c 86a> And I believe <c 86b> that we're in the process of starting to rebuild on that foundation.
	86b	that		we		
87	87			That foundation		<c 87> That foundation is our trust in God.
88	88			That		<c 88> That's what this service is all about.
89	89a	And		in that faith	we	<c 89a> And in that faith we have the strength [<c 89b> to endure something as difficult and horrendous <c 89c> as what we've experienced this week.]
90	90			This		<c 90> This has been a terrible week with many tears.
91	91	But also		it		<c 91> But also it's been a week of great faith..
92	92			Churches all across the country		<c 92> Churches all across the country have called prayer meetings.
93	93	And		today		<c 93a> And today is a day [<c 93b> that they're celebrating not only in this country, but in many parts of the world.]
94	94a	And		the words of [that familiar hymn that Andrew Young quoted]	it	<c 94a> And the words of that familiar hymn [<c 94b>that Andrew Young quoted,] it says <c 94c> 'Fear not, <c 94d> I am with thee
	94c			Fear not		
	94d			I		
95	95a		Oh	be not dismayed		<c 95a> Oh be not dismayed <c 95b> for I am thy God <c 95c> and will give thee aid.
	95b	for		I		
	95c	and				
96	96a			I		<c 96a> I'll strengthen thee, <c 96b> help thee, <c 96c> and cause thee to stand upon my righteous, omnipotent hand.'
	96b					
	96c	and				
97	97a			My prayer		<c 97a> My prayer today is [<c 97b> that we will feel the loving arms of God wrapped around us <c 97c> and
	97b	and				
	97c	that		He		

Theme-rheme structure of

Billy Graham's Address at the National Prayer and Memorial Service, 14 September 2001.

Sent#	Cl#	Theme				Clause
		Textual	Inter-personal	Topical/ Existential	displaced	
	97d	as		we		will know in our hearts <c 97d> that He will never forsake us <c 97e> as we trust in Him.]
98	98a			We		<c 98a> We also know <c 98b> that God is going to give wisdom, and courage, and strength to the President, and those around him.
	98b	that		God		
99	99	And		this		<c 99a> And this is going to be a day [<c 99b> that we will remember as a day of victory.]
100	100		May	God		<c 100> May God bless you all.

11 Visualizing the architeXture of the text: Analyzing Obama's first inaugural address and Nixon's second inaugural address

11.1 Introduction

Common among functional approaches is the idea that a text is composed of functionally-significant text spans. A functionally-significant text span is a lexico-grammatically cohesive unit. It is characterized by distinctive lexicogrammatical patterning, or in other words, its own weave, its own texture.

The style of representation used here (see Figure 11.1) is borrowed from RST with some modification. Instead of extending downward from text on top to constituent clauses on the bottom, we begin with the text as ground and build upward, showing how the text builds span by span up to each constituent paragraph at the top. Taking the text as ground and building span by span up to each constituent paragraph allows a different perspective on the text as semantic unit which we like to refer to as the 'architeXture' of the text.

Particularly in writing or in the published transcripts of speeches, the notion of 'paragraph' offers a convenient typographically obvious way of identifying spans (larger than a clause or clause-complex) whose own constituent spans develop a particular idea. When it comes to representing the hypotactic and paratactic relations between constituents of a paragraph, however, we have kept the traditional RST top-down approach for representing relations between spans, preferring to show how the paragraph (as a functionally significant span) breaks down into its constituent spans, which are for the most part lexico-grammatical rather than semantic in character.

Like RST, hypotaxis between spans is indicated by an arc extending from the dependent span or satellite – as it is referred to in RST – to the main span or nucleus which is linked with a span on the layer below by a straight line. Parataxis is indicated when two or more spans are linked by straight lines with the same span on the layer below.

Unlike, RST, we do not identify the relations between spans other than to indicate whether the relationship involves elaboration – indicated by an equal sign (=), extension – indicated by a plus sign (+), enhancement – indicated by a multiplication sign (×), or projection – indicated by double quotes ("). Elaboration, extension, enhancement and projection are terms used in systemic-functional grammar (Halliday and Matthiessen, 2004).

11.2 Nixon's second Inaugural Address

The following extract from Nixon's second inaugural illustrates the interplay between parataxis and hypotaxis in the span of paragraphs between paragraphs 3 to 11.

Nixon begins by introducing the subject of peace in the world in paragraph 3, and then, in paragraphs 4 through 11 elaborates further on what this peace is (and is not) and what America's role should be in maintaining world peace.

> *<p 3> <c 6> This past year saw far-reaching results from our new policies for peace. <c 7a> By continuing to revitalize our traditional friendships, and by our missions to Peking and to Moscow, <c 7b> we were able [<c 7c> to establish the base for a new and more durable pattern of relationships among the nations of the world.] <c 8> Because of America's bold initiatives, 1972 will be long remembered as the year of the greatest progress since the end of World War II toward* ***a lasting peace in the world.***

> *<p 4> <c 9a>* ***The peace*** [<c 9b> ***we seek***] ***in the world*** *is not the flimsy peace [<c 9c> which is merely an interlude between wars], but a peace [<c 9d> which can endure for generations to come.] <c 10a> It is important [<c 10b> that we understand both the necessity and the limitations of America's role [<c 10c> in maintaining that peace.] <c 11a> Unless we in America work <c 11b> to preserve the peace, <c 11c> there will be no peace. <c 12a> Unless we in America work <c 12b> to preserve freedom, <c 12c> there will be no freedom.*

The conjunction 'but' at the beginning of paragraph 5 concedes the necessity of America's role in maintaining world peace, while setting out in paragraphs 6–11 to define what America's new role should be. The same phrase, 'we shall' is repeated at the beginning of paragraphs 6 through 9, reinforcing the sense that these paragraphs form a series of paratactically-related spans.

> *<p 5> <c 13a>* ***But*** *let us clearly understand the new nature of America's role, as a result of the new policies [<c 13b> we have adopted over these past four years:]*

> *<p 6> <c 14>* ***We shall*** *respect our treaty commitments.*

> *<p 7> <c 15a>* ***We shall*** *support vigorously the principle [<c 15b> that no country has the right [<c 15c> to impose its will or rule on another by force.]]*

<p 8> <c 16a> ***We shall*** *continue, in this era of negotiation, to work for the limitation of nuclear arms, <c 16b> and to reduce the danger of confrontation between the great powers.*

<p 9> <c 17a> ***We shall*** *do our share [<c 17b> in defending peace and freedom in the world. <c 18a> But we shall expect others <c 18b> to do their share.*

Finally paragraphs 10 and 11 jointly elaborate on the point raised in paragraph 9 about each nation doing their share for peace. Similar phrasing at the end of paragraph 10 and the beginning of paragraph 11, contributes a sense of symmetry to both paragraphs:

<p 10> <c 19a> The time has passed <c 19b> when America will make every other nation's conflict our own, <c 19c> or make every other nation's future our responsibility, <c 19d> or presume <c 19e> to tell the people of other nations <c 19f> how to manage their own affairs.

<c 20a> ***Just as we*** *respect the right of each nation [<c 20b> to determine its own future,] <c 20c> we also recognize the responsibility of each nation [<c 20d> to secure its own future.]*

<p 11> <c 21a> ***Just as*** *America's role is indispensable <c 21b> in preserving the world's peace, <c 21c> so is each nation's role indispensable <c 21d> in preserving its own peace.*

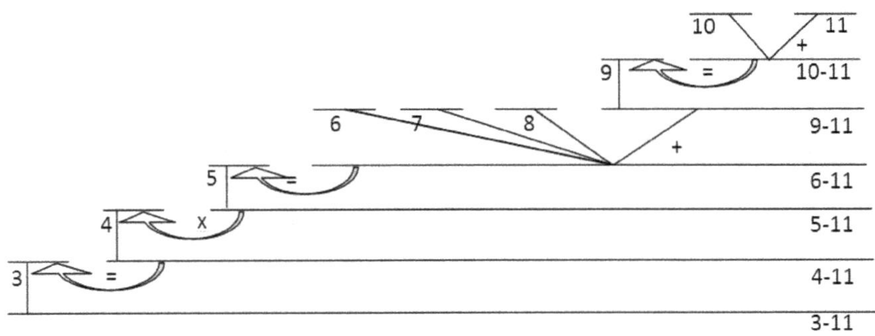

Figure 11.1: Paragraphs 3–11 in Nixon's second inaugural address

The visualization of this span of paragraphs, in which Nixon elaborates on world peace, reveals a climactic rise, after which he returns to exhorting his listeners to action, repeating the first person exclamation, 'let us' or 'let each of us', 22 times throughout the inaugural. In contrast, this first-person exclamation occurs only once in the span of paragraphs from paragraphs 3 to 11, and not as a call to action but rather to 'understand' (note para.5, clause 13: 'But let us clearly understand …'.

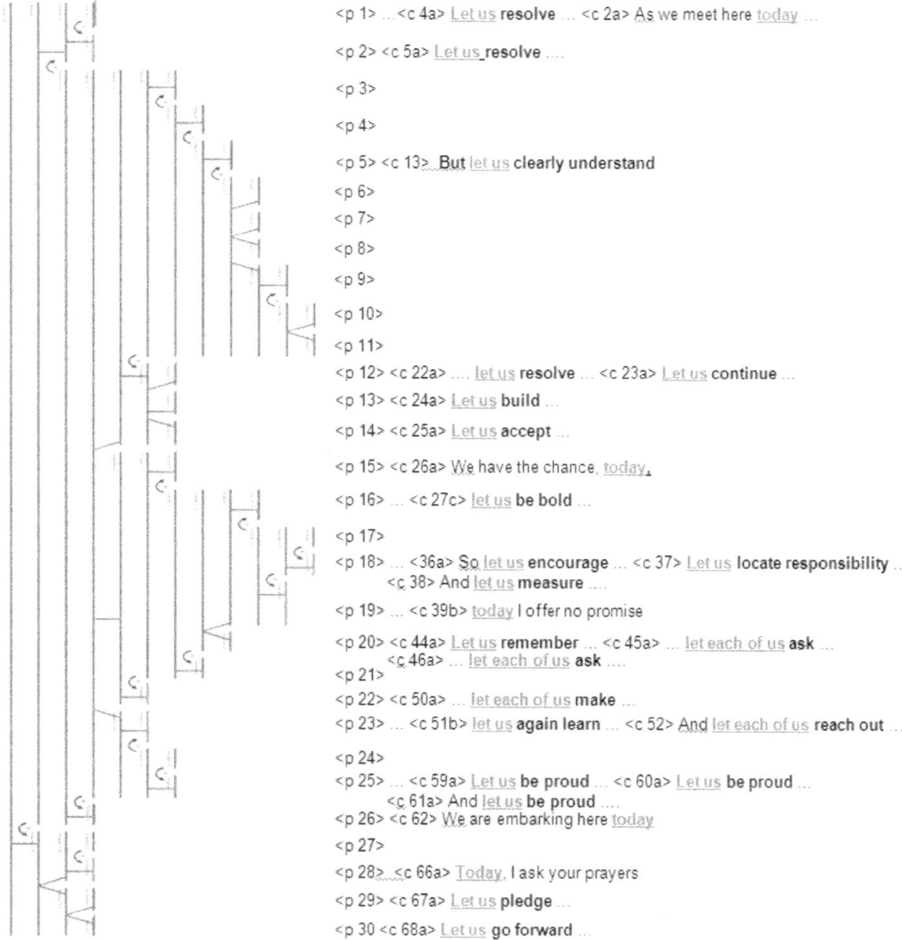

Figure 11.2: Architecture of Nixon's Second Inaugural

The rhetorical structure of the text – its architecture – is consistent with lexico-grammatical choices made by the speaker/writer. There is a unity of lexis and grammar which extends beyond constituent clauses to the text as a whole. The spans are defined by the cohesiveness achieved here through the frequent or infrequent reiteration of the same phrase.

11.3 Analysing Obama's Inaugural

Literary critic, Stanley Fish, writing in the *Opinionator*, an exclusive online commentary from the *New York Times* (22 January 2009), noted how radio and television commentators criticized Obama's inaugural address for its lack of eloquence, especially as compared with his earlier speeches, such as the one given on the night he won the presidency, i.e. Obama's victory speech. Fish goes on to describe the inaugural address as 'a framework on which a succession of verbal ornaments was hung, and we were being invited not to move forward but to stop and ponder significances only hinted at'.

Referring to Obama's Inaugural, Fish complains: 'There are few transitions and those there are – "for," "nor," "as for," "so," "and so" – seem just stuck in, providing a pause, not a marker of logical progression. Obama doesn't deposit us at a location he has in mind from the beginning; he carries us from meditative bead to meditative bead, and invites us to contemplate.'

Citing the *Oxford English Dictionary* definition for the technical term 'parataxis' – i.e. 'the placing of propositions or clauses one after the other without indicating ... the relation of co-ordination or subordination between them' – as opposed to 'hypotaxis' where relations between propositions and clauses are marked by 'connectives that point backward or forward', Fish describes Obama's inaugural address as 'surely more paratactic than hypotactic', as 'incantatory rather than progressive; the cadences ask for assent to each proposition ("That we are in the midst of crisis is now well understood") rather than to a developing argument. The power is in discrete moments rather than in a thesis proved by the marshaling of evidence'.

Comparing the two styles, Fish writes:

> One kind of prose is additive – here's this and now here's that; the other asks the reader or hearer to hold in suspension the components of an argument that will not fully emerge until the final word. It is the difference between walking through a museum and stopping as long as you like at each picture, and being hurried along by a guide who wants you to see what you're looking at as a stage in a developmental arc she is eager to trace for you.

Blogging two days later in the *Language Log* ('Presidential parataxis?', 24 January 2009), Mark Liberman, founder and director of the *Linguistic Data Consortium*, criticizes Fish's terminology as 'arguably misleading'. 'Hypotaxis,' argues Liberman, 'is not crucially characterized by the use of connectives, but by the use of explicit grammatical embedding, hierarchical structuring that 'places' (= *-taxis*) some words or phrases 'beneath' (= *hypo-*) others.'

Unlike Liberman, however, I take -taxis, whether parataxis or hypotaxis, to indicate a relationship between functionally-significant spans of like or equal grammatical status. Embedded clauses, on the other hand, are rank-shifted units functioning at a rank below clause level, such as when a nominalized clause takes on the role of grammatical Subject in another clause.

Table 11.3 shows the result of comparing instances of –taxis and embedding across Nixon's second inaugural and resignation speeches, as well as three of Obama's speeches: the concession speech he gave on 8 January 2008 after losing the New Hampshire primary to Hillary Clinton, often referred to as the original 'Yes we can' speech; his Victory speech, another 'Yes we can' speech; and Obama's Inaugural address.

From Table 11.3 we observe that Nixon's resignation speech had the fewest simple clauses and highest percentage of embedded (or rank-shifted) clauses. Among complex clauses, only Obama's Inaugural was characterized by a near 50–50 split between hypotaxis and parataxis, the other speeches clearly favouring hypotaxis over parataxis.

Table 11.3 shows percentages of parataxis, hypotaxis and embedding.

Table 11.3

		Nixon		**Obama**		
		2nd Inaugural	**Resignation**	**NH Yes We Can**	**Victory**	**Inaugural**
simple (vs. complex) clauses		21%	5%	18%	14%	24%
complex clauses	**parataxis**	23%	31%	34%	36%	41%
	hypotaxis	77%	69%	66%	64%	59%
embedding		21%	31%	25%	20%	18%

The Fish vs. Liberman debate confines the discussion over parataxis and hypotaxis to inter-clausal relations only. By our own reckoning of taxis and embedding between clauses, Obama's Inaugural is arguably more paratactic than either his NH-'Yes we can' or his Victory speeches. Still it is doubtful whether inter-clausal relations alone, whether paratactic or hypotactic, can adequately explain why listeners responded the way they did.

If we take the broader view that parataxis occurs not just between conjoined, independent clauses, but also wherever there is a symmetrical juxtaposition of like-with-like, be it at clause, or even phrase level, then parataxis can be seen to figure significantly in Obama's Victory speech as well.

For example, the span of text from paragraph 36 to the end of the Obama's Victory speech demonstrates how paratactic repetition helps to establish a rhythm that gradually builds into the climactic conclusion whose impact was clearly evident in the chants and on the faces of his listeners.

<p 36> ...<c 57b> that America ***can change****.*

<c 58> Our union ***can be perfected****. ...*

<p 44> <c 74a> ***<u>A man touched down on the Moon,</u>***

<c 74b> ***<u>a wall came down in Berlin,</u>***

<c 74c> ***<u>a world was connected by our own science and imagination</u>****.*

<p 45> <c 77> America, ***<u>we have come so far.</u>***

<c 78> ***<u>We have seen so much</u>****.*

<c 79> But there is so much more to do.

<p 46>...<c 80b> ***<u>if</u>*** *our children should live <c 80c>* ***<u>to see</u>*** *the next century;*

<c 80d> ***<u>if</u>*** *my daughters should be so lucky* ***<u>to live</u>*** *as long ...*

<c 80e> ***<u>what change will they see</u>****?*

<c 81> ***<u>What progress will we have made</u>****?*

<p 47> <c 82a> ***<u>This is our chance</u>*** *...*

<c83> ***<u>This is our moment</u>****.*

<p 48> <c 84a> ***<u>This is our time</u>*** *–*

<c 84b> ***<u>to put</u>*** *our people back to work <c 84c>* ***<u>and open</u>*** *doors ...*

<c 84d> ***<u>to restore</u>*** *prosperity <c 84e>* ***<u>and promote</u>*** *...*

<c 84f> ***<u>to reclaim</u>*** *the American dream <c 84g>* ***and reaffirm*** *...*

11.4 Taxis beyond the clause

The answer to the question of why Obama's Victory speech won acclaim for its eloquence, while his Inaugural was criticized for being flat and diffuse, may be related to taxis, but not just at clause level, but also above clause level.

Figure 11.3 displays only a partial picture of Obama's Inaugural from the text-as-ground up to that point in the speech where the block of paragraphs 6 through 64 divides into seven paratactically-joined spans. Each of the seven spans which together form the main block of paragraphs 6 through 64 reveals a unique texture. This unique weave to each block likely contributed to what some described as the speech's diffuseness and flatness. It was almost

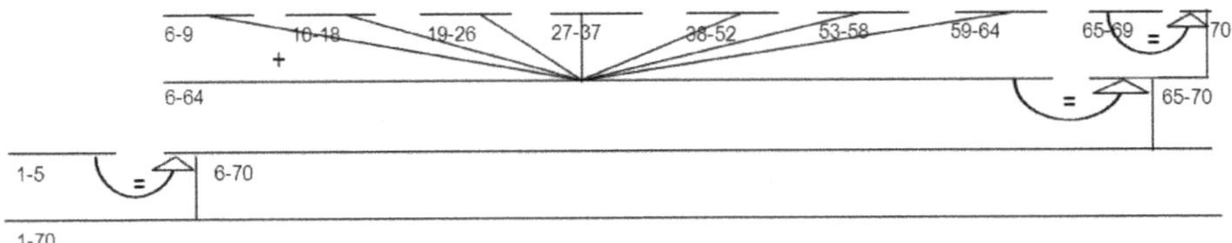

Figure 11.3: Obama's Inaugural – paragraphs 1–70

as though different writers had written each block, resulting in a kind of patchwork quilt of a speech.

Paragraphs 38 through 51, for example, combine to form a single span of text. Throughout these paragraphs, Obama explicitly addresses other than the American people, continually switching between two patterns of address: (1) *to* so-and-so: *know...*; (2) *for/to* so-and-so, *we say/seek/pledge ...*

> *<p 38> <c 65a> And so, to all the other peoples and governments [<c 65b>who are watching today, from the grandest capitals to the small village [<c65c> where my father was born:]] know ...*
>
> *<p 44> <c 75a> And for those [<c 75b> who seek to advance their aims by inducing terror and slaughtering innocents,] <c 75a> we say to you now ...*
>
> *<p 47> <c 79> To the Muslim world, we seek ...*
>
> *<p 48> <c 80a> To those leaders around the globe [c 80b>who seek to sow conflict, <c 80c> or blame their society's ills on the West,] know ...*
>
> *<p 49> <c 81a> To those [<c 81b> who cling to power through corruption and deceit and the silencing of dissent,] know ...*
>
> *<p 50> <c 82a> To the people of poor nations, we pledge ...*
>
> *<p 51> <c 83a> And to those nations like ours [<c 83b> that enjoy relative plenty,] we say...*

In fact, a similar pattern also appeared in John F. Kennedy's inaugural:

> *To those old allies whose cultural and spiritual origins we share, we pledge ...*
>
> *To those new states whom we welcome to the ranks of the free, we pledge ...*
>
> *To those people in the huts and villages of half the globe struggling to break the bonds of mass misery, we pledge ...*
>
> *To our sister republics south of our border, we offer a special pledge ...*
>
> *To that world assembly of sovereign states, the United Nations, our last best hope in an age where the instruments of war have far outpaced the instruments of peace, we renew our pledge of support ...*
>
> *Finally, to those nations who would make themselves our adversary, we offer not a pledge but a request: ...*

In paragraphs 52 through 57, after referring to those serving in the military, whom 'we remember ...'; 'we honor ...', Obama repeats another pattern beginning with *it is ... that/which*, or what we might refer to as cleft sentences or predicated theme.

> *<p 54> <c 88a> And yet at this moment, a moment [<c 88b> that will define a generation,] it is precisely this spirit [<c 88c> that must inhabit us all.]*

<p 55> <c 89a> For as much as government can do, <c 89b> and must do, <c 89c> it is ultimately the faith and determination of the American people [<c 89d> upon which this nation relies.]

<p 56> <c 90a> It is the kindness [<c 90b> to take in a stranger <c 90c> when the levees break,] the selflessness of workers [<c 90d> who would rather cut their hours <c 90e> than see <c 90f> a friend lose their job] <c 90g> which sees us through our darkest hours.

<p 57> <c 91a> It is the firefighter's courage [<c 91b> to storm a stairway [<c 91c> filled with smoke,]] but also a parent's willingness [<c 91d> to nurture a child] [<c 91e> that finally decides our fate.]

Unlike the flat rhetorical architecture of Obama's Inaugural, Obama's Victory Speech, is a very different semantic construct. Each successive span builds on the previous span, culminating in Obama's resounding 'Yes, we can.' Relations between larger spans are more hypotactic than paratactic. But then as the spans become smaller, the relations between spans become more paratactic. Unlike the flatter, paratactic structure evident in the architecture of the Inaugural, the Victory Speech displays a step-by-step architecture, building upward, through hypotactic links, from one span to another (see Figure 11.4).

Obama's Inaugural Address: paragraph level

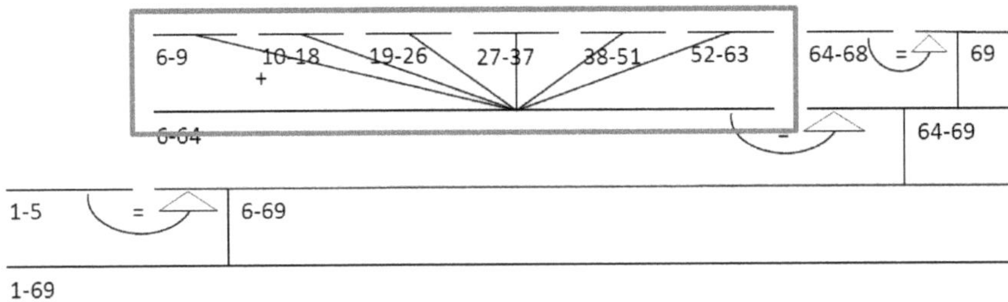

Paragraphs 1-69

Obama's Victory Speech: paragraph level

Figure 11.4: Comparison of Obama's speeches at paragraph level

11.5 Conclusion

A text is an instance of meaning created by patterns of choice at both clause level and above. By exploring various ways of visualizing the representation of such patterns, we gain new perspectives on the text.

From our analysis of Obama's and Nixon's speeches, we have observed how the patterning of relations between functionally significant text spans at both clause level and above plays a significant role in contributing to the reader's response to the text.

How one responds to a text depends on a variety of factors, including those lexicogrammatical patterns that contribute to its texture, and the rhetorical patterns that are reflected in its architecture.

Appendix 11.1

Barack Obama's First Inaugural Address
(Transcript source: http://www.nytimes.com/2009/01/20/us/politics/20text-obama.html?pagewanted=1&_r=2)

<p 1> <c 1a> I stand here today <c 1b> humbled by the task before us, <c 1c> grateful for the trust [<c 1d> you've bestowed], <c 1e> mindful of the sacrifices [<c 1f> borne by our ancestors.]

<p 2> <c 2a> I thank President Bush for his service to our nation – (applause) – as well as the generosity and cooperation [<c 2b>he has shown throughout this transition.]

<p 3> <c 3> Forty-four Americans have now taken the presidential oath.

<p 4> <c 4> The words have been spoken during rising tides of prosperity and the still waters of peace. <c 5> Yet, every so often, the oath is taken amidst gathering clouds and raging storms. <c 6a> At these moments, America has carried on not simply because of the skill or vision of those in high office, <c 6b> but because we, the people, have remained faithful to the ideals of our forebears <c 6c> and true to our founding documents.

<p 5> <c 7a> So it has been, <c 7b> so it must be with this generation of Americans.

<p 6> <c 8a> [<c 8b> That we are in the midst of crisis] is now well understood. <c 9> Our nation is at war against a far-reaching network of violence and hatred. <c 10a> Our economy is badly weakened, a consequence of greed and irresponsibility on the part of some, but also our collective failure [<c 10b> to make hard choices <c 10c> and prepare the nation for a new age].

<p 7> <c 11a> Homes have been lost, <c 11b> jobs shed, <c 11c> businesses shuttered. <c 12a> Our health care is too costly, <c 12b> our schools fail too many – <c 12c> and each day brings further evidence [<c 12d> that the ways [<c 12e> we use energy] strengthen our adversaries <c 12f> and threaten our planet.]

<p 8> <c 13> These are the indicators of crisis, subject to data and statistics. <c 14a> Less measurable, but no less profound, is a sapping of confidence across our land; a nagging fear [<c 14b> that America's decline is inevitable, <c 14c> that the next generation must lower its sights.]

<p 9> <c 15a> Today I say to you <c 15b> that the challenges [<c 15c> we face] are real. <c 16a> They are serious <c 16b> and they are many. <c 17> They will not be met easily or in a short span of time. <c 18a> But know this America: <c 18b> They will be met. (Applause.)

<p 10> <c 19a> On this day, we gather <c 19b> because we have chosen hope over fear, unity of purpose over conflict and discord.

<p 11> <c 20a> On this day, we come <c 20b> to proclaim an end to the petty grievances and false promises, the recriminations and worn-out dogmas [<c 20c> that for far too long have strangled our politics.]

<p 12> <c 21> We remain a young nation. <c 22> But in the words of Scripture, <c 22a> the time has come <c 22b> to set aside childish things. <c 23a> The time has come <c 23b> to reaffirm our enduring spirit; <c 23c> to choose our better history; <c 23d> to carry forward that precious gift, that noble idea [<c 23e> passed on from generation to generation:] the God-given promise [<c 23f> that all are equal, <c 23g> all are free, <c 23h> and all deserve a chance [<c 23i> to pursue their full measure of happiness.]] (Applause.)

<p 13> <c 24a> In reaffirming the greatness of our nation <c 24b> we understand <c 24c> that greatness is never a given. <c 25> It must be earned. <c 26> Our journey has never been one of short-cuts or settling for less.

<p 14> <c 27a> It has not been the path for the faint-hearted, for those [<c 27b> that prefer leisure over work, <c 27c> or seek only the pleasures of riches and fame.]

<p 15> <c 28a> Rather, it has been the risk-takers, the doers, the makers of things – some celebrated, but more often men and women obscure in their labor –[<c 28b> who have carried us up the long rugged path towards prosperity and freedom.]

<p 16> <c 29> For us <c 29a> they packed up their few worldly possessions <c 29b> and traveled across oceans in search of a new life. <c 30> For us <c 30a> they toiled in sweatshops, <c 30b> and settled the West, <c 30c> endured the lash of the whip <c 30d> and plowed the hard earth.

<p 17> <c 31> For us, <c 31a> they fought <c 31b> and died in places like Concord and Gettysburg, Normandy and Khe Sahn.

<p 18> <c 32a> Time and again these men and women struggled <c 32b> and sacrificed <c 32c> and worked <c 32d> till their hands were raw <c 32e>so that we might live a better life. <c 33> They saw America as bigger

than the sum of our individual ambitions, greater than all the differences of birth or wealth or faction.

<p 19> <c 34a> This is the journey [<c 34b> we continue today.] <c 35> We remain the most prosperous, powerful nation on Earth. <c 36a> Our workers are no less productive <c 36b> than when this crisis began. <c 37a> Our minds are no less inventive, <c 37b> our goods and services no less needed <c 37c> than they were last week, or last month, or last year. <c 38> Our capacity remains undiminished. <39a> But our time [<c 39b> of standing pat, <c 39c> of protecting narrow interests <c 39d> and putting off unpleasant decisions]– that time has surely passed.

<p 20> <c 40a> Starting today, <c 40b> we must pick ourselves up, <c 40c> dust ourselves off, <c 40d> and begin again the work of remaking America. (Applause.)

<p 21> <c 41a> For everywhere [<c 41b> we look], there is work [<c 41c> to be done.]

<p 22> <c 42> The state of our economy calls for action, bold and swift. <c 43a> And we will act, <c 43b> not only to create new jobs, <c 43c> but to lay a new foundation for growth.

<p 23> <c 44a> We will build the roads and bridges, the electric grids and digital lines [<c 44b> that feed our commerce <c 44c> and bind us together.]

<p 24> <c 45a> We'll restore science <c 45b> and wield technology's wonders <c 45c> to raise health care's quality <c 45d> and lower its cost.

<p 25> <c 46a> We will harness the sun and the winds and the soil <c 46b> to fuel our cars <c 46c> and run our factories. <c 47a> And we will transform our schools and colleges and universities <c 47b> to meet the demands of a new age.

<p 26> <c 48> All this we can do. <c 49> All this we will do.

<p 27> <c 50a> Now, there are some [<c 50b> who question the scale of our ambitions, <c 50c> who suggest <c 50d> that our system cannot tolerate too many big plans.] c 51a> Their memories are short, <c 51b> for they have forgotten <c 51c> what this country has already done, <c 51d> what free men and women can achieve <c 51e> when imagination is joined to common purpose, and necessity to courage.

<p 28> <c 52a> [<c 52b>What the cynics fail to understand] is [<c 52c> that the ground has shifted beneath them, <c 52d> that the stale political arguments [<c 52e> that have consumed us for so long] no longer apply.]

<p 29> <c 53a> The question [<c 53b> we ask today] is not [<c 53c> whether our government is too big or too small,] but [<c 53d> whether it works – <c 53e> whether it helps families <c 53f> find jobs at a decent wage, care [<c 53g> they can afford], a retirement [<c 53h> that is dignified.]]

<p 30> <c 54a> Where the answer is yes, <c 54b> we intend <c 54c> to move forward. <c 55a> Where the answer is no, <c 55b> programs will end.

<p 31> <c 56a> And those of us [<c 56b> who manage the public's dollars] will be held to account,<c 56c> to spend wisely, <c 56d> reform bad habits, <c 56e> and do our business in the light of day, <c 56f> because only then can we restore the vital trust between a people and their government.

<p 32> <c 57a> Nor is the question before us [<c 57b> whether the market is a force for good or ill.] <c 58a> Its power [<c 58b> to generate wealth <c 58c> and expand freedom] is unmatched.

<p 33> <c 59a> But this crisis has reminded us <c 59b> that without a watchful eye, the market can spin out of control. <c 60a> The nation cannot prosper long <c 60b> when it favors only the prosperous.

<p 34> <c 61a> The success of our economy has always depended not just on the size of our gross domestic product, but on the reach of our prosperity, on the ability [<c 61b> to extend opportunity to every willing heart –] <c 61c> not out of charity, but because it is the surest route to our common good. (Applause.)

<p 35> <c 62> As for our common defense, we reject as false the choice between our safety and our ideals.

<p 36> <c 63a> Our Founding Fathers – (applause) – our Founding Fathers, … drafted a charter <63b> faced with perils [<63c> that we can scarcely imagine], <c 63d> to assure the rule of law and the rights of man – a charter [<c 63e> expanded by the blood of generations.]

<p 37> <c 64a> Those ideals still light the world, <c 64b> and we will not give them up for expedience sake. (Applause)

<p 38> <c 65a> And so, to all the other peoples and governments [<c 65b> who are watching today, from the grandest capitals to the small village [<c 65c> where my father was born]]: know <c 65d> that America is a friend of each nation, and every man, woman and child [<c 65e>who seeks a future of peace and dignity.] <c 66a> And we are ready [<c 66b> to lead once more.] (Applause.)

<p 39> <c 67a> Recall <c 67b> that earlier generations faced down fascism and communism not just with missiles and tanks, but with the sturdy alliances and enduring convictions.

<p 40> <c 68a> They understood <c 68b> that our power alone cannot protect us, <c 68c> nor does it entitle us <c 68d> to do <c 68e> as we please. <c 69a> Instead they knew <c 69b> that our power grows through its prudent use; <c 69c> our security emanates from the justness of our cause, the force of our example, the tempering qualities of humility and restraint.

<p 41> <c 70> We are the keepers of this legacy. <c 71a> Guided by these principles <c 71b> once more we can meet those new threats [<c 71c> that demand even greater effort, even greater cooperation and understanding between nations.] <c 72a> We will begin to responsibly leave Iraq to its people <c 72b> and forge a hard-earned peace in Afghanistan.

<p 42> <c 73a> With old friends and former foes, we'll work tirelessly <c 73b> to lessen the nuclear threat, <c 73c> and roll back the specter of a warming planet.

<p 43> <c 74a> We will not apologize for our way of life, <c 74b> nor will we waver in its defense.

<p 44> <c 75a> And for those [<c 75b> who seek <c 75c> to advance their aims by inducing terror and slaughtering innocents,] <c 75a> we say to you now <c 75d> that our spirit is stronger <c 75e> and cannot be broken – <c 75f> you cannot outlast us, <c 75g> and we will defeat you. (Applause.)

<p 45> <c 76a> For we know <c 76b> that our patchwork heritage is a strength, not a weakness.

<p 46> <c 77> We are a nation of Christians and Muslims, Jews and Hindus, and non-believers. <c 78a> We are shaped by every language and culture, <c 78b> drawn from every end of this Earth; <c 78c> and because we have tasted the bitter swill of civil war and segregation, <c 78d> and emerged from that dark chapter stronger and more united, <c 78e> we cannot help but believe <c 78f> that the old hatreds shall someday pass; <c 78g> that the lines of tribe shall soon dissolve; <c 78h> that as the world grows smaller, <c 78i> our common humanity shall reveal itself; <c 78j> and that America must play its role <c 78k> in ushering in a new era of peace.

<p 47> <c 79> To the Muslim world, we seek a new way forward, based on mutual interest and mutual respect.

<p 48> <c 80a> To those leaders around the globe [c 80b>who seek <c 80c> to sow conflict, <c 80d> or blame their society's ills on the West,] know <c 80e> that your people will judge you on [<c 80f> what you can build, not <c 80g> what you destroy.] (Applause.)

<p 49> <c 81a> To those [<c 81b> who cling to power through corruption and deceit and the silencing of dissent,] know <c 81c> that you are on the wrong side of history, <c 81d> but that we will extend a hand <c 81e> if you are willing to unclench your fist. (Applause.)

<p50><c 82a> To the people of poor nations, we pledge <c 82b> to work alongside you <c 82c> to make your farms flourish <c 82d> and let clean waters flow; <c 82e> to nourish starved bodies <c 82f> and feed hungry minds.

<p 51> <c 83a> And to those nations like ours [<c 83b> that enjoy relative plenty,] we say <c 83c> we can no longer afford indifference to the suffering outside our borders, <c 83d> nor can we consume the world's resources without regard to effect. <c 84a> For the world has changed, <c 84b> and we must change with it.

<p 52><c 85a> As we consider the role [<c 85b> that unfolds before us], <c 85c> we remember with humble gratitude those brave Americans [<85d> who at this very hour patrol far-off deserts and distant mountains]. <c 86a> They have something to tell us, <c 86b> just as the fallen heroes [<c 86c> who lie in Arlington] whisper through the ages.

<p 53> <c 87a> We honor them <c 87b> not only because they are the guardians of our liberty, <c 87c> but because they embody the spirit of service – willingness to find meaning in something greater than themselves.

<p 54> <c 88a> And yet at this moment, a moment [<88b> that will define a generation,] it is precisely this spirit [<c 88c> that must inhabit us all.]

<p 55> <c 89a> For as much as government can do, <c 89b> and must do, <c 89c> it is ultimately the faith and determination of the American people [<c 89d> upon which this nation relies.]

<p 56> <c 90a> It is the kindness [<c 90b> to take in a stranger <c 90c> when the levees break,] the selflessness of workers [<c 90d> who would rather cut their hours <c 90e> than see <c 90f> a friend lose their job] [<c 90g> which sees us through our darkest hours.]

<p 57> <c 91a> It is the firefighter's courage [<c 91b> to storm a stairway [<c 91c> filled with smoke,]] but also a parent's willingness [<c 91d> to nurture a child] [<c 91e> that finally decides our fate.]

<p 58> <c 92> Our challenges may be new. <c 93a> The instruments [<c 93b> with which we meet them] may be new. <c 94a> But those values [<c 94b> upon which our success depends – honesty and hard work, courage and fair play, tolerance and curiosity, loyalty and patriotism] – these things are old.

<p 59> <c 95> These things are true. <c 96> They have been the quiet force of progress throughout our history.

<p 60> <c 97a> [<c 97b> What is demanded, then,] is a return to these truths. <c 98a> [<c 98b> What is required of us, now,] is a new era of responsibility – a recognition on the part of every American [<c 98c> that we have duties to ourselves, our nation and the world; duties [<c 98d> that we do not grudgingly accept, <c 98e> but rather seize gladly, firm in the knowledge [<c 98f> that there is nothing so satisfying to the spirit, so defining of our character <c 98g> than giving our all to a difficult task.]]]

<p 61> <c 99> This is the price and the promise of citizenship.

<p 62> <c 100a> This is the source of our confidence – the knowledge [<c 100b> that God calls on us to shape an uncertain destiny.]

<p 63> <c 101a> This is the meaning of our liberty and our creed, <c 101b> why men and women and children of every race and every faith can join in celebration across this magnificent mall; <c 101c> and why a man [<c 101d> whose father less than 60 years ago might not have been served in a local restaurant] can now stand before you <c 101e> to take a most sacred oath. (Applause.)

<p 64> <c 102a> So let us mark this day with remembrance of [<c 102b> who we are <c 102c> and how far we have traveled.]

<p 65> <c 103> In the year of America's birth, in the coldest of months, a small band of patriots huddled by dying campfires on the shores of an icy river.

<p 66> <c 104> The capital was abandoned. <c 105> The enemy was advancing. <c 106> The snow was stained with blood.

<p 67> <c 107a> At the moment [<c 107b> when the outcome of our revolution was most in doubt,] the father of our nation ordered <c 107c> these words to be read to the people:

<p 68> —

<p 69> <c 108> America: In the face of our common dangers, in this winter of our hardship, let us remember these timeless words. <c 109a> With hope and virtue, let us brave once more the icy currents, <c 109b> and endure [<c 109c> what storms may come.] <c 110a> Let it be said by our children's children <c 110b> that when we were tested <c 110c> we refused <c 110d> to let this journey end, <c 110e> that we did not turn back <c 110f> nor did we falter; <c 110g> and with eyes fixed on the horizon and God's grace upon us, <c 110h> we carried forth that great gift of freedom <c 110i> and delivered it safely to future generations.

Appendix 11.2

Transitivity Structure of Barack Obama's First Inaugural Address

Para#	Cl#	Transitivity Structure				Clause (Complex)
		Process (type)	Participant(s)		Circumstance(s)	
			X…	Roles		
1	1a	stand (behavioural)	I	Behaver	today; here	<c 1a> I stand here today <c 1b> humbled by the task before us, <c 1c> grateful for the trust [<c 1d> you've bestowed], <c 1e> mindful of the sacrifices [<c 1f> borne by our ancestors.]
	1b	humbled (material)			by the task before us	
	1c		grateful	Attribute	for the trust [<c 1d>]	
	1d	bestowed (material)	you	Actor		
	1e		mindful	Attribute	of the sacrifices [<c 1f>]	
	1f	borne (material)	our ancestors	Actor		
2	2a	thank (material)	I	Actor	for his service to our nation -- (applause) -- as well as the generosity and cooperation [<c 2b>]	<c 2a> I thank President Bush for his service to our nation -- (applause) -- as well as the generosity and cooperation [<c 2b>he has shown throughout this transition.]
			President Bush	Goal		
	2b	shown (material)	he	Actor	throughout this transition	
3	3	taken (material)	Forty-four Americans	Actor	now	<c 3> Forty-four Americans have now taken the presidential oath.
			the presidential oath.	Goal		
4	4	spoken (material)	The words	Goal	during rising tides of prosperity and the still waters of peace.	<c 4> The words have been spoken during rising tides of prosperity and the still waters of peace.
	5	taken (material)	the oath	Goal	amidst gathering clouds and raging storms.	<c 5> Yet, every so often, the oath is taken amidst gathering clouds and raging storms.
	6a	carried on (material)	America	Actor	At these moments	<c 6a> At these moments, America has carried on not simply because of the skill or vision of those in high office, <c 6b> but because we, the people, have remained faithful to the ideals of our forebears <c 6c> and true to our founding documents.
	6b	remained (relational)	we, the people,	Carrier	to the ideals of our forebears	
			faithful	Attribute		
	6d		true	Attribute	to our founding documents.	

Transitivity Structure of Barack Obama's First Inaugural Address

Para#	Cl#	Transitivity Structure				Clause (Complex)
		Process (type)	Participant(s)		Circumstance(s)	
			X…	Roles		
5	7a	been (relational)	it	Identified		<c 7a> So it has been; <c 7b> so it must be with this generation of Americans.
			so	Identifier		
	7b	be (relational)	it	Identified	with this generation of Americans.	
			so	Identifier		
6	8a	is (relational)	<c 8b>	Carrier		<c 8a> [<c 8b> That we are in the midst of crisis] is now well understood.
			now well understood	Attribute		
	8b	are (relational)	we	Carrier		
			in the midst of crisis	Attribute		
	9	is (relational)	Our nation	Carrier	against a far-reaching network of violence and hatred.	<c 9> Our nation is at war against a far-reaching network of violence and hatred.
			at war	Attribute		
	10a	is (relational)	Our economy	Carrier		<c 10a> Our economy is badly weakened, a consequence of greed and irresponsibility on the part of some, but also our collective failure [<c 10c> to make hard choices <c 10b> and prepare the nation for a new age].
			badly weakened	Attribute		
	10b	make (material)	hard choices	Goal		
	10c	prepare (material)	the nation	Goal	for a new age	
7	11a	lost (material)	Homes	Goal		<c 11a> Homes have been lost, <c 11b> jobs shed, <c 11c> businesses shuttered.
	11b	shed (material)	jobs	Goal		
	11c	shuttered (material)	businesses	Goal		
	12a	is (relational)	Our health care	Carrier		<c 12a> Our health care is too costly,<c 12b> our schools fail too many –<c 12c> and each day brings further evidence [<c 12d> that the ways [<c 12e> we use energy] strengthen our adversaries <c 12f> and threaten our planet.]
			too costly	Attribute		
	12b	fail (material)	our schools	Actor		
			too many	Goal		
	12c	brings (material)	each day	Actor		

Transitivity Structure of Barack Obama's First Inaugural Address

Para#	Cl#	Transitivity Structure				Clause (Complex)
		Process (type)	Participant(s)		Circumstance(s)	
			X…	Roles		
			further evidence [<c 12d> [<c 12e>]<c 12f>]	Goal		
	12d	strengthen (material)	the ways [<c 12e>]	Actor		
			our adversaries	Goal		
	12e	use (material)	we	Actor		
			energy	Goal		
	12f	threaten (material)	our planet	Goal		
8	13	are (relational)	These	Identified	subject to data and statistics.	<c 13> These are the indicators of crisis, subject to data and statistics.
			the indicator of crisis	Identifier		
	14a	is (relational)	Less measurable, but no less profound	Attribute		<c 14a> Less measurable, but no less profound, is a sapping of confidence across our land; a nagging fear [<c 14b> that America's decline is inevitable, <c 14c> that the next generation must lower its sights.]
			a sapping of confidence across our land;	Carrier		
	14b	is (relational)	America's decline	Carrier		
			inevitable	Attribute		
	14c	lower (material)	the next generation	Actor		
			its sights	Goal		
9	15a	say (verbal)	I	Sayer	Today	<c 15a> Today I say to you <c 15b> that the challenges [<c 15c> we face] are real.
			you	Receiver		
			<c 15b> [<c 15c>]	Verbiage		
	15b	are (relational)	the challenges [<c 15c>]	Carrier		
			real	Attribute		
	15c	face (material)	we	Actor		

Transitivity Structure of Barack Obama's First Inaugural Address

Para#	Cl#	Transitivity Structure				Clause (Complex)
		Process (type)	Participant(s)		Circumstance(s)	
			X…	Roles		
	16a	are (relational)	They	Carrier		<c 16a> They are serious <c 16b> and they are many.
			serious	Attribute		
	16b	are (relational)	they	Carrier		
			many	Attribute		
	17	met (material)	They	Goal	easily or in a short span of time.	<c 17> They will not be met easily or in a short span of time.
	18a	know (mental)	America	Senser		<c 18a> But know this America: <c 18b> They will be met. (Applause.)
			this	Phenomenon		
	18b	met (material)	They	Goal		
10	19a	gather (material)	we		On this day	<c 19a> On this day, we gather <c 19b> because we have chosen hope over fear, unity of purpose over conflict and discord.
	19b	chosen (material)	we	Actor		
			hope over fear, unity of purpose over conflict and discord.	Goal		
11	20a	come (material)	we	Actor	On this day	<c 20a> On this day, we come <c 20b> to proclaim an end to the petty grievances and false promises, the recriminations and worn-out dogmas [<c 20c> that for far too long have strangled our politics.]
	20b	proclaim (verbal)	an end to the petty grievances and false promises, the recriminations and worn-out dogmas [<c 20c>]	Verbiage		
	20c	strangled (material)	our politics	Goal	for far too long	
12	21	remain (relational)	we	Carrier		<c 21> We remain a young nation.
			a young nation	Attribute		
	22a	come (material)	the time	Actor	But in the words of Scripture,	<c 22a> But in the words of Scripture, the time has come <c 22b> to set aside childish things.
	22b	set aside (material)	childish things	Goal		

Transitivity Structure of Barack Obama's First Inaugural Address

Para#	Cl#	Transitivity Structure				Clause (Complex)
		Process (type)	Participant(s)		Circumstance(s)	
			X…	Roles		
	23a	come (material)	The time	Actor		<c 23a> The time has come <c 23b> to reaffirm our enduring spirit;<c 23c> to choose our better history; <c 23d> to carry forward that precious gift, that noble idea [<c 23e> passed on from generation to generation:] the God-given promise [<c 23f> that all are equal, <c 23g> all are free, <c 23h> and all deserve a chance [<c 23i> to pursue their full measure of happiness.]] (Applause.)
	23b	reaffirm (material)	our enduring spirit	Goal		
	23c	choose (material)	our better history	Goal		
	23d	carry forward (material)	that precious gift, that noble idea [<c 23e>] the God-given promise [<c 23f-h[<c 23i>>]]	Goal		
	23e	passed on (material)			from generation to generation	
	23f	are (relational)	all	Carrier		
			equal	Attribute		
	23g	are (relational)	all	Carrier		
			free	Attribute		
	23h	deserve (relational)	all	Possessor		
			a chance	Possessed		
	23i	pursue (material)	their full measure of happiness	Goal		
13	24a	reaffirming (material)	the greatness of our nation	Goal		<c 24a> In reaffirming the greatness of our nation <c 24b> we understand <c 24c> that greatness is never a given.
	24b	understand (mental)	we	Senser		
	24c	is (relational)	greatness	Carrier		
			a given	Attribute		
	25	be earned (material)	It	Goal		<c 25> It must be earned.
	26	been (relational)	Our journey	Carrier		<c 26> Our journey has never been one of short-cuts or settling for less.
			one of short-cuts or settling for less	Attribute		

Transitivity Structure of Barack Obama's First Inaugural Address

Para#	Cl#	Transitivity Structure				Clause (Complex)
		Process (type)	Participant(s)		Circumstance(s)	
			X…	Roles		
14	27a	been (relational)	It	Identifier		<c 27a> It has not been the path for the faint-hearted, for those [<c 27b> that prefer leisure over work, <c 27c> or seek only the pleasures of riches and fame.]
			the path for the faint-hearted, for those [<c 27b-c>]	Identified		
	27b	prefer (mental)	leisure over work	Phenomenon		
	27c	seek (material)	only the pleasures of riches and fame	Goal		
15	28a	been (relational)	it = the risk-takers, the doers, the makers of things -- some celebrated, but more often men and women obscure in their labor	Identified		<c 28a> Rather, it has been the risk-takers, the doers, the makers of things -- some celebrated, but more often men and women obscure in their labor –[<c 28b> who have carried us up the long rugged path towards prosperity and freedom.]
			<c 28b>	Identifier		
	28b	carried (material)	us	Goal	up the long rugged path towards prosperity and freedom.	
16	29				For us	<c 29>For us <c 29a> they packed up their few worldly possessions <c 29b> and traveled across oceans in search of a new life.
	29a	packed up (material)	they	Actor		
			their few worldly possessions	Goal		
	29b	traveled (material)			across oceans in search of a new life	
	30				For us	<c 30> For us <c 30a> they toiled in sweatshops, <c 30b> and settled the West, <c 30c> endured the lash of the whip <c 30d> and plowed the hard earth.
	30a	toiled (material)	They	Actor	in sweatshops	
	30b	settled (material)	the West	Goal		
	30c	endured (material)	the lash of the whip	Goal		
	30d	plowed (material)	the hard earth	Goal		

Transitivity Structure of Barack Obama's First Inaugural Address

Para#	Cl#	Transitivity Structure				Clause (Complex)
		Process (type)	Participant(s)		Circumstance(s)	
			X…	Roles		
17	31				For us	<31> For us, <31a> they fought <31b> and died in places like Concord and Gettysburg, Normandy and Khe Sahn.
	31a	fought (material)	they	Actor		
	31b	died (behavioural)			in places like Concord and Gettysburg, Normandy and Khe Sahn	
18	32a	struggled (material)	these men and women	Actor	Time and again	<c 32a> Time and again these men and women struggled <c 32b> and sacrificed <c 32c> and worked <c 32d> till their hands were raw <c 32e>so that we might live a better life.
	32b	sacrificed (material)				
	32c	worked (material)				
	32d	were (relational)	their hands	Carrier		
			raw	Attribute		
	32e	live (behavioural)	we	Behaver		
			a better life	Range		
	33	saw (mental)	They	Senser		<c 33> They saw America as bigger than the sum of our individual ambitions, greater than all the differences of birth or wealth or faction.
			America as bigger than the sum of our individual ambitions, greater than all the differences of birth or wealth or faction.	Phenomenon		
19	34a	is (relational)	This	Identified		<c 34a> This is the journey [<c 34b> we continue today.]
			the journey [<c 34b>]	Identifier		
	34b	continue (material)	we	Actor	today	
	35	remain (relational)	We	Identified		<c 35> We remain the most prosperous, powerful nation on Earth.
			the most prosperous, powerful nation on Earth.	Identifier		

Transitivity Structure of Barack Obama's First Inaugural Address

Para#	Cl#	Transitivity Structure				Clause (Complex)
		Process (type)	Participant(s)		Circumstance(s)	
			X…	Roles		
	36a	are (relational)	Our workers	Carrier		<c 36a> Our workers are no less productive <c 36b> than when this crisis began.
			no less productive	Attribute		
	36b	began (material)	this crisis	Actor		
	37a	are (relational)	Our minds	Carrier		<c 37a> Our minds are no less inventive, <c 37b> our goods and services no less needed <c 37c> than they were last week, or last month, or last year.
			no less inventive	Attribute		
	37b		our goods and services	Carrier		
			no less needed	Attribute		
	37c	were (relational)	they	Carrier	last week, or last month, or last year.	
	38	remains (relational)	Our capacity	Carrier		<c 38> Our capacity remains undiminished.
			undiminished	Attribute		
	39a	passed (material)	our time [<c 39b-d>]	Goal		<39a> But our time [<c 39b> of standing pat, <c 39c> of protecting narrow interests <c 39d> and putting off unpleasant decisions]-- that time has surely passed.
	39b	standing (material)			pat	
	39c	protecting (material)	narrow interests	Goal		
	39d	putting off (material)	unpleasant decisions	Goal		
20	40a	Starting (material)			today	<c 40a> Starting today, <c 40b> we must pick ourselves up, <c 40c> dust ourselves off, <c 40d> and begin again the work of remaking America. (Applause.)
	40b	pick X up (material)	we	Actor		
			ourselves	Goal		
	40c	dust X off (material)	ourselves	Goal		
	40d	begin (material)	the work of remaking America	Goal	again	
21	41a	is (existential)	there		everywhere [<c 41b>]	<c 41a> For everywhere [<c 41b> we look] there is work [<41c> to be done.]
			work [< c41c>]	Existent		
	41b	look (behavioural)	we	Behaver		

Transitivity Structure of Barack Obama's First Inaugural Address

Para#	Cl#	Transitivity Structure				Clause (Complex)
		Process (type)	Participant(s)		Circumstance(s)	
			X…	Roles		
	41c	done (material)				
22	42	call for (material)	The state of our economy	Actor	bold and swift	<c 42> The state of our economy calls for action, bold and swift.
			action	Goal		
	43a	act (material)	we	Actor		<c 43a> And we will act, <c 43b> not only to create new jobs, <c 43c> but to lay a new foundation for growth.
	43b	create (material)	new jobs	Goal		
	43c	lay (material)	a new foundation for growth	Goal		
23	44a	build (material)	We	Actor		<c 44a> We will build the roads and bridges, the electric grids and digital lines [<44b> that feed our commerce <44c> and bind us together.]
			the roads and bridges, the electric grids and digital lines [<c 44b-c>]	Goal		
	44b	feed (material)	our commerce	Goal		
	44c	bind (material)	us	Goal	together	
24	45a	restore (material)	We	Actor		<c 45a> We'll restore science <c 45b> and wield technology's wonders <c 45c> to raise health care's quality <c 45d> and lower its cost.
			science	Goal		
	45b	wield (material)	technology's wonders	Goal		
	45c	raise (material)	health care's quality	Goal		
	45d	lower (material)	its cost	Goal		
25	46a	harness (material)	We	Actor		<c 46a> We will harness the sun and the winds and the soil <c 46b> to fuel our cars <c 46c> and run our factories.
			the sun and the winds and the soil	Goal		
	46b	fuel (material)	our cars	Goal		
	46c	run (material)	our factories	Goal		
	47a	transform (material)	we	Actor		<c 47a> And we will transform our schools and colleges and universities <c 47b> to meet the demands of a new age.
			our schools and colleges and universities	Goal		

Transitivity Structure of Barack Obama's First Inaugural Address

Para#	Cl#	Transitivity Structure				Clause (Complex)
		Process (type)	Participant(s)		Circumstance(s)	
			X…	Roles		
	47b	meet (material)	the demands of a new age	Goal		
26	48	do (material)	we	Actor		<c 48> All this we can do.
			All this	Goal		
	49	do (material)	we	Actor		<c 49> All this we will do.
			All this	Goal		
27	50a	are (existential)	there		Now	<c 50a> Now, there are some [<c 50b> who question the scale of our ambitions, <c 50c> who suggest <c 50d> that our system cannot tolerate too many big plans.]
			some [<c50b-d>]	Existent		
	50b	question (material)	who	Actor		
			the scale of our ambitions	Goal		
	50c	suggest (verbal)	who	Sayer		
			<c 50d>	Verbiage		
	50d	tolerate (material)	our system	Actor		
			too many big plans	Goal		
	51a	are (relational)	Their memories	Carrier		<c 51a> Their memories are short, <c 51b> for they have forgotten <c 51c> what this country has already done, <c 51d> what free men and women can achieve <c 51e> when imagination is joined to common purpose, and necessity to courage.
			short	Attribute		
	51b	forgotten (mental)	they	Senser		
			<c 51c-e>	Phenomenon		
	51c	done (material)	this country	Actor		
	51d	achieve (material)	free men and women	Actor		
	51e	joined (material)	imagination	Goal	to common purpose, and necessity to courage.	
28	52a	is (relational)	[<c 52bc>]	Identified		<c 52a> [<c 52b>What the cynics fail <c 52c> to understand] is [<c 52d> that the ground has shifted beneath them, <c 52e> that the stale
			[<c 52d><c 52e> [<c 52f>]]	Identifier		
	52b	fail (material)	the cynics	Actor		

Transitivity Structure of Barack Obama's First Inaugural Address

Para#	Cl#	Transitivity Structure				Clause (Complex)
		Process (type)	Participant(s)		Circumstance(s)	
			X…	Roles		
	52c	to understand (mental)	the cynics	Senser		political arguments [<c 52f> that have consumed us for so long] no longer apply.]
	52d	shifted (material)	the ground	Actor	beneath them	
	52e	apply (material)	the stale political arguments [<c 52e>]	Actor	no longer	
	52f	consumed (material)	us	Goal	for so long	
29	53a	is (relational)	The question [<c 53b>]	Identified		<c 53a> The question [<c 53b> we ask today] is [not [<c 53c> whether our government is too big or too small,] but [<c 53d> whether it works– <c 53e> whether it helps families <c 53f> find jobs at a decent wage, care [<c 53g> they can afford], a retirement [<c 53h> that is dignified.]]
			[not [<c 53c>] but [<c 53d> – <c 53e> <c 53f> [<c 53g>][<c 53h]]	Identifier		
	53b	ask (verbal)	we	Sayer	today	
	53c	is (relational)	our government	Carrier		
			too big or too small	Attribute		
	53d	works (material)	it	Actor		
	53e	helps (material)	it	Actor		
			families	Goal		
	53f	find (material)	jobs	Goal	at a decent wage	
	53g	afford (material)	they	Actor		
	53h	is (relational)	dignified	Attribute		
30	54a	is (relational)	the answer	Identified		<c 54a> Where the answer is yes, <c 54b> we intend <c 54c> to move forward.
			yes	Identifier		
	54b	intend (mental)	we	Senser		
			<c 54c>	Phenomenon		
	54c	move (material)	we	Actor	forward	

Transitivity Structure of Barack Obama's First Inaugural Address

Para#	Cl#	Transitivity Structure				Clause (Complex)
		Process (type)	Participant(s)		Circumstance(s)	
			X…	Roles		
	55a	is (relational)	the answer	Identified		<c 55a> Where the answer is no, <c 55b> programs will end.
			no	Identifier		
	55b	end (material)	the programs	Goal		
31	56a	held to account (material)	those of us [<c 56b>]	Goal		<c 56a> And those of us [<c 56b> who manage the public's dollars] will be held to account,<c 56c> to spend wisely, <c 56d> reform bad habits, <c 56e> and do our business in the light of day, <c 56f> because only then can we restore the vital trust between a people and their government.
	56b	manage (material)	the public's dollars	Goal		
	56c	spend (material)			wisely	
	56d	reform (material)	bad habits	Goal		
	56e	do (material)	our business	Goal	in the light of day	
	56f	restore (material)	we	Actor	only then	
			the vital trust between a people and their government.	Goal		
32	57a	is (relational)	the question before us	Identified		<c 57a> Nor is the question before us [<c 57b> whether the market is a force for good or ill.]
			[<c 57b>]	Identifier		
	57b	is (relational)	the market	Carrier		
			a force for good or ill	Attribute		
	58a	is (relational)	Its power [<c 58bc>]	Carrier		<c 58a> Its power [<c 58b> to generate wealth <c 58c> and expand freedom] is unmatched.
			unmatched	Attribute		
	58b	generate (material)	wealth	Goal		
	58c	expand (material)	freedom	Goal		
33	59a	reminded (verbal)	this crisis	Sayer		<c 59a> But this crisis has reminded us <c 59b> that without a watchful eye, the market can spin out of control.
			us	Recipient		
			<c 59b>	Verbiage		

Transitivity Structure of Barack Obama's First Inaugural Address

Para#	Cl#	Transitivity Structure				Clause (Complex)
		Process (type)	Participant(s)		Circumstance(s)	
			X…	Roles		
	59b	spin (material)	the market	Actor	without a watchful eye; out of control	
	60a	prosper (material)	The nation	Actor	long	<c 60a> The nation cannot prosper long <c 60b> when it favors only the prosperous.
	60b	favours (material)	it	Actor		
			only the prosperous	Goal		
34	61a	depended (relational)	The success of our economy	Carrier	not just on the size of our gross domestic product, but on the reach of our prosperity, on the ability [<c 61b>]	<c 61a> The success of our economy has always depended not just on the size of our gross domestic product, but on the reach of our prosperity, on the ability [<c 61b> to extend opportunity to every willing heart –] <c 61c> not out of charity, but because it is the surest route to our common good. (Applause.)
	61b	extend (material)	opportunity	Goal	to every willing heart –	
	61c	is (relational)	it	Identified		
			the surest route to our common good.	Identifier		
35	62	reject (material)	we	Actor	as false	<c 62> As for our common defense, we reject as false the choice between our safety and our ideals.
			the choice between our safety and our ideals	Goal		
36	63a	drafted (material)	Our Founding Fathers	Actor		<c 63a> Our Founding Fathers -- (applause) -- our Founding Fathers, … drafted a charter <63b> faced with perils [<63c> that we can scarcely imagine], <c 63d> to assure the rule of law and the rights of man -- a charter [<c 63e> expanded by the blood of generations.]
			a charter	Goal		
	63b	faced (material)			with perils [<c 63c>]	
	63c	imagine (mental)	we	Senser		
	63d	assure (material)	the rule of law and the rights of man -- a charter [<c 63e>]	Goal		
	63e	expanded (material)	the blood of generations	Actor		
37	64a	light (material)	Those ideals	Actor		<c 64a> Those ideals still light the world, <c 64b> and we will not give them up for
			the world	Goal		

Transitivity Structure of Barack Obama's First Inaugural Address

Para#	Cl#	Transitivity Structure				Clause (Complex)
		Process (type)	Participant(s)		Circumstance(s)	
			X…	Roles		
	64b	give X up (material)	we	Actor	for expedience sake	expedience sake. (Applause.)
			them	Goal		
38	65a	know (mental)	<c 65d>[<c 65e>]	Phenomenon	to all the other peoples and governments [<c 65b>], from the grandest capitals to the small village [<c 65c>]	<c 65a> And so, to all the other peoples and governments [<c 65b> who are watching today, from the grandest capitals to the small village [<c 65c> where my father was born:]] know <c 65d> that America is a friend of each nation, and every man, woman and child [<c 65e>who seeks a future of peace and dignity.]
	65b	watching (material)			today	
	65c	born (material)	my father	Range		
	65d	is (relational)	America	Carrier		
			a friend of each nation, and every man, woman and child [<c 65e>]	Attribute		
	65e	seeks (material)	a future of peace and dignity	Goal		
	66a	are (relational)	we	Carrier	once more	<c 66a> And we are ready [<c 66b> to lead once more.] (Applause.)
			ready [<c 66b>]	Attribute		
	66b	lead (material)				
39	67a	Recall (mental)	<c 67b>	Phenomenon		<c 67a> Recall <c 67b> that earlier generations faced down fascism and communism not just with missiles and tanks, but with the sturdy alliances and enduring convictions.
	67b	faced down (material)	earlier generations	Actor	not just with missiles and tanks, but with the sturdy alliances and enduring convictions	
			fascism and communism	Goal		
40	68a	understood (mental)	they	Senser		<c 68a> They understood <c 68b> that our power alone cannot protect us, <c 68c> nor does it entitle us <c 68d> to do <c 68e> as we please.
			<c 68b>	Phenomenon		
	68b	protect (material)	our power	Actor	alone	
			us	Goal		

Transitivity Structure of Barack Obama's First Inaugural Address

Para#	Cl#	Transitivity Structure				Clause (Complex)
		Process (type)	Participant(s)		Circumstance(s)	
			X…	Roles		
	68c	entitle (material)	it	Actor		
			us	Goal		
	68d	do (material)				
	68e	please (mental)	we	Senser		
	69a	knew (mental)	they	Senser		<c 69a> Instead they knew <c 69b> that our power grows through its prudent use; <c 69c> our security emanates from the justness of our cause, the force of our example, the tempering qualities of humility and restraint.
			<c 69b>; <c 69c>	Phenomenon		
	69b	grows (material)	our power	Actor	through its prudent use	
	69c	emanates (material)	our security	Actor	from the justness of our cause, the force of our example, the tempering qualities of humility and restraint	
41	70	are (relational)	we	Identified		<c 70> We are the keepers of this legacy.
			the keepers of this legacy	Identifier		
	71a	Guided (material)	these principles	Actor		<c 71a> Guided by these principles <c 71b> once more we can meet those new threats [<c 71c> that demand even greater effort, even greater cooperation and understanding between nations.]
	71b	meet (material)	we	Actor	once more	
			those new threats [<c 71c>]	Goal		
	71c	demand (material)	even greater effort, even greater cooperation and understanding between nations	Goal		
	72a	begin (material)	we	Actor	to its people	<c 72a> We will begin <c 72b> to responsibly leave Iraq to its people <c 72c> and forge a hard-earned peace in Afghanistan.
	72b	leave (material)	Iraq	Goal		
	72c	forge (material)	a hard-earned peace	Goal	in Afghanistan	
42	73a	work (material)	we	Actor	With old friends and former foes; tirelessly	<c 73a> With old friends and former foes, we'll work tirelessly <c 73b> to lessen the nuclear

Transitivity Structure of Barack Obama's First Inaugural Address

Para#	Cl#	Transitivity Structure				Clause (Complex)
		Process (type)	Participant(s)		Circumstance(s)	
			X…	Roles		
	73b	lessen (material)	the nuclear threat	Goal		threat, <c 73c> and roll back the specter of a warming planet.
	73c	roll back (material)	the specter of a warming planet	Goal		
43	74a	apologize (material)	we	Actor	for our way of life	<c 74a> We will not apologize for our way of life, <c 74b> nor will we waver in its defense.
	74b	waver (material)	we	Actor	in its defense	
44	75a	say (verbal)	we	Sayer	And for those [<c 75b>]; now	<c 75a> And for those [<c 75b> who seek <c 75c> to advance their aims by inducing terror and slaughtering innocents,] <c 75a> we say to you now <c 75d> that our spirit is stronger <c 75e> and cannot be broken – <c 75f> you cannot outlast us, <c 75g> and we will defeat you. (Applause.)
			you	Receiver		
			<c 75d-g>	Verbiage		
	75b	seek (material)	<c 75c>	Goal		
	75c	advance (material)	their aims	Goal	by inducing terror and slaughtering innocents	
	75d	is (relational)	our spirit	Carrier		
			stronger	Attribute		
	75e	broken (material)				
	75f	outlast (material)	you	Actor		
			us	Goal		
	75g	defeat (material)	we	Actor		
			you	Goal		
45	76a	know (mental)	we	Senser		<c 76a> For we know <c 76b> that our patchwork heritage is a strength, not a weakness.
			<c 76b>	Phenomenon		
	76b	is (relational)	our patchwork heritage	Carrier		
			a strength, not a weakness	Attribute		

Transitivity Structure of Barack Obama's First Inaugural Address

Para#	Cl#	Transitivity Structure				Clause (Complex)
		Process (type)	Participant(s)		Circumstance(s)	
			X…	Roles		
46	77	are (relational)	we	Carrier		<c 77> We are a nation of Christians and Muslims, Jews and Hindus, and non-believers.
			a nation of Christians and Muslims, Jews and Hindus, and non-believers.	Attribute		
	78a	shaped (material)	we	Goal		<c 78a> We are shaped by every language and culture, <c 78b> drawn from every end of this Earth; <c 78c> and because we have tasted the bitter swill of civil war and segregation, <c 78d> and emerged from that dark chapter stronger and more united, <c 78e> we cannot help but believe <c 78f> that the old hatreds shall someday pass; <c 78g> that the lines of tribe shall soon dissolve; <c 78h> that as the world grows smaller, <c 78i> our common humanity shall reveal itself; <c 78j> and that America must play its role <c 78k> in ushering in a new era of peace.
			every language and culture	Actor		
	78b	drawn (material)			from every end of this Earth	
	78c	tasted (material)	we	Actor		
			the bitter swill of civil war and segregation	Goal		
	78d	emerged (material)	stronger and more united	Attribute	from that dark chapter	
	78e	believe (mental)	we	Senser		
			<c 78f-k>	Phenomenon		
	78f	pass (material)	the old hatreds	Affected	someday	
	78g	dissolve (material)	the lines of tribe	Affected	soon	
	78h	grows (relational)	the world	Carrier		
			smaller	Attribute		
	78i	reveal (material)	our common humanity	Actor		
			itself	Goal		
	78j	play (material)	America	Actor		
			its role	Goal		
	78k	ushering in (material)	a new era of peace	Goal		
47	79	seek (material)	we	Actor	To the Muslim world; based on mutual interest and mutual respect	<c 79> To the Muslim world, we seek a new way forward, based on mutual interest and mutual respect.
			a new way forward	Goal		

Transitivity Structure of Barack Obama's First Inaugural Address

Para#	Cl#	Transitivity Structure				Clause (Complex)
		Process (type)	Participant(s)		Circumstance(s)	
			X…	Roles		
48	80a	know (mental)	<c 80e>[<c 80fg>]	Phenomenon	To those leaders around the globe [<c 80b-d>]	<c 80a> To those leaders around the globe [c 80b>who seek <c 80c> to sow conflict, <c 80d> or blame their society's ills on the West,] know <c 80e> that your people will judge you on [<c 80f> what you can build, not <c 80g> what you destroy.] (Applause.)
	80b	seek (material)	<c 80c>			
	80c	sow (material)	conflict	Goal		
	80d	blame (material)	their society's ills	Goal	on the West	
	80e	judge (material)	your people	Actor	on [<c 80fg>]	
			you	Goal		
	80f	build (material)	you	Actor		
	80g	destroy (material)	you	Actor		
49	81a	know (mental)	<c 81c-e>	Phenomenon	To those [<c 81b >]	<c 81a> To those [<c 81b> who cling to power through corruption and deceit and the silencing of dissent,] know <c 81c> that you are on the wrong side of history, <c 81d> but that we will extend a hand <c 81e> if you are willing to unclench your fist. (Applause.)
	81c	are (relational)	you	Carrier		
			on the wrong side of history	Attribute		
	81d	extend (material)	we	Actor		
			a hand	Goal		
	81e	unclench (material)	you	Actor		
			your fist	Goal		
50	82a	pledge (verbal)	we	Sayer	To the people of poor nations	<c 82a> To the people of poor nations, we pledge <c 82b> to work alongside you <c 82c> to make your farms flourish <c 82d> and let clean waters flow; <c 82e> to nourish starved bodies <c 82f> and feed hungry minds.
			<c 82b-f>	Verbiage		
	82b	work (material)			along side you	
	82c	make (material)	your farms	Goal		
			flourish	Target		
	82d	let X flow (material)	clean waters	Goal		
	82e	nourish (material)	starved bodies	Goal		
	82f	feed (material)	hungry minds	Goal		

Transitivity Structure of Barack Obama's First Inaugural Address

Para#	Cl#	Transitivity Structure				Clause (Complex)
		Process (type)	Participant(s)		Circumstance(s)	
			X…	Roles		
51	83a	say (verbal)	we	Sayer	And to those nations like ours [<c 83b>]	<c 83a> And to those nations like ours [<c 83b> that enjoy relative plenty,] we say <c 83c> we can no longer afford indifference to the suffering outside our borders, <c 83d> nor can we consume the world's resources without regard to effect.
			<c 83c-d>	Verbiage		
	83b	enjoy (material)	relative plenty	Goal		
	83c	afford (material)	we	Actor		
			indifference to the suffering outside our borders	Goal		
	83d	consume (material)	we	Actor	without regard to effect	
			the world's resources	Goal		
	84a	changed (material)	the world	Actor		<c 84a> For the world has changed, <c 84b> and we must change with it.
	84b	change (material)	we	Actor	with it	
52	85a	consider (mental)	we	Senser		<c 85a> As we consider the role [<c 85b> that unfolds before us], <c 85c> we remember with humble gratitude those brave Americans [<85d> who at this very hour patrol far-off deserts and distant mountains].
			the role [<c 85b>]	Phenomenon		
	85b	unfolds (material)			before us	
	85c	remember (mental)	we	Senser	with humble gratitude	
			those brave Americans [<c 85d>]	Phenomenon		
	85d	patrol (material)	far-off deserts and distant mountains	Goal		
	86a	have (relational)	they	Possessor		<c 86a> They have something to tell us, <c 86b> just as the fallen heroes [<c 86c> who lie in Arlington] whisper through the ages.
			something to tell us	Possessed		
	86b	whisper (verbal)	the fallen heroes [<c 86c>]	Sayer	through the ages	
	86c	lie (relational)	in Arlington	Attribute		
53	87a	honor (material)	we	Actor		<c 87a> We honor them <c 87b> not only because they are the guardians of our liberty,
			them	Goal		

Transitivity Structure of Barack Obama's First Inaugural Address

Para#	Cl#	Transitivity Structure				Clause (Complex)
		Process (type)	Participant(s)		Circumstance(s)	
			X...	Roles		
	87b	are (relational)	they	Identified		<c 87c> but because they embody the spirit of service -- a willingness to find meaning in something greater than themselves.
			the guardians of our liberty	Identifier		
	87c	embody (relational)	they	Possessor		
			the spirit of service	Possessed		
54	88a	is (relational)	it	Identified	And yet at this moment, a moment [<c 88b>]	<c 88a> And yet at this moment, a moment [<88b> that will define a generation,] it is precisely this spirit [<c 88c> that must inhabit us all.]
			this spirit [<c 88c>]	Identifier		
	88b	define (material)	a new generation	Goal		
	88c	inhabit (material)	us	Goal		
55	89a	do (material)	government	Actor	as much as	<c 89a> For as much as government can do, <c 89b> and must do, <c 89c> it is ultimately the faith and determination of the American people [<c 89d> upon which this nation relies.]
	89b	do (material)				
	89c	is (relational)	it	Identified		
			the faith and determination of the American people [<c 89d>]	Identifier		
	89d	relies (material)	this nation	Actor		
56	90a	is (relational)	It	Identified		<c 90a> It is the kindness [<c 90b> to take in a stranger <c 90c> when the levees break,] the selflessness of workers [<c 90d> who would rather cut their hours <c 90e> than see <c 90f> a friend lose their job] [<c 90g> which sees us through our darkest hours.]
			the kindness [<c 90bc>] the selflessness of workers [<c 90df][<c 90g>]	Identifier		
	90b	take in (material)	a stranger	Goal		
	90c	break (material)	the levees	Affected		
	90d	cut (material)	their hours	Goal		
	90e	see (mental)	a friend <c 90f>	Phenomenon		
	90f	lose (material)	their job	Goal		
	90g	see (material)	us	Goal	through our darkest hours	

Transitivity Structure of Barack Obama's First Inaugural Address

Para#	Cl#	Transitivity Structure				Clause (Complex)
		Process (type)	Participant(s)		Circumstance(s)	
			X...	Roles		
57	91a	is (relational)	It	Identified		<c 91a> It is the firefighter's courage [<c 91b> to storm a stairway [<c 91c> filled with smoke,]] but also a parent's willingness [<c 91d> to nurture a child] [<c 91e> that finally decides our fate.]
			the firefighter's courage [<c 91b> [<c 91c>]] but also a parent's willingness [<c 91d>] [<c 91e>]	Identifier		
	91b	storm (material)	a stairway	Goal		
	91c	filled (material)			with smoke	
	91d	nurture (material)	a child	Goal		
	91e	decides (material)	our fate	Goal		
58	92	be (relational)	Our challenges	Carrier		<c 92> Our challenges may be new.
			new	Attribute		
	93a	be (relational)	The instruments [<c 93b>]	Carrier		<c 93a> The instruments [<c 93b> with which we meet them] may be new.
			new	Attribute		
	93b	meet (material)	we	Actor		
			them	Goal		
	94a	are (relational)	But those values [<c 94b>] -- these things	Carrier		<c 94a> But those values [<c 94b> upon which our success depends -- honesty and hard work, courage and fair play, tolerance and curiosity, loyalty and patriotism] -- these things are old.
			old	Attribute		
	94b	depends upon (material)	our success	Actor		
59	95	are (relational)	These things	Carrier		<c 95> These things are true.
			true	Attribute		
	96	have been (relational)	they	Identified		<c 96> They have been the quiet force of progress throughout our history.
			the quiet force of progress throughout our history	Identifier		

Transitivity Structure of Barack Obama's First Inaugural Address

Para#	Cl#	Transitivity Structure				Clause (Complex)
		Process (type)	Participant(s)		Circumstance(s)	
			X…	Roles		
60	97a	is (relational)	<c 97b>	Identified		<c 97a> [<c 97b> What is demanded, then,] is a return to these truths.
			a return to these truths	Identifier		
	97b	demanded (material)	What	Goal	then	
	98a	is (relational)	<c 98b>	Identified		<c 98a> [<c 98b> What is required of us now] is a new era of responsibility -- a recognition on the part of every American [<c 98c> that we have duties to ourselves, our nation and the world; duties [<c 98d> that we do not grudgingly accept, <c 98e> but rather seize gladly, firm in the knowledge [<c 98f> that there is nothing so satisfying to the spirit, so defining of our character <c 98g> than giving our all to a difficult task.]]]
			a new era of responsibility -- a recognition on the part of every American [<c 98c>; duties [<c 98d>, <c 98e> [<c 98f> <c 98g>]]]	Identifier		
	98b	required (material)	what	Goal	now || of us	
	98c	have (relational)	we	Possessor		
			duties to ourselves, our nation and the world; duties [<c 98d>, <c 98e> [<c 98f> <c 98g>]]	Possessed		
	98d	accept (mental)	we	Senser		
	98e	seize (material)			gladly, firm in the knowledge [<c 98f-g>]	
	98f	is (existential)	there			
			nothing so satisfying to the spirit, so defining of our character <c 98g>	existent		
	98g	giving (material)	our all	Goal	to a difficult task	
61	99	is (relational)	This	Identified		<c 99> This is the price and the promise of citizenship.
			the price and the promise of citizenship	Identifier		

Transitivity Structure of Barack Obama's First Inaugural Address

Para#	Cl#	Transitivity Structure				Clause (Complex)
		Process (type)	Participant(s)		Circumstance(s)	
			X…	Roles		
62	100a	is (relational)	This	Identified		<c 100a> This is the source of our confidence -- the knowledge [<100b> that God calls on us <c 100c> to shape an uncertain destiny.]
			the source of our confidence -- the knowledge [<c 100bc>]	Identifier		
	100b	calls on (material)	God	Actor		
			us	Goal		
	100c	shape (material)	an uncertain destiny	Goal		
63	101a	is (relational)	This	Identified		<c 101a> This is the meaning of our liberty and our creed, <c 101b> why men and women and children of every race and every faith can join in celebration across this magnificent mall; <c 101c> and why a man [<c 101d>whose father less than 60 years ago might not have been served in a local restaurant] can now stand before you<c 101e> to take a most sacred oath. (Applause.)
			the meaning of our liberty and our creed	Identifier		
	101b	join (material)	men and women and children of every race and every faith	Actor	in celebration across this magnificent mall	
	101c	stand (behavioural)	a man [< c 101d>]	Behaver	before you	
	101d	served (material)	whose father	Goal	less than 60 years ago; in a local restaurant	
	101e	to take (material)	a most sacred oath	Goal		
64	102a	let X mark (material)	us	Actor	with remembrance of [<c 102bc>]	<c 102a> So let us mark this day with remembrance of [<c 102b> who we are <c 102c> and how far we have traveled.]
			this day	Goal		
	102b	are (relational)	we	Identified		
	102c	traveled (material)	we	Actor	how far	
65	103	huddled (behavioural)	a small band of patriots	Behaver	In the year of America's birth, in the coldest of months,; by dying campfires on the shores of an icy river	<c 103> In the year of America's birth, in the coldest of months, a small band of patriots huddled by dying campfires on the shores of an icy river.
66	104	abandoned (material)	The capital	Goal		<c 104> The capital was abandoned.
	105	advancing (material)	The enemy	Actor		<c 105> The enemy was advancing.

Transitivity Structure of Barack Obama's First Inaugural Address

Para#	Cl#	Transitivity Structure				Clause (Complex)
		Process (type)	Participant(s)		Circumstance(s)	
			X…	Roles		
	106	stained (material)	The snow	Goal	with blood	<c 106> The snow was stained with blood.
67	107a	ordered (material)	the father of our nation	Actor	At the moment [<c 107b>]	<c 107a> At the moment [<c 107b> when the outcome of our revolution was most in doubt,] the father of our nation ordered <c 107c> these words to be read to the people:
			<c 107c>	Goal		
	107b	was (relational)	the outcome of our revolution	Carrier		
			most in doubt	Attribute		
	107c	read (material)	these words	Goal	to the people	
68						<missing>
69	108	remember (mental)	us	Senser	In the face of our common dangers, in this winter of our hardship	<c 108> America: In the face of our common dangers, in this winter of our hardship, let us remember these timeless words.
			these timeless words	Phenomenon		
	109a	brave (material)	us	Actor	With hope and virtue; once more	<c 109a> With hope and virtue, let us brave once more the icy currents, <c 109b> and endure [<c 109c> what storms may come.]
			the icy currents	Goal		
	109b	endure (material)	[<c 109c>]	Goal		
	109c	come (material)	what storms	Actor		
	110a	said (verbal)	it	Verbiage		<c 110a> Let it be said by our children's children <c 110b> that when we were tested <c 110c> we refused <c 110d> to let this journey end,<c 110e> that we did not turn back <c 110f> nor did we falter; <c 110g> and with eyes fixed on the horizon and God's grace upon us, <c 110h> we carried forth that great gift of freedom <c 110i> and delivered it safely to future generations.
			our children's children	Sayer		
	110b	tested (material)	we	Goal		
	110c	refused (verbal)	we	Sayer		
			<c 110d>	Verbiage		
	110d	let X end (material)	journey	Goal		
	110e	turn back (material)	we	Actor		
	110f	falter (material)	we	Actor		
	110g	fixed (material)	eyes	Goal	on the horizon and God's grace upon us	

Transitivity Structure of Barack Obama's First Inaugural Address

Para#	Cl#	Transitivity Structure				Clause (Complex)
		Process (type)	Participant(s)		Circumstance(s)	
			X…	Roles		
	110h	carried forth (material)	we	Actor		
			that great gift of freedom	Goal		
	110i	delivered (material)	it	Goal	safely to future generations	

Appendix 11.3

Logical structure of Barack Obama's First Inaugural Address.

Paragraph	Simple clause	Clause complex											
		Paratactic				Hypotactic							
		Expansion			Projection	Expansion						Projection	
		Elaboration	Extension	Enhancement		Elaboration		Extension		Enhancement			
						α	β	α	β	α	β	α	β
1	1		1b + 1c + 1d			1a	1b-d						
2	2a[b]												
3	3												
4	4												
	5												
	6		6b + 6c							6a	6b,c		
5	7		7a + 7b										
6	8a[b]												
	9												
	10a[bc]												
7	11		11a + 11b + 11c										
	12		12a + 12b + 12c[d[e]f]										
8	13												
	14a[bc]												
9	15											15a	15b[c]
	16		16a + 16b										
	17												
	18											18a	18b
10	19									19a	19b		
11	20									20a	20b[c]		
12	21												
	22									22a	22b		
	23		23b + 23c + 23d[e][fgh[i]]							23a	23b-i		
13	24					24b,c	24a					24b	24c
	25												

Logical structure of Barack Obama's First Inaugural Address.

Paragraph	Simple clause	Clause complex											
		Paratactic				Hypotactic							
		Expansion			Projection	Expansion						Projection	
		Elaboration	Extension	Enhancement		Elaboration		Extension		Enhancement			
						α	β	α	β	α	β	α	β
	26												
14	27a[bc]												
15	28a[b]												
16	29		29a + 29b										
	30		30a + 30b + 30c + 30d										
17	31		31a + 31b										
18	32		32a + 32b + 32c							32a-c	32d		
										32a-d	32e		
	33												
19	34a[b]												
	35												
	36									36a	36b		
	37		37a + 37bc							37b	37c		
	38												
	39a[b-d]												
20	40		40b + 40c + 40d							40b-d	40a		
21	41[b][c]												
22	42												
	43		43b + 43c							43a	43b,c		
23	44a[bc]												
24	45		45a + 45b							45a,b	45c,d		
			45c + 45d										
25	46		46b + 46c							46a	46b,c		
	47									47a	47b		
26	48												
	49												
27	50a[b-d]												

Logical structure of Barack Obama's First Inaugural Address.

Paragraph	Simple clause	Clause complex											
		Paratactic				Hypotactic							
		Expansion			Projection	Expansion						Projection	
		Elaboration	Extension	Enhancement		Elaboration		Extension		Enhancement			
						α	β	α	β	α	β	α	β
	51		51c + 51de							51a	51b-e	51b	51c-e
										51d	51e		
28	52a[b][c d[e]]												
29	53a[b][c][def[g][h]]												
30	54					54b	54c			54b,c	54a		
	55									55b	55a		
	56									56a[b]	56c-f		
										56c-e	56f		
32	57a[b]												
	58a[bc]												
33	59											59a	59b
	60									60a	60b		
34	61									61a[b]	61c		
35	62												
36	63					63a	63b[c]			63a-b[c]	63d[e]		
37	64		64a + 64b										
38	65											65a[b[c]]	65d[e]
	66a[b]												
39	67											67a	67b
40	68		68b + 68ce							68c	68d,e	68a	68b-e
										68d	68e		
	69		69b + 69c									69a	69bc
41	70												
	71					71b[c]	71a						
	72		72a + 72b										
42	73		73b + 73c							73a	73b,c		
43	74		74a + 74b										

Logical structure of Barack Obama's First Inaugural Address.

Paragraph	Simple clause	Clause complex											
		Paratactic				Hypotactic							
		Expansion			Projection	Expansion						Projection	
		Elaboration	Extension	Enhancement		Elaboration		Extension		Enhancement			
						α	β	α	β	α	β	α	β
44	75		75d + 75e									75a[bc]	75d-g
			75f + 75g										
45	76											76a	76b
46	77												
	78		78ab + 78c-k			78a	78b			78e-k	78c,d	78e	78f-k
			78c + 78d										
			78f + 78g + 78hi + 78jk										
47	79												
48	80											80a[bcd]	80[e[fg]]
49	81		81c + 81de							81d	81e	81a[b]	81c-e
50	82		82b-d + 82ef									82a	82b-f
			82b+ 82c + 82d										
			82e + 82f										
51	83		83c + 83d									83a[b]	83c,d
	84		84a + 84b										
52	85									85c[d]	85a[b]		
	86									86a	86b[c]		
53	87		87b + 87c							87a	87b,c		
54	88 a[b][c]												
55	89		89a + 89b							89c[d]	89a,b		
56	90a[bc][def][g]												
57	91[b[c]][d][e]												
58	92												
	93a[b]												
	94a[b]												
59	95												

Logical structure of Barack Obama's First Inaugural Address.

Paragraph	Simple clause	Clause complex											
		Paratactic				Hypotactic							
		Expansion			Projection	Expansion						Projection	
		Elaboration	Extension	Enhancement		Elaboration		Extension		Enhancement			
						α	β	α	β	α	β	α	β
	96												
60	97a[b]												
	98a[b][c[de[fg]]]												
61	99												
62	100a[b]												
63	101		101b + 101c-e							101a	101b-e		
										101c[d]	101e		
64	102a[bc]												
65	103												
66	104												
	105												
	106												
67	107									107c	107a[b]		
68	108												
69	109		109a + 109b[c]										
	110		110b-d + 110e-f							110c-d	110b	110a	110b-i
			110b-f + 110g-i							110c	110d		
										110h,i	110g		

Appendix 11.4

Theme-rheme structure of Barack Obama's First Inaugural Address

Sent #	Cl#	Theme				Clause
		Textual	Inter-personal	Topical/ Existential	displaced	
1	1a			I		<c 1a> I stand here today <c 1b> humbled by the task before us, <c 1c> grateful for the trust [<c 1d> you've bestowed], <c 1e> mindful of the sacrifices [<c 1 f> borne by our ancestors.]
	1b					
	1c					
	1d					
2	2a			I		<c 2a> I thank President Bush for his service to our nation -- (applause) -- as well as the generosity and cooperation [<c 2b>he has shown throughout this transition.]
3	3			Forty-four Americans		<c 3> Forty-four Americans have now taken the presidential oath.
4	4			The words		<c 4> The words have been spoken during rising tides of prosperity and the still waters of peace.
5	5	Yet		every so often	the oath	<c 5> Yet, every so often, the oath is taken amidst gathering clouds and raging storms.
6	6a			At these moments	America	<c 6a> At these moments, America has carried on not simply because of the skill or vision of those in high office, <c 6b> but because we, the people, have remained faithful to the ideals of our forebears <c 6c> and true to our founding documents.
	6b	but because		we, the people		
	6c	and				
7	7a			So		<c 7a> So it has been; <c 7b> so it must be with this generation of Americans.
	7b			so		
8	8			[<c 8b> That we are in the midst of crisis]		<c 8a> [<c 8b> That we are in the midst of crisis] is now well understood.
9	9			Our nation		<c 9> Our nation is at war against a far-reaching network of violence and hatred.
10	10a			Our economy		<c 10a> Our economy is badly weakened, a consequence of greed and irresponsibility on the part of some, but also our collective failure [<c 10b> to make hard choices <c 10c> and prepare the nation for a new age].
11	11a			Homes		<c 11a> Homes have been lost, <c 11b> jobs shed, <c 11c> businesses shuttered.
	11b			jobs		
	11c			businesses		

Theme-rheme structure of Barack Obama's First Inaugural Address

Sent #	Cl#	Theme				Clause
		Textual	Inter-personal	Topical/ Existential	displaced	
12	12a			Our health care		<c 12a> Our health care is too costly,<c 12b> our schools fail too many –<c 12c> and each day brings further evidence [<c 12d> that the ways [<c 12e> we use energy] strengthen our adversaries <c 12f> and threaten our planet.]
	12b			our schools		
	12c	and		each day		
13	13			These		<c 13> These are the indicators of crisis, subject to data and statistics.
14	14a			Less measurable, but no less profound		<c 14a> Less measurable, but no less profound, is a sapping of confidence across our land; a nagging fear [<c 14b> that America's decline is inevitable, <c 14c> that the next generation must lower its sights.]
15	15a			Today	I	<c 15a> Today I say to you <c 15b> that the challenges [<c 15c> we face] are real.
	15b	that		that the challenges [<c 15c> we face]		
16	16a			They		<c 16a> They are serious <c 16b> and they are many.
	16b	and		they		
17	17			They		<c 17> They will not be met easily or in a short span of time.
18	18a	But	know			<c 18a> But know this America: <c 18b> They will be met. (Applause.)
	18b			They		
19	19a			On this day	we	<c 19a> On this day, we gather <c 19b> because we have chosen hope over fear, unity of purpose over conflict and discord.
	19b	because		we		
20	20a			On this day	we	<c 20a> On this day, we come <c 20b> to proclaim an end to the petty grievances and false promises, the recriminations and worn-out dogmas [<c 20c> that for far too long have strangled our politics.]
	20b					
21	21			We		<c 21> We remain a young nation.
22	22a	But		in the words of Scripture	the time	<c 22a> But in the words of Scripture, the time has come <c 22b> to set aside childish things.
	22b					
23	23a			The time		<c 23a> The time has come <c 23b> to reaffirm our enduring spirit;<c 23c> to choose our better history; <c 23d>
	23b					
	23c					

Theme-rheme structure of Barack Obama's First Inaugural Address

Sent #	Cl#	Theme				Clause
		Textual	Inter-personal	Topical/ Existential	displaced	
	23d					to carry forward that precious gift, that noble idea [<c 23e> passed on from generation to generation:] the God-given promise [<c 23f> that all are equal, <c 23g> all are free, <c 23h> and all deserve a chance [<c 23i> to pursue their full measure of happiness.]] (Applause.)
24	24a					<c 24a> In reaffirming the greatness of our nation <c 24b> we understand <c 24c> that greatness is never a given.
	24b			we		
	24c	that		greatness		
25	25			It		<c 25> It must be earned.
26	26			Our journey		<c 26> Our journey has never been one of short-cuts or settling for less.
27	27a			It		<c 27a> It has not been the path for the faint-hearted, for those [<c 27b> that prefer leisure over work, <c 27c> or seek only the pleasures of riches and fame.]
28	28	Rather		it		<c 28a> Rather, it has been the risk-takers, the doers, the makers of things -- some celebrated, but more often men and women obscure in their labor –[<c 28b> who have carried us up the long rugged path towards prosperity and freedom.]
29	29			For us		<c 29>For us <c 29a> they packed up their few worldly possessions <c 29b> and traveled across oceans in search of a new life.
	29a			they		
	29b	and				
30	30			For us		<c 30> For us <c 30a> they toiled in sweatshops, <c 30b> and settled the West, <c 30c> endured the lash of the whip <c 30d> and plowed the hard earth.
	30a			they		
	30b	and				
	30c					
	30d	and				
31	31			For us		<31> For us, <31a> they fought <31b> and died in places like Concord and Gettysburg, Normandy and Khe Sahn.
	31a			they		
	31b	and				
32	32a			Time and again	these men and women	<c 32a> Time and again these men and women struggled <c 32b> and sacrificed <c 32c> and worked <c 32d> till their hands were raw <c 32e>so that we might live a better life.
	32b	and				
	32c	and				
	32d	till		their hands		
	32e	so that		we		

Theme-rheme structure of Barack Obama's First Inaugural Address

Sent #	Cl#	Theme				Clause
		Textual	Inter-personal	Topical/ Existential	displaced	
33	33			They		<c 33> They saw America as bigger than the sum of our individual ambitions, greater than all the differences of birth or wealth or faction.
34	34			This		<c 34a> This is the journey [<c 34b> we continue today.]
35	35			We		<c 35> We remain the most prosperous, powerful nation on Earth.
36	36a			Our workers		<c 36a> Our workers are no less productive <c 36b> than when this crisis began.
	36b	than when		this crisis		
37	37a			Our minds		<c 37a> Our minds are no less inventive, <c 37b> our goods and services no less needed <c 37c> than they were last week, or last month, or last year.
	37b			our goods and services		
	37c	than		they		
38	38			Our capacity		<c 38> Our capacity remains undiminished.
39	39	But		our time [<c 39b> of standing pat, <c 39c> of protecting narrow interests <c 39d> and putting off unpleasant decisions]-- that time		<39a> But our time [<c 39b> of standing pat, <c 39c> of protecting narrow interests <c 39d> and putting off unpleasant decisions]-- that time has surely passed.
40	40a					<c 40a> Starting today, <c 40b> we must pick ourselves up, <c 40c> dust ourselves off, <c 40d> and begin again the work of remaking America. (Applause.)
	40b			we		
	40c					
	40d	and				
41	41a	For		everywhere we look	there	<c 41a> For everywhere [<c 41b> we look] there is work [<41c> to be done.]
42	42			The state of our economy		<c 42> The state of our economy calls for action, bold and swift.
43	43a	And		we		<c 43a> And we will act, <c 43b> not only to create new jobs, <c 43c> but to lay a new foundation for growth.
	43b	not only				
	43c	but				
44	44a			We		<c 44a> We will build the roads and bridges, the electric grids and digital lines [<44b> that feed our commerce <44c> and bind us together.]
45	45a			We		<c 45a> We'll restore science <c 45b> and wield technology's wonders <c
	45b	and				

Theme-rheme structure of Barack Obama's First Inaugural Address

Sent #	Cl#	Theme				Clause
		Textual	Inter-personal	Topical/ Existential	displaced	
	45c					45c> to raise health care's quality <c 45d> and lower its cost.
	45d	and				
46	46a			We		<c 46a> We will harness the sun and the winds and the soil <c 46b> to fuel our cars <c 46c> and run our factories.
	46b					
	46c	and				
47	47a	And		we		<c 47a> And we will transform our schools and colleges and universities <c 47b> to meet the demands of a new age.
	47b					
48	48			All this	we	<c 48> All this we can do.
49	49			All this	we	<c 49> All this we will do.
50	50a			Now	there	<c 50a> Now, there are some [<c 50b> who question the scale of our ambitions, <c 50c> who suggest <c 50d> that our system cannot tolerate too many big plans.]
51	51a			Their memories		<c 51a> Their memories are short, <c 51b> for they have forgotten <c 51c> what this country has already done, <c 51d> what free men and women can achieve <c 51e> when imagination is joined to common purpose, and necessity to courage.
	51b	for		they		
	51c			what	this country	
	51d			what	free man and women	
	51e			when	imagination	
52	52a			[<c 52b>What the cynics fail to understand]		<c 52a> [<c 52b>What the cynics fail to understand] is [<c 52c> that the ground has shifted beneath them, <c 52d> that the stale political arguments [<c 52e> that have consumed us for so long] no longer apply.]
53	53a			The question [<c 53b> we ask today]		<c 53a> The question [<c 53b> we ask today] is [not [<c 53c> whether our government is too big or too small,] but [<c 53d> whether it works– <c 53e> whether it helps families <c 53f> find jobs at a decent wage, care [<c 53g> they can afford], a retirement [<c 53h> that is dignified.]]
54	54a			Where	the answer	<c 54a> Where the answer is yes, <c 54b> we intend <c 54c> to move forward.
	54b			we		
55	55a			Where	the answer	<c 55a> Where the answer is no, <c 55b> programs will end.
	55b			programs		
56	56a	And		those of us [<c 56b> who manage the public's dollars]		<c 56a> And those of us [<c 56b> who manage the public's dollars] will be held to account,<c 56c> to spend wisely, <c 56d> reform

Theme-rheme structure of Barack Obama's First Inaugural Address

Sent #	Cl#	Theme				Clause
		Textual	Inter-personal	Topical/ Existential	displaced	
	56c					bad habits, <c 56e> and do our business in the light of day, <c 56f> because only then can we restore the vital trust between a people and their government.
	56d					
	56e	and				
	56f	because		only then		
57	57a	Nor				<c 57a> Nor is the question before us [<c 57b> whether the market is a force for good or ill.]
58	58a			<c 58a> Its power [<c 58b> to generate wealth <c 58c> and expand freedom]		<c 58a> Its power [<c 58b> to generate wealth <c 58c> and expand freedom] is unmatched.
59	59a	But		this crisis		<c 59a> But this crisis has reminded us <c 59b> that without a watchful eye, the market can spin out of control.
	59b	that		without a watchful eye	the market	
60	60a			The nation		<c 60a> The nation cannot prosper long <c 60b> when it favors only the prosperous.
	60b	when		it		<c 60a> The nation cannot prosper long <c 60b> when it favors only the prosperous.
61	61a			The success of our economy		<c 61a> The success of our economy has always depended not just on the size of our gross domestic product, but on the reach of our prosperity, on the ability [<c 61b> to extend opportunity to every willing heart –] <c 61c> not out of charity, but because it is the surest route to our common good. (Applause.)
	61c			not out of charity		
62	62	As for		our common defense	we	<c 62> As for our common defense, we reject as false the choice between our safety and our ideals.
63	63a			Our Founding Fathers		<c 63a> Our Founding Fathers -- (applause) -- our Founding Fathers, ... drafted a charter <63b> faced with perils [<63c> that we can scarcely imagine], <c 63d> to assure the rule of law and the rights of man -- a charter [<c 63e> expanded by the blood of generations.]
	63b					
	63d					
64	64a			Those ideals		<c 64a> Those ideals still light the world, <c 64b> and we will not give them up for expedience sake. (Applause.)
	64b	and		we		

Theme-rheme structure of Barack Obama's First Inaugural Address

Sent #	Cl#	Theme				Clause
		Textual	Inter-personal	Topical/ Existential	displaced	
65	65a	And so		to all the other peoples and governments [<c 65b> who are watching today]		<c 65a> And so, to all the other peoples and governments [<c 65b> who are watching today, from the grandest capitals to the small village [<c 65c> where my father was born:]] know <c 65d> that America is a friend of each nation, and every man, woman and child [<c 65e> who seeks a future of peace and dignity.]
	65d	that		America		
66	66a	And		we		<c 66a> And we are ready [<c 66b> to lead once more.] (Applause.)
67	67a		Recall			<c 67a> Recall <c 67b> that earlier generations faced down fascism and communism not just with missiles and tanks, but with the sturdy alliances and enduring convictions.
	67b	that		earlier generations		
68	68a			They		<c 68a> They understood <c 68b> that our power alone cannot protect us, <c 68c> nor does it entitle us <c 68d> to do <c 68e> as we please.
	68b	that		our power alone		
	68c	nor				
	68d	as		we		
69	69a	Instead		they		<c 69a> Instead they knew <c 69b> that our power grows through its prudent use; <c 69c> our security emanates from the justness of our cause, the force of our example, the tempering qualities of humility and restraint.
	69b	that		our power		
	69c			our security		
70	70			We		<c 70> We are the keepers of this legacy.
71	71a					<c 71a> Guided by these principles <c 71b> once more we can meet those new threats [<c 71c> that demand even greater effort, even greater cooperation and understanding between nations.]
	71b			once more	we	
72	72a			We		<c 72a> We will begin to responsibly leave Iraq to its people <c 72b> and forge a hard-earned peace in Afghanistan.
	72b	and				
73	73a			With old friends and former foes	we	<c 73a> With old friends and former foes, we'll work tirelessly <c 73b> to lessen the nuclear threat, <c 73c> and roll back the specter of a warming planet.
	73b					
	73c	and				
74	74a			We		<c 74a> We will not apologize for our way of life, <c 74b> nor will we waver in its defense.
	74b	nor				

Theme-rheme structure of Barack Obama's First Inaugural Address

Sent #	Cl#	Theme				Clause
		Textual	Inter-personal	Topical/ Existential	displaced	
75	75a	And for		those [<c 75b> who seek <c 75c> to advance their aims by inducing terror and slaughtering innocents,]	we	<c 75a> And for those [<c 75b> who seek <c 75c> to advance their aims by inducing terror and slaughtering innocents,] <c 75a> we say to you now <c 75d> that our spirit is stronger <c 75e> and cannot be broken – <c 75f> you cannot outlast us, <c 75g> and we will defeat you. (Applause.)
	75c					
	75d	that		our spirit		
	75e	and				
	75f			you		
	75g	and		we		
76	76a	For		we		<c 76a> For we know <c 76b> that our patchwork heritage is a strength, not a weakness.
	76b	that		our patchwork heritage		
77	77			We		<c 77> We are a nation of Christians and Muslims, Jews and Hindus, and non-believers.
78	78a			We		<c 78a> We are shaped by every language and culture, <c 78b> drawn from every end of this Earth; <c 78c> and because we have tasted the bitter swill of civil war and segregation, <c 78d> and emerged from that dark chapter stronger and more united, <c 78e> we cannot help but believe <c 78f> that the old hatreds shall someday pass; <c 78g> that the lines of tribe shall soon dissolve; <c 78h> that as the world grows smaller, <c 78i> our common humanity shall reveal itself; <c 78j> and that America must play its role <c 78k> in ushering in a new era of peace.
	78b					
	78c	and because		we		
	78d	and				
	78e			we		
	78f	that		the old hatreds		
	78g	that		the lines of tribe		
	78h	that as		the world		
	78i			our common humanity		
	78j	and that		America		
	78k					
79	79			To the Muslim world	we	<c 79> To the Muslim world, we seek a new way forward, based on mutual interest and mutual respect.
80	80a			To those leaders around the globe [<c 80b-d>]		<c 80a> To those leaders around the globe [<c 80b> who seek <c 80c> to sow conflict, <c 80d> or blame their society's ills on the West,] know <c 80e> that your people will judge you on [<c 80f> what you can build, not <c 80g> what you destroy.] (Applause.)
	80e	that		your people		

Theme-rheme structure of Barack Obama's First Inaugural Address

Sent #	Cl#	Theme				Clause
		Textual	Inter-personal	Topical/ Existential	displaced	
81	81a			To those [<c 81b> who cling to power through corruption and deceit and the silencing of dissent,]		<c 81a> To those [<c 81b> who cling to power through corruption and deceit and the silencing of dissent,] know <c 81c> that you are on the wrong side of history, <c 81d> but that we will extend a hand <c 81e> if you are willing to unclench your fist. (Applause.)
	81c	that		you		
	81d	but that		we		
	81e	if		you		
82	82a			To the people of poor nations	we	<c 82a> To the people of poor nations, we pledge <c 82b> to work alongside you <c 82c> to make your farms flourish <c 82d> and let clean waters flow; <c 82e> to nourish starved bodies <c 82f> and feed hungry minds.
	82b					
	82c					
	82d	and				
	82e					
	82f	and				
83	83a	And		to those nations like ours [<c 83b> that enjoy relative plenty,]	we	<c 83a> And to those nations like ours [<c 83b> that enjoy relative plenty,] we say <c 83c> we can no longer afford indifference to the suffering outside our borders, <c 83d> nor can we consume the world's resources without regard to effect.
	83c			we		
	83d	nor				
84	84a	For		the world		<c 84a> For the world has changed, <c 84b> and we must change with it.
	84b	and		we		
85	85a	As		we		<c 85a> As we consider the role [<c 85b> that unfolds before us], <c 85c> we remember with humble gratitude those brave Americans [<85d> who at this very hour patrol far-off deserts and distant mountains].
	85c			we		
86	86a			They		<c 86a> They have something to tell us, <c 86b> just as the fallen heroes [<86c> who lie in Arlington]whisper through the ages.
	86b	just as		the fallen heroes [<86c> who lie in Arlington]		
87	87a			We		<c 87a> We honor them <c 87b> not only because they are the guardians of our liberty, <c 87c> but because they embody the spirit of service -- a willingness to find meaning in something greater than themselves.
	87b	not only because		they		
	87c	but because		they		
88	88	And yet		at this moment		<c 88a> And yet at this moment, a moment [<88b> that will define a generation,] it is precisely this spirit [<c 88c> that must inhabit us all.]
89	89a	For as much as		government		<c 89a> For as much as government can do, <c 89b> and must do, <c 89c>

Theme-rheme structure of Barack Obama's First Inaugural Address

Sent #	Cl#	Theme				Clause
		Textual	Inter-personal	Topical/ Existential	displaced	
	89b	and				it is ultimately the faith and determination of the American people [<c 89d> upon which this nation relies.]
	89c			it		
90	90a			It		<c 90a> It is the kindness [<c 90b> to take in a stranger <c 90c> when the levees break,] the selflessness of workers [<c 90d> who would rather cut their hours <c 90e> than see <c 90f> a friend lose their job] [<c 90g> which sees us through our darkest hours.]
91	91a			It		<c 91a> It is the firefighter's courage [<c 91b> to storm a stairway [<c 91c> filled with smoke,]] but also a parent's willingness [<c 91d> to nurture a child] [<c 91e> that finally decides our fate.]
92	92			Our challenges		<c 92> Our challenges may be new.
93	93a			The instruments [<c 93b> with which we meet them]		<c 93a> The instruments [<c 93b> with which we meet them] may be new.
94	94a	But		those values [<c 94b> upon which our success depends -- honesty and hard work, courage and fair play, tolerance and curiosity, loyalty and patriotism] -- these things		<c 94a> But those values [<c 94b> upon which our success depends -- honesty and hard work, courage and fair play, tolerance and curiosity, loyalty and patriotism] -- these things are old.
95	95			These things		<c 95> These things are true.
96	96			They		<c 96> They have been the quiet force of progress throughout our history.
97	97			[<c 97b> What is demanded then]		<c 97a> [<c 97b> What is demanded then,] is a return to these truths.

Theme-rheme structure of Barack Obama's First Inaugural Address

Sent #	Cl#	Theme				Clause
		Textual	Inter-personal	Topical/ Existential	displaced	
98	98a			[<c 98b> What is required of us now]		<<c 98a> [<c 98b> What is required of us, now] is a new era of responsibility -- a recognition on the part of every American [<c 98c> that we have duties to ourselves, our nation and the world; duties [<c 98d> that we do not grudgingly accept, <c 98e> but rather seize gladly, firm in the knowledge [<c 98f> that there is nothing so satisfying to the spirit, so defining of our character <c 98g> than giving our all to a difficult task.]]]
99	99			This		<c 99> This is the price and the promise of citizenship.
100	100a			This		<c 100a> This is the source of our confidence -- the knowledge [<100b> that God calls on us <c 100c> to shape an uncertain destiny.]
101	101a			This		<c 101a> This is the meaning of our liberty and our creed, <c 101b> why men and women and children of every race and every faith can join in celebration across this magnificent mall; <c 101c> and why a man [<c 101d>whose father less than 60 years ago might not have been served in a local restaurant] can now stand before you<c 101e> to take a most sacred oath. (Applause.)
	101b			why	men and women and children of every race and every faith	
	101c	and		why	a man whose father less than 60 years ago might not have been served in a local restaurant	
	101e					
102	102a	So	let us			<c 102a> So let us mark this day with remembrance of [<c 102b> who we are <c 102c> and how far we have traveled.]
103	103			In the year of America's birth, in the coldest of months	a small band of patriots	<c 103> In the year of America's birth, in the coldest of months, a small band of patriots huddled by dying campfires on the shores of an icy river.
104	104			The capital		<c 104> The capital was abandoned.
105	105			The enemy		<c 105> The enemy was advancing.
106	106			The snow		<c 106> The snow was stained with blood.

Theme-rheme structure of Barack Obama's First Inaugural Address

Sent #	Cl#	Theme				Clause
		Textual	Inter-personal	Topical/ Existential	displaced	
107	107a			At the moment [<c 107b> when the outcome of our revolution was most in doubt]	the father of our nation	<c 107a> At the moment [<c 107b> when the outcome of our revolution was most in doubt,] the father of our nation ordered <c 107c> these words to be read to the people:
	107c			these words		
108	108		America	In the face of our common dangers, in this winter of our hardship	let us	<c 108> America: In the face of our common dangers, in this winter of our hardship, let us remember these timeless words.
109	109a			With hope and virtue	let us	<c 109a> With hope and virtue, let us brave once more the icy currents, <c 109b> and endure [<c 109c> what storms may come.]
	109b	and				
110	110a		Let	it		<c 110a> Let it be said by our children's children <c 110b> that when we were tested <c 110c> we refused <c 110d> to let this journey end,<c 110e> that we did not turn back <c 110f> nor did we falter; <c 110g> and with eyes fixed on the horizon and God's grace upon us, <c 110h> we carried forth that great gift of freedom <c 110i> and delivered it safely to future generations.
	110b	that when				
	110c			we		
	110d					
	110e	that		we		
	110f	nor				
	110g	and		with eyes fixed on the horizon and God's grace upon us		
	110h			we		
	110i	and				

Appendix 11.5

Richard M. Nixon's Second Inaugural address

(Transcript source: http://www.americanrhetoric.com/speeches/richardnixonsecondinaugural.htm)

Mr. Vice President, Mr. Speaker, Mr. Chief Justice, Senator Cook, Mrs. Eisenhower, and my fellow citizens of this great and good country we share together:

<p 1> <c 1a>When we met here four years ago, <c 1b> America was bleak in spirit, <c 1c> depressed by the prospect of seemingly endless war abroad and of destructive conflict at home. <c 2a> As we meet here today, <c 2b> we stand on the threshold of a new era of peace in the world. <c 3a> The central question before us is: <c 3b> How shall we use that peace? <c 4a> Let us resolve <c 4b> that this era [<c 4c> we are about <c 4d> to enter] will not be what other postwar periods have so often been: a time of retreat and isolation [<c 4e> that leads to stagnation at home <c 4f> and invites new danger abroad.]

<p2> <c 5a> Let us resolve <c 5b> that this will be [<c 5c> what it can become]: a time of great responsibilities greatly borne, <c 5d> in which we renew the spirit and the promise of America <c 5e> as we enter our third century as a nation.

<p3> <c 6> This past year saw far-reaching results from our new policies for peace. <c 7a> By continuing to revitalize our traditional friendships, and by our missions to Peking and to Moscow, <c 7b> we were able [<c 7c> to establish the base for a new and more durable pattern of relationships among the nations of the world.] <c 8> Because of America's bold initiatives, 1972 will be long remembered as the year of the greatest progress since the end of World War II toward a lasting peace in the world.

<p4> <c 9a> The peace [<c 9b> we seek] in the world is not the flimsy peace [<c 9c> which is merely an interlude between wars,] but a peace [<c 9d> which can endure for generations to come.] <c 10a> It is important [<c 10b>that we understand both the necessity and the limitations of America's role in maintaining that peace.] <c 11a> Unless we in America work <c 11b> to preserve the peace, <c 11c> there will be no peace. <c 12a> Unless we in America work <c 12b> to preserve freedom, <c 12c> there will be no freedom.

<p5> <c 13> But let us clearly understand the new nature of America's role, as a result of the new policies [<c 13b> we have adopted over these past four years:]

<p6> <c14> We shall respect our treaty commitments.

<p7> <c 15> We shall support vigorously the principle [<c 15b> that no country has the right [<c 15c> to impose its will or rule on another by force.]]

<p8> <c 16a> We shall continue, in this era of negotiation, to work for the limitation of nuclear arms, <c 16b> and to reduce the danger of confrontation between the great powers.

<p9> <c 17> We shall do our share in [<c 17b> defending peace and freedom in the world. <c 18a> But we shall expect <c 18b> others to do their share.

<p10> <c 19a> The time has passed <c 19b>when America will make every other nation's conflict our own, <c 19c> or make every other nation's future our responsibility, <c 19d> or presume <c 19e> to tell the people of other nations <c 19f> how to manage their own affairs. <c 20a> Just as we respect the right of each nation [<c 20b> to determine its own future,] <c 20c> we also recognize the responsibility of each nation [<c 20d> to secure its own future.]

<p 11> <c 21a> Just as America's role is indispensable <c 21b> in preserving the world's peace, <c 21c> so is each nation's role indispensable <c 21d> in preserving its own peace.

<p12> <c 22a> Together with the rest of the world, let us resolve <c 22b> to move forward from the beginnings [<c 22c> we have made.] <c 23a> Let us continue to bring down the walls of hostility [<c 23b> which have divided the world for too long,] <c 23c> and to build in their place bridges of understanding, <c 23d> so that despite profound differences between systems of government, the people of the world can be friends.

<p13> <c 24a> Let us build a structure of peace in the world <c 24b> in which the weak are as safe as the strong – <c24c> in which each respects the right of the other [<c 24d> to live by a different system –]<c 24e> in which those [<c 24f> who would influence others] will do so by the strength of their ideas, and not by the force of their arms.

<p14> <c 25a> Let us accept that high responsibility not as a burden, but gladly – <c 25b> gladly because the chance [<c 25c> to build such a peace] is the noblest endeavor [<c 25d> in which a nation could engage;] <c 25e> and gladly, also, because only will we remain a great nation, <c 25f> – if

we act greatly [<c 25g> in meeting our responsibilities abroad] <c 25h> and only if we remain a great nation <c 25i> will we act greatly [<c 25j> in meeting our challenges at home.]

<p15> <c 26a> We have the chance, today, <c 26b> to do more than ever before in our history <c 26c> to make life better in America <c 26d> – to ensure better education, better health, better housing, better transportation, a cleaner environment <c 26e> – to restore respect for law, <c 26f> to make our communities more livable <c 26g> – and to insure the God-given right of every American to full and equal opportunity.

<p16> <c 27a> Because the range of our needs is so great, <c 27b> because the reach of our opportunities is so great, <c 27c> let us be bold in our determination [<c 27d> to meet those needs in new ways.] <c 28a> Just as [<c 28b> building a structure of peace abroad] has required [<c 28c> turning away from old policies [<c 28d> that had failed,]] <c 28e> so [<c 28f> building a new era of progress at home] requires [<c 28g> turning away from old policies [<c 28h> that have failed.]] <c 29> Abroad, the shift from old policies to new has not been a retreat from our responsibilities, but a better way to peace. <c 30> And at home, the shift from old policies to new will not be a retreat from our responsibilities, but a better way to progress. <c 31> Abroad and at home, the key to those new responsibilities lies in the placing and the division of responsibility.

<p17> <c 32a> We have lived too long with the consequences [<c 32b> of attempting to gather all power and responsibility in Washington.] <c 33a> Abroad and at home, the time has come [<c 33b> to turn away from the condescending policies of paternalism – of "Washington knows best."]

<p18> <c 34a> A person can be expected < c 34b> to act responsibly <c 34c> only if he has responsibility. <c 35> This is human nature. <c 36a> So let us encourage individuals at home and nations abroad <c 36b> to do more for themselves, <c 36c> to decide more for themselves. <c 37> Let us locate responsibility in more places. <c 38a> And let us measure [<c 38b> what we will do for others] by [<c 38c> what they will do for themselves.]

<p19> <c 39a> That is [<c 39b> why today I offer no promise of a purely governmental solution for every problem.] <c 40> We have lived too long with that false promise. <c 41a> In trusting too much in government, <c 41b> we have asked of it <c 41c> more than it can deliver. <c 42a> This leads only to inflated expectations, to reduced individual effort, and to a disappointment and frustration that erode confidence both in

[<c 42b> What government can do] and in [<c 42c> what people can do.] <c 43a> Government must learn <c 43b> to take less from people <c 43c> so that people can do more for themselves.

<p 20> <c 44a> Let us remember <c 44b> that America was built not by government, but by people; not by welfare, but by work; not by [<c 44c> shirking responsibility], but by [<c 44d> seeking responsibility]. <c 45a> In our own lives, let each of us ask, not just <c 45b> what will government do for me, <c 45c> but what can I do for myself? <c 46a> In the challenges we face together, let each of us ask, not just <c 46b> how can government help, <c 46c> but how can I help?

<p 21> <c 47> Your National Government has a great and vital role to play. <c 48a> And I pledge to you <c 48b> that where this Government should act, <c 48c> we will act boldly <c48d> and we will lead boldly. <c 49a> But just as important is the role [<c 49b> that each and every one of us must play], as an individual and as a member of his own community.

<p 22> <c 50a> From this day forward, let each of us make a solemn commitment in his own heart: <c 50b> to bear his responsibility, <c 50c> to do his part, <c 50d> to live his ideals, <c 50e> so that together we can see the dawn of a new age of progress for America, <c 50f> and together, as we celebrate our 200th anniversary as a nation, <c 50g> we can do so proud in the fulfillment of our promise to ourselves and to the world.

<p 23> <c 51a> As America's longest and most difficult war comes to an end, <c 51b> let us again learn <c 51c> to debate our differences with civility and decency. <c 52a> And let each of us reach out for that one precious quality [<c 52b> government cannot provide] – a new level of respect for the rights and feelings of one another, a new level of respect for the individual human dignity [<c 52c> which is the cherished birthright of every American.] <c 53a> Above all else, the time has come [<c 53b> for us to renew our faith in ourselves and in America.]

<p 24> <c 54> In recent years, that faith has been challenged. <c 55a> Our children have been taught <c 55b> to be ashamed of their country, ashamed of their parents, ashamed of America's record at home and its role in the world. <c 56a> At every turn, we have been beset by those [<c 56b> who find everything wrong with America and little [<c56c> that is right.]] <c 57a> But I am confident <c 57b> that this will not be the judgment of history on these remarkable times[<c 57c> in which we are privileged [<c 57d> to live.]]

<p 25> <c 58> America's record in this century has been unparalleled in the world's history for its responsibility, for its generosity, for its creativity and for its progress. <c 59a> Let us be proud <c 59b> that our system has produced <c 59c> and provided more freedom and more abundance, more widely shared, than any other system in the history of the world. <c 60a> Let us be proud <c 60b> that in each of the four wars [<c 60c> in which we have been engaged in this century, <c 60d> including the one [<c 60e> we are now bringing to an end,]] <c 60b> we have fought not for our selfish advantage, <c 60f> but to help <c 60g > others resist aggression. <c 61a> And let us be proud. <c 61b> that by our bold, new initiatives, by our steadfastness for peace with honor, we have made a break-through <c 61c> toward creating in the world [<c 61d> what the world has not known before – a structure of peace [<c 61 e> that can last, not merely for our time, but for generations to come.]]

<p 26> <c 62a> We are embarking here today on an era [<c 62b> that presents challenges <c 62c> as great as those any nation, or any generation, has ever faced.] <c 63a> We shall answer to God, to history, and to our conscience for the way [<c 63b> in which we use these years.]

<p 27> <c 64a> As I stand in this place, <c 64b> so hallowed by history, <c 64c> I think of others [<c 64d> who have stood here before me.] <c 65a> I think of the dreams [<c 65b> they had for America,] <c 65c> and I think of [<c 65d> how each recognized <c 65e> that he needed help far beyond himself <c 65f> in order to make <c 65g> those dreams come true.]

<p 28> <c 66a> Today, I ask your prayers <c 66b> that in the years ahead I may have God's help <c 66c> in making decisions [<c 66d> that are right for America,] <c 66e> and I pray for your help <c 66f> so that together we may be worthy of our challenge.

<p 29> <c 67a> Let us pledge together <c 67b> to make these next four years the best four years in America's history, <c 67c> so that on its 200th birthday America will be as young and as vital and as bright a beacon of hope for all the world <c 67d> as when it began.

<p 30> <c 68a> Let us go forward from here confident in hope, strong in our faith in one another, [<c 68b> sustained by our faith in God [<c 68c> who created us,]] <c 68d> and striving always <c 68e> to serve His purpose.

Appendix 11.6

Transitivity Structure of RM Nixon's Second Inaugural Address

Para#	Cl #	Transitivity Structure				Clause (Complex)
		Process (type)	Participant(s)		Circumstance(s)	
			X...	Roles		
1	1a	met (material)	we	Actor	here four years ago,	Mr. Vice President, Mr. Speaker, Mr. Chief Justice, Senator Cook, Mrs. Eisenhower, and my fellow citizens of this great and good country we share together: <c 1a> When we met here four years ago, <c 1b> America was bleak in spirit, <c 1c> depressed by the prospect of seemingly endless war abroad and of destructive conflict at home.
	1b	was (relational)	America	Carrier		
			bleak in spirit	Attribute		
	1c	depressed (material)	by the prospect of seemingly endless war abroad and of destructive conflict at home.	Actor		
	2a	meet (material)	we	Actor	here today,	<c 2a> As we meet here today, <c 2b> we stand on the threshold of a new era of peace in the world.
	2b	stand (material)	we	Actor	on the threshold of a new era of peace in the world.	
	3a	is (relational)	The central question before us	Identified		<c 3a> The central question before us is: <c 3b> How shall we use that peace?
			<c 3b>	Identifier		
	3b	use (material)	we	Actor		
			that peace	Goal		
	4a	resolve (mental)	us	Senser		<c 4a> Let us resolve <c 4b> that this era [<c 4c> we are about <c 4d> to enter] will not be what other postwar periods have so often been: a time of retreat and isolation [<c 4e> that leads to stagnation at home <c 4f> and invites new danger abroad.]
			<c 4b>[<c 4c-d>][<c 4e-f>]	Phenomenon		
	4b	be (relational)	this era [<c 4c>]	Carrier		
			what other postwar periods have so often been: a time of retreat and isolation [<c 4e>]	Attribute		
	4c	are (relational)	we	Carrier		
			about <c 4d>	Attribute		
	4d	enter (material)				

Transitivity Structure of RM Nixon's Second Inaugural Address

Para#	Cl #	Transitivity Structure				Clause (Complex)
		Process (type)	Participant(s)		Circumstance(s)	
			X…	Roles		
	4e	leads to (material)	stagnation at home	Goal		
	4f	invites (material)	new danger	Goal	abroad	
2	5a	resolve (mental)	us	Senser		<c 5a> Let us resolve <c 5b> that this will be [<c 5c> what it can become]: a time of great responsibilities greatly borne, <c 5d> in which we renew the spirit and the promise of America <c 5e> as we enter our third century as a nation.
			<c 5b-e>	Phenomenon		
	5b	be (relational)	this	Identified		
			[<c 5c>]: <c 5d-e>	Identifier		
	5c	become (relational)	it	Carrier		
			what	Attribute		
	5d	renew (material)	we	Actor		
			the spirit and the promise of America	Goal		
	5e	enter (material)	we	Actor	as a nation.	
			our third century	Goal		
3	6	saw (mental)	This past year	Senser	from our new policies for peace.	<c 6> This past year saw far-reaching results from our new policies for peace.
			far-reaching results	Phenomenon		
	7a	continuing to revitalize (material)	our traditional friendships	Goal		<c 7a> By continuing to revitalize our traditional friendships, and by our missions to Peking and to Moscow, <c 7b> we were able [<c 7c> to establish the base for a new and more durable pattern of relationships among the nations of the world.]
	7b	were (relational)	we	Carrier		
			able [<c 7c>]	Attribute		
	7c	establish (material)	the base for a new and more durable pattern of relationships among the nations of the world,	Goal		

Transitivity Structure of RM Nixon's Second Inaugural Address

Para#	Cl #	Transitivity Structure				Clause (Complex)
		Process (type)	Participant(s)		Circumstance(s)	
			X…	Roles		
	8	remembered (mental)	1972… as the year of the greatest progress since the end of World War II toward a lasting peace in the world.	Phenomenon		<c 8> Because of America's bold initiatives, 1972 will be long remembered as the year of the greatest progress since the end of World War II toward a lasting peace in the world.
4	9a	is (relational)	The peace [<c 9b>] in the world	Identified		<c 9a> The peace [<c 9b> we seek] in the world is not the flimsy peace [<c 9c> which is merely an interlude between wars], but a peace [<c 9d> which can endure for generations to come.]
			the flimsy peace [<c 9c>]	Identifier		
	9b	seek (material)	we	Actor		
	9c	is (relational)	an interlude between wars	Attribute		
	9d	endure (relational)			for generations to come	
	10a	is (relational)	It….[<c 10b>]	Carrier		<c 10a> It is important [<c 10b>that we understand both the necessity and the limitations of America's role in maintaining that peace.]
			important	Attribute		
	10b	understand (mental)	we	Senser		
			both the necessity and the limitations of America's role in maintaining that peace	Phenomenon		
	11a	work (material)	we in America	Actor		<c 11a> Unless we in America work <c 11b> to preserve the peace, <c 11c> there will be no peace.
	11b	preserve (material)	the peace	Goal		
	11c	be (existential)	there			
			no peace	Existent		
	12a	work (material)	we in America	Actor		<c 12a> Unless we in America work <c 12b> to preserve freedom,<c 12c> there will be no freedom.
	12b	preserve (material)	freedom	Goal		
	12c	be (existential)	there			
			no freedom	Existent		

Transitivity Structure of RM Nixon's Second Inaugural Address

Para#	Cl #	Transitivity Structure				Clause (Complex)
		Process (type)	Participant(s)		Circumstance(s)	
			X…	Roles		
5	13a	understand (mental)	us	Senser	as a result of the new policies [<c 13b>]	<c 13a> But let us clearly understand the new nature of America's role, as a result of the new policies [<c 13b> we have adopted over these past four years:]
			the new nature of America's role,	Phenomenon		
	13b	adopted (material)	we	Actor	over these past four years	
6	14	respect (material)	we	Actor		<c 14> We shall respect our treaty commitments.
			our treaty commitments.	Goal		
7	15a	support (material)	we	Actor	vigorously	<c 15> We shall support vigorously the principle [<c 15b> that no country has the right [<c 15c> to impose its will or rule on another by force.]]
			the principle [<c 15b>]	Goal		
	15b	has (relational)	no country	Possessor		
			the right [<c 15c>]	Possessed		
	15c	impose (material)	its will or rule on another	Goal	by force	
8	16a	continue (material)	we	Actor	for the limitation of nuclear arms,	<c 16a> We shall continue, in this era of negotiation, <c 16b> to work for the limitation of nuclear arms, <c 16c> and to reduce the danger of confrontation between the great powers.
	16b	to work (material)				
	16c	reduce (material)	the danger of confrontation between the great powers.	Goal		
9	17a	do (material)	we	Actor	in [<c 17b>]	<c 17a> We shall do our share in [<c 17b> defending peace and freedom in the world.]
			our share	Goal		
	17b	defending (material)	peace and freedom	Goal	in the world	
	18a	expect (mental)	we	Senser		<c 18a> But we shall expect <c 18b> others to do their share.
			others <c 18b>	Phenomenon		
	18b	do (material)	their share	Goal		
10	19a	passed (material)	The time	Affected		<c 19a> The time has passed <c 19b> when America will make every other nation's conflict

Transitivity Structure of RM Nixon's Second Inaugural Address

Para#	Cl #	Transitivity Structure				Clause (Complex)
		Process (type)	Participant(s)		Circumstance(s)	
			X…	Roles		
	19b	make (material, relational)	America	Actor		our own, <c 19c> or make every other nation's future our responsibility, <c 19d> or presume <c 19e> to tell the people of other nations <c 19f> how to manage their own affairs.
			every other nation's conflict	Carrier		
			our own	Attribute		
	19c	make (material, relational)	every other nation's future	Carrier		
			our responsibility	Attribute		
	19d	presume (mental)	<c 19e>	Phenomenon		
	19e	tell (verbal)	the people of other nations	Receiver		
			<c 19f>	Verbiage		
	19f	manage (material)	their own affairs	Goal		
	20a	respect (mental)	we	Actor		<c 20a> Just as we respect the right of each nation [<c 20b> to determine its own future,]<c 20c> we also recognize the responsibility of each nation [<c 20d> to secure its own future.]
			the right of each nation [<c 20b>]	Goal		
	20b	determine (material)	its own future	Goal		
	20c	recognize (mental)	we	Actor		
			the responsibility of each nation [<c 20d>]	Goal		
	20d	secure (material)	its own future	Goal		
11	21a	is (relational)	America's role	Carrier		<c 21a> Just as America's role is indispensable <c 21b> in preserving the world's peace, <c 21c> so is each nation's role indispensable <c 21d> in preserving its own peace.
			indispensable	Attribute		
	21b	preserving (material)	the world's peace	Goal		
	21c	is (relational)	each nation's role	Carrier		
			indispensable	Attribute		
	21d	preserving (material)	its own peace	Goal		

Transitivity Structure of RM Nixon's Second Inaugural Address

Para#	Cl #	Transitivity Structure				Clause (Complex)
		Process (type)	Participant(s)		Circumstance(s)	
			X…	Roles		
12	22a	resolve (mental)	us	Senser	Together with the rest of the world	<c 22a> Together with the rest of the world, let us resolve <c 22b> to move forward from the beginnings [<c 22c> we have made.]
			<c 22b>			
	22b	move (material)		Phenomenon	forward from the beginnings [<c 22c>]	
	22c	made (material)	we	Actor		
	23a	continue to bring down (material)	us	Actor		<c 23a> Let us continue to bring down the walls of hostility [<c 23b> which have divided the world for too long,] <c 23c> and to build in their place bridges of understanding, <c 23d> so that despite profound differences between systems of government, the people of the world can be friends.
			the walls of hostility [<c 23b>]	Goal		
	23b	divided (material)	the world	Goal	for too long,	
	23c	build (material)	bridges of understanding,	Goal	in their place	
	23d	be (relational)	the people of the world	Carrier	despite profound differences between systems of government,	
			friends	Attribute		
13	24a	build (material)	us	Actor		<c 24a> Let us build a structure of peace in the world <c 24b> in which the weak are as safe as the strong – <c24c> in which each respects the right of the other [<c 24d> to live by a different system –]<c 24e> in which those [<c 24f> who would influence others] will do so by the strength of their ideas, and not by the force of their arms.
			a structure of peace in the world	Goal		
	24b	are (relational)	the weak	Carrier		
			as safe as the strong –	Attribute		
	24c	respects (mental)	each	Senser		
			the right of the other [<c 24d>]	Phenomenon		
	24d	live (behavioural)			by a different system	
	24e	do (material)	those [<c 24f>]	Actor	by the strength of their ideas, and not by the force of their arms.	
			so	Goal		

Transitivity Structure of RM Nixon's Second Inaugural Address

Para#	Cl #	Transitivity Structure				Clause (Complex)
		Process (type)	Participant(s)		Circumstance(s)	
			X...	Roles		
	24f	influence (material)	others	Goal		
14	25a	accept (material)	us	Actor	not as a burden, but gladly –	<c 25a> Let us accept that high responsibility not as a burden, but gladly – <c 25b> gladly because the chance [<c 25c> to build such a peace] is the noblest endeavor [<c 25d> in which a nation could engage;] <c 25e> and gladly, also, because only will we remain a great nation, <c 25f> -- if we act greatly [<c 25g> in meeting our responsibilities abroad] <c 25h> and only if we remain a great nation <c 25i> will we act greatly [<c 25j>in meeting our challenges at home.]
			that high responsibility	Goal		
	25b	is (relational)	the chance to build such a peace	Identifier		
			the noblest endeavor [<c 25d>];	Identified		
	25c	build (material)	such a peace	Goal		
	25d	engage (material)	a nation	Actor		
	25e	remain (relational)	we	Carrier		
			a great nation	Attribute		
	25f	act (material)	we	Actor	greatly [<c 25g>]	
	25g	meeting (material)	our responsibilities	Goal	abroad	
	25h	remain (relational)	we	Carrier		
			a great nation	Attribute		
	25i	act (material)	we	Actor	greatly [<c 25j>]	
	25j	meeting (material)	our challenges	Goal	at home	
15	26a	have (relational)	we	Possessor	today	<c 26a> We have the chance, today, <c 26b> to do more than ever before in our history <c 26c> to make life better in America <c 26d> -- to ensure better education, better health, better housing, better transportation, a cleaner environment <c 26e> -- to restore respect for law, <c 26f> to make our communities more livable <c 26g> -- and to insure the God-given right of every American to full and equal
			the chance, ... [<c 26b>]	Possessed		
	26c	make... (material, relational)	life	Carrier	in America	
			better	Attribute		
	26d	ensure (material)	better education, better health, better housing, better transportation, a cleaner environment	Goal		

Transitivity Structure of RM Nixon's Second Inaugural Address

Para#	Cl #	Transitivity Structure				Clause (Complex)
		Process (type)	Participant(s)		Circumstance(s)	
			X...	Roles		
	26e	restore (material)	respect for law	Goal		opportunity
	26f	make (material, relational)	our communities	Carrier		
			more livable	Attribute		
	26f	insure (material)	the God-given right of every American to full and equal opportunity.	Goal		
16	27a	is (relational)	the range of our needs	Carrier		<c 27a> Because the range of our needs is so great, <c 27b> because the reach of our opportunities is so great, <c 27c> let us be bold in our determination [<c 27d> to meet those needs in new ways.]
			so great	Attribute		
	27b	is (relational)	the reach of our opportunities	Carrier		
			so great	Attribute		
	27c	be (relational)	us	Carrier	in our determination [<c 27d>]	
			bold	Attribute		
	27d	meet (material)	those needs	Goal	in new ways	
	28a	required (material)	<c 28b>	Actor		<c 28a> Just as [<c 28b> building a structure of peace abroad] has required [<c 28c> turning away from old policies [<c 28d> that had failed,]] <c 28e> so [<c 28f> building a new era of progress at home] requires [<c 28g> turning away from old policies [<c 28h> that have failed.]]
			<c 28c[d]>	Range		
	28b	building (material)	a structure of peace abroad	Goal		
	28c	turning away (material)			from old policies [<c 28d>]	
	28d	failed (material)				
	28e	requires (material)	<c 28f>	Actor		
			<c 28g[h]>	Range		
	28f	building (material)	a new era of progress at home	Goal		
	28g	failed (material)				
	29	been (relational)	the shift from old policies to new	Carrier	Abroad	<c 29> Abroad, the shift from old policies to new has not been a retreat from our

Transitivity Structure of RM Nixon's Second Inaugural Address

Para#	Cl #	Transitivity Structure				Clause (Complex)
		Process (type)	Participant(s)		Circumstance(s)	
			X…	Roles		
			a retreat from our responsibilities, but a better way to peace.	Attribute		responsibilities, but a better way to peace.
	30	be (relational)	the shift from old policies to new	Carrier		<c 30> And at home, the shift from old policies to new will not be a retreat from our responsibilities, but a better way to progress.
			a retreat from our responsibilities, but a better way to progress.	Attribute		
	31	lies in (relational)	the key to those new responsibilities	Identified	Abroad and at home,	<c 31> Abroad and at home, the key to those new responsibilities lies in the placing and the division of responsibility.
			the placing and the division of responsibility.	Identifier		
17	32a	lived (behavioural)	we	Behaver	too long with the consequences [<c 32b>]	<c 32a> We have lived too long with the consequences [<c 32b> of attempting to gather all power and responsibility in Washington.]
	32b	attempting to gather (material)	all power and responsibility	Goal	in Washington	
	33a	come (material)	the time [<c 33b>]	Actor	Abroad and at home	<c 33a> Abroad and at home, the time has come [<c 33b> to turn away from the condescending policies of paternalism -- of "Washington knows best."]
	33b	turn away (material)			from the condescending policies of paternalism -- of "Washington knows best."	
18	34a	expected (mental)	A person	Phenomenon		<c 34a> A person can be expected < c 34b> to act responsibly<c 34c> only if he has responsibility.
	34b	act (material)	(A person)	Actor	responsibly	
	34c	has (relational)	he	Possessor		
			responsibility	Possessed		
	35	is (relational)	This	Identified		<c 35> This is human nature.
			human nature	Identifier		

Transitivity Structure of RM Nixon's Second Inaugural Address

Para#	Cl #	Transitivity Structure				Clause (Complex)
		Process (type)	Participant(s)		Circumstance(s)	
			X…	Roles		
	36a	encourage (material)	us	Actor		<c 36a> So let us encourage individuals at home and nations abroad <c 36b> to do more for themselves, <c 36c> to decide more for themselves.
			individuals at home and nations abroad	Goal		
	36b	do (material)	more	Goal	for themselves	
	36c	decide (mental)	more	Phenomenon	for themselves	
	37	locate (material)	us	Actor	in more places.	<c 37> Let us locate responsibility in more places.
			responsibility	Goal		
	38a	measure (material)	us	Actor	by [<c 38c>]	<c 38a> And let us measure [<c 38b> what we will do for others] by [<c 38c> what they will do for themselves.]
			[<c 38b>]	Goal		
	38b	do (material)	we	Actor	for others	
	38c	do (material)	they	Actor	for themselves	
19	39a	is (relational)	That	Identified		<c 39a> That is [<c 39b> why today I offer no promise of a purely governmental solution for every problem.]
			[<c 39b>]	Identifier		
	39b	offer (material)	I	Actor	today	
			no promise of a purely governmental solution for every problem.	Goal		
	40	lived (behavioural)	we	Behaver	too long with that false promise.	<c 40> We have lived too long with that false promise.
	41a	trusting (mental)	in government	Phenomenon	too much	<c 41a> In trusting too much in government, <c 41b> we have asked of it <c 41c> more than it can deliver.
	41b	asked (verbal)	we	Sayer		
			<c 41c>	Verbiage		
			of it	Receiver		
	41c	deliver (material)	it	Actor		

Transitivity Structure of RM Nixon's Second Inaugural Address

Para#	Cl #	Transitivity Structure				Clause (Complex)
		Process (type)	Participant(s)		Circumstance(s)	
			X…	Roles		
	42a	leads (material)	This	Actor	only to inflated expectations, to reduced individual effort, and to a disappointment and frustration that erode confidence both in in [<c 42b>] and in [<c 42c>]	<c 42a> This leads only to inflated expectations, to reduced individual effort, and to a disappointment and frustration that erode confidence both in [<c 42b> what government can do] and in [<c 42c> what people can do.]
	42b	do (material)	government	Actor		
	42c	do (material)	people	Actor		
	43a	learn (mental)	Government	Senser		<c 43a> Government must learn <c 43b> to take less from people <c 43c> so that people can do more for themselves.
	43b	take (material)	less from people	Goal		
	43c	do (material)	people	Actor	for themselves.	
			more	Goal		
20	44a	remember (mental)	us	Senser		<c 44a> Let us remember <c 44b> that America was built not by government, but by people; not by welfare, but by work; not by [<c 44c> shirking responsibility], but by [<c 44d> seeking responsibility].
			<c 44b>-[<c 44cd>]	Phenomenon		
	44b	built (material)	America	Goal		
			not by government, but by people; not by welfare, but by work; not by [<c 44c>], but by [<c 44d>].	Actor		
	44c	shirking (material)	responsibility	Goal		
	44d	seeking (material)	responsibility	Goal		
	45a	ask (verbal)	each of us	Sayer	In our own lives,	<c 45a> In our own lives, let each of us ask, not just <c 45b> what will government do for me, <c 45c> but what can I do for myself?
			<c 45[bc]>	Verbiage		
	45b	do (material)	government	Actor	for me,	
			what	Goal		
	45c	do (material)	I	Actor	for myself?	
			what	Goal		

Transitivity Structure of RM Nixon's Second Inaugural Address

Para#	Cl #	Transitivity Structure				Clause (Complex)
		Process (type)	Participant(s)		Circumstance(s)	
			X…	Roles		
	46a	ask (verbal)	each of us	Sayer	In the challenges we face together	<c 46a> In the challenges we face together, let each of us ask, not just <c 46b> how can government help, <c 46c> but how can I help?
			<c 46[bc]>	Verbiage		
	46b	help (material)	government	Actor		
	46c	help (material)	I	Actor		
21	47	has (relational)	Your National Government	Possessor		<c 47> Your National Government has a great and vital role to play.
			a great and vital role to play	Possessed		
	48a	pledge (verbal)	I	Sayer		<c 48a> And I pledge to you <c 48b> that where this Government should act, <c 48c> we will act boldly <c48d> and we will lead boldly.
			you	Receiver		
	48b	act (material)	this Government	Actor	where	
	48c	act (material)	we	Actor	boldly	
	48d	lead (material)	we	Actor	boldly	
	49a	is (relational)	the role [<c 49b>]	Carrier		<c 49a> But just as important is the role [<c 49b> that each and every one of us must play], as an individual and as a member of his own community.
			important	Attribute		
	49b	play (material)	each and every one of us	Actor	as an individual and as a member of his own community.	
22	50a	make (material)	each of us	Actor	From this day forward	<c 50a> From this day forward, let each of us make a solemn commitment in his own heart: <c 50b> to bear his responsibility, <c 50c> to do his part, <c 50d> to live his ideals, <c 50e> so that together we can see the dawn of a new age of progress for America, <c 50f> and together, as we celebrate our 2th anniversary as a nation, <c 50g> we can do so proud in the fulfillment of our promise to ourselves and to the world
			a solemn commitment in his own heart:	Goal		
	50b	bear (material)	his responsibility,	Goal		
	50c	do (material)	his part,	Goal		
	50d	live (behavioural)	his ideals	Range		
	50e	see (mental)	we	Senser	together	
			the dawn of a new age of progress for America,	Phenomenon		

Transitivity Structure of RM Nixon's Second Inaugural Address

Para#	Cl #	Transitivity Structure				Clause (Complex)
		Process (type)	Participant(s)		Circumstance(s)	
			X…	Roles		
	50f	celebrate (material)	we	Actor	together	
			our 200th anniversary as a nation,	Goal		
	50g	do (material)	we	Actor	proud in the fulfillment of our promise to ourselves and to the world	
			so	Goal		
23	51a	comes (material)	America's longest and most difficult war	Actor	to an end,	<c 51a> As America's longest and most difficult war comes to an end, <c 51b> let us again learn <c 51c> to debate our differences with civility and decency.
	51b	learn (mental)	us	Senser		
			<c 51c>	Phenomenon		
	51c	debate (material)	our differences	Goal	with civility and decency.	
	52a	reach out (material)	each of us	Actor	for that one precious quality [<c 52b>] -- a new level of respect for the rights and feelings of one another, a new level of respect for the individual human dignity [<c 52c>]	<c 52a> And let each of us reach out for that one precious quality [<c 52b> government cannot provide] -- a new level of respect for the rights and feelings of one another, a new level of respect for the individual human dignity [<c 52c> which is the cherished birthright of every American.]
	52b	provide (material)	government	Actor		
	52c	is (relational)	the cherished birthright of every American	Identifier		
	53a	come (material)	the time	Actor	Above all else	<c 53a> Above all else, the time has come [<c 53b> for us to renew our faith in ourselves and in America.]
					[<c 53b>]	
	53b	renew (material)	us	Actor		
			our faith in ourselves and in America	Goal		

Transitivity Structure of RM Nixon's Second Inaugural Address

Para#	Cl #	Transitivity Structure				Clause (Complex)
		Process (type)	Participant(s)		Circumstance(s)	
			X…	Roles		
24	54	challenged (material)	that faith	Goal	In recent years,	<c 54> In recent years, that faith has been challenged.
	55a	taught (verbal)	Our children	Receiver		<c 55a> Our children have been taught <c 55b> to be ashamed of their country, ashamed of their parents, ashamed of America's record at home and its role in the world.
			<c 55b>	Verbiage		
	55b	be (relational)	ashamed of their country, ashamed of their parents, ashamed of America's record at home and its role in the world.	Attribute		
	56a	beset (material)	we	Goal	At every turn,	<c 56a> At every turn, we have been beset by those [<c 56b> who find everything wrong with America and little [<c56c> that is right.]]
			by those [<c 56b>[<c 56c>]]	Actor		
	56b	find (mental)	everything wrong with America and little [<c56c>]	Phenomenon		
	57a	am (relational)	I	Carrier		<c 57a> But I am confident <c 57b> that this will not be the judgment of history on these remarkable times[<c 57c> in which we are privileged [<c 57d> to live.]]
			confident	Attribute		
	57b	be (relational)	this	Identifier		
			the judgment of history on these remarkable times[<c 57c[d]>].	Identified		
	57c	privileged (material)	we	Goal		
	57d	live (behavioural)				
25	58	been (relational)	America's record in this century	Carrier	for its responsibility, for its generosity, for its creativity and for its progress.	<c 58> America's record in this century has been unparalleled in the world's history for its responsibility, for its generosity, for its creativity and for its progress.
			unparalleled in the world's history	Attribute		

Transitivity Structure of RM Nixon's Second Inaugural Address

Para#	Cl #	Transitivity Structure				Clause (Complex)
		Process (type)	Participant(s)		Circumstance(s)	
			X…	Roles		
	59a	be (relational)	us	Carrier		<c 59a> Let us be proud <c 59b> that our system has produced <c 59c> and provided more freedom and more abundance, more widely shared, than any other system in the history of the world.
			proud	Attribute		
	59b	produced and provided (material)	our system	Actor		
			more freedom and more abundance, more widely shared, than any other system in the history of the world.	Goal		
	59c	provided (material)				
	60a	be (relational)	us	Carrier		<c 60a> Let us be proud <c 60b> that in each of the four wars [<c 60c> in which we have been engaged in this century], <c 60d> including the one [<c 60e> we are now bringing to an end,] <c 60b> we have fought not for our selfish advantage,<c 60f> but to help <c 60g > others resist aggression.
			proud	Attribute		
	60b	fought (material)	we	Actor	that in each of the four wars [<c 60c>], <c 60d> including the one [<c 60e>]; for our selfish advantage,<c 60f> but to help others <c 60g > resist aggression.	
	60c	engaged (material)	we	Actor	in this century	
	60d	including (relational)	the one [<c 60e>]	Possessed		
	60e	bringing (material)			to an end	
	60f	help (material)	others	Goal		
	60g	resist (material)	aggression	Goal		
	61a	be (relational)	us	Carrier		<c 61a> And let us be proud <c 61b> that by our bold, new initiatives, by our steadfastness for peace with honor, we have made a break-through <c 61c> toward creating in the world [<c 61d> what the world has not known before -- a structure of peace [<c 61 e> that can last,
			proud	Attribute		

Transitivity Structure of RM Nixon's Second Inaugural Address

Para#	Cl #	Transitivity Structure				Clause (Complex)
		Process (type)	Participant(s)		Circumstance(s)	
			X...	Roles		
	61b	made (material)	we	Actor	by our bold, new initiatives, by our steadfastness for peace with honor,	not merely for our time, but for generations to come.]]
			a break-through toward <c 61c> creating in the world [<c 61d> [<c 61 e>]]	Goal		
	61c	creating (material)	[<c 61d> [<c 61 e>]]	Goal	in the world	
	61d	known (mental)	the world	Senser	before	
			a structure of peace [<c 61 e>]	Phenomenon		
	61e	last (relational)			not merely for our time, but for generations to come.	
26	62a	embarking (material)	we	Actor	here today on an era [<c 62b> <c 62c>]	<c 62a> We are embarking here today on an era [<c 62b> that presents challenges <c 62c> as great as those any nation, or any generation, has ever faced.]
	62b	presents (material)	challenges <c 62c>	Goal		
	62c	faced (material)	any nation, or any generation	Actor		
	63a	answer (verbal)	we	Sayer	for the way [<c 63b>].	<c 63a> We shall answer to God, to history, and to our conscience for the way [<c 63b> in which we use these years.]
			to God, to history, and to our conscience	Receiver		
	63b	use (material)	we	Actor		
			these years	Goal		
27	64a	stand (material)	I	Actor	in this place	<c 64a> As I stand in this place, <c 64b> so hallowed by history, <c 64c> I think of others [<c 64d> who have stood here before me.]
	64b	hallowed (material)	by history	Actor		
	64c	think (mental)	I	Senser		
			of others [<c 64d>]	Phenomenon		
	64d	stood (material)			here before me	
	65a	think (mental)	I	Senser		<c 65a> I think of the dreams [<c 65b> they had for America,] <c 65c> and I think of [<c
			of the dreams [<c 65b>]	Phenomenon		

Transitivity Structure of RM Nixon's Second Inaugural Address

Para#	Cl #	Transitivity Structure				Clause (Complex)
		Process (type)	Participant(s)		Circumstance(s)	
			X…	Roles		
	65b	had (relational)	they	Possessor	for America	65d> how each recognized <c 65e> that he needed help far beyond himself <c 65f> in order to make <c 65g> those dreams come true.]
	65c	think (mental)	I	Senser		
			of <c 65d>	Phenomenon		
	65d	recognized (mental)	each	Senser		
			<c 65e-g>	Phenonenon		
	65e	needed (relational)	he	Possessor		
			help far beyond himself	Possessed		
	65f	make (material)	<c 65g>	Goal		
	65g	come (material)	those dreams	Actor		
			True	Range		
28	66a	ask (verbal)	I	Sayer		<c 66a> Today, I ask your prayers <c 66b> that in the years ahead I may have God's help <c 66c> in making decisions [<c 66d> that are right for America,] <c 66e> and I pray for your help <c 66f> so that together we may be worthy of our challenge.
			your prayers	Verbiage		
	66b	have (relational)	I	Possessor	in the years ahead	
			God's help <c 66c[d]>	Possessed		
	66c	making (material)	decisions [<c 66d]	Goal		
	66d	are (relational)	right	Attribute	for America	
	66e	pray (verbal)	I	Sayer		
			for your help	Verbiage		
	66f	be (relational)	we	Carrier	together	
			worthy of our challenge	Attribute		
29	67a	pledge (verbal)	us	Sayer	together	<c 67a> Let us pledge together <c 67b> to make these next four years the best four years in America's history, <c 67c> so that on its 2th birthday America will be as young and as vital…. and as bright a beacon of hope for all
			<c 67b>	Verbiage		

Transitivity Structure of RM Nixon's Second Inaugural Address

Para#	Cl #	Transitivity Structure				Clause (Complex)
		Process (type)	Participant(s)		Circumstance(s)	
			X…	Roles		
	67b	make (material, relational)	these next four years	Identified		the world. <c 67d> as when it began.
			the best four years in America's history,	Identifier		
	67c	be (relational)	America	Carrier	on its 200th birthday	
			as young and as vital …. and as bright a beacon of hope for all the world.	Attribute		
	67d	began (existential)	it	Existent		
30	68a	go (material)	us	Actor	forward from here confident in hope, strong in our faith in one another, [<c 68b> [<c 68c>]]	<c 68a> Let us go forward from here confident in hope, strong in our faith in one another, [<c 68b> sustained by our faith in God [<c 68c> who created us,]] <c 68d> and striving always <c 68e> to serve His purpose.
	68b	sustained (material)	by our faith in God [<c 68c>]	Actor		
	68c	created (material)	us	Goal		
	68d	striving (material)			always	
	68e	serve (material)	His purpose	Goal		

Appendix 11.7

Logical structure of Nixon's Second Inaugural Address.

Paragraph	Simple clause	Clause complex											
		Paratactic				Hypotactic							
		Expansion			Projection	Expansion						Projection	
		Elaboration	Extension	Enhancement		Elaboration		Extension		Enhancement			
						α	β	α	β	α	β	α	β
1	1					1b	1c			1bc	1a		
	2									2b	2a		
	3	3a = 3b											
	4											4a	4b[cd[ef]
2	5					5b	5de			5d	5e	5a	5b-e
3	6												
	7									7b[c]	7a		
	8												
4	9[b] [c][d]												
	10a[b]												
	11									11c	11ab		
										11a	11b		
	12									12c	12ab		
										12a	12b		
5	13a[b]												
6	14												
7	15 a[b[c]]												
8	16		16a + 16b										
9	17a[b]												
	18											18a	18b
10	19		19b + 19c + 19d-f							19a	19b-f	19d	19ef
												19e	19f
	20									20c[d]	20a[b]		

Logical structure of Nixon's Second Inaugural Address.

Paragraph	Simple clause	Clause complex											
		Paratactic				Hypotactic							
		Expansion			Projection	Expansion						Projection	
		Elaboration	Extension	Enhancement		Elaboration		Extension		Enhancement			
						α	β	α	β	α	β	α	β
11	21					21a	21b	21cd	21ab				
						21c	21d						
12	22											22a	22b[c]
	23		23a[b]+ 23c							23 a[b]c	23d		
13	24		24b + 24c[d] + 24e[f]			24a	24b-f						
14	25		25b[c][d] + 25ef[g],h,i[j]							25a	25 b[c][d]-25e-i[j]		
			25ef[g] + 25hi[j]							25e	25f[g]		
										25i[j]	25h		
15	26		26b+26c+26d+ 26e+26f+26g							26a	26b-g		
16	27		27a + 27b							27c[d]	27ab		
	28		28a[b][c[d]] + 28e[f][g[h]]										
	29												
	30												
	31												
17	32a[b]												
	33a[b]												
18	34									34ab	34c	34a	34b
	35												
	36		36b + 36c									36a	36bc
	37												
	38 a[b][c]												

Logical structure of Nixon's Second Inaugural Address.

Paragraph	Simple clause	Clause complex											
		Paratactic				Hypotactic							
		Expansion			Projection	Expansion						Projection	
		Elaboration	Extension	Enhancement		Elaboration		Extension		Enhancement			
						α	β	α	β	α	β	α	β
19	39a[b]												
	40												
	41					41b	41c			41b-c	41a		
	42 a[b][c]												
	43					43a	43b-c			43b	43c		
20	44											44a	44 b[c][d]
	45		45b + 45c									45a	45b-c
	46		46b + 46c									46a	46b-c
21	47												
	48		48c + 48d							48cd	48b	48a	48b-d
	49a[b]									50b-d	50e-g		
22	50		50b+50c+50d 50e + 50fg			50a	50b-g			50g	50f		
23	51									51bc 51b	51a 51c		
	52 a[b][c]												
	53a[b]												
24	54												
	55					55a	55b						
	56 a[b[c]]												
	57					57a	57b[c[d]]						
25	58												
	59		59b + 59c			59a	59bc						
	60					60f-g	60ab [cd[e]]						

Logical structure of Nixon's Second Inaugural Address.

Paragraph	Simple clause	Clause complex											
		Paratactic				Hypotactic							
		Expansion			Projection	Expansion						Projection	
		Elaboration	Extension	Enhancement		Elaboration		Extension		Enhancement			
						α	β	α	β	α	β	α	β
						60a	60b[cd[e]]						
						60g	60f						
	61					61a	61bc[d[e]]						
						61b	61c[d[e]]						
26	62a[bc]												
	63a[b]												
	64					64a	64b			64c[d]	64a,b		
	65		65a[b] + 65c[efg]										
28	66		66abc[d] + 66ef			66b	66c[d]			66a	66b-f		
										66e	66f		
29	67									67ab	67c,d	67a	67b
										67c	67d		
30	68		68a[b[c]] + 68dc							68d	68e		

Appendix 11.8

Theme-rheme structure of RM Nixon's Second Inaugural Address

Sent#	Cl#	Theme				Clause
		Textual	Inter-personal	Topical/ Existential	displaced	
1	1a	When		we		Mr. Vice President, Mr. Speaker, Mr. Chief Justice, Senator Cook, Mrs. Eisenhower, and my fellow citizens of this great and good country we share together: <c 1a> When we met here four years ago, <c 1b> America was bleak in spirit, <c 1c> depressed by the prospect of seemingly endless war abroad and of destructive conflict at home.
	1b			America		
	1c					
2	2a	As		we		<c 2a> As we meet here today, <c 2b> we stand on the threshold of a new era of peace in the world.
	2b			we		
3	3a			The central question before us		<c 3a> The central question before us is: <c 3b> How shall we use that peace?
	3b		How shall			
4	4a		Let us			<c 4a> Let us resolve <c 4b> that this era [<c 4c> we are about <c 4d> to enter] will not be what other postwar periods have so often been: a time of retreat and isolation [<c 4e> that leads to stagnation at home <c 4f> and invites new danger abroad.]
	4b	that		this era [<c 4cd>]		
5	5a		Let us			<c 5a> Let us resolve <c 5b> that this will be [<c 5c> what it can become]: a time of great responsibilities greatly borne, <c 5d> in which we renew the spirit and the promise of America <c 5e> as we enter our third century as a nation.
	5b	that		this		
	5d	in which		we		
	5e	as		we		
6	6			This past year		<c 6> This past year saw far-reaching results from our new policies for peace.
7	7a					<c 7a> By continuing to revitalize our traditional friendships, and by our missions to Peking and to Moscow, <c 7b> we were able to establish the base for a new and more durable pattern of relationships among the nations of the world.
	7b			we		
8	8			Because of America's bold initiatives,	1972	<c 8> Because of America's bold initiatives, 1972 will be long remembered as the year of the greatest progress since the end of World War II toward a lasting peace in the world.

Theme-rheme structure of RM Nixon's Second Inaugural Address

Sent#	Cl#	Theme				Clause
		Textual	Inter-personal	Topical/ Existential	displaced	
9	9			The peace [<c 9b>] in the world		<c 9a> The peace [<c 9b> we seek] in the world is not the flimsy peace [<c 9c> which is merely an interlude between wars], but a peace [<c 9d> which can endure for generations to come.]
10	10			It		<c 10> It is important that we understand both the necessity and the limitations of America's role in maintaining that peace.
11	11a	Unless		we in America		<c 11a> Unless we in America work <c 11b> to preserve the peace, <c 11c> there will be no peace.
	11c			there		
12	12a	Unless		we in America		<c 12a> Unless we in America work <c 12b>to preserve freedom, <c 12c> there will be no freedom.
	12c			there		
13	13	But	let us			<c 13>But let us clearly understand the new nature of America's role, as a result of the new policies [<c 13b> we have adopted over these past four years:]
14	14			We		<c 14>We shall respect our treaty commitments.
15	15			We		<c 15> We shall support vigorously the principle [<c 15b> that no country has the right [<c 15c> to impose its will or rule on another by force.]]
16	16a			We		<c 16a> We shall continue, in this era of negotiation, to work for the limitation of nuclear arms, <c 16b> and to reduce the danger of confrontation between the great powers.
	16b	and				
17	17			We		<c 17a> We shall do our share in [<c 17b> defending peace and freedom in the world.]
18	18a	But		we		<c 18a> But we shall expect <c 18b> others to do their share.
	18b					
19	19a			The time		<c 19a> The time has passed <c 19b> when America will make every other nation's conflict our own, <c 19c> or make every other nation's future our responsibility, <c 19d> or presume <c 19e> to tell the people of other nations <c 19f> how to manage their own affairs.
	19b	when		America		
	19c	or				
	19d	or				
	19e					
	19f					

Theme-rheme structure of RM Nixon's Second Inaugural Address

Sent#	Cl#	Theme				Clause
		Textual	Inter-personal	Topical/ Existential	displaced	
20	20a	Just as		we		<c 20a> Just as we respect the right of each nation [<c 20b> to determine its own future,] <c 20c> we also recognize the responsibility of each nation [<c 20d> to secure its own future.]
	20c			we		
21	21a	Just as		America's role		<c 21a> Just as America's role is indispensable <c 21b> in preserving the world's peace, <c 21c> so is each nation's role indispensable <c 21d> in preserving its own peace.
	21b					
	21c	so				
	21d					
22	22a		let us		Together with the rest of the world,	<c 22a> Together with the rest of the world, let us resolve <c 22b> to move forward from the beginnings [<c 22c> we have made.]
	22b					
23	23a		Let us			<c 23a> Let us continue to bring down the walls of hostility [<c 23b> which have divided the world for too long,] <c 23c> and to build in their place bridges of understanding, <c 23d> so that despite profound differences between systems of government, the people of the world can be friends.
	23c	and				
	23d	so that		despite profound differences between systems of government	the people of the world	
24	24a		Let us			<c 24a> Let us build a structure of peace in the world <c 24b> in which the weak are as safe as the strong – <c24c> in which each respects the right of the other [<c 24d> to live by a different system –]<c 24e> in which those [<c 24f> who would influence others] will do so by the strength of their ideas, and not by the force of their arms.
	24b	in which		the weak		
	24c	in which		each		
	24e	in which		those [<c 24f>]		
25	25a		Let us			<c 25a> Let us accept that high responsibility not as a burden, but gladly – <c 25b> gladly because the chance [<c 25c> to build such a peace] is the noblest endeavor [<c 25d> in which a nation could engage;] <c 25e> and gladly, also, because only will we remain a great nation, <c 25f> -- if we act greatly [<c 25g> in meeting our responsibilities abroad] <c 25h> and only if we remain a great nation <c 25i> will we act greatly [<c 25j>in meeting our challenges at home.]
	25b	because	gladly	the chance [<c 25c> to build such a peace]		
	25c					
	25e	and, also because		only will we	gladly	
	25f	if		we		
	25h	and only if		we		
	25i			will we		
26	26a			We		<c 26a> We have the chance, today, [<c 26b> to do more than ever before in our history] <c 26c> to make life
	26c					
	26d					

Theme-rheme structure of RM Nixon's Second Inaugural Address

Sent#	Cl#	Theme				Clause
		Textual	Inter-personal	Topical/ Existential	displaced	
	26e					better in America <c 26d> -- to ensure better education, better health, better housing, better transportation, a cleaner environment <c 26e> -- to restore respect for law, <c 26f> to make our communities more livable <c 26g> -- and to insure the God-given right of every American to full and equal opportunity
	26f					
	26g	and				
27	27a	Because		the range of our needs		<c 27a> Because the range of our needs is so great, <c 27b> because the reach of our opportunities is so great, <c 27c> let us be bold in our determination [<c 27d> to meet those needs in new ways.]
	27b	because		the reach of our opportunities		
	27c		let us			
28	28a	Just as		[<c 28b>]		<c 28a> Just as [<c 28b> building a structure of peace abroad] has required [<c 28c> turning away from old policies [<c 28d> that had failed,]] <c 28e> so [<c 28f> building a new era of progress at home] requires [<c 28g> turning away from old policies [<c 28h> that have failed.]]
	28e	so		[<c 28f>]		
29	29			Abroad	the shift from old policies to new	<c 29> Abroad, the shift from old policies to new has not been a retreat from our responsibilities, but a better way to peace.
30	30	And		at home	the shift from old policies to new	<c 30> And at home, the shift from old policies to new will not be a retreat from our responsibilities, but a better way to progress.
31	31			Abroad and at home	the key to those new responsibili-ties	<c 31> Abroad and at home, the key to those new responsibilities lies in the placing and the division of responsibility.
32	32a			We		<c 32a> We have lived too long with the consequences [<c 32b> of attempting to gather all power and responsibility in Washington.]
33	33a			Abroad and at home	the time	<c 33a> Abroad and at home, the time has come [<c 33b> to turn away from the condescending policies of paternalism -- of "Washington knows best."]
34	34a			A person		<c 34a> A person can be expected < c 34b> to act responsibly<c 34c> only if he has responsibility.
	34b					
	34c	only if		he		
35	35			This		<c 35> This is human nature.

Theme-rheme structure of RM Nixon's Second Inaugural Address

Sent#	Cl#	Theme				Clause
		Textual	Inter-personal	Topical/ Existential	displaced	
36	36a	So	let us			<c 36a> So let us encourage individuals at home and nations abroad to do more for themselves, <c 36b> to do more for themselves, <c 36c> to decide more for themselves.
	36b					
	36c					
37	37		Let us			<c 37> Let us locate responsibility in more places.
38	38a	And	let us			<c 38a> And let us measure [<c 38b> what we will do for others] by [<c 38c> what they will do for themselves.]
39	39a			That		<c 39a> That is [<c 39b> why today I offer no promise of a purely governmental solution for every problem.]
40	40			We		<c 40> We have lived too long with that false promise.
41	41a					<c 41a> In trusting too much in government, <c 41b> we have asked of it <c 41c> more than it can deliver.
	41b			we		
42	42			This		<c 42a> This leads only to inflated expectations, to reduced individual effort, and to a disappointment and frustration that erode confidence both in [<c 42b> government can do] and in [<c 42c> what people can do.]
43	43a			Government		<c 43a> Government must learn <c 43b> to take less from people <c 43c> so that people can do more for themselves.
	43b					
	43c	so that		people		
44	44a		Let us			<c 44a> Let us remember <c 44b> that America was built not by government, but by people; not by welfare, but by work; not by [<c 44c> shirking responsibility], but by [<c 44d> seeking responsibility].
	44b	that		America		
45	45a			In our own lives,		<c 45a> In our own lives, let each of us ask, not just [<c 45b> what will government do for me,] <c 45c> but what can I do for myself?
46	46a			In the challenges we face together,		<c 46a> In the challenges we face together, let each of us ask, not just [<c 46b> how can government help], <c 46c> but how can I help?
47	47			Your National Government		<c 47> Your National Government has a great and vital role to play.

Theme-rheme structure of RM Nixon's Second Inaugural Address

Sent#	Cl#	Theme				Clause
		Textual	Inter-personal	Topical/ Existential	displaced	
48	48a	And		I		<c 48a> And I pledge to you <c 48b> that where this Government should act, <c 48c> we will act boldly <c48d> and we will lead boldly.
	48b	that where		this Government		
	48c			we		
	48d	and		we		
49	49	But		just as important		<c 49a> But just as important is the role [<c 49b> that each and every one of us must play], as an individual and as a member of his own community.
50	50a			From this day forward		<c 50a> From this day forward, let each of us make a solemn commitment in his own heart: <c 50b> to bear his responsibility, <c 50c> to do his part, <c 50d> to live his ideals, <c 50e> so that together we can see the dawn of a new age of progress for America, <c 50f> and together, as we celebrate our 200th anniversary as a nation, <c 50g> we can do so proud in the fulfillment of our promise to ourselves and to the world
	50b					
	50c					
	50d					
	50e	so that		together	we	
	50f	and		together	we	
	50g			we		
51	51a	As		America's longest and most difficult war		<c 51a> As America's longest and most difficult war comes to an end, <c 51b> let us again learn <c 51c> to debate our differences with civility and decency.
	51b		let us			
	51c					
52	52	And	let each of us			<c 52a> And let each of us reach out for that one precious quality [<c 52b> government cannot provide] -- a new level of respect for the rights and feelings of one another, a new level of respect for the individual human dignity [<c 52c> which is the cherished birthright of every American.]
53	53		Above all else	the time		<c 53a> Above all else, the time has come [<c 53b> for us to renew our faith in ourselves and in America.]
54	54			In recent years	that faith	<c 54> In recent years, that faith has been challenged.
55	55a			Our children		<c 55a> Our children have been taught <c 55b> to be ashamed of their country, ashamed of their parents, ashamed of America's record at home and its role in the world.
	55b					
56	56a			At every turn	we	<c 56a> At every turn, we have been beset by those [<c 56b> who find everything wrong with America and little [<c56c> that is right.]]

Theme-rheme structure of RM Nixon's Second Inaugural Address

Sent#	Cl#	Theme				Clause
		Textual	Inter-personal	Topical/ Existential	displaced	
57	57a	But		I		<c 57a> But I am confident <c 57b> that this will not be the judgment of history on these remarkable times[<c 57c> in which we are privileged [<c 57d> to live.]]
	57b	that		this		
58	58			America's record in this century		<c 58> America's record in this century has been unparalleled in the world's history for its responsibility, for its generosity, for its creativity and for its progress.
59	59a		Let us			<c 59a> Let us be proud <c 59b> that our system has produced and provided more freedom and more abundance, more widely shared, than any other system in the history of the world.
	59b	that		our system		
60	60a		Let us			<c 60a> Let us be proud <c 60b> that in each of the four wars [<c 60c> in which we have been engaged in this century], <c 60d> including the one [<c 60e> we are now bringing to an end,] <c 60b> we have fought not for our selfish advantage,<c 60f> but to help others <c 60g > resist aggression.
	60b	that		in each of the four wars [<c 60c>]	we	
	60f	but				
	60g					
61	61a	And	let us			<c 61a> And let us be proud <c 61b> that by our bold, new initiatives, by our steadfastness for peace with honor, we have made a break-through <c 61c> toward creating in the world [<c 61d> what the world has not known before -- a structure of peace [<c 61 e> that can last, not merely for our time, but for generations to come.]]
	61b	that		by our bold, new initiatives, by our steadfastness for peace with honor	we	
62	62			We		<c 62a> We are embarking here today on an era [<c 62b> that presents challenges <c 62c> as great as those any nation, or any generation, has ever faced.]
63	63			We		<c 63a> We shall answer to God, to history, and to our conscience for the way [<c 63b> in which we use these years.]
64	64a	As		I		<c 64a> As I stand in this place, <c 64b> so hallowed by history, <c 64c> I think of others [<c 64d> who have stood here before me.]
	64b					
	64c			I		

Theme-rheme structure of RM Nixon's Second Inaugural Address

Sent#	Cl#	Theme				Clause
		Textual	Inter-personal	Topical/ Existential	displaced	
65	65a			I		<c 65a> I think of the dreams [<c 65b> they had for America,] <c 65c> and I think of [<c 65d> how each recognized <c 65e> that he needed help far beyond himself <c 65f> in order to make <c 65g> those dreams come true.]
	65c	and		I		
66	66a			Today	I	<c 66a> Today, I ask your prayers <c 66b> that in the years ahead I may have God's help <c 66c> in making decisions [<c 66d> that are right for America,] <c 66e> and I pray for your help <c 66f> so that together we may be worthy of our challenge.
	66b	that		in the years ahead	I	
	66e	and		I		
	66f	so that		together	we	
67	67a		Let us			<c 67a> Let us pledge together <c 67b> to make these next four years the best four years in America's history, <c 67c> so that on its 200th birthday America will be as young and as vital and as bright a beacon of hope for all the world. <c 67d> as when it began,
	67b					
	67c	so that		on its 200th birthday	America	
	67d	as when		it		
68	68a		Let us			<c 68a> Let us go forward from here confident in hope, strong in our faith in one another, [<c 68b> sustained by our faith in God [<c 68c> who created us,]] <c 68d> and striving always <c 68e> to serve His purpose.
	68d	and				
	68e					

12 Arriving at a theory of the text: A case study of the commencement addresses delivered by Steve Jobs and Susan Rice

12.1 Introduction

Both speeches analysed here are commencement speeches which were given at Stanford University. Steve Jobs, the founder of Apple, gave the commencement speech in 2005; Susan Rice, the current United States Ambassador to the United Nations, delivered her commencement speech in 2010. Table 12.1 lists the commencement speakers at Stanford University for the years 2003–2012. The list includes well-known speakers from government, business and entertainment.

Because commencement speeches are addressed to new graduates on the occasion of their graduation, such speeches are expected to be inspirational in nature, typically exhorting them to make the most of their lives following graduation.

Some speakers put the focus on their own personal life story. Steve Jobs, for example, uses his own life experience to tell graduates how they should live their lives going forward. In his speech, Jobs exhorts by his own personal example, encouraging students to adopt his own approach to experiencing life: 'Stay Hungry. Stay Foolish.' Jobs' focus on his own personal narrative is reflected in the high percentage of first person singular pronouns in his speech.

A study of the use of personal pronouns in Stanford University commencement speeches (see Table 12.2) reveals a relatively higher proportion (above 5% of the total number of words, compared with most other speakers who ranged between 1% and 2%) of first-person singular pronouns in the speeches of Alejandro Toledo (5.8%), Steve Jobs (6.2%), Oprah Winfrey (6.4%) and Cory Booker (6.3%). Of these, only Jobs' speech is similar in length to other speakers (between 2,000 and 3,000 words), the rest – Toledo, Winfrey and Booker – all tended to give longer speeches (as measured by word count).

Instead of focusing on their own personal narrative, some speakers choose to focus on the current state of the world, exhorting graduates to help make the world a better place. Speaking from her own personal experience about the problems the world is facing (thus accounting for the fact that 3.2% of the words are first person singular pronouns), Susan Rice's speech is less about her biography, and more a call to action. Rice challenges students to become agents of change in solving the world's problems.

12.2 Steve Jobs

Steve Jobs' commencement speech is very deliberately crafted to make use of familiar rhetorical techniques (see, for example, Andrew Dlugan's critique at http://sixminutes.dlugan.com/video-critique-steve-jobs-stanford-2005). Some of the techniques noted by Dlugan include repeating things in threes – the 'rule of three'; and frequent use of semantic opposites.

Examples of things in three's: 'the rule of three'

> *<p 7> ... <c 35a> Because I had dropped out <c 35b> and didn't have to take the normal classes, <c 35c> I decided <c 35d> to take a calligraphy class <c 35e> learn [<c 35f> how to do this.] <c 36a> I learned* ***about serif and san serif typefaces, about [c 36b> varying the amount of space between different letter combinations], about [<c 36c> what makes great typography great.]*** *<c 37a> It was* ***beautiful, historical, artistically subtle*** *in a way [<c 37b> that science can't capture, <c 37c> and I found it fascinating.]*

> *<p 18> ... <c 102a> Because almost everything —* ***all external expectations, all pride, all fear of embarrassment or failure*** *— these things just fall away in the face of death, <c 102b> leaving only [<c 102c> what is truly important.] ...*

> *<p 19> ... <c 111a>* ***It means [<c 111b> to try*** *to tell your kids everything [<c 111c> you thought <c 111d> you'd have the next 10 years <c 111e> to tell them in just a few months.]] <c 112a>* ***It means [<c 112b> to make*** *sure <c 112c> everything is buttoned up <c 112d> so that it will be as easy as possible for your family.] <c 113a>* ***It means [<c 113b> to say*** *your goodbyes.]*

> *<p 22> <c 129a> Your time is limited, <c 129b> so* ***don't*** *waste it <c 129c> living someone else's life. <c 130a>* ***Don't*** *be trapped by dogma — <c 130b> which is living with the results of other people's thinking. <c 131>* ***Don't*** *let the noise of others' opinions drown out your own inner voice....*

Examples of semantic opposites:

> *<p 5> ... <c 27a> The minute [<c 27b> I* ***dropped out****] I could stop taking the required classes [<c 27c> that didn't interest me,] <c 27d> and begin* ***dropping in*** *on the ones [<c 27e> that looked interesting.]*

> *<p 8> ... <c 44a > If I had never* ***dropped out****, <c 44b> I would have never* ***dropped in*** *on this calligraphy class, <c 44c> and personal computers might not have the wonderful typography [<c 44d> that they do.]*

> *<p 9> <c 47a> Again, you can't connect the dots <c 47b>* ***looking forward;*** *<c 47c> you can only connect them <c 47d>* ***looking backwards.*** *...*
>
> *<p 13> ... <c 74a>* ***The heaviness*** *[<c 74b> of being successful] <c 74a> was replaced by* ***the lightness*** *[<c 74c> of being a beginner again, less sure about everything.] ...*
>
> *<p 21> ... <c 126a> It clears out* ***the old*** *<c 126b> to make way for* ***the new.*** *...*

The word cloud for Steve Jobs' commencement speech at Stanford University (2005) reveals some of his most prominent motifs: *life, college, Apple.* In fact, these three motifs correspond to the clear division of his speech into three stories from his own personal narrative.

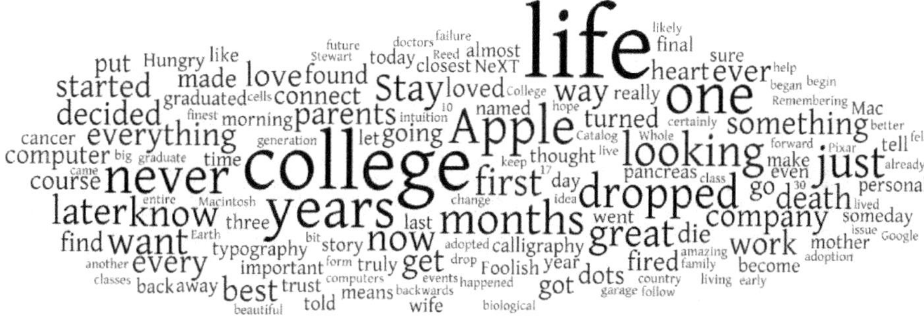

Figure 12.1: Word cloud for Steve Jobs' Commencement Speech

Introducing his speech, Steve Jobs informs his audience that he wants to tell them three stories from his life. The word clouds for the three stories are shown in Figures 12.2–12.4. The first story relates his experience having dropped out of college; the second story is about his being fired by Apple; the third talks about the time he faced death due to cancer.

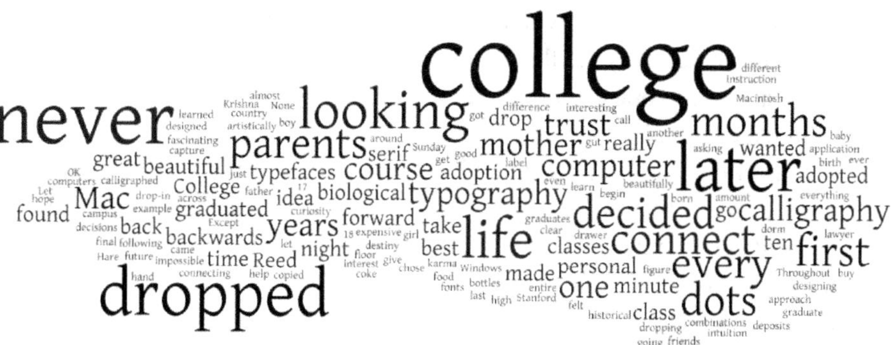

Figure 12.2: Jobs' Story 1 'Connecting the dots' <c 8> to <c 48>

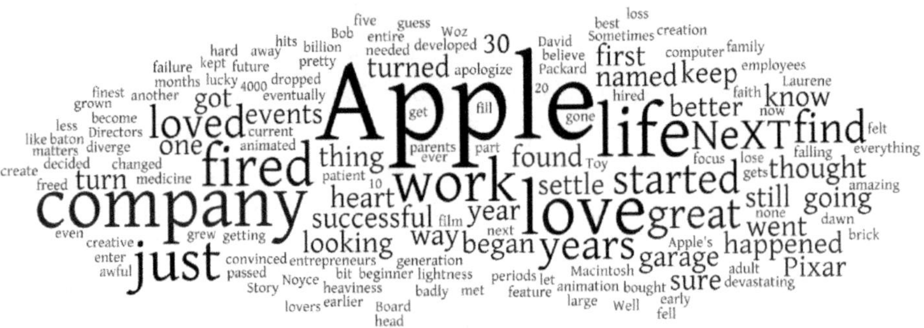

Figure 12.3: Jobs' Story 2 'love and loss' <c 49> to <c 92>

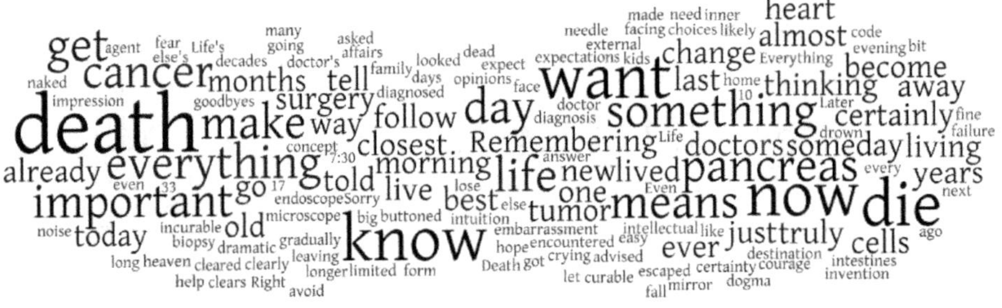

Figure 12.4: Jobs' Story 3 'death' <c 93> to <c 132>

Table 12.3 shows the processes by type (relational, material, mental, verbal) and by story. Story 1 is the most material-oriented – 56% (compared with 51% for Story 2, and 30% for Story 3). The Actor in over half of those material processes is the first-person singular 'I' (compared with 20% in Story 2, and 14% in Story 3). In fact, Steve Jobs is the most in control of events in his life in Story 1, as compared to when he was fired by Apple (Story 2), or had to deal with cancer (Story 3). Story 3 is the most relational and least material of the three, perhaps because he is making the point that there is nothing one can do about death, it simply is a fact of life which we all must eventually face.

Based on Table 12.4.1 and 12.4.2, we note that there are significantly more complex than simple clauses in Steve Jobs commencement speech. The percentage of simple clauses is slightly higher in the second story. Story 2 contains relatively more parataxis than either of the other two stories. Also, as noted in Table 5, Story 2 is the shortest – in terms of word count – of the three, and employs double the percentage of paratactic conjunctions, 'and' and 'but'.

Table 12.3: Processes by Type and by Story in Steve Jobs commencement speech

	Steve Jobs		
	First story	**Second Story**	**Third story**
relational	27 (24%)	31 (30%)	49 (40%)
material	62 (56%) [21 (33%) = 'I']	54 (51%) [11 (20%) = 'I']	36 (30%) [5 (14%) = 'I']
mental	14 (13%)	20 (19%)	16 (13%)
verbal	3 (3%)		8 (7%)

Table 12.4.1: Clause relations by Story in Steve Jobs commencement speech

		Steve Jobs		
simple (vs. complex clauses)		**First story**	**Second Story**	**Third story**
		21%	24%	17%
complex clauses	parataxis	38%	47%	32%
	hypotaxis	62%	53%	68%

Table 12.4.2: Clause relations by Story in Steve Jobs commencement speech (noting projection)

		Steve Jobs		
simple (vs. complex clauses)		**First story**	**Second Story**	**Third story**
		21%	24%	17%
complex clauses	parataxis	27%	47%	32%
	hypotaxis	49%	29%	55%
	projection	24%	24%	13%

Table 12.5: Count of words, 'and', 'but' in Steve Jobs commencement speech

	Story 1 – connecting the dots	**Story 2 – love and loss**	**Story 3 – death**
# of words	727	438	639
# 'and'	19	23	15
# 'but'	5	5	4
% of 'and' & 'but'	24/727 = 3%	28/438 = 6%	19/639 = 3%

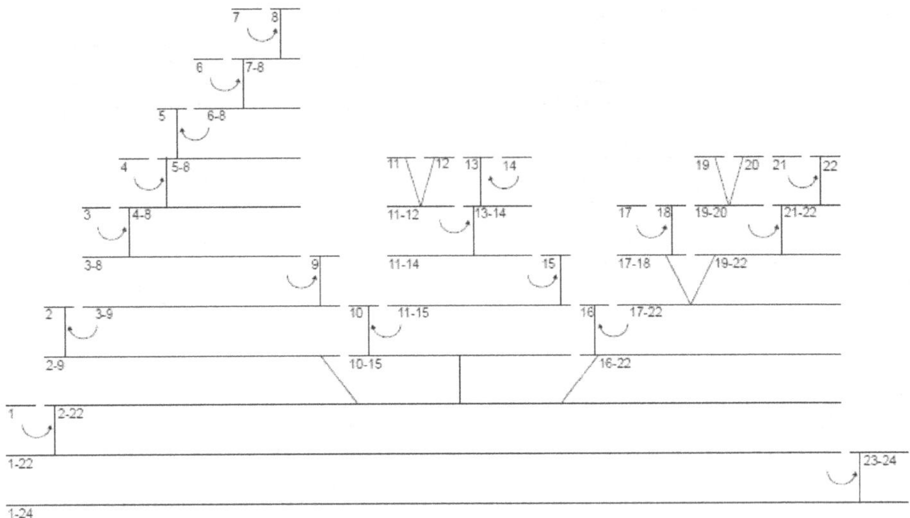

Figure 12.5: RST mapping (paragraph and above) for the three stories in Steve Jobs commencement speech

Observing the differences in the mapping of the three stories, we note that all begin with a brief introduction, and conclude with a final exhortation summing up the main point of that particular story.

There is an interesting pattern with respect to Jobs' use of the word 'best'. The word occurs only five times in the speech.

> *<p 5> ... <c 26a> It was pretty scary at the time, <c 26b> but looking back <c 26c> it was one of the* ***best*** *decisions [<c 26d> I ever made.] <c 27a> The minute [<c 27b> I* ***dropped out****] I could stop taking the required classes [<c 27c> that didn't interest me,] <c 27d> and begin* ***dropping in*** *on the ones [<c 27e> that looked interesting.]*

> *<p 7> <c 33> Reed College at that time offered perhaps the* ***best*** *calligraphy instruction in the country. ...*

> *<p 13> <c 73a> I didn't see it then, <c 73b> but it turned out <c 73c> that [<c 73d> getting fired from Apple] was the* ***best*** *thing [<c 73e> that could have ever happened to me]. <c 74a>* ***The heaviness*** *[<c 74b> of being successful] <c 74a> was replaced by* ***the lightness*** *[<c 74c> of being a beginner again, less sure about everything.] <c 75a> It freed me <c 75b> to enter one of the most creative periods of my life.*

> *<p 18> ... <c 103a> [<c 103b> Remembering <c 103c> that you are going to die] is the* ***best*** *way [<c 103d> I know] [<c 103e> to avoid the trap [<c 103f> of thinking <c 103g> you have something [<c 103h> to*

> *lose]]]. <c 104> You are already naked. <c 105a> There is no reason [<c 105b> not to follow your heart].*
>
> *<p 21> ... <c 123> No one has ever escaped it. <c 124a> And that is [<c 124b> as it should be], <c 124c> because Death is very likely the single **best** invention of Life. <c 125> It is Life's change agent. <c 126a> It clears out **the old** <c 126b> to make way for **the new.** ...*

Among the five occurrences of the word 'best', just three occur in conjunction with a pair of semantic opposites:

> Paragraph 5: 'one of the **best** decisions I ever made'; 'dropped out'/'dropping in'
>
> Paragraph 13: 'the **best** thing that could have ever happened to me'; 'heaviness'/'lightness'
>
> Paragraph 21: 'the single **best** invention of Life'; 'the old'/'the new'

Noting where these three instances occur within the speech, it appears that this pattern coincides with what we have identified as the more central/core paragraphs within each story.

Another lexicogrammatical pattern which appears to correlate with the rhetorical structure of the text as a whole is the occurrence of the second person pronoun. In the first two stories, usage of the second person pronoun comes both in the beginning and concluding paragraphs of a story. The only exception is the final sentence of paragraph 6 – midway through the first story – when Jobs introduces the example – 'Let me give you one example:' – which he then goes on to elaborate in the subsequent two paragraphs. Paragraph 15, which concludes the second story, stands out with the most occurrences of the second person pronoun, and the most imperative clauses. In fact, it seems as though the speech climaxes at this point, and from here on Jobs increasingly directs his words to his audience. In the third story, the second person pronoun repeatedly occurs in every paragraph except for paragraph 20.

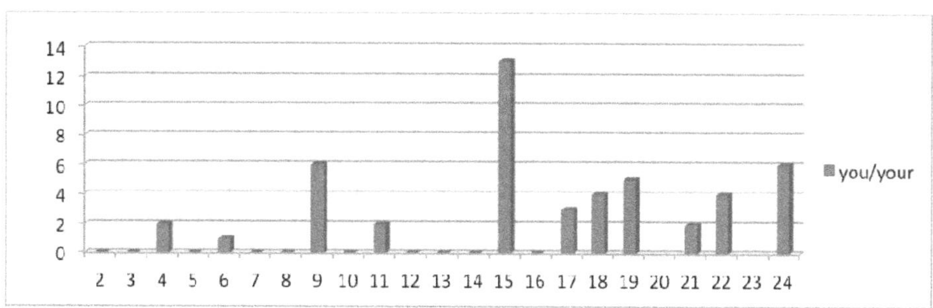

Figure 12.6: Occurrences of second person pronoun (*you, your)* across paragraphs in Jobs' commencement speech.

12.3 Susan Rice

For this analysis, I have excluded the opening remarks in the paragraphs prior to where she turns her attention to the graduates as signalled by her saying: 'Now graduates: …' The excluded paragraphs include some reminiscing about her student days at Stanford, and her gratefully acknowledging the parents of graduates in the audience. Instead I will focus on that portion directed primarily at the graduates.

The word 'world' is the most prominent in the word cloud for Susan Rice's commencement speech at Stanford (2010). Less prominent, but still frequent are words like 'child', 'change', 'Stanford', 'just', 'deserves'.

Figure 12.7: Word cloud for Susan Rice's Commencement Speech

Table 12.6: Process types by personal pronouns and other for Susan Rice's speech (all paragraphs)

	I	you	we	OTHER	
relational (=74)	6/74 = 8%	6/74 = 8%	1/74 = 2%	61/74 = 82%	74/203 = 37%
material (=78)	16/78 = 24%	12/78 = 18%	–/78	45/78 = 58%	78/203 = 38%
mental (=32)	13/32 = 44%	8/32 = 25%	2/32 = 6%	8/32 = 25%	32/203 = 16%
verbal (=6)	2/6 = 34%	–/6	–/6	4/6 = 66%	6/203 = 3%
existential (=4)	–/4	–/4	–/4	4/4 = 100%	4/203 = 2%
behavioural (=9)	1/9 = 12%	–/9	–/9	8/9 = 99%	9/203 = 4%
	38/203= 19%	26/203 = 13%	3/203 = 1%	128/203 = 63%	

Table 12.7: Processes by type and particiapant for span from paragraphs 23 – 29 only

	I	you	we	OTHER	
relational (=23)	5/23= 22%	2/23= 9%	–/23	16/23= 69%	23/56 = 40%
material (=19)	8/19= 42%	3/19= 18%	–/19	7/19= 40%	19/56 = 34%
mental (=14)	6/14 = 42%	4/14 = 29%	–/14	4/14 = 29%	14/56 = 25%
verbal (=2)	–/2	–/2	2/2 = 100%	–/2	2/56 = 1%
	19/56 = 34%	9/56 = 16%	2/56 = 4%	27/56 = 48%	

Taking into account the speech as a whole, over half of the Actors are OTHER (63%) than Rice and her listening audience, i.e. 'I', 'you' or 'we' (33%).

Compare this with the span of the speech from paragraph 23 through 29 (see Table 12.7). 'I' is the Actor in 42% of material processes, up from 24%. Adding together the percentages of first- (singular and plural) and second-person Actors in this portion of the speech, the sum is 60%, up from 42%, reflecting the increased role of Rice and her listeners in the material activity described in the closing paragraphs of the speech. Similar to Steve Jobs' commencement speech, Rice's message becomes more 'we'- / i.e. both 'you'-and-'I'-centred, as the speech progresses and as she exhorts listeners to follow her example.

Aside from the introductory (paragraphs 1–2) and concluding paragraphs (paragraphs 30–32) of Rice's commencement speech, the main body of her speech can be divided into three spans as shown in Figure 12.8. The larger span from paragraph 3 to 22 divides at the point where Rice directly addresses the graduates:

> *<p 11> <c 41a> So, here's my challenge to you: <c 41b> become agents of change. <c 42a> Be driven by a passion [<c 42b> to lift up the most vulnerable and <c 42c> to serve those with the least, both at home and around the world.]*

In what follows, from paragraphs 12 to 22, Rice shares the reason for why this imperative is personal. As reflected in the word cloud for paragraphs 11–22 (see Figure 12.10), other than the word 'world', the two other most prominent words are 'child' and 'deserves', both of which consistently appear in the Theme of the initial clause of each paragraph from 17–22.

The span between 11 and 22 is also distinguished by a higher proportion of simple (48%) to complex clauses (compared with 27% for paragraphs 3–10; 28% for paragraphs 23–29) – see Table 12.8.

Table 12.8: Clause relations by span

		Susan Rice commencement speech		
		para. 3-10	**para. 11-22**	**para. 23-29**
simple (vs. complex) clauses		27%	48%	28%
complex clauses	parataxis	44%	42%	38%
	hypotaxis	56%	58%	62%

Many of the simple clauses, however, contain embedding, either post-modifying relative or *to*-infinitive clauses (shown below **in bold**).

> *<p 11>...<c 42a> Be driven by a passion* ***[<c 42b> to lift up the most vulnerable and <c 42c> to serve those with the least, both at home and around the world.]***
>
> *<p 13> <c 44a> One of those reasons is a little boy* ***[<c 44b> whom I met in war-ravaged Angola in1995.]*** *<c 45> I don't even know his name. <c 46a> He was one face in a friendly mob of destitute little kids* ***[<c 46b> who greeted our delegation at a dusty camp for internally displaced persons in the middle of nowhere.]*** *...*
>
> *<p 14>...<c 54a> But he could well have become one of the 9 million children under the age of 5* ***[<c 54b> who die each year, mostly from preventable and treatable afflictions.]***
>
> *<p 15> <c 55a> Yet he has every right* ***[<c 55b>to live with the same dignity, hope, and security [<c 55c> that my own son enjoys.]]*** *<c 56> They are both children of God, of equal worth, equal consequence, and equal rights.*
>
> *<p16> <c 57> That little boy's future is tied to ours; <c 58> our security is ultimately linked to his well-being. <c 59a> So we must shape the world* ***[<c 59b> that he deserves.]***
>
> *<p 17> <c 60a> That child deserves a world without the poverty* ***[<c 60b> that crushes the dreams of hundreds of millions.]*** *<c 61> Half of humanity lives on less than $2.50 a day.*
>
> *<p 18> <c 62a>That child deserves a world without extreme hunger and dependence* ***[<c 62b> that it fosters.]*** *<c 63a> So we are investing in building poor countries' capacity* ***[<c 63b> to feed themselves.]*** *<c 64a> Agricultural research has produced stronger crops* ***[<c 64b> that yield more, <c 64c> adapt faster, <c 64d> and better resist drought, disease, and pests.]*** *...*

> *<p 19> <c 67a> That child deserves a world* ***[<c 67b> where everyone can get a quality education.]****...*

The extent of embedding is generally higher across the span of paragraphs from 11–29 (34%) – see Table 12.9 – than the span from paragraphs 3–10 (4%), and the span from paragraphs 30–33 (16%).

Table 12.9: Clauses with embedding by span

span	para. 3–10	para. 11–22	para. 23–29	para. 30–33
clauses with embedding	4%	39%	29%	16%
			34%	

Lexicogrammatically speaking, the span of paragraphs from 3–10 is very different from what follows in paragraphs 11–29. The span from 3–10 is grammatically more complex (fewer simple clauses), and with much less embedding. Such distinctive texture defines a span, no matter that span be a clause, clause complex, combination of several clauses, a paragraph, or larger.

Noteworthy is the fact that speech – particularly spontaneous speech – is typically more complex grammatically than written language, suggesting that the span from 3–10 may be considered more speech-like than the rest of the text.

The span of paragraphs from 11–22 climaxes in a paratactic series of paragraphs beginning with the same phrasing: 'That/The child (also) deserves a world ...'

> *<p 17> <c 60a> That child deserves a world without the poverty* ***[<c 60b> that crushes the dreams of hundreds of millions.]*** *...*
>
> *<p 18> <c 62a>That child deserves a world without extreme hunger and dependence* ***[<c 62b> that it fosters.]*** *...*
>
> *<p 19> <c 67a>That child deserves a world* ***[<c 67b>where everyone can get a quality education.]*** *...*
>
> *<p 20> <c 70a> The child deserves a world* ***[<c 70b> in which we find new cures for old plagues.]*** *...*
>
> *<p 21> <c 72a> The child also deserves a world* ***[<c 72b> whose climate isn't collapsing, <c 72c> whose air isn't chocked by soot–<c 72d> and whose waters aren't polluted with spewing oil.]*** *...*
>
> *<p 22> <c76> That child, every child, deserves a world of greater opportunity, democracy and hope ...*

Patterning can also be seen in how paragraphs conclude. Paragraphs 23–25 similarly conclude with a concessive 'but' joining the final two clauses of the paragraph:

> *<p 23> <c 78a> Sometimes we innovate in great strides; <c 78b> sometimes we progress by slow and steady advances. <c 79>* ***But*** *progress we must.*
>
> *<p 24> ...<c 82> The aim is ambitious. <c 83>* ***But*** *so are you.*
>
> *<p 25> ...<c 89a> Graduating from Stanford is great, <c 89b>* ***but*** *it's just the beginning.*

What distinguishes the span of paragraphs 26 and 27 from the immediately preceding three paragraphs (23–25) and those following (28–29) is the frequent first-person reference (19 occurrences of 'I') as compared with its absence in the paragraphs before and after – see Table 12.10.

Table 12.10: Use of first-person singular pronoun 'I' throughout Rice speech

Paragraph #	1	3	5	13	14	**26**	**27**	32
Occurrences of the first-person pronoun 'I'	5	1	2	9	2	**11**	**8**	1

This span – paragraphs 26–27 – begins with the conjunction 'so', and the last sentence of paragraph of 27 also begins with 'so'. Her personal story, which she offers by way of example, is bookended by clauses conveying what she wants listeners to conclude.

Paragraphs 28 and 29 both begin with an imperative clause with a relational process. The span of paragraphs 11–29 begins as it now concludes with imperatives formed with relational processes:

> *<p 11> <c 41a> So, here's my challenge to you: <c 41b> become agents of change. <c 42a> Be driven by a passion [<c 42b> to lift up the most vulnerable and <c 42c> to serve those with the least, both at home and around the world.]*
>
> ...
>
> *<p28> <c 101> Be fearless. ...*
>
> *<p29> <c 108> Be about more than money. ...*

12.4 Texture and architeXture

Patterns of lexicogrammatical choice contribute to establishing texture, on the basis of which one can identify the spans that together form the text as a whole. Lexicogrammatical choice may be experiential (choices from the system of transitivity), logical (choices related to clausal taxis), interpersonal (choices from systems of mood and modality), and textual (choices related to theme-rheme and information structures).

Sometimes the speaker's choices are deliberate – such as choosing to repeat clauses with the same thematic structure at the beginning of each in a series of paragraphs. Some lexicogrammatical choices – such as repeating the first-person singular pronoun in an autobiographical account – are less deliberate and instead result from choices on another level about what one wants to say.

The architeXture of a text is the outcome of lexicogrammatical choices and can be determined from their patterning.

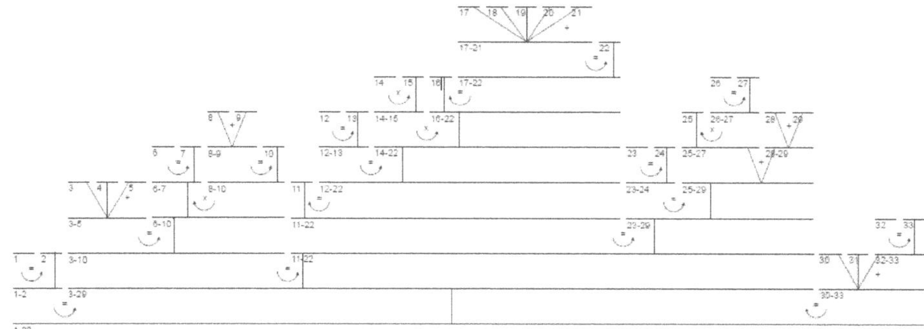

Figure 12.8: RST mapping of Rice's Stanford commencement speech

Figure 12.9: Word Cloud for Rice Commencement Speech paragraphs 3–10

Figure 12.10: Word Cloud for Rice Commencement Speech paragraphs 11–10

Figure 12.11: Word Cloud for Rice Commencement Speech paragraphs 23–29

Table 12.1: Stanford University Commencement Speakers – 2003 to 2012

Speakers	Year	Speaker's Title	Word Count
Alejandro Toledo	2003	President of Peru	3512
Sandra Day O'Connor	2004	US Supreme Court Associate Justice	2668
Steve Jobs	2005	CEO and Co-Founder of Apple Computer and of Pixar Animation Studios	2248
Tom Brokaw	2006	Broadcast-news icon and author	2602
Dana Gioia	2007	Chairman of the National Endowment for the Arts	2414
Oprah Winfrey	2008	Global media leader and philanthropist	4334
Anthony Kennedy	2009	US Supreme Court Associate Justice	2037
Susan E. Rice	2010	US Ambassador to the United Nations	2147
Felipe Calderón	2011	President of Mexico	1872
Cory Booker	2012	Mayor of Newark, NJ	6849

Table 12.2: Use of personal pronouns by Stanford University Commencement Speakers – 2003 to 2012

		First person Singular			**Second Person Singular/Plural**		**Third Person Singular**					**First Person Plural**			**Third Person Plural**		
Speaker (Year)	**Word count**	***I***	***Me***	***my/ mine***	***you***	***your(s)***	***he/she***	***him/ her***	***his/ her(s)***	***it***	***its***	***we***	***us***	***our(s)***	***they***	***them***	***Their (s)***
Toledo 2003	3512	128 (3.6%)	29 (0.8%)	49/1 (=50) (1.4%)	48 (1.4%)	10 (0.3%)	4+2 (=6) (0.2%)	1/-- (0.03%)	4/-- (0.1%)	36 (1.4%)	--	19 (0.5%)	4 (0.1%)	7 (0.2%)	19 (0.5%)	15 (0.4%)	7 (0.2%)
		(5.8%)			**(1.7%)**		**(1.7%)**					**(0.8%)**			**(1.1%)**		
O'Connor 2004	2668	35 (1.3%)	7 (0.3%)	8/-- (0.3%)	33 (1.2%)	17 (0.6%)	24/-- (0.9%)	3/-- (0.1%)	13/-- (0.5%)	23 (0.9%)	5 (0.2%)	11 (0.4%)	3 (0.1%)	16 (0.6%)	12 (0.4%)	3 (0.1%)	9 (0.3%)
		(1.9%)			**(1.8%)**		**(2.6%)**					**(1.1%)**			**(0.8%)**		
Jobs 2005	2248	93 (4.1%)	18 (0.8%)	30/-- (1.3%)	35 (1.6%)	16 (0.7%)	1/4 (=5) (0.2%)	2/-- (0.08%)	3/-- (0.1%)	55 (2.4%)	1 (0.04%)	9 (0.4%)	1 (0.05%)	3 (0.1%)	9 (0.4%)	3 (0.1%)	3 (0.1%)
		(6.2%)			**(2.3%)**		**(2.8%)**					**(0.6%)**			**(0.6%)**		
Brokaw 2006	2602	42 (1.6%)	4 (0.2%)	10/-- (0.4%)	36 (1.4%)	22 (0.8%)	2/-- (0.07%)	2/1 (=4) (1.2%)	2/1 (=3) (0.1%)	25 (1%)	2 (0.08%)	20 (0.8%)	8 (0.3%)	8 (0.3%)	20 (0.8%)	7 (0.3%)	19 (0.7%)
		(2.2%)			**(2.2%)**		**(2.5%)**					**(1.4%)**			**(1.8%)**		
Gioia 2007	2414	44 (1.8%)	8 (0.3%)	15/-- (0.6%)	17 (0.7%)	4 (0.2%)	7/3 (=10) (0.4%)	1/1 (=2) (0.08%)	6/2 (=8) (0.3%)	20 (0.8%)	2 (0.08%)	14 (0.6%)	8 (0.3%)	15 (0.6%)	9 (0.4%)	3 (0.1%)	6 (0.2%)
		(2.7%)			**(0.9%)**		**(1.7%)**					**(1.5%)**			**(0.7%)**		
Winfrey 2008	4334	202 (4.6%)	28 (0.6%)	54/-- (1.2%)	155 (3.6%)	28 (0.6%)	8/11 (=19) (0.4%)	--/6 (0.1%)	1/9 (=10) (0.2%)	5 (1.3%)	--	15 (0.3%)	--	8 (0.2%)	22 (0.5%)	2 (0.05%)	12 (0.3%)
		(6.4%)			**(4.2%)**		**(2%)**					**(0.5%)**			**(0.9%)**		
Kennedy 2009	2037	5 (0.2%)	2 (0.09%)	2/-- (0.1%)	40 (2%)	22 (1.1%)	1/4 (=5) (0.2%)	1/2 (=3) (0.1%)	1/1 (=2) (0.1%)	21 (1%)	3 (0.1%)	24 (1.2%)	6 (0.3%)	18 (0.8%)	2 (0.1%)	4 (0.2%)	7 (0.3%)
		(0.4%)			**(3.1%)**		**(1.5%)**					**(2.3%)**			**(0.6%)**		
Rice 2010	2147	39 (1.8%)	10 (0.5%)	19/-- (0.9%)	39 (1.8%)	21 (1%)	10/-- (0.5%)	3/-- (0.1%)	7/-- (0.3%)	24 (1.1%)	3 (0.1%)	14 (0.7%)	5 (0.2%)	12 (0.5%)	5 (0.2%)	3 (0.1%)	3 (0.1%)
		(3.2%)			**(2.8%)**		**(2.1%)**					**(1.4%)**			**(0.4%)**		
Calderon 2011	1872	16 (0.8%)	5 (0.3%)	6/-- (0.3%)	43 (2.3%)	24 (1.3%)	3/-- (0.2%)	3/-- (0.2%)	2/1 (=3) (0.2%)	18 (1%)	1 (0.05%)	17 (0.9%)	2 (0.1%)	5 (0.3%)	6 (0.3%)	6 (0.3%)	2 (0.1%)
		(1.4%)			**(3.6%)**		**(2.6%)**					**(1.3%)**			**(0.7%)**		
Booker 2012	6849	218 (3.1%)	103 (1.5%)	114/1 (=115) (1.7%)	125 (1.8%)	31 (0.5%)	82/36 (=118) (1.7%)	30/4 (=34) (0.5%)	45/17 (=62) (0.9%)	79 (1.2%)	2 (0.03%)	40 (0.6%)	12 (0.2%)	12 (0.2%)	61 (0.9%)	16 (0.2%)	15 (0.2%)
		(6.3%)			**(2.3%)**		**(4.3%)**					**(1%)**			**(1.3%)**		
Total	30683																

Appendix 12.1

Susan Rice's commencement speech at Stanford University

Good morning, Stanford! Thank you very much, President Hennessy, for that very warm introduction. It is wonderful to be back at Stanford. Having gotten around a bit over the last few years, I am more convinced than ever – that this is the best university on the face of the planet.

It's particularly gratifying to be back in this stadium, which is a rather special place for me. It happens to be the spot where my husband and I had our first romantic moment. It was just as the Band was playing 'Alright Now'. (But my kids are in the audience, so I'm not going to give you any more detail.)

Stanford has had an enormous impact on my life. Not only is it where I met my husband, but it's where I met the people, took the courses, and championed the causes that ultimately led me to make my career in international affairs. Stanford also taught me focus and discipline. Once you've learned to study in a bathing suit on the grass with muscled men throwing frisbees over your head, you can accomplish almost anything.

Let me join President Hennessy and start by recognizing the parents here today. For many families, your kids have been living far away from home. I grew up in Washington, DC, and I think my mother got over my decision to go to Stanford about three weeks ago. I still understand your pride in your children has no bounds. You have made great sacrifices to enable your kids to get such a tremendous education. So this is your day too. Parents, grandparents, family and friends, thank you for all you've done.

<p 1> <c 1> Now, graduates: first and foremost, congratulations. <c 2a> I suspect <c 2b> you're feeling pretty good about yourselves right now. <c 3a> I remember <c 3b> feeling pretty good about myself too <c 3c> when I was sitting in your seats. <c 4a> In fact, I might have been feeling a little too good — <c 4b> judging from [<c 4c> how much I remember about my commencement speech.]

<p 2> <c 5a> Hold on to this jubilant moment <c 5b> and cherish your memories of this extraordinary place.<c 6a> Nurture the friendships [<c 6b> you have made here.] <c 7a> The warmth and security of Stanford can sustain you <c 7b>as you face an economy [<c 7c> still climbing out of a deep hole] <c 7d>and enter a world [<c 7e> changing at a furious pace.]

<p 3> <c 8a> Imagine the world and [<c 8b> what it will be like] <c 8c> when one of you comes back a quarter century from now <c 8d> to deliver

the commencement address. <c 9a> In 1986, when I graduated, <c 9b> the Soviet Union was bristling with 45,000 nuclear weapons, <c 9c> and the Berlin Wall was impenetrable. <c 10> Nelson Mandela was clocking his 23rd year in prison in apartheid South Africa. <c 11a> Osama bin Laden was fighting the Soviets in Afghanistan, <c 11b> and al-Qaeda didn't exist. <c 12> Almost nobody had heard of global warming. <c 13a> Japan was the daunting economic powerhouse, <c 13b> and China's share of global GDP was 2 percent. <c 14> There were some 30 fewer countries in the world, and 2 billion fewer people on the planet.

<p 4> <c 15> We've seen amazing technological advances. <c 16a> In 1986, only 0.2 percent of the US population had a cell phone, <c 16b> which were bricks about 10 inches long. <c 17a> IBM announced its first laptop, <c 17b> which weighed 12 pounds. <c 18> Twenty-four-hour cable news was in its infancy.

<p 5> <c 19> The face of America has changed too. <c 20a> In 1986, 8 percent of the U.S. population was Hispanic; <c 20b> today, it's about 15 percent. <c 21a> The number of African Americans [<c 21b>serving in Congress] has doubled, <c 21c> and the number of women and Latinos has tripled. <c 22a> And, <c 22b> if on my graduation day, someone had told me <c 22c>that I would live <c 22d> to see the first African American president, <c 22e>much less serve in his cabinet, <c 22a>I would have asked them <c 22f>what they were smoking.

<p 6> <c 23a>So much change has transpired just in my adult lifetime, <c 23b>and you will see so much more in yours. <c 24>But it doesn't just happen. <c 25>Progress is the product of human agency. <c 26a>Things get better <c 26b>because we make them better; <c 26c>and things go wrong <c 26d>when we get too comfortable, <c 26e>when we fail <c 26f>to take risks <c 26g>or seize opportunities. <c 27a>Never trust <c 27b>that the abstract forces of history will end a war, <c 27c>or that luck will cure a disease, <c 27d>or that prayers alone will save a child.

<p 7> <c 28a>If you want change, <c 28b>you have to make it. <c 29a>If we want progress, <c 29b>we have to drive it.

<p 8> <c 30>Technology and trade helped transform a bipolar world into the deeply interconnected global community of the 21st century. <c 31>Yet the planet is still divided by fundamental inequalities. <c 32a>Some of us live in peace, freedom, and comfort <c 32b>while billions are condemned to conflict, poverty, and repression.<c 33a>These massive disparities erode our common security <c 33b>and corrode our common humanity.

<p 9> <c 34>We cannot afford to live in contempt of each other's welfare. <c 35>It's not just wrong. <c 36>It's dangerous. <c 37a>When a country is wracked by war <c 37b> or weakened by want, <c 37c>its people suffer first. <c 38a>But poor and fragile states can incubate threats [<c 38b>that spread far beyond their borders – terrorism, pandemic disease, nuclear proliferation, criminal networks, climate change, genocide, and more.] <c 39>In our interconnected age, a threat to development anywhere is a threat to security everywhere.

<p 10> <c 40>That makes the fight against global poverty not only one of the great moral challenges of all time but also one of the great national security challenges of our time.

<p 11> <c 41a> So, here's my challenge to you: <c 41b> become agents of change. <c 42a> Be driven by a passion [<c 42b> to lift up the most vulnerable and <c 42c> to serve those with the least, both at home and around the world.]

<p 12> <c 43> For me, for so many reasons, that is a personal as well as a professional imperative.

<p 13> <c 44a> One of those reasons is a little boy [<c 44b> whom I met in war-ravaged Angola in 1995.] <c 45> I don't even know his name. <c 46a> He was one face in a friendly mob of destitute little kids [<c 46b> who greeted our delegation at a dusty camp for internally displaced persons in the middle of nowhere.] <c 47a> He was perhaps 3 or 4 years old, with pencil-thin legs and a distended belly, and only a torn T-shirt [<c 47b> to wear.] <c 48a> But he stood out <c 48b> because he had the most amazingly infectious smile. <c 49a> I walked up to him <c 49b> before realizing <c 49c> that the only thing [<c 49d> I had <c 49e> to give him] <c 49c> was the worn baseball cap [<c 49f> I was wearing.] <c 50a> I took it off, <c 50b> and put it gently on his head. <c 51> The joy on his face remains etched in my mind to this day. <c 52a> But I had to leave that camp, <c 52b> and when I did, <c 52c> I left that little boy in hell.

<p 14> <c 53a> I like <c 53b> to think – <c 53c> and I sure hope – <c 53d> that kid is OK. <c 54a> But he could well have become one of the 9 million children under the age of 5 [<c 54b> who die each year, mostly from preventable and treatable afflictions.]

<p 15> <c 55a> Yet he has every right [<c 55b>to live with the same dignity, hope, and security [<c 55c> that my own son enjoys.]] <c 56> They are both children of God, of equal worth, equal consequence, and equal rights.

<p16> <c 57> That little boy's future is tied to ours; <c 58> our security is ultimately linked to his well-being. <c 59a> So we must shape the world [<c 59b> that he deserves.]

<p 17> <c 60a> That child deserves a world without the poverty [<c 60b> that crushes the dreams of hundreds of millions.] <c 61> Half of humanity lives on less than $2.50 a day.

<p 18> <c 62a> That child deserves a world without extreme hunger and dependence [<c 62b> that it fosters.] <c 63a> So we are investing <c 63b> in building poor countries' capacity [<c 63c> to feed themselves.] <c 64a> Agricultural research has produced stronger crops [<c 64b> that yield more, <c 64c> adapt faster, <c 64d> and better resist drought, disease, and pests.] <c 65> Yet Africa's crop production remains the lowest in the world. <c 66> With your generation's leadership and ingenuity, you can make it the highest.

<p 19> <c 67a> That child deserves a world [<c 67b> where everyone can get a quality education.] <c 68a> More than 70 million kids are not enrolled in primary school today, <c 68b> and 60 percent of them are girls. <c 69a> You can help close this gap – you can help close this gap <c 69b> by joining Teach for America here at home or the Peace Corps abroad, <c 69c> by providing lunches for rural girls' schools, <c 69d> by working <c 69e> to end child labor, forced marriage, and human trafficking, <c 69f> and by creating educational systems [<c 69g> that reach all of our children.]

<p 20> <c 70a> The child deserves a world [<c 70b> in which we find new cures for old plagues.] <c71a> You can be the generation [<c 71b> to develop new vaccines for tuberculosis and HIV/ AIDS, <c 71c> to use technology <c 71d> to create smart therapies [<c 71e> that kill cancer cells and <c 71f> leave their healthy neighbors untouched,] <c 71g> to provide needle-free immunizations <c 71h> to stop pandemics in their tracks.]

<p 21> <c 72a> The child also deserves a world [<c 72b> whose climate isn't collapsing, <c 72c> whose air isn't choked by soot---<c 72d> and whose waters aren't polluted with spewing oil.] <c 73a> Imagine deploying clean-energy technologies to poor countries <c 73b> to power development without fossil fuels – <c 73c> much as China and Africa largely skipped landlines and <c 73d> leapfrogged to cell phones. <c 74a> You can be the generation [<c 74b> that makes a green economy reality – <c 74c> that turns the fight against climate change into a boon for the developing world, not just a burden.] <c 75a> You can be the generation [<c 75b> that actually reverses global warming.]

<p 22> <c76> That child, every child, deserves a world of greater opportunity, democracy and hope. <c 77a> And that is the world [<c 77b> you can help forge.]

<p 23><c 78a> Sometimes we innovate in great strides; <c 78b> sometimes we progress by slow and steady advances. <c 79> But progress we must.

<p 24><c 80a> The fight against poverty is a challenge worthy of your generation [<c 80b> that grew up in this interlinked age.] <c 81a> The goal of a world free of famine and mass misery may seem distant – <c 81b> but once, so were the moon and the microchip. <c 82> The aim is ambitious. <c 83> But so are you.

<p 25><c 84a> As you go about changing the world, <c 84b> continuously challenge yourselves. <c 85> Get out of your comfort zone. <c 86a> Go travel the world [<c 86b> we share.] <c 87> Learn more languages. <c 88> Get grit in your eyes, and sand in your hair, and service in your soul. <c 89a> [<c 89b> Graduating from Stanford] is great, <c 89c> but it's just the beginning.

<p 26> <c 90> So, don't settle on a single path too soon. <c 91a> The last time [<c 91b> I really was sure <c 91c> I knew [<c 91d> what I wanted <c 91e> to do with my life]] was my senior year at Stanford. <c 92a> I was sure <c 92b> I wanted <c 92c> to be a United States Senator. <c 93a> I left for Oxford, certain <c 93b> I would go on to law school. <c 94a> To round myself out, <c 94b> I decided <c 94c> to study international affairs. <c 95a> After Oxford, I decided <c 95b> to skip law school <c 95c> and decided <c 95d> to sample the business world at McKinsey and Company, <c 95e> and I did so precisely <c 95f> because I was never any good at math <c 95g> and had literally never met a spreadsheet.

<p27> <c 96> I've not followed a pre-ordained path. <c 97a> Rather, I've tried <c 97b> to push myself, <c 97c> stretch myself, <c 97d> and learn new skills [<c 97e> that would serve me whichever path [<c 97f> I took.]] <c 98a> I've changed course <c 98b> and I've taken unexpected turns <c 98c> when my gut dictated. <c 99a> That's led me to places [<c 99b> I never expected] – <c 99c> but I'm grateful [<c 99d> I've been.] <c 100a> So focus on [<c 100b> what stirs your soul,] <c 100c> because it's hard [<c 100d> to excel at anything [<c 100e> that you don't love.]]

<p28> <c 101> Be fearless. <c 102a> It is hard [<c 102b> to make progress] <c 102c> without breaking at least a little crockery. <c 103a> And don't be afraid <c 103b> to go down <c 103c> fighting, <c 103d> if you're fighting

a righteous battle. <c 104> Stick to your guns and to your principles. <c 105a> Remember: <c 105b> you should never want something so badly <c 105c> that you do something [<c 105d> you don't believe in] <c 105e> to get it. <c 106a> At the same time, don't sweat too much [<c 106b> what other folks may think of you.] <c 107a> As Dr Seuss said, <c 107b> 'Be [<c 107c> who you are] <c 107d> and say [<c 107e> what you feel,] <c 107f> because those [<c 107g> who mind] don't matter <c 107h> and those [<c 107i> who matter] don't mind.'

<p29> <c 108> Be about more than money. <c 109a> Comfort and economic security are good, <c 109b> but they're not enough. <c 110a> You should be [<c 110b> about creating change, <c 110c> not just counting it.]

<p 30> <c 111a> And finally, as you're changing the world, <c 111b> never neglect family. <c 112a> They're not just your foundation; <c 112b>they're the source of life's greatest fulfillment, <c 112c> as all the parents here can testify. <c 113> Both my parents were recently struck by serious illnesses. <c 114a> My colleagues were tremendous [<c 114b> about stepping in for me at the halls of the United Nations,] <c 114c> but nobody could step in for me or for my brother at the hospital. <c 115a> There's usually somebody else [<c 115b>who can do your job,] <c 115c> but there's nobody else [<c 115d>who can be a loving child or a devoted parent.]

<p 31> <c 116a> Like those before you, your generation will contribute; <c 116b> it will innovate; <c 116c> and it will serve in unique ways. <c 117> But today, change is coming faster than ever. <c 118> And you must shape that change. <c 119> You can be that change – not for an election, but for a lifetime.

<p 32> <c 120a> If you remember nothing else of [<c 120b> what I've said,] <c 120c> try to remember that little boy. <c 121a> Remember <c 121b> that he is someone's beloved son. <c 122a> Remember <c 122b> that he counts as much as any of us. <c 123a> Remember <c 123b> that we cannot afford to sleep easy <c 123c> while he suffers. <c 124a> Remember <c 124b>that you can make his life better. <c 125a> Above all, remember <c 125b> that each of us, each of us, has a profound responsibility [<c 125c> to try – with all our skill, all our smarts, and all our soul.]

<p 33> <c 126> Make him safe. <c 127> Make progress. <c 128> Make us proud.

Appendix 12.2

Transitivity Structure of Susan Rice Commencement Speech

Para#	Cl #	Transitivity Structure				Clause (Complex)
		Process (type)	Participant(s)		Circumstance(s)	
			X…	Roles		
1	1					<c 1>Now, graduates: first and foremost, congratulations.
	2a	suspect (mental)	I	Senser		<c 2a> I suspect <c 2b>you're feeling pretty good about yourselves right now.
			<c 2b>	Phenomenon		
	2b	feeling (mental)	you	Senser	right now	
			pretty good about yourselves	Phenomenon		
	3a	remember (mental)	I	Senser		<c 3a>I remember <c 3b> feeling pretty good about myself too <c 3c>when I was sitting in your seats.
			<c 3bc>	Phenomenon		
	3b	feeling. (mental)				
			pretty good about myself	Phenomenon		
	3c	sitting (material)	I	Actor	in your seats	
	4a	feeling (mental)	I	Senser		<c 4a> In fact, I might have been feeling a little too good — <c 4b>judging from [<c 4c>how much I remember about my commencement speech.]
			a little too good	Phenomenon		
	4b	judging (material)			from [<c 4c>]	
	4c	remember (mental)	I	Senser		
			about my commencement speech	Phenomenon		
2	5a	Hold on to (material)				<c 5a>Hold on to this jubilant moment <c 5b> and cherish your memories of this extraordinary place.
			this jubilant moment	Goal		
	5b	cherish (mental)				
			your memories…. place.	Phenomenon		

Transitivity Structure of Susan Rice Commencement Speech

Para#	Cl #	Transitivity Structure				Clause (Complex)
		Process (type)	Participant(s)		Circumstance(s)	
			X…	Roles		
	6a	Nurture (material)	the friendships	Goal		.<c 6a>Nurture the friendships [<c 6b> you have made here.]
	6b	made (material)	you	Actor	here	
	7a	sustain (material)	The warmth and security of Stanford	Actor		<c 7a>The warmth and security of Stanford can sustain you <c 7b>as you face an economy [<c 7c>still climbing out of a deep hole] <c 7d>and enter a world [<c 7e>changing at a furious pace.]
			you	Goal		
	7b	face (material)	you	Actor		
			an economy	Goal		
	7c	climbing (material)			out of a deep hole	
	7d	enter (material)	a world	Goal		
	7e	changing (material)			at a furious pace	
3	8a	Imagine (mental)	the world and [<c 8b>]	Phenomenon		<c 8a> Imagine the world and [<c 8b> what it will be like] <c 8c>when one of you comes back a quarter century from now <c 8d>to deliver the commencement address.
	8b	be (relational)	it	Carrier		
			like what	Attribute		
	8c	comes back (material)	one of you	Actor	a quarter century from now	
	8d	deliver (material)	the commencement address.	Goal		
	9a	graduated (material)	I	Actor	In 1986,	<c 9a> In 1986, when I graduated, <c 9b>the Soviet Union was bristling with 45, nuclear weapons, <c 9c>and the Berlin Wall was impenetrable.
	9b	was (relational)	the Soviet Union	Carrier		
			bristling with 45,000 nuclear weapons	Attribute		
	9c	was (relational)	the Berlin Wall	Carrier		
			impenetrable	Attribute		
	10	clocking (material)	Nelson Mandela	Actor	in prison in apartheid South Africa.	<c 10>Nelson Mandela was clocking his 23rd year in prison in apartheid South Africa.
			his 23rd year	Goal		
	11a	fighting (material)	Osama bin Laden	Actor	in Afghanistan	<c 11a>Osama bin Laden was fighting the Soviets in Afghanistan, <c 11b>and al-Qaeda
			the Soviets,	Goal		

Transitivity Structure of Susan Rice Commencement Speech

Para#	Cl #	Transitivity Structure				Clause (Complex)
		Process (type)	Participant(s)		Circumstance(s)	
			X…	Roles		
	11b	exist (existential)	al-Qaeda	Existent		didn't exist.
	12	heard (mental)	nobody	Senser		<c 12>Almost nobody had heard of global warming.
			of global warming	Phenomenon		
	13a	was (relational)	Japan	Identified		<c 13a> Japan was the daunting economic powerhouse, <c 13b> and China's share of global GDP was 2 percent.
			the daunting economic powerhouse	Identifier		
	13b	was (relational)	China's share of global GDP	Carrier		
			2 percent	Attribute		
	14a	were (existential)	some 30 fewer countries	Existent	in the world	<c 14a> There were some 3 fewer countries in the world, <c 14b> and 2 billion fewer people on the planet.
	14b		2 billion fewer people	Existent	on the planet	
4	15	seen (mental)	We	Senser		<c 15>We've seen amazing technological advances.
			amazing technological advances	Phenomenon		
	16a	had (relational)	0.2 percent of the U.S. population	Possessor	In 1986	<c 16a> In 1986, only .2 percent of the U.S. population had a cell phone, <c 16b> which were bricks about 1 inches long.
			a cell phone	Possessed		
	16b	were (relational)	which	Carrier	In 1986	
			bricks about 10 inches long	Attribute		
	17a	announced (material)	IBM	Actor		<c 17a> IBM announced its first laptop, <c 17b> which weighed 12 pounds.
			first laptop	Goal		
	17b	weighed (relational)	which	Carrier		
			12 pounds	Attribute		
	18	was (relational)	Twenty-four-hour cable news	Carrier		<c 18>Twenty-four-hour cable news was in its infancy.
			in its infancy	Attribute		

Transitivity Structure of Susan Rice Commencement Speech

Para#	Cl #	Transitivity Structure				Clause (Complex)
		Process (type)	Participant(s)		Circumstance(s)	
			X…	Roles		
5	19	changed (material)	The face of America	Goal		<c 19>The face of America has changed too.
	20a	was (relational)	8 percent of the U.S. population	Carrier	In 1986	<c 20a> In 1986, 8 percent of the U.S. population was Hispanic; <c 20b>today, it's about 15 percent.
			Hispanic	Attribute		
	20b	is (relational)	it	Carrier	today,	
			about 15 percent.	Attribute		
	21a	doubled (material)	The number of African Americans	Goal		<c 21a> The number of African Americans [<c 21b>serving in Congress] has doubled, <c 21c> and the number of women and Latinos has tripled.
	21b	serving (material)			in Congress	
	21c	tripled (material)	the number of women and Latinos	Affected		
	22a	asked (verbal)	I	Sayer		<c 22a> And, <c 22b> if on my graduation day, someone had told me <c 22c>that I would live <c 22d> to see the first African American president, <c 22e>much less serve in his cabinet, <c 22a>I would have asked them <c 22f>what they were smoking.
			them	Receiver		
			<c 22f>	Verbiage		
	22b	told (verbal)	someone	Sayer	on my graduation day	
			me	Receiver		
			<c 22c-e>	Verbiage		
	22c	live (behavioural)	I	Behaver		
	22d	see (mental)	the first African American president	Phenomenon		
	22e	serve (material)		Actor	in his cabinet	
	22f	smoking (material)	they	Actor		
			what	Goal		

Transitivity Structure of Susan Rice Commencement Speech

Para#	Cl #	Transitivity Structure				Clause (Complex)
		Process (type)	Participant(s)		Circumstance(s)	
			X…	Roles		
6	23a	transpired (material)	So much change	Affected	just in my adult lifetime	<c 23a>So much change has transpired just in my adult lifetime, <c 23b>and you will see so much more in yours.
	23b	see (mental)	you	Senser	in yours.	
			so much more	Phenomenon		
	24	happen (material)	It	Goal		<c 24>But it doesn't just happen.
	25	is (relational)	Progress	Identified		<c 25>Progress is the product of human energy.
			the product of human agency	Identifier		
	26a	get (relational)	Things	Carrier		<c 26a>Things get better <c 26b>because we make them better; <c 26c>and things go wrong <c 26d>when we get too comfortable, <c 26e>when we fail <c 26f>to take risks <c 26g>or seize opportunities.
			better	Attribute		
	26b	make (material)	we	Actor		
			them	Goal/Carrier		
			better	Attribute		
	26c	go (relational)	things	Carrier		
			wrong	Attribute		
	26d	get (relational)	we	Carrier		
			too comfortable	Attribute		
	26e	fail (material)	we	Actor		
	26f	take (material)	risks	Goal		
	26g	seize (material)	opportunities	Goal		
	27a	trust (mental)	<c 27b-d>	Phenomenon		<c 27a>Never trust <c 27b>that the abstract forces of history will end a war, <c 27c>or that luck will cure a disease, <c 27d>or that prayers alone will save a child.
	27b	end (material)	abstract forces of history	Actor		
			a war	Goal		
	27c	cure (material)	luck	Actor		
			a disease	Goal		

Transitivity Structure of Susan Rice Commencement Speech

Para#	Cl #	Transitivity Structure				Clause (Complex)
		Process (type)	Participant(s)		Circumstance(s)	
			X…	Roles		
	27d	save (material)	prayers alone	Actor		
			a child	Goal		
7	28a	want (mental)	You	Senser		<c 28a>If you want change, <c 28b>you have to make it.
			change	Phenomenon		
	28b	make (material)	you	Actor		
			it	Goal		
	29a	want (mental)	we	Senser		<c 29a>If we want progress, <c 29b>we have to drive it.
			progress	Phenomenon		
	29b	have to drive (material)	we	Actor		
			it	Goal		
8	30	helped transform (material)	Technology and trade	Actor	into the deeply interconnected global community of the 21st century	<c 30>Technology and trade helped transform a bipolar world into the deeply interconnected global community of the 21st century.
			a bipolar world	Goal		
	31	divided (material)	the planet	Goal		<c 31>Yet the planet is still divided by fundamental inequalities.
			by fundamental inequalities	Actor		
	32a	live (behavioural)	Some of us	Behaver	in peace, freedom, and comfort	<c 32a>Some of us live in peace, freedom, and comfort <c 32b>while billions are condemned to conflict, poverty, and repression.
	32b	condemned (material)	billions	Goal	to conflict, poverty, and repression	
	33a	erode (material)	These massive disparities	Actor		<c 33a>These massive disparities erode our common security <c 33b>and corrode our common humanity.
			our common security	Goal		
	33b	corrode (material)	our common humanity	Goal		
9	34	afford to live (behavioural)	We	Behaver	in contempt of each others' welfare	<c 34>We cannot afford to live in contempt of each others' welfare.

Transitivity Structure of Susan Rice Commencement Speech

Para#	Cl #	Transitivity Structure				Clause (Complex)
		Process (type)	Participant(s)		Circumstance(s)	
			X…	Roles		
	35	's (relational)	it	Carrier		<c 35>It's not just wrong.
			not just wrong	Attribute		
	36	's (relational)	It	Carrier		<c 36>It's dangerous.
			dangerous	Attribute		
	37a	wracked (material)	a country	Goal		<c 37a>When a country is wracked by war <c 37b> or weakened by want, <c 37c>its people suffer first.
			by war	Actor		
	37b	weakened (material)	by want	Actor		
	37c	suffer (material)	its people	Affected		
	38a	incubate (material)	poor and fragile states	Actor		<c 38a>But poor and fragile states can incubate threats [<c 38b>that spread far beyond their borders—terrorism, pandemic disease, nuclear proliferation, criminal networks, climate change, genocide, and more.]
			threats [<c 38b>]	Goal		
	38b	spread (material)			far beyond their borders—terrorism, pandemic disease, nuclear proliferation, criminal networks, climate change, genocide, and more	
	39	is (relational)	a threat to development anywhere	Carrier	In our interconnected age	<c 39>In our interconnected age, a threat to development anywhere is a threat to security everywhere.
			a threat to security everywhere	Attribute		
10	40	makes (material/relational)	That	Actor	not only one of the great moral challenges of all time but also one of the great national security challenges of our time.	<c 40>That makes the fight against global poverty not only one of the great moral challenges of all time but also one of the great national security challenges of our time.
			the fight against global poverty	Goal/Identified		
			the great moral challenges of all time but also one of the great national security challenges of our time	Identifier		

Transitivity Structure of Susan Rice Commencement Speech

Para#	Cl #	Transitivity Structure				Clause (Complex)
		Process (type)	Participant(s)		Circumstance(s)	
			X…	Roles		
11	41a	is (relational)	my challenge to you	Existent		<c 41a> So, here's my challenge to you: <c 41b> become agents of change.
	41b	become (relational)	agents of change	Attribute		
	42a	driven (material)	by a passion [<c 42bc>.]			<c 42a> Be driven by a passion [<c 42b> to lift up the most vulnerable and <c 42c> to serve those with the least, both at home and around the world.]
	42b	lift up (material)	the most vulnerable	Goal		
	42c	serve (material)	those with the least, both at home and around the world	Goal		
12	43	is (relational)	that	Carrier	For me, for so many reasons,	<c 43> For me, for so many reasons, that is a personal as well as a professional imperative.
			a personal as well as a professional imperative.	Attribute		
13	44a	is (relational)	One of those reasons	Carrier		<c 44a> One of those reasons is a little boy [<c 44b> whom I met in war-ravaged Angola in1995.]
			a little boy [<c 44b>]	Attribute		
	44b	met (material)	whom	Goal	in war-ravaged Angola in1995	
			I	Actor		
	45	know (mental)	I	Senser		<c 45> I don't even know his name.
			his name	Phenomenon		
	46a	was (relational)	He	Identified		<c 46a> He was one face in a friendly mob of destitute little kids [<c 46b> who greeted our delegation at a dusty camp for internally displaced persons in the middle of nowhere.]
			one face in a friendly mob of destitute little kids [<c 46b>]	Identifier		
	46b	greeted (material)	our delegation	Goal	at a dusty camp for internally displaced persons in the middle of nowhere	
	47a	was (relational)	He	Carrier	with pencil-thin legs and a distended belly, and only a torn T-shirt [<c 47b>]	<c 47a> He was perhaps 3 or 4 years old, with pencil-thin legs and a distended belly, and only a torn T-shirt [<c 47b> to wear.]
			perhaps 3 or 4 years old	Attribute		
	47b	wear (material)				
	48a	stood out (material)	he	Actor		<c 48a> But he stood out <c 48b> because he

Transitivity Structure of Susan Rice Commencement Speech

Para#	Cl #	Transitivity Structure				Clause (Complex)
		Process (type)	Participant(s)		Circumstance(s)	
			X…	Roles		
	48b	had (relational)	he	Possessor		had the most amazingly infectious smile.
			the most amazingly infectious smile.	Possessed		
	49a	walked up (material)	I	Actor	to him	<c 49a> I walked up to him <c 49b> before realizing <c 49c> that the only thing [<c 49d> I had <c 49e> to give him] <c 49c> was the worn baseball cap [<c 49f> I was wearing.]
	49b	realizing (mental)	that the only thing [<c 49de>] was the worn baseball cap [<c 49f>]	Phenomenon		
	49c	was (relational)	the only thing [<c 49de>]	Identified		
			the worn baseball cap [I was wearing.]	Identifier		
	49d	had (relational)	I	Possessor		
	49e	give (material)	him	Recipient		
	49f	wearing (material)	I	Actor		
	50a	took… off (material)	I	Actor		<c 50a> I took it off, <c 50b> and put it gently on his head.
			it	Goal		
	50b	put (material)	it	Goal	gently on his head.	
	51	remains (relational)	The joy on his face	Carrier	in my mind to this day	<c 51> The joy on his face remains etched in my mind to this day.
			etched	Attribute		
	52a	had to leave (material)	I	Actor		<c 52a> But I had to leave that camp, <c 52b> and when I did, <c 52c> I left that little boy in hell.
			that camp	Goal		
	52b	did (material)	I	Actor		
	52c	left (material)	I	Actor	in hell	
			that little boy	Goal		
14	53a	like (mental)	I	Senser		<c 53a> I like <c 53b> to think -- <c 53c> and

Transitivity Structure of Susan Rice Commencement Speech

Para#	Cl #	Transitivity Structure				Clause (Complex)
		Process (type)	Participant(s)		Circumstance(s)	
			X…	Roles		
	53b	think (mental)				I sure hope--<c 53d> that kid is OK.
	53c	hope (mental)	I	Senser		
			<c 13d>	Phenomenon		
	53d	is (relational)	that kid	Carrier		
			ok	Attribute		
	54a	become (relational)	he	Identified		<c 54a> But he could well have become one of the 9 million children under the age of 5 [<c 54b> who die each year, mostly from preventable and treatable afflictions.]
			one of the 9 million children under the age of 5 [<c 54b>.]	Identifier		
	54b	die (behavioural)			each year, mostly from preventable and treatable afflictions	
15	55a	has (relational)	he	Possessor		<c 55a> Yet he has every right [<c 55b>to live with the same dignity, hope, and security [<c 55c> that my own son enjoys.]]
			every right [<c 55>[<c 55c>]]	Possessed		
	55b	live (behavioural)			with the same dignity, hope, and security <c 55c>	
	55c	enjoys (mental)	my own son	Senser		
	56	are (relational)	They	Carrier		<c 56> They are both children of God, of equal worth, equal consequence, and equal rights.
			both children of God, of equal worth, equal consequence, and equal rights.	Attribute		
16	57	tied (material)	That little boy's future	Goal	to ours;	<c 57> That little boy's future is tied to ours;
	58	linked (material)	our security	Goal	to his well-being.	<c 58> our security is ultimately linked to his well-being.
	59a	shape (material)	we	Actor		<c 59a> So we must shape the world [<c 59b> that he deserves.]
			the world [<c 59c>.]	Goal		
	59b	deserves (relational)	he	Possessor		

Transitivity Structure of Susan Rice Commencement Speech

Para#	Cl #	Transitivity Structure				Clause (Complex)
		Process (type)	Participant(s)		Circumstance(s)	
			X…	Roles		
17	60a	deserves (relational)	That child	Possessor		<c 60a> That child deserves a world without the poverty [<c 60b> that crushes the dreams of hundreds of millions.]
			a world without the poverty [<c 60b>.]	Possessed		
	60b	crushes (material)	the dreams of hundreds of millions	Goal		
	61	lives (behavioural)	Half of humanity	Behaver	on less than $2.50 a day.	<c 61> Half of humanity lives on less than $2.5 a day.
18	62a	deserves (relational)	That child	Possessor		<c 62a>That child deserves a world without extreme hunger and dependence [<c 62b>that it fosters.]
			a world without extreme hunger and dependence [<c 62b>]	Possessed		
	62b	fosters (material)	it	Actor		
	63a	investing (material)	we	Actor	<c 63b>[<c 63c>]	<c 63a> So we are investing <c 63b> in building poor countries' capacity [<c 63c> to feed themselves.]
	63b	building (material)	poor countries' capacity [<c 63b>]	Goal		
	63c	feed (material)	themselves	Goal		
	64a	produced (material)	Agricultural research	Actor		<c 64a> Agricultural research has produced stronger crops [<c 64b>that yield more, <c 64c>adapt faster, <c 64d>and better resist drought, disease, and pests.]
			stronger crops [<c 64b-d>]	Goal		
	64b	yield (material)			more	
	64c	adapt (material)			faster	
	64d	resist (material)	dreought, disease, and pests	Goal	better	
	65	remains (relational)	Africa's crop production	Identified		<c 65>Yet Africa's crop production remains the lowest in the world.
			the lowest in the world.	Identifier		
	66	make (material/relational)	you	Actor	With your generation's	<c 66>With your generation's leadership and

Transitivity Structure of Susan Rice Commencement Speech

Para#	Cl #	Transitivity Structure				Clause (Complex)
		Process (type)	Participant(s)		Circumstance(s)	
			X…	Roles		
			it	Goal/Identified	leadership and ingenuity,	ingenuity, you can make it the highest.
			the highest	Identifier		
19	67a	deserves (relational)	That child	Possessor		<c 67a>That child deserves a world [<c 67b>where everyone can get a quality education.]
			a world [<c 67b>]	Possessed		
	67b	get (relational)	everyone	Possessor		
			a quality education	Possessed		
	68a	enrolled (material)	More than 70 million kids	Goal	in primary school today,	<c 68a>More than 7 million kids are not enrolled in primary school today, <c 68b> and 6 percent of them are girls.
	68b	are (relational)	60 percent of them	Carrier		
			girls	Attribute		
	69a	help close (material)	You	Actor		<c 69a> You can help close this gap — you can help close this gap <c 69b> by joining Teach for America here at home or the Peace Corps abroad, <c 69c> by providing lunches for rural girls' schools, <c 69d> by working <c 69e> to end child labor, forced marriage, and human trafficking, <c 69f>and by creating educational systems [<c 69g>that reach all of our children.]
			this gap	Goal		
	69b	joining (material)	Teach for America here at home or the Peace Corps abroad	Goal	here at home… abroad	
	69c	providing (material)	lunches for rural girls' schools,	Goal		
	69d	working (material)				
	69e	end (material)	child labor, forced marriage, and human trafficking	Goal		
	69f	creating (material)	educational systems [<c 69g>.]	Goal		
	69g	reach (material)	all of our children	Goal		
20	70a	deserves (relational)	The child	Possessor		<c 70a> The child deserves a world [<c 7b> in which we find new cures for old plagues.]
			a world [<c 70b>.]	Possessed		
	70b	find (material)	we	Actor		

Transitivity Structure of Susan Rice Commencement Speech

Para#	Cl #	Transitivity Structure				Clause (Complex)
		Process (type)	Participant(s)		Circumstance(s)	
			X...	Roles		
			new cures for old plagues	Goal		
	71a	be (relational)	You	Identifying		<c71a> You can be the generation [<c 71b> to develop new vaccines for tuberculosis and HIV/ AIDS, <c 71c> to use technology <c 71d> to create smart therapies [<c 71e> that kill cancer cells and <c 71f> leave their healthy neighbors untouched,] <c 71g> to provide needle-free immunizations <c 71h> to stop pandemics in their tracks.]
			the generation [<c 71b-d> [<c 71ef>] <c 71gh>.]	Identified		
	71b	develop (material)	new vaccines	Goal	for tuberculosis and HIV/ AIDS	
	71c	use (material)	technology	Goal		
	71d	create (material)	smart therapies [<c 71ef>]	Goal		
	71e	kill (material)	cancer cells	Goal		
	71f	leave X untouched (material)	their healthy neighbors	Goal		
	71g	provide (material)	needle-free immunizations	Goal		
	71h	stop (material)	pandemics	Goal	in their tracks	
21	72a	deserves (relational)	The child	Possessor		<c 72a> The child also deserves a world [<c 72b> whose climate isn't collapsing, <c 72c> whose air isn't choked by soot---<c 72d>and whose waters aren't polluted with spewing oil.]
			a world [<72b-d>]	Possessed		
	72b	collapsing (material)	whose climate	Affected		
	72c	choked (material)	whose air	Affected		
			by soot	Actor		
	72d	polluted (material)	whose waters	Affected	with spewing oil	
	73a	Imagine (mental)	deploying clean-energy technologies [<c 73b>]	Phenomenon	to poor countries	<c 73a> Imagine deploying clean-energy technologies to poor countries [<c 73b> to power development without fossil fuels] — <c 73c> much as China and Africa largely skipped landlines and <c 73d> leapfrogged to cell phones.
	73b	power (material)	development	Goal	without fossil fuels	
	73c	skipped (material)	China and Africa	Actor		
			landlines	Goal		
	73d	leapfrogged (material)			to cell phones	

Transitivity Structure of Susan Rice Commencement Speech

Para#	Cl #	Transitivity Structure				Clause (Complex)
		Process (type)	Participant(s)		Circumstance(s)	
			X…	Roles		
	74a	be (relational)	You	Identified		<c 74a> You can be the generation [<c 74b>that makes a green economy reality -- <c 74c> that turns the fight against climate change into a boon for the developing world, not just a burden.]
			the generation [<c 74b-c>]	Identifier		
	74b	makes (material/ relational)	a green economy	Goal/Identified		
			reality	Identifier		
	74c	turns (material)	the fight against climate change	Goal	into a boon for the developing world, not just a burden	
	75a	be (relational)	You	Identified		<c 75a> You can be the generation [<c 75b> that actually reverses global warming.]
			the generation [<c 75b>]	Identifier		
	75b	reverses (material)	global warming	Goal		
22	76	deserves (relational)	That child, every child,	Possessor		<c76> That child, every child, deserves a world of greater opportunity, democracy and hope.
			a world of greater opportunity, democracy and hope.	Possessed		
	77a	is (relational)	that	Identified		<c 77a> And that is the world [<c 77b> you can help forge.]
			the world [<c 77b>]	Identifier		
	77b	help forge (material)	you	Actor		
23	78a	innovate (material)	we	Actor	in great strides	<c 78a> Sometimes we innovate in great strides; <c 78b> sometimes we progress by slow and steady advances.
	78b	progress (material)	we	Actor	by slow and steady advances.	
	79	progress (material)	we	Actor		<c 79> But progress we must.
24	80a	is (relational)	The fight against poverty	Carrier		<c 80a> The fight against poverty is a challenge worthy of your generation [<c 80b> that grew up in this interlinked age.]
			a challenge worthy of your generation [<c 80b>.]	Attribute		
	80b	grew up (material)			in this interlinked age.	

Transitivity Structure of Susan Rice Commencement Speech

Para#	Cl #	Transitivity Structure				Clause (Complex)
		Process (type)	Participant(s)		Circumstance(s)	
			X…	Roles		
	81a	seem (relational)	The goal of a world free of famine and mass misery	Carrier		<c 81a> The goal of a world free of famine and mass misery may seem distant— <c 81b> but once, so were the moon and the microchip.
			distant	Attribute		
	81b	were (relational)	the moon and the microchip	Carrier		
	82	is (relational)	The aim	Carrier		<c 82> The aim is ambitious.
			ambitious	Attribute		
	83	are (relational)	you	Carrier		<c 83> But so are you.
25	84a	go about changing (material)	you	Actor		<c 84a> As you go about changing the world, <c 84b> continuously challenge yourselves.
			the world	Goal		
	84b	challenge (material)	yourselves	Goal	continuously	
	85	Get out (material)			of your comfort zone	<c 85> Get out of your comfort zone.
	86a	Go travel (material)	the world	Goal		<c 86a> Go travel the world [<c 86b> we share.]
	86b	share (material)	we	Actor		
	87	Learn (material)	more languages	Goal		<c 87> Learn more languages.
	88	Get (material)	grit, sand, service	Goal	in your eyes, in your hair, service in your soul.	<c 88> Get grit in your eyes, and sand in your hair, and service in your soul.
	89a	is (relational)	[<c 89b>]	Carrier		<c 89a> [<c 89b> Graduating from Stanford] is great, <c 89c> but it's just the beginning.
			great	Attribute		
	89b	Graduating (material)			from Stanford	
	89c	's (relational)	it	Identified		
			the beginning.	Identifier		
26	90	settle (material)			on a single path too soon.	<c 90> So, don't settle on a single path too soon.

Transitivity Structure of Susan Rice Commencement Speech

Para#	Cl #	Transitivity Structure				Clause (Complex)
		Process (type)	Participant(s)		Circumstance(s)	
			X…	Roles		
	91a	was (relational)	The last time [<c 91b> [<c 91c> [<c 91de>]]	Identified		<c 91a> The last time [<c 91b> I really was sure <c 91c> I knew [<c 91d> what I wanted <c 91e> to do with my life]] was my senior year at Stanford.
			my senior year at Stanford.	Identifier		
	91b	was (relational)	I	Carrier		
			sure	Attribute		
	91c	knew (mental)	I	Senser		
			<c 91de>	Phenomenon		
	91d	wanted (mental)	I	Senser		
	91e	do (material)	what	Goal	with my life	
	92a	was (relational)	I	Carrier		<c 92a> I was sure <c 92b> I wanted <c 92c> to be a United States Senator.
			sure [<c 92bc>.]	Attribute		
	92b	wanted (mental)	I	Senser		
	92c	be (relational)	a United States Senator	Attribute		
	93a	left (material)	I	Actor	for Oxford, certain [<c 93b>]	<c 93a> I left for Oxford, certain <c 93b> I would go on to law school.
	93b	go on (material)	I	Actor	to law school	
	94a	round X out (material)	myself	Goal		<c 94a> To round myself out, <c 94b> I decided <c 94c> to study international affairs.
	94b	decided (mental)	I	Senser		
			<c 94c>	Phenomenon		
	94c	study (material)	international affairs	Goal		
	95a	decided (mental)	I	Senser	After Oxford	<c 95a> After Oxford, I decided <c 95b> to skip law school <c 95c> and decided <c 95d> to sample the business world at McKinsey and Company, <c 95e> and I did so precisely <c 95f> because I was never any good at math <c 95g> and had literally never met a spreadsheet.
			<c 95b>	Phenomenon		
	95b	skip (material)	law school	Goal		
	95c	decided (mental)	<c 95d>	Phenomenon		
	95d	sample (material)	the business world	Goal	at McKinsey and Company	

Transitivity Structure of Susan Rice Commencement Speech

Para#	Cl #	Transitivity Structure				Clause (Complex)
		Process (type)	Participant(s)		Circumstance(s)	
			X…	Roles		
	95e	did (material)	I	Actor		
			so	Goal		
	95f	was (relational)	I	Carrier	at math	
			never any good	Attribute		
	95g	met (material)	a spreadsheet	Goal		
27	96	followed (material)	I	Actor		<c 96> I've not followed a pre-ordained path.
			a pre-ordained path	Goal		
	97a	tried (material)	I	Actor		<c 97a> Rather, I've tried <c 97b> to push myself, <c 97c> stretch myself, <c 97d> and learn new skills [<c 97e> that would serve me whichever path [<c 97f> I took.]]
	97b	push (material)	myself	Goal		
	97c	stretch (material)	myself	Goal		
	97d	learn (material)	new skills [<c 97d[<c 97f>]]	Goal		
	97e	serve (material)	me	Goal		
	97f	took (material)	I	Actor		
	98a	changed (material)	I	Actor		<c 98a> I've changed course <c 98b> and I've taken unexpected turns <c 98c> when my gut dictated.
			course	Goal		
	98b	taken (material)	I	Actor		
			unexpected turns	Goal		
	98c	dictated (material)	my gut	Actor		
	99a	led (material)	That	Actor	to places [<c 99b>] — <c 99c> [<c 99d>]	<c 99a> That's led me to places [<c 99b> I never expected] — <c 99c> but I'm grateful [<c 99d> I've been.]
			me	Goal		
	99b	expected (mental)	I	Senser		
	99c	'm (relational)	I	Carrier		
			grateful [<c 99d>.]	Attribute		
	99d	been (relational)	I	Carrier		

Transitivity Structure of Susan Rice Commencement Speech

Para#	Cl #	Transitivity Structure				Clause (Complex)
		Process (type)	Participant(s)		Circumstance(s)	
			X…	Roles		
	100a	focus on (material)	<c 100b>	Goal		<c 100a> So focus on [<c 100b> what stirs your soul,] <c 100c> because it's hard [<c 100d> to excel at anything [<c 100e> that you don't love.]]
	100b	stirs (material)	what	Actor		
			your soul	Goal		
	100c	's (relational)	it	Carrier		
			hard [<c 100d> [<c 100e.]]	Attribute		
	100d	excel at (material)	anything	Goal		
	100e	love (mental)	you	Senser		
28	101	Be (relational)	fearless	Attribute		<c 101> Be fearless.
	102a	is (relational)	It	Carrier		<c 102a> It is hard [<c 102b> to make progress] <c 102c> without breaking at least a little crockery.
			hard [<c 102b>]	Attribute		
	102b	make (material)	progress	Goal		
	102c	breaking (material)	a little crockery	Goal		
	103a	be (relational)	afraid [<c 103b>]	Attribute		<c 103a> And don't be afraid [<c 103b> to go down <c 103c> fighting], <c 103d> if you're fighting a righteous battle.
	103b	go down (material)				
	103c	fighting (material)				
	103d	fighting (material)	you	Actor		
			a righteous battle.	Goal		
	104	Stick (material)			to your guns and to your principles.	<c 104> Stick to your guns and to your principles.
	105a	Remember (mental)	<c 105b-e>	Phenomenon		<c 105a> Remember: <c 105b> you should never want something so badly <c 105c> that you do something [<c 105d> you don't believe in] <c 105e> to get it.
	105b	want (mental)	you	Senser	so badly	
			something	Phenomenon		

Transitivity Structure of Susan Rice Commencement Speech

Para#	Cl #	Transitivity Structure				Clause (Complex)
		Process (type)	Participant(s)		Circumstance(s)	
			X…	Roles		
	105c	do (material)	you	Actor		
			something [<c 105d>]	Goal		
	105d	believe (mental)	you	Senser	in	
	105e	get (material)	it	Goal		
	106a	sweat (behavioural)	[<c 106b>]	Range	too much	<c 106a> At the same time, don't sweat too much [<c 106b> what other folks may think of you.]
	106b	think (mental)	other folks	Senser	of you	
			what	Phenomenon		
	107a	said (verbal)	Dr. Seuss	Sayer		<c 107a> As Dr. Seuss said, <c 107b> 'Be [<c 107c> who you are] <c 107d> and say [<c 107e> what you feel,] <c 107f> because those [<c 107g> who mind] don't matter <c 107\h> and those [<c 107i> who matter] don't mind.'
			<c 107b-i>	Verbiage		
	107b	Be (relational)	[<c 107c>]	Identifier		
	107c	are (relational)	who	Identified		
			you	Identifier		
	107d	say (verbal)	<c 107d>	Verbiage		
	107e	feel (mental)	you	Senser		
			what	Phenomenon		
	107f	matter (relational)	those [<c 107g>]	Carrier		
	107g	mind (mental)	who	Senser		
	107h	mind (mental)	those [<c 107i>]	Senser		
	107i	matter (relational)	who	Carrier		
29	108	Be (relational)	about more than money.	Attribute		<c 108> Be about more than money.
	109a	are (relational)	Comfort and economic security	Carrier		<c 109a> Comfort and economic security are good, <c 109b> but they're not enough.
			good	Attribute		

Transitivity Structure of Susan Rice Commencement Speech

Para#	Cl #	Transitivity Structure				Clause (Complex)
		Process (type)	Participant(s)		Circumstance(s)	
			X…	Roles		
	109b	‘re (relational)	they	Carrier		
			not enough	Attribute		
	110a	be (relational)	You	Carrier		<c 110a> You should be [<c 110b> about creating change, <c 11c> not just counting it.]
			[<c 110bc>]	Attribute		
	110b	creating (material)	change	Goal		
	110c	counting (material)	it	Goal		
30	111a	changing (material)	you	Actor		<c 111a> And finally, as you’re changing the world, <c 111b> never neglect family.
			the world	Goal		
	111b	neglect (material)	family	Goal		
	112a	‘re (relational)	they	Identified		<c 112a> They’re not just your foundation; <c 112b>they’re the source of life’s greatest fulfillment, <c 112c> as all the parents here can testify.
			your foundation	Identifier		
	112b	‘re (relational)	they	Identified		
			the source of life’s greatest fulfillment,	Identifier		
	112c	testify (verbal)	all the parents here	Sayer		
	113	recently struck (material)	Both my parents	Goal		<c 113> Both my parents were recently struck by serious illnesses.
			serious illnesses	Actor		
	114a	were (relational)	My colleagues	Carrier		<c 114a> My colleagues were tremendous [<c 114b> about stepping in for me at the halls of the United Nations,] <c 114c> but nobody could step in for me or for my brother at the hospital.
			tremendous [<c 114b>]	Attribute		
	114b	stepping in (material)	for me	Beneficiary	at the halls of the United Nations	
	114c	step in (material)	for me or for my brother	Beneficiary	at the hospital.	
	115a	‘s (existential)	somebody else [<c 115b>]	Existent		<c 115a> There’s usually somebody else [<c 115b>who can do your job,] <c 115c> but there’s nobody else [<c 115d>who can be a
	115b	do (material)	your job	Goal		
	115c	‘s (existential)	nobody else [<c 115d>]	Existent		

Transitivity Structure of Susan Rice Commencement Speech

Para#	Cl #	Transitivity Structure				Clause (Complex)
		Process (type)	Participant(s)		Circumstance(s)	
			X…	Roles		
	115d	be (relational)	a loving child or a devoted parent	Attribute		loving child or a devoted parent.]
31	116a	contribute (material)	your generation	Actor	in unique ways	<c 116a> Like those before you, your generation will contribute; <c 116b> it will innovate; <c 116c> and it will serve in unique ways.
	116b	innovate (material)	it	Actor		
	116c	serve (material)	it	Actor		
	117	coming (material)	change	Actor		<c 117> But today, change is coming faster than ever.
	118	shape (material)	you	Actor		<c 118> And you must shape that change.
			that change	Goal		
	119	be (relational)	You	Identified	not for an election, but for a lifetime.	<c 119> You can be that change—not for an election, but for a lifetime.
			that change—	Identifier		
32	120a	remember (mental)	you	Senser		<c 120a> If you remember nothing else of [<c 120b> what I've said,] <c 120c> try to remember that little boy.
			nothing else of [<c 120b>]	Phenomenon		
	120b	said (verbal)	I	Sayer		
			what	Verbiage		
	120c	try to remember (mental)	that little boy	Phenomenon		
	121a	Remember (mental)	<c 121b>	Phenomenon		<c 121a>Remember <c 121b>that he is someone's beloved son.
	121b	is (relational)	he	Carrier		
			someone's beloved son	Attribute		
	122a	Remember (mental)	<c 122b>	Phenomenon		<c 122a> Remember <c 122b> that he counts as much as any of us.
	122b	counts (relational)	he	Carrier		
			as much as any of us.	Attribute		

Transitivity Structure of Susan Rice Commencement Speech

Para#	Cl #	Transitivity Structure				Clause (Complex)
		Process (type)	Participant(s)		Circumstance(s)	
			X…	Roles		
	123a	Remember (mental)	<c 123b>	Phenomenon		<c 123a> Remember <c 123b> that we cannot afford to sleep easy <c 123c> while he suffers.
	123b	afford to sleep (behavioural)	we	Behaver		
	123c	suffers (behavioural)	he	Behaver		
	124a	Remember (mental)	<c 124b>	Phenomenon		<c 124a> Remember <c 124b>that you can make his life better.
	124b	make (material/ relational)	you	Actor		
			his life	Goal/ Carrier		
			better	Attribute		
	125a	remember (mental)	[you]	Senser		<c 125a> Above all, remember <c 125b> that each of us, each of us, has a profound responsibility [<c 125c> to try—with all our skill, all our smarts, and all our soul.]
			125b	Phenomenon		
	125b	has (relational)	each of us	Possesser		
			a profound responsibility [<c 125c>.]	Possessed		
	125c	try (material)			with all our skill, all our smarts, and all our soul	
33	126	Make (material/ relational)	him	Goal/ Carrier		<c 126>Make him safe.
			safe	Attribute		
	127	Make (material/ relational)	progress	Goal		<c 127>Make progress.
	128	Make (material/ relational)	us	Goal/ Carrier		<c 128>Make us proud.
			proud	Attribute		

Appendix 12.3

Logical structure of Susan Rice's Commencement Speech

Para	Simple clause	Clause complex											
		Paratactic				Hypotactic							
		Expansion			Projection	Expansion						Projection	
		Elaboration	Extension	Enhancement		Elaboration		Extension		Enhancement			
						α	β	α	β	α	β	α	β
1	1												
	2											2a	2b
	3									3b	3c	3a	3bc
	4					4a	4b[c]						
2	5		5a + 5b										
	6a[b]												
	7		7b[c] + 7d[e]							7a	7b-e		
3	8									8a[b]	8cd		
										8c	8d		
	9		9b + 9c							9bc	9a		
	10												
	11		11a + 11b										
	12												
	13		13a + 13b										
	14												
4	15												
	16					16a	16b						
	17					17a	17b						
	18												
5	19												
	20		20a + 20b										
	21		21a[b] + 21c										
	22		22d + 22e							22af	22b-e	22b	22c-e
										22c	22de	22a	22f
6	23		23a + 23b										
	24												

Logical structure of Susan Rice's Commencement Speech

Para	Simple clause	Clause complex											
		Paratactic				Hypotactic							
		Expansion			Projection	Expansion						Projection	
		Elaboration	Extension	Enhancement		Elaboration		Extension		Enhancement			
						α	β	α	β	α	β	α	β
	25												
	26		26a-b + 26c-g							26a	26b		
			26f + 26g							26c	26d-g		
			26d + 26e-g										
	27		27b + 27c + 27d									27a	27b-d
7	28									28b	28a		
	29									29b	29a		
8	30												
	31												
	32									32a	32b		
	33		33a + 33b										
9	34												
	35												
	36												
	37									37c	37a,b		
	38a[b]												
	39												
10	40												
11	41	41a = 41b											
	42a[bc]												
12	43												
13	44												
	45												
	46a[b]												
	47a[b]												
	48									48a	48b		
	49									49a	49b-f	49b	49c[de][f]
	50		50a + 50b										

Logical structure of Susan Rice's Commencement Speech

Para	Simple clause	Clause complex											
		Paratactic				Hypotactic							
		Expansion			Projection	Expansion						Projection	
		Elaboration	Extension	Enhancement		Elaboration		Extension		Enhancement			
						α	β	α	β	α	β	α	β
	51												
	52		52a + 52b-c							52c	52b		
14	53		53a-b + 53c-d									53a	53b
												53c	53d
	54a[b]												
15	55 a[b[c]]												
	56												
16	57												
	58												
	59a[b]												
17	60a[b]												
	61												
18	62a[b]												
	63					63a	63b[c]						
	64 a[b-d]												
	65												
	66												
19	67a[b]												
	68		68a + 68b										
	69		69b + 69c + 69d-e + 69f[g]							69a	69b-[g]		
										69d	69e		
20	70a[b]												
	71[b-d[ef] gh]												
21	72a[b-d]												
	73		73c + 73d							73a	73b		

Logical structure of Susan Rice's Commencement Speech

Para	Simple clause	Clause complex											
		Paratactic				Hypotactic							
		Expansion			Projection	Expansion						Projection	
		Elaboration	Extension	Enhancement		Elaboration		Extension		Enhancement			
						α	β	α	β	α	β	α	β
	74a[bc]												
	75a[b]												
22	76												
	77a[b]												
23	78		78a + 78b										
	79												
24	80a[b]												
	81		81a + 81b										
	82												
	83												
25	84									84b	84a		
	85												
	86a[b]												
	87												
	88												
	89		89a[b] + 89c										
26	90												
	91 a[bc[de]]												
	92					92b	92c					92a	92bc
	93											93a	93b
	94									94bc	94a	94b	94c
	95		95 ab + 95 cd 95a-d + 95e-g 95f + 95g							95e	95fg	95a 95c	95b 95d
27	96												
	97		97b + 97c + 97d[e[f]]			97a	97b-d						

Logical structure of Susan Rice's Commencement Speech

Para	Simple clause	Clause complex											
		Paratactic				Hypotactic							
		Expansion			Projection	Expansion						Projection	
		Elaboration	Extension	Enhancement		Elaboration		Extension		Enhancement			
						α	β	α	β	α	β	α	β
	98		98a + 98b							98ab	98c		
	99		99a[b] + 99c[d]										
	100									100a[b]	100c[d[e]]		
28	101												
	102					102 a[b]	102c						
	103					103 a	103b			103a-b	103c		
	104												
	105									105b 105c[d]	105c-e 105e	105a	105b-e
	106a[b]												
	107		107b[c] + 107d[e] 107f[g] + 107h[i]							107 b-[e]	107 f-h[i]	107a	107b-h[i]
29	108												
	109			109a x 109b									
	110a[bc]												
30	111									111b	111a		
	112		112a + 112bc							112b	112c		
	113												
	114		114a[b] + 114c										
	115		115a[b] + 115c[d]										
31	116		116a+116b+116c										
	117												

Logical structure of Susan Rice's Commencement Speech

Para	Simple clause	Clause complex											
		Paratactic				Hypotactic							
		Expansion			Projection	Expansion						Projection	
		Elaboration	Extension	Enhancement		Elaboration		Extension		Enhancement			
						α	β	α	β	α	β	α	β
	118												
	119												
32	120									120c	120a[b]		
	121											121a	121b
	122											122a	122b
	123									123b	123c	123a	123b,c
	124											124a	124b
	125											125a	125b[c]
33	126												
	127												
	128												

Appendix 12.4

Theme-rheme Structure of Susan Rice Commencement Speech

Sent#	Cl#	Theme				Clause
		Textual	Inter-personal	Topical/ Existential	displaced	
1	1	Now	graduates			<c 1>Now, graduates: first and foremost, congratulations.
2	2a			I		<c 2a> I suspect <c 2b>you're feeling pretty good about yourselves right now.
	2b			you		
3	3a			I		<c 3a>I remember <c 3b> feeling pretty good about myself too <c 3c>when I was sitting in your seats.
	3b					
	3c	when		I		
4	4a		In fact	I		<c 4a> In fact, I might have been feeling a little too good — <c 4b>judging from [<c 4c>how much I remember about my commencement speech.]
	4b					
5	5a		Hold on			<c 5a>Hold on to this jubilant moment <c 5b> and cherish your memories of this extraordinary place.
	5b	and	cherish			
6	6a		Nurture			.<c 6a>Nurture the friendships [<c 6b> you have made here.]
7	7a			The warmth and security of Stanford		<c 7a>The warmth and security of Stanford can sustain you <c 7b>as you face an economy [<c 7c>still climbing out of a deep hole] <c 7d>and enter a world [<c 7e>changing at a furious pace.]
	7b	as		you		
	7d	and				
8	8a		Imagine			<c 8a> Imagine the world and [<c 8b> what it will be like] <c 8c>when one of you comes back a quarter century from now <c 8d>to deliver the commencement address.
	8c	when		one of you		
	8d					
9	9a			In 1986		<c 9a> In 1986, when I graduated, <c 9b>the Soviet graduated, <c 9b> the Soviet Union was bristling with 45,000 nuclear weapons, <c 9c>and the Berlin Wall was impenetrable.
	9b			the Soviet Union		
	9c	and		the Berlin Wall		
10	10			Nelson Mandela		<c 10>Nelson Mandela was clocking his 23rd year in prison in apartheid South Africa.
11	11a			Osama bin Laden		<c 11a> Osama bin Laden was fighting the Soviets in Afghanistan, <c 11b>and al-Qaeda didn't exist.
	11b	and		al-Qaeda		
12	12			Almost nobody		<c 12>Almost nobody had heard of global warming.

Theme-rheme Structure of Susan Rice Commencement Speech

Sent#	Cl#	Theme				Clause
		Textual	Inter-personal	Topical/ Existential	displaced	
13	13a			Japan		<c 13a> Japan was the daunting economic powerhouse, <c 13b> and China's share of global GDP was 2 percent.
	13b			China's share of global GDP		
14	14			There		<c 14> There were some 30 fewer countries in the world, and 2 billion fewer people on the planet.
15	15			We		<c 15>We've seen amazing technological advances.
16	16a			In 1986	only 0.2 percent of the U.S. population	<c 16a> In 1986, only 0.2 percent of the U.S. population had a cell phone, <c 16b> which were bricks about 10 inches long.
	16b	which				
17	17a			IBM		<c 17a> IBM announced its first laptop, <c 17b> which weighed 12 pounds.
	17b	which				
18	18			Twenty-four-hour cable news		<c 18>Twenty-four-hour cable news was in its infancy.
19	19			The face of America		<c 19>The face of America has changed too.
20	20a			In 1986	8 percent of the U.S. population	<c 20a> In 1986, 8 percent of the U.S. population was Hispanic; <c 20b>today, it's about 15 percent.
	20b			today	it	
21	21a			The number of African Americans [serving in Congress]		<c 21a> The number of African Americans [<c 21b>serving in Congress] has doubled, <c 21c> and the number of women and Latinos has tripled.
	21c	and		the number of women and Latinos		
22	22a	And		I		<c 22a> And, <c 22b> if on my graduation day, someone had told me <c 22c>that I would live <c 22d> to see the first African American president, <c 22e>much less serve in his cabinet, <c 22a>I would have asked them [<c 22f>what they were smoking.]
	22b	if		on my graduation day,	someone	
	22c	that		I		
	22d					
	22e					
23	23a			So much change		<c 23a>So much change has transpired just in my adult lifetime, <c 23b>and you will see so much more in yours.
	23b	and		you		
24	24	But		it		<c 24>But it doesn't just happen.
25	25			Progress		<c 25>Progress is the product of human energy.

Theme-rheme Structure of Susan Rice Commencement Speech

Sent#	Cl#	Theme				Clause
		Textual	Inter-personal	Topical/ Existential	displaced	
26	26a			Things		<c 26a>Things get better <c 26b>because we make them better; <c 26c>and things go wrong <c 26d>when we get too comfortable, <c 26e>when we fail <c 26f>to take risks <c 26g>or seize opportunities.
	26b	because		we		
	26c	and		things		
	26d	when		we		
	26e	when		we		
	26f					
	26g	or				
27	27a		Never trust			<c 27a>Never trust <c 27b>that the abstract forces of history will end a war, <c 27c>or that luck will cure a disease, <c 27d>or that prayers alone will save a child.
	27b	that		the abstract forces of history		
	27c	or that		luck		
	27d	or that		prayers		
28	28a	If		you		<c 28a>If you want change, <c 28b>you have to make it.
	28b			you		
29	29a	If		we		<c 29a>If we want progress, <c 29b>we have to drive it.
	29b			we		
30	30			Technology and trade		<c 30>Technology and trade helped transform a bipolar world into the deeply interconnected global community of the 21st century.
31	31	Yet		the planet		<c 31>Yet the planet is still divided by fundamental inequalities.
32	32a			Some of us		<c 32a>Some of us live in peace, freedom, and comfort <c 32b>while billions are condemned to conflict, poverty, and repression.
	32b	while		billions		
33	33a			These massive disparities		<c 33a>These massive disparities erode our common security <c 33b>and corrode our common humanity.
	33b	and				
34	34			We		<c 34>We cannot afford to live in contempt of each others' welfare.
35	35			It		<c 35>It's not just wrong.
36	36			It		<c 36>It's dangerous.
37	37a	When		a country		<c 37a>When a country is wracked by war <c 37b> or weakened by want, <c 37c>its people suffer first.
	37b	or				
	37c			its people		
38	38a	But		poor and fragile states		<c 38a>But poor and fragile states can incubate threats [<c 38b>that spread far beyond their borders—terrorism, pandemic disease, nuclear proliferation, criminal networks, climate change, genocide, and more.]

Theme-rheme Structure of Susan Rice Commencement Speech

Sent#	Cl#	Theme				Clause
		Textual	Inter-personal	Topical/ Existential	displaced	
39	39			In our interconnected age,	a threat to development anywhere	<c 39>In our interconnected age, a threat to development anywhere is a threat to security everywhere.
40	40			That		<c 40>That makes the fight against global poverty not only one of the great moral challenges of all time but also one of the great national security challenges of our time.
41	41a	So		here		<c 41a> So, here's my challenge to you: <c 41b> become agents of change.
	41b		become			
42	42a		Be driven			<c 42a> Be driven by a passion [<c 42b> to lift up the most vulnerable and <c 42c> to serve those with the least, both at home and around the world.]
43	43			For me, for so many reasons,	that	<c 43> For me, for so many reasons, that is a personal as well as a professional imperative.
44	44a			One of those reasons		<c 44a> One of those reasons is a little boy [<c 44b> whom I met in war-ravaged Angola in1995.]
45	45			I		<c 45> I don't even know his name.
46	46a			He		<c 46a> He was one face in a friendly mob of destitute little kids [<c 46b> who greeted our delegation at a dusty camp for internally displaced persons in the middle of nowhere.]
47	47a			He		<c 47a> He was perhaps 3 or 4 years old, with pencil-thin legs and a distended belly, and only a torn T-shirt [<c 47b> to wear.]
48	48a	But		He		<c 48a> But he stood out <c 48b> because he had the most amazingly infectious smile.
	48b	because		he		
49	49a			I		<c 49a> I walked up to him <c 49b> before realizing <c 49c> that the only thing [<c 49d> I had <c 49e> to give him] <c 49c> was the worn baseball cap [<c 49f> I was wearing.]
	49b					
	49c	that		the only thing [<c 49d> <e 49e>]]		
50	50a			I		<c 50a> I took it off, <c 50b> and put it gently on his head.
	50b	and				
51	51			The joy on his face		<c 51> The joy on his face remains etched in my mind to this day.
52	52a	But		I		<c 52a> But I had to leave that camp, <c 52b> and when I did, <c 52c> I left that little boy in hell.
	52b	and when		I		
	52c			I		

Theme-rheme Structure of Susan Rice Commencement Speech

Sent#	Cl#	Theme				Clause
		Textual	Inter-personal	Topical/ Existential	displaced	
53	53a			I		<c 53a> I like <c 53b> to think -- <c 53c> and I sure hope--<c 53d> that kid is OK.
	53b					
	53c	and		I		
	53d			that kid		
54	54a	But		he		<c 54a> But he could well have become one of the 9 million children under the age of 5 [<c 54b> who die each year, mostly from preventable and treatable afflictions.]
55	55a	Yet		he		<c 55a> Yet he has every right [<c 55b>to live with the same dignity, hope, and security[<c 55c> that my own son enjoys.]]
56	56			They		<c 56> They are both children of God, of equal worth, equal consequence, and equal rights.
57	57			That little boy's future		<c 57> That little boy's future is tied to ours;
58	58			our security		<c 58> our security is ultimately linked to his well-being.
59	59a	So		we		<c 59a> So we must shape the world [<c 59b> that he deserves.]
60	60a			That child		<c 60a> That child deserves a world without the poverty [<c 60b> that crushes the dreams of hundreds of millions.]
61	61			Half of humanity		<c 61> Half of humanity lives on less than $2.50 a day.
62	62a			That child		<c 62a>That child deserves a world without extreme hunger and dependence [<c 62b>that it fosters.]
63	63a	So		we		<c 63a> So we are investing in <c 63b>building poor countries' capacity [<c 63c> to feed themselves.]
64	64a			Agricultural research		<c 64a> Agricultural research has produced stronger crops [<c 64b>that yield more, <c 64c>adapt faster, <c 64d>and better resist drought, disease, and pests.]
65	65	Yet		Africa's crop production		<c 65>Yet Africa's crop production remains the lowest in the world.
66	66			With your generation's leadership and ingenuity	you	<c 66>With your generation's leadership and ingenuity, you can make it the highest.

Theme-rheme Structure of Susan Rice Commencement Speech

Sent#	Cl#	Theme				Clause
		Textual	Inter-personal	Topical/ Existential	displaced	
67	67a			That child		<c 67a>That child deserves a world [<c 67b>where everyone can get a quality education.]
68	68a			More than 70 million kids		<c 68a>More than 70 million kids are not enrolled in primary school today, <c 68b> and 60 percent of them are girls.
	68b	and		60 percent of them		
69	69a			You		<c 69a> You can help close this gap — you can help close this gap <c 69b> by joining Teach for America here at home or the Peace Corps abroad, <c 69c> by providing lunches for rural girls' schools, <c 69d> by working <c 69e> to end child labor, forced marriage, and human trafficking, <c 69f>and by creating educational systems [<c 69g>that reach all of our children.]
	69b					
	69c					
	69d					
	69e					
	69f					
70	70a			The child		<c 70a> The child deserves a world [<c 70b> in which we find new cures for old plagues.]
71	71a			You		<c71a> You can be the generation [<c 71b> to develop new vaccines for tuberculosis and HIV/ AIDS, <c 71c> to use technology [<c 71d> to create smart therapies <c 71e> that kill cancer cells and <c 71f> leave their healthy neighbors untouched,] <c 71g> to provide needle-free immunizations [<c 71h> to stop pandemics in their tracks.]]
72	72a			The child		<c 72a> The child also deserves a world [<c 72b> whose climate isn't collapsing, <c 72c> whose air isn't chocked by soot---<c 72d>and whose waters aren't polluted with spewing oil.]
73	73a		Imagine			<c 73a> Imagine deploying clean-energy technologies to poor countries <c 73b> to power development without fossil fuels — <c 73c> much as China and Africa largely skipped landlines and <c 73d> leapfrogged to cell phones.
	73c	much as		China and Africa		
	73d					

Theme-rheme Structure of Susan Rice Commencement Speech

Sent#	Cl#	Theme				Clause
		Textual	Inter-personal	Topical/ Existential	displaced	
74	74a			You		<c 74a> You can be the generation [<c 74b>that makes a green economy reality -- <c 74c> that turns the fight against climate change into a boon for the developing world, not just a burden.]
75	75a			You		<c 75a> You can be the generation [<c 75b> that actually reverses global warming.]
76	76			That child, every child		<c76> That child, every child, deserves a world of greater opportunity, democracy and hope.
77	77a	And		that		<c 77a> And that is the world [<c 77b> you can help forge.]
78	78a			Sometimes	we	<c 78a> Sometimes we innovate in great strides; <c 78b> sometimes we progress by slow and steady advances.
	78b			sometimes	we	
79	79	But		progress		<c 79> But progress we must.
80	80a			The fight against poverty		<c 80a> The fight against poverty is a challenge worthy of your generation [<c 80b> that grew up in this interlinked age.]
81	81a			The goal of a world free of famine and mass misery		<c 81a> The goal of a world free of famine and mass misery may seem distant— <c 81b> but once, so were the moon and the microchip.
	81b	but once		so	the moon and the microchip.	
82	82			The aim		<c 82> The aim is ambitious.
83	83	But so		are	you	<c 83> But so are you.
84	84a	As		you		<c 84a> As you go about changing the world, <c 84b> continuously challenge yourselves.
	84b		continuously challenge			
85	85		Get out			<c 85> Get out of your comfort zone.
86	86a		Go travel			<c 86a> Go travel the world [<c 86b> we share.]
87	87		Learn			<c 87> Learn more languages.
88	88		Get			<c 88> Get grit in your eyes, and sand in your hair, and service in your soul.
89	89a			<c 89b>		<c 89a> [<c 89b> Graduating from Stanford] is great, <c 89c> but it's just the beginning.
	89c	but		it		
90	90	So	don't settle			<c 90> So, don't settle on a single path too soon.

Theme-rheme Structure of Susan Rice Commencement Speech

Sent#	Cl#	Theme				Clause
		Textual	Inter-personal	Topical/ Existential	displaced	
91	91a			The last time [<c 91b-e>]		<c 91a> The last time [<c 91b> I really was sure <c 91c> I knew [<c 91d> what I wanted <c 91e> to do with my life]] was my senior year at Stanford.
92	92a			I		<c 92a> I was sure <c 92b> I wanted <c 92c> to be a United States Senator.
	92b			I		
93	93a			I		<c 93a> I left for Oxford, certain <c 93b> I would go on to law school.
	93b			I		
94	94a					<c 94a> To round myself out, <c 94b> I decided <c 94c> to study international affairs.
	94b			I		
	94c					
95	95a			After Oxford	I	<c 95a> After Oxford, I decided <c 95b> to skip law school <c 95c> and decided <c 95d> to sample the business world at McKinsey and Company, <c 95e> and I did so precisely <c 95f> because I was never any good at math <c 95g> and had literally never met a spreadsheet.
	95b					
	95c	and				
	95d					
	95e	and		I		
	95f	because		I		
	95g	and				
96	96			I		<c 96> I've not followed a pre-ordained path.
97	97a	Rather		I		<c 97a> Rather, I've tried <c 97b> to push myself, <c 97c> stretch myself, <c 97d> and learn new skills [<c 97e> that would serve me whichever path [<c 97f> I took.]]
	97b					
	97c					
	97d	and				
98	98a			I		<c 98a> I've changed course <c 98b> and I've taken unexpected turns <c 98c> when my gut dictated.
	98b	and		I		
	98c	when		my gut		
99	99a			That		<c 99a> That's led me to places [<c 99b> I never expected] — <c 99c> but I'm grateful [<c 99d> I've been.]
	99c	but		I		
100	100a	So	focus			<c 100a> So focus on [<c 100b> what stirs your soul,] <c 100c> because it's hard [<c 100d> to excel at anything [<c 100e> that you don't love.]]
	100c	because		it		
101	101		Be			<c 101> Be fearless.
102	102a			it		<c 102a> It is hard [<c 102b> to make progress] <c 102c> without breaking at least a little crockery.
	102c					

Theme-rheme Structure of Susan Rice Commencement Speech

Sent#	Cl#	Theme				Clause
		Textual	Inter-personal	Topical/ Existential	displaced	
103	103a	And	don't be			<c 103a> And don't be afraid <c 103b> to go down fighting, <c 103c> if you're fighting a righteous battle.
	103c	if		you		
104	104		Stick			<c 104> Stick to your guns and to your principles.
105	105a		Remember			<c 105a> Remember: <c 105b> you should never want something so badly <c 105c> that you do something [<c 105d> you don't believe in] <c 105e> to get it.
	105b				you	
	105c	that			you	
	105d				you	
106	106a			At the same time		<c 106a> At the same time, don't sweat too much [<c 106b> what other folks may think of you.]
107	107a	As		Dr. Seuss		<c 107a> As Dr. Seuss said, <c 107b> 'Be who you are <c 107c> and say [<c 107d> what you feel,] <c 107e> because those [<c 107f> who mind] don't matter <c 107g> and those [<c 107h> who matter] don't mind.'
	107b		Be			
	107c	and	say			
	107e	because		those [<c 107f>]		
	107g	and		those [<c 107h>]		
108	108		Be			<c 108> Be about more than money.
109	109a			Comfort and economic security		<c 109a> Comfort and economic security are good, <c 109b> but they're not enough.
	109b	but		they		
110	110a			You		<c 110a> You should be [<c 110b> about creating change, <c 110c> not just counting it.]
111		And finally				<c 111a> And finally, as you're changing the world, <c 111b> never neglect family.;
	111a	as		you		
	111b		never neglect			
112	112a			They		<c 112a> They're not just your foundation; <c 112b>they're the source of life's greatest fulfillment, <c 112c> as all the parents here can testify.
	112b			they		
	112c	as		all the parents here		
113	113			Both my parents		<c 113> Both my parents were recently struck by serious illnesses.
114	114 a[b]			My colleagues		<c 114a> My colleagues were tremendous [<c 114b> about stepping in for me at the halls of the United Nations,] <c 114c> but nobody could step in for me or for my brother at the hospital.
	114c	but		nobody		

Theme-rheme Structure of Susan Rice Commencement Speech

Sent#	Cl#	Theme				Clause
		Textual	Inter-personal	Topical/ Existential	displaced	
115	115 a[b]			There		<c 115a> There's usually somebody else [<c 115b>who can do your job,] <c 115c> but there's nobody else [<c 115d>who can be a loving child or a devoted parent.]
	115 c[d]	but		there		
116	116a			Like those before you	your generation	<c 116a> Like those before you, your generation will contribute; <c 116b> it will innovate; <c 116c> and it will serve in unique ways.
	116b			it		
	116c	and		it		
117	117	But		today	change	<c 117> But today, change is coming faster than ever.
118	118	And		you		<c 118> And you must shape that change.
119	119			You		<c 119> You can be that change—not for an election, but for a lifetime.
120	120 a[b]	If		you		<c 120a> If you remember nothing else of [<c 120b> what I've said,] <c 120c> try to remember that little boy.
	120c		try to remember			
121	121a		Remember			<c 121a>Remember <c 121b>that he is someone's beloved son.
	121b	that		he		
122	122a		Remember			<c 122a> Remember <c 122b> that he counts as much as any of us.
	122b	that		he		
123	123a		Remember			<c 123a> Remember <c 123b> that we cannot afford to sleep easy <c 123c>while he suffers.
	123b	that		we		
	123c	while		he		
124	124a		Remember			<c 124a> Remember <c 124b>that you can make his life better.
	124b	that		you		
125	125a	Above all	remember			<c 125a> Above all, remember <c 125b> that each of us, each of us, has a profound responsibility [<c 125c> to try—with all our skill, all our smarts, and all our soul.]
	125 b[c]	that		each of us, each of us,		
126	126		Make			<c 126>Make him safe.
127	127		Make			<c 127>Make progress.
128	128		Make			<c 128>Make us proud.

Index

Abercrombie, D. 3
adjective 14, 28, 79–82, 140, 142–143, 147–150, 157, 160, 171, 176
adjunct 21, 52–53, 111–114, 126, 135, 137–8, 186–187, 221, 232, 234–235
adverb 28, 110, 126, 128, 133, 136, 139–140, 176, 184, 234
adverbial 14, 24, 28–29, 42, 110–117, 127, 138, 184, 186, 194
ambiguity 62–63, 89–90, 123, 145, 153, 165, 167, 208
    ambiguous 11, 19, 86, 88, 90, 123
anaphoric 9–10, 21, 226
architecture 275, 280–281, 379
Bühler, K. 4–5, 8
Chinese 147, 150, 152, 154
cognition, cognitive 6, 25, 56, 61–2, 65, 67, 70, 75, 163, 165–6
coherence, coherent 9, 151, 183, 190, 195, 200, 207, 235
cohesion, cohesive 12, 14, 19–20, 74, 183, 186–187, 197, 235, 272
complement 21, 60, 92, 111–112, 117–118, 126–127, 138, 163, 187–188, 194, 234
conative 4–5, 8
congruent 75, 149, 170
culture 44, 108–109, 286, 327
declarative 21–22, 71, 76, 170, 185–187, 234, 238
decoding 87–94, 98–101
deictic, deixis 68, 101, 139, 143–145, 226–227
English 7, 14–16, 19, 21, 24–50, 52, 56, 60, 63–64, 69, 72–75, 78–79, 82, 89, 92, 95–96, 101–114, 118, 121, 124–138, 139–155, 159, 163–165, 170, 172, 175, 184–187, 191, 234, 276
ergative 38–46, 54–55, 75, 114, 118–119, 124, 129, 134, 165, 227
experiential 7, 9, 11, 15, 17–20, 23, 24–25, 28–29, 43, 47, 59, 64–65, 73, 96, 102, 108, 114, 123, 133–134, 137, 144, 146, 149, 221–222, 235, 238, 378
expressive 4–5, 8, 14
fuzzy 141, 146, 174–175
grammar 10, 12–23, 24–25, 28, 42, 47–48, 50, 52, 54, 56–58, 88, 102, 105, 108, 128, 130–132, 134, 136, 140, 142, 145, 147–151, 164, 170, 175, 177, 183, 198, 233, 238, 273, 275
grammatical
    function 26–28, 134
    metaphor 75, 140, 148, 150–151, 155
    structure 25–27, 161, 170
    subject 20, 52, 195, 226, 276
    system 13, 108
hypotactic, hypotaxis 14, 68–70, 72–73, 76–77, 133, 136, 147, 164, 186, 207–208, 228–32, 272–273, 276–277, 280, 371, 376
ideational 9, 12, 15–23, 24, 60, 140, 156–157, 176, 185–186, 192–193, 195, 219, 221, 227, 235, 238
Identifier 80–81, 85–8, 91–92, 94, 97–102, 188, 223, 225
imperative 71, 76, 170–178, 206, 234, 373, 375, 378, 384
imperfective 82, 100
indeterminacy 18–20, 103, 105, 117, 153, 160, 173, 178
intensive 78, 96–99, 101, 104, 157
interpersonal 8–9, 11–12, 14–16, 19–23, 24, 108, 137–138, 140–141, 156–158, 170, 174, 186, 194, 219, 233–235, 238, 378
interrogative 8, 11, 21, 63, 71–72, 76, 170–171, 175, 177–178, 185–186, 234, 238
intransitive 25, 30–1, 34–45, 53–55, 64, 66, 94, 102, 119, 124, 147
lexical 14,16, 19–20, 28, 57, 82, 108, 140–141, 150, 157, 161, 171, 178, 184, 197, 238

lexicogrammar, lexicogrammatical 47, 60–61, 69, 139–140, 146, 163–165, 179, 207, 238, 272, 275, 281, 373, 378–379
literary 72, 109
logical 9, 13–20, 23, 24, 69, 73, 76, 88, 103, 105, 108, 132–133, 221, 227, 238, 276, 337, 378
material (process) 27, 42–45, 47, 51–52, 55, 66–67, 74, 79–81, 84, 94, 96–97, 102–110, 124, 126, 128, 134, 138, 147, 162–163, 166–168, 221–227, 370–371, 375
metaphor 140, 148, 150–151, 155
  metaphoric(al) 39, 75, 132, 150–151, 153–154, 163
modal 19, 22, 111–113, 118, 126, 138, 171–178, 186, 220, 234–235
modality 19, 159, 170–179, 234, 378
mood 8, 11, 15, 21–23, 33, 43, 71, 76, 111–112, 118, 126, 173, 177, 234, 378
multinuclear 199, 202, 206, 212
narrative 7–8, 21, 72–73, 77, 164, 203, 367
nominal 11–12, 14, 24, 28–29, 42, 55, 60, 62, 74, 79, 101, 110–117, 119, 124, 127, 129, 137–138, 147–149, 165, 167, 184–185
nominalization 61–63, 75, 151, 155, 166–167, 188, 190, 221, 226
non-finite 96, 111, 148, 171, 176
noun 12, 17–18, 28, 49, 62, 71, 74, 79–81, 110, 138–162, 166–168, 171, 184, 221
  noun-like 118, 137
paratactic, parataxis 14, 69, 72–73, 76–77, 147, 164, 207–208, 228–232, 272–273, 276–278, 280, 370–371, 376–377
passive 35–36, 41–44, 52–53, 55–57, 64–67, 80–84, 91–93, 98–100, 113–114, 116, 121, 126, 135, 165, 171, 176–177, 185
possessive 11, 78, 82, 95–97, 99–101, 104
predicator 21, 68, 111–113, 126, 188, 234
preposition 53, 84, 97–8, 110–111, 114–130, 132, 136, 138, 147–148, 165, 221
  prepositional 28–29, 110–117, 122–124, 128, 133, 136, 138–139, 148
pronoun(s) 35, 39, 72, 74, 79–81, 112, 122, 142, 144, 184, 187, 189–190, 195, 221, 226, 238, 367–368, 373, 375, 378–379, 381
rank-shifted 70, 276–277
Rheme 22, 123, 183–184, 188, 191, 194–197, 232
rhetorical 73, 190, 198, 200–201, 207, 215, 229, 232, 275, 280–281, 360, 373
RST 198–204, 208–209, 272, 372, 379
semantic
  category (-ies) 47, 100, 168
  construct 54, 280
  features 76, 82, 175, 188
  level 61, 163–164
  opposites 368, 373
  structure 104–105, 108, 163
  system 46–47, 96, 168–169, 222
speech act(s) 4–5, 8, 15, 20
tense 14, 28, 50, 66, 72, 82, 114, 132, 135, 171–172, 175–176, 227, 233
thematic, Theme 21–3, 29, 42–3, 48–9, 53, 65, 90, 106–7, 123, 125, 136, 178, 183–197, 204, 226, 232–236, 238, 264–271, 279, 320–330, 359, 375, 379, 416–417, 420
tonic 22, 73, 83, 85, 87–88, 98, 121, 189
transitive 30–31, 34–46, 53–35, 59, 64–66, 74, 94, 102–103, 114, 119, 124, 147
transitivity 20, 22–23, 25, 28–31, 33, 39, 42–47, 53, 60, 101–102, 106–115, 120, 123, 126, 137–138, 184, 222–226, 238, 243, 378
verb(s) 11, 14, 17, 28, 30–36, 40–45, 48–50, 52–58, 62, 64, 73–74, 76, 78–79, 81–85, 91–92, 96–100, 103, 110–111, 114, 116–117, 129, 132, 137, 139–143, 147–150, 156–157, 162, 164, 168, 171, 176, 184–188, 220–221, 227, 234
verbal process(es) 52, 68–77, 83, 104, 109, 137–138, 147, 163, 165–166, 221, 227–228
verbalization 68–76, 83, 103, 133

www.ingramcontent.com/pod-product-compliance
Lightning Source LLC
Chambersburg PA
CBHW062113270925
33188CB00003B/24

* 9 7 8 1 9 0 4 7 6 8 4 8 7 *